MORE
BAD
NEWS

The authors are
Peter Beharrell
Howard Davis
John Eldridge
John Hewitt
Jean Oddie
Greg Philo
Paul Walton
Brian Winston

Previous works by the research team (all are co-authors of Bad News, *Routledge & Kegan Paul, 1976)*

Peter Beharrell *Lecturer in Sociology, Liverpool College of Higher Education*
Co-editor of *Trade Unions and the Media*, Macmillan, 1977

Howard Davis, *Lecturer in Sociology, University of Kent*
Beyond Class Images, Croom Helm, 1979

John Eldridge *Professor of Sociology, Glasgow University*

Industrial Disputes, Routledge & Kegan Paul, 1968
Max Weber: The Interpretation of Social Reality, Michael Joseph, 1971/ Nelson, 1972
Sociology and Industrial Life, Michael Joseph 1971/Nelson, 1972
A Sociology of Organisations (with A. Crombie), Allen & Unwin, 1975

John Hewitt *Lecturer in Sociology, Liverpool College of Higher Education*
Contributor to *Trade Unions and the Media*, Macmillan, 1977

Greg Philo *Lecturer in Sociology, University of Glasgow*
Co-editor of *Trade Unions and the Media*, Macmillan, 1977

Paul Walton *Reader in Communications, Goldsmiths' College, University of London*
Situating Marx (with S. Hall), Chaucer Press, 1971
From Alienation to Surplus Value (with A. Gamble), Sheed & Ward, 1972/PB, 1976
The New Criminology (with J. Young and I. Taylor), Routledge & Kegan Paul, 1973
Critical Criminology (with J. Young and I. Taylor), Routledge & Kegan Paul, 1974
Capitalism in Crisis (with A. Gamble), Macmillan, 1976

Brian Winston *Professor of Film, State University of New York*
Dangling Conversations –the Image of the Media, Davis Poynter, 1973
Dangling Conversations –Hardware/Software, Davis Poynter, 1974

Volume 2 of *Bad News*
Glasgow University Media Group

Routledge & Kegan Paul
London, Boston and Henley

First published in 1980
by Routledge & Kegan Paul Ltd
39 Store Street,
London WC1E 7DD,
Broadway House,
Newtown Road,
Henley-on-Thames,
Oxon RG9 1EN and
9 Park Street,
Boston, Mass. 02108, USA
Photoset in 10 on 12 Linoterm Times by
Kelly Typesetting Ltd, Bradford-on-Avon, Wiltshire
and printed in Great Britain by
Unwin Brothers Ltd,
The Gresham Press, Old Woking, Surrey
A member of the Staples Printing Group

British Library Cataloguing in Publication Data

University of Glasgow. Media Group
Bad news.
Vol. 2: More bad news
1. Television broadcasting of news – Great
Britain
I. Title II. Beharrell, Peter
III. More bad news
791.45'5   PN5124.T4   79–42911

ISBN 0 7100 0414 1

In memory of Neill Williamson,
who helped on this and many other projects,
in the hope that the balance may be made more favourable

'The cabinet decision is really a negative one. They want to be able to say that they did not commandeer us, but they know that they can trust us not to be really impartial.'

Lord Reith: 11 May 1926

Contents

Acknowledgments

We would like to thank the following people for their encouragement, advice and help: Christine Douglas, Margaret Hall, Pru Larsen and Ann Taggart of the University of Glasgow; the Staff of the University Television Service and the University Administration for financial help and general support; the Social Science Research Council for financing the Project for two years; the staff of the BBC's Audience Research Department: the staffs of the BBC's newsrooms in London and Glasgow, ITN and Scottish Television Limited; Dave Bridges; Tom Burns; Rex Cathcart; Umberto Eco; Robin Fox; David Frisby; Andrew Gamble; Erving Goffman; Al Gouldner; John Gray; Toni Griffiths; Stuart Hall; Caroline Heller; Richard Hoggart; Elihu Katz; Roy Lockett; Des McNulty; Graham Murdock; Brian Murphy; Henrietta Resler; Franco Rositi; Ian Roxborough; Alan Sapper; Anthony Smith; Ian Taylor; Laurie Taylor; John Westergaard; Steve White; Philip Whitehead; Colin Young; Jock Young.

We have also benefited from discussions and seminars at the following universities and organisations: the Institute of Education, the University of London; the Department of Sociology and the Centre for Mass Communication Research, the University of Leicester; the Institute for Workers Control, the University of Sheffield; the Industrial Relations Unit, the University of Nottingham; the Centre for Television Research, the University of Leeds; the Department of Communications, Glasgow College of Technology; the Science and Technology Groups, the University of Sussex; Broadcasting Symposia, the University of Manchester; the National Deviancy Symposium, the University of Cardiff; the Criminology Unit, the University of Sheffield; the British Sociological Association, Industrial Sociology and Mass Media Study Groups; the Academic Section of the Prix Italia, 1975, at

Florence; the press and publicity departments of national and regional conferences of NALGO; interested members of the General Council of the TUC; the Sociology Departments of the Universities of Edinburgh and Glasgow; and the Centre for Contemporary Cultural Studies, the University of Birmingham.

Special mention must be made of Stella McGarrity for timely help; Phillipa Carter; Yusuf Ahmad for adding a local dimension to the study; and Alison McNaughton who freely and unstintingly gave of her time and energy during the first year of the project and thereby contributed enormously to the work.

We would like gratefully to acknowledge the advice and technical help of photographers Lawrence Sparham and Paul Taylor. We especially thank Jill Matthews for her help in the latter stages of the research and production of this volume, and Dave Jordan and the Low Pay Unit for providing information and assistance.

Figure 1.1 is reproduced by kind permission of the *Sunday Times*, Figure 6.1 by kind permission of the IBA.

Finally we would like to thank all those academics and audiences who bore with, and were critically helpful in the production and reception of, Volume 1 and therefore helped make Volume 2 a better book.

The Glasgow Media Group
The University
Glasgow

Introduction

> Good evening. For the first time in many months we have some
> good news.
>
> ITN, *News at Ten*, 24 January 1975

Our argument in *Bad News*, Volume 1 of this study, was that
routine news practices led to the production of bad news. For
example, viewers were given a misleading portrayal of industrial
disputes in the UK when measured against the independent reality
of events. They were given restricted accounts and somewhat one-
sided evaluations of such events. In general we examined the
routine practices of television news production as they appeared on
the screen. This second volume continues that work, but by way of
introduction we would like to indicate an area which, although not
routine, can be said to represent a type of bad news. On those rare
occasions when individuals who cannot reply in kind are singled out
for attack on the major information medium in our society we can
then see clearly the most dramatic extremes of the contours of the ·
working ideology of news producers. It is difficult to see how, in
terms of professional journalistic codes or cultural doctrines of
fairness, this can be justified. We do not argue that such examples
are a product of routine practices, but when they do occur then that
is really bad news. The following instance is taken from the
coverage of the London dock strike on ITN's main bulletin on 27
March 1975. Brian Nicholson is defined as 'the man at the centre of
the London dock strike' and as 'a controversial figure during two
dock meetings where the voting's been disputed'. The newscaster
then hands over to the correspondent, who reports as follows:

> Brian Nicholson has attracted the attention of the cameras only
> during the last few weeks as leader of the latest dock strike, but

he's been a major political force in the docks for many years. In 1969 he was largely responsible for the Bristow Committee reporting on the ports, at the time their proposals were shelved; and in 1972 when Bernie Steer and Vic Turner were briefly imprisoned for being in contempt of the Industrial Relations Court, Nicholson was thought to be the mastermind behind the dispute at the time. He is chairman of the Docks Group of the Transport and General Workers' Union. The recent disputes over who should run the container depots have been largely in the hands of the shop stewards, led by Vic Turner, but in the last few weeks Nicholson has taken over, in his role as local union chairman, even though the strike is unofficial. This has been his bid for ultimate power in the London docks.

Brian Nicholson lives in Hackney; he's divorced and he has three children; he's a member of the Labour party and of the national executive of the transport union. For the four months prior to this dispute he's been on sick leave with an injured leg. Nicholson's main political affiliation is to the Institute for Workers' Control, an organisation based in Nottingham, which has the late Bertrand Russell as its honorary President. Nicholson is a vice chairman of the Institute, whose members include the Minister of State for Northern Ireland, Mr Stan Orme, and whose conference this year will be addressed by the Industry Secretary, Mr Tony Benn.

Brian Nicholson has written a number of pamphlets on the docks, urging total workers' control throughout Britain so that dock employees can have complete power to dictate terms and conditions of employment. His involvement in recent days in disputed vote-counting may have been a setback to his ambition as a dockers' leader. (ITN, 22.10, 27 March 1975)

What basis is there for asserting that Nicholson was largely responsible for the Bristow Committee being set up? By whom was Nicholson thought to be the mastermind behind the 1972 dispute and on what evidence? What is the relevance to the story of telling us that he is divorced with three children and that he has been on sick leave for four months? Are we meant to infer that he is abusing his role as branch chairman of the union by the part he is playing in the strike? On what possible grounds can one define one local union official as making a bid for 'ultimate power' in the London docks? What is one expected to understand concretely by such a term in the context of the overall organisational structure of the London docks (about which we are told nothing)?

It is the case that, without the basic methodological approach we have taken, such isolated examples cannot be turned into evidence of the continuing nature of such reporting. The sense in which we call these volumes 'Bad News' refers, then, to the more routine failures of the bulletins to be consistent with their own proclaimed standards of neutrality and impartiality. What has to be examined is the ways in which this may happen.

The present volume is focused on three main levels of analysis: the story, the language and the visuals. The first is the presentation in the bulletins of the British economy in crisis and its thematic linkage with the Social Contract during the first four months of 1975. Whereas in Volume 1 we were especially concerned to look at the range of industries covered in news stories and their content, here we focus on a theme which cuts through many stories.

Debates about the state of the British economy are no new thing. Arguments about what should be done are the stuff of politics. What we show so far as television news is concerned is that there are organising principles which lead to a presentation of items dealing with inflation, unemployment, wages and the Social Contract in a generally consistent but highly restricted manner. In order to show with precision that this is so we have done several things. We have indicated the broad range of economic judgments concerning what is wrong with the economy and what political and/or economic actions are required to put things right. Against this kind of reality-testing we show that the news focused predominantly on a particular view of the role of wages as causing inflation, and that this was then linked to editorial comments on wage claims and settlements. These comments were themselves geared into news journalists' own views as to what did or did not break the Social Contract.

Whether, then, we examine the ways in which routine coverage shapes interpretation of wages and prices statistics, which throughout the period were continually being juxtaposed in very definite ways, or whether we look at the extended treatment of the miners' pay claim, it is the same frame of reference that operates. We will show in some detail how this is done.

In presenting the Social Contract/economic crisis theme, we are inevitably drawn into questions of language: the structuring of information, the imputation of causes, the pattern of interviewer questions, the use of rhetoric, and so on. It is through such devices that accounts of the world are filtered. It is this which is involved in encoding and which is not really summarised in a term like bias.

This process of encoding receives more particular attention in Part II. In analysing the structure of news talk, which has particular but not exclusive reference to industrial news, we examine features such as the use of headlines and boundary markers, the way in which talk is organised within a news item, the use of reported speech. We also look closely at the vocabulary of industrial news talk. Such elements may be separated for the purpose of careful scrutiny but they form the texture of a continuing flow of news. We conclude that news talk is in several senses a 'restricted' code. There is a high degree of predictability in the way the talk is organised; the plurality of meanings inherent in conflict situations is typically reduced to simple formulae and frames of reference; there is a high level of redundancy in the language but, at the same time, an absence of information relevant for understanding the items under discussion; and a lexical and syntactical form that is weighted against trades union and labour points of view. With only two exceptions in our sample, complex industrial disputes were described in such a way that the hearer could only attribute their cause to the 'unreasonable' because unexplained action of labour.

Some of the discussion in that section is somewhat technical but we think the implications are substantial. It does not follow that when we refer to some 'deep structure' of news talk that such structures cannot be changed; but it is the case that codes and conventions do tend to hide the necessary selectivity and editing of news and create the appearance of a natural neutrality.

Part III has to do with the visual organisation of news. It represents an exploratory attempt to uncover the rules governing its visual presentation. This has proved very difficult and arduous. For reasons later elaborated we have concentrated on one week of total news bulletins (not only industrial but all news). At the heart of the analysis is the use of the shot as the basic unit – the visual equivalent of the 'lexeme'. By breaking down the sample into shots which were then indexed by category of input it is possible to begin to describe the visual content of television news in some detail.

How does the flow of visual presentation proceed? What are the rules for opening and ending programmes? How are news presenters themselves presented? How are correspondents and reporters shown to the viewer? What visual rules govern interviewing? To what extent do the normative rules of film-editing apply? While there may be formal professional guidelines, the answers to these questions are not known in any empirical sense. What we have tried to do is to deduce what ground rules appear to be operating.

Some of these visual rules we have illustrated in action by the use of photographs. However, although for some purposes the visual aspect of news presentation can be isolated, it is necessary to show how visual treatment meshes together with news talk: not least, because all images can serve symbolic, indexical and iconic purposes. Hence the attempt is made in the text to depict image (i.e. shot) changes against news talk, to reconstruct on the page the verbal and visual interaction of the television broadcast. It must be emphasised that this part of our work is breaking new ground and we have no desire to overstate the findings. On the other hand we do think they provide an instance of methodological innovations which bears scrutiny and should provide a basis for further work to be undertaken. This is perhaps underscored by the continuing arguments about the visual aspects of news. The matter has been well summarised recently by Tom Burns:[1]

> because television news and current affairs programmes convey action, movement, facial expression and demeanour, scenes and actors, as well as verbal messages, they seem *more* complete, *more* satisfactory than any account provided by newspapers. 'Viewability' is easily construed as reliability because any intervention by broadcasters is largely invisible, and because the dramatic intensity of film and video recording carries conviction and guarantees authenticity in ways which words cannot. And the constant striving for 'viewability' sets its own traps.

So, then, it is because television news can be seen as simply reflecting events and as therefore being 'natural', as simply reporting facts and as therefore being 'neutral', and as filming what happened and as therefore being 'reliable' that we have thought it worthwhile to study whether the appearance is also the reality. In so far as we discover that the majority of most bulletins consist of news personnel addressing the camera, we find that the case for 'viewability' cannot be sustained. Whoever is setting 'traps', it is not the masters of what might be called 'the visual imperative'.

What is clear in what follows is that the news is not a neutral and natural phenomenon: it is rather the manufactured production of ideology.

This present volume fulfils in large measure the plan of work that we outlined initially. The exception to this is our last chapter, in which we address ourselves to the continuing debate about the function and purpose of television news, of which, since the publication of our first volume, we have ourselves been part.

PART I

REPORTING THE ECONOMIC CRISIS AND THE SOCIAL CONTRACT: A CASE STUDY

The quadrilateral of full employment, free collective bargaining, free elections and reasonably stable prices, has become a figure of unstable forces.

The Times, 18 October 1974

1 Introduction: The Economic Background

We have argued throughout our study that news is never simply a series of facts or a simple mirror of external reality. Rather it is a cultural product and the accounts and descriptions of the world which it gives are produced from within specific interpretative frameworks. By this we mean that its accounts are formulated from within limited assumptions as to the nature of the social and industrial world. These assumptions are guided by beliefs about what the problems of our society are and how those problems might and should be solved. These beliefs give order and form to news accounts – they determine what information is to be included and what excluded. They are at the heart of what is to be declared as 'newsworthy' and are implicit in the normal practices of journalists.

Tom Burns has observed that by the 1970s[1]

> The television news journalists slipped easily into the set of 'attitudes and expectations, truisms and commonplaces' current not among their audience (of whom they knew no more than did any one else in Britain) but among colleagues in the BBC, in ITN and in the newspaper world. By the mid-seventies, that is, television news had become indeed a mirror, at least mentally, but a mirror reflecting not society at large, but the *Weltanschauung* – the vision of society – held by television journalists.

Thus it is that television news as the major source of news information for the mass of our society fulfils its most crucial role: it sets social agendas and priorities.

In what follows we will illustrate the buried conventions and beliefs which shaped the television news coverage of the Social Contract during the first four months of 1975. They reveal how the

most routine and apparently factual accounts had as their organising principle severely limited perspectives and interpretations
about the nature of the social world and what is important,
necessary and possible within it.

Television news has played a central role in disseminating information and comment on the causes of the 'British' economic crisis and
the variety of ways in which it could be resolved. These two themes
– the cause and possible cure of the crisis – were central concerns of
television news and underpinned much of the routine coverage of
inflation, unemployment, the state of industry and finance, and
crucially, the negotiation and development of the Social Contract.
Outside the television newsroom, in the press, in Parliament, and
elsewhere, the debate on these themes was vigorous, and marked
divisions of opinion emerged between sections of the population,
including political groups and trade unions.
  A vital point is that the divisions between these groups were not
merely about the range of possible cures, but over what had caused
the problem in the first place. Whichever explanation of the crisis
was embraced implied quite different attitudes to its resolution.
More crucial, perhaps, are the effects on the population at large; for
explanations affect attitudes and in turn can become central in the
acceptance or rejection of policies and solutions. A simple example
would be that if most people were convinced that inflation was
caused by 'excessive' wage increases, the policy of cutting wages to
reduce inflation then might appear as socially just and acceptable.
If, however, it was shown that prices were rising because of
'excessive' profits, or from the activities of speculators and
financiers, or the collapse in world trade, then a policy of lowering
wages to resolve the crisis might not have the same public approval
and support. Therefore the question of how the crisis is explained is
central to the formation of public attitudes and policies, and
conditions whether or not particular policies might gain wide social
approval.

The explanation of the crisis

The most obvious manifestation of Britain's economic decline has
been the persistent and widespread growth of inflation and
unemployment. There are three major strands of academic opinion
which have been aired in recent years as to the nature and possible

causes of this. These three main areas of debate have a long academic pedigree. While the differences between and within these approaches have all kinds of complexities, they do divide very clearly over the cause of inflation and the relation of wages to this.

The first of the approaches is *orthodox marginal economics* (and some *neo-Keynesian* approaches to inflation, which share certain assumptions – notably that a causal relationship exists between wage increases and price increases). The second, which we will term the *critical approach*, sees inflation as a manifestation of a basic problem of productivity in the Western economy. The third is the *monetarist school*, which ascribes inflation essentially to the failure of governments adequately to control the money supply – the effect of which is to allow massive increases in prices.[2]

The first of these approaches has been concerned to demonstrate that a relationship exists between the level of money, wages and inflation. Its best-known theories involve the demand-pull/cost-push explanations.[3] The 'demand-pull' situation is presented as occurring when there is a shortage of labour (i.e. it is 'in demand' in an economy with full employment). In this situation, it is suggested that employers compete with one another to pay higher wages, and thus average earnings rise. The shortage may apply not only to labour, but also to capital or any other factor of production, but because there is a shortage, the price will rise. According to this theory, the higher wage costs are then passed on as higher prices. The demand for labour is thus seen as 'pulling' up prices. The cost-push side of this argument focuses on the monopoly power of modern companies which have the ability to fix prices almost as they wish. The cost-push theorists also argue that the increasing strength of trade unions enables them to fix wage rates at levels higher than their market value, which are then passed on to the consumer as enforced higher prices by the large corporations. The solutions which flow from such analysis usually involve the increase of unemployment as a way of reducing the increase in wage rates.

These explanations have begun to look unlikely as accounts of the rapid inflation which has afflicted the British economy in the 1970s. There is now a considerable group of opinion on both the 'right' and 'left' wing of economic debate, which disputes the argument that it is the rate of wage increases which is the prime mover of this inflation. Empirically, it is the case that 'real' wages (after deductions for tax and cost-of-living increases) have not in fact risen significantly in the last four years and in two of these, 1973 and 1975, they appear to have fallen for most people. Money wages were rising rapidly, but as the *Financial Times* noted in August 1973:[4]

> The discovery that according to the Government's own figures, living standards have actually begun to fall because the pay freeze has been holding back incomes while prices continued to rise will naturally tend to have the effect of arousing suspicions in this respect. It must be expected to make a still greater impact . . . as it begins to be realised that the rise in prices has been accompanied by a spectacular advance in profits.

In a study of real income, published in 1976, Frances Cairncross concluded that: 'The purchasing power of the average male worker's earnings has been virtually unchanged for four years.'[5] We

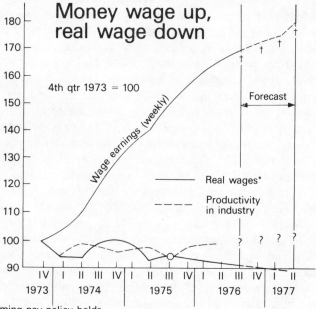

†Assuming pay policy holds
*After national insurance and tax assuming married couple with one child

Figure 1.1   Weekly earnings and real wages (after *Sunday Times*, 5 December 1976).

will deal with the use of official figures in the television news in the next chapter. It may be noted here, however, that Figure 1.1, used by Malcolm Crawford, economics editor of the *Sunday Times*, illustrates the trends in real wages as against money wages, and shows that throughout the period of our study they were declining. The demand-pull/cost-push explanations might show how a general increase in prices might lead to demands for higher wages, which would then affect specific prices. In other words it could reveal how inflation is sustained. But if real wages are relatively constant or falling, it cannot show what is causing the problem in the first place.

Other theorists have therefore argued that the source of the problem must be elsewhere. The simplest definition of inflation is of a situation in which too much money is chasing too few goods. In this situation manufacturers and retailers will increase prices to absorb the excess money, and of course their customers must be prepared to pay more for what is available. However, as many economists argue, the key question when this occurs is not why there is so much paper money, but why there are so few goods to be purchased. For if more goods are produced and productivity is high enough then there need be no crisis of inflation. In the case of Britain the economic crisis essentially involves the decline of its productive capacity and of the relative inefficiency of industry. *The Economist* noted as early as 1972: 'It has been Britain's failure of productivity rather than wages that has made us more inflation-prone than other countries.'[6] This is why the second group of economists, the critical theorists, have turned to the problems of production in the post-war period as a source for their prime explanations.[7]

The central problem of the post-war economy was how to achieve stable growth and full employment. The governments of the Western world realised that it would be politically catastrophic to return to the booms and slumps of the pre-war economy and to the social disruption which had characterised the 1920s and the Great Depression. If this was to be avoided, then governments would have to intervene to manage and control the economy. The importance of Keynes in this period was that as early as the late 1930s he had outlined a general theory by which this might be accomplished. The essence of Keynes's position was that if the government ensured an adequate money supply at the right interest rate, then production would be stimulated. In other words, if the population at large has plenty of income, then capitalists will produce commodities to sell to them. Keynes suggested that the initial stimulus should be provided by government spending on anything from roads to armaments. Simultaneously the government could expand credit and overdraft facilities and make hire-purchase easier, which would also have the effect of stimulating the economy by increasing incomes, and thus increasing demand. In addition, the government could give guaranteed contracts to industrialists, enabling them to plan investment ahead for the production of steel, plastics, electronics, chemicals, etc. For a time, in the post-war period, this system ensured stability and growth.

Keynes had expected a small amount of inflation to result from these policies, but thought that as long as private investment and production was stimulated, then enough commodities would be made to hold this in check. If governments overspent and inflation increased, it was believed that it would be possible simply to reverse the policy and cut back on such expenditure. The theory appeared to work as long as investment in British industry was growing at a rate which matched that of its foreign competitors. Theorists such as D. Yaffe have noted a crucial problem which has beset all the economies of the West and Britain in particular, namely that there has been a persistent decline in the rate of profit. In Britain, between 1950 and 1970, the average annual rate of profit in industrial and commercial enterprise fell from 16.5 per cent to 9.7 per cent. This decline in the profitability of British capital was accompanied by an extremely low level of investment, especially in manufacturing industries, relative to other industrial nations. Investment as a percentage of gross national product between 1960 and 1972 ranged between 30 and 35 per cent in Japan, 23 and 27 per cent in France and 16 and 18 per cent in Britain. What this means in practice is, for example, that each Toyota car worker in Japan works with £11,780 worth of machinery, whereas a British Leyland worker only works with approximately £1,000 worth. As a result, it takes each Leyland worker forty-seven days to produce £1,000 worth of car whereas a Toyota worker only takes nine days to produce the same amount.[8]

In Britain from 1960 to 1972, between 16 and 18 per cent of the gross national product was reinvested. Of this, only 7 per cent was invested in plant and machinery in the productive sector.[9]

The decline in this rate of profit applied mainly to industrial production. In areas of the economy which did not require heavy expenditure on machinery and raw materials, such as banking and entertainment, it was possible to receive much higher returns. These areas therefore began to attract money from speculative investors and there arose the potential danger of a relative decline in investment in the more central parts of the economy for which the rate of profit was lower. In the long-run, this could only lead to an uncompetitive industrial sector and unemployment.

This crisis of investment in the vital areas of industrial production was resolved temporarily in the 1950s and 1960s by governments increasingly taking on responsibility for the investment and the promotion of economic growth that the owners of capital were failing to do for themselves. By doing this, governments were forced increasingly into 'deficit financing' – i.e. they were spending more than they received in taxation. This in Britain was to prove highly inflationary. Government expenditure that was intended as an encouragement to private investment became more and more of a substitute for it. Governments were obliged to give direct investment grants to ensure that production took place at all in some areas. In Britain, for example, firms such as Rolls-Royce, British Leyland, Chrysler and Upper Clyde Shipbuilders have received massive injections of government money to sustain otherwise insolvent concerns. By 1975 government intervention and the giving of direct subsidies to industry, both public and private, had reached unparalleled heights. The *Observer* reported in May 1975 that public borrowing by the government to finance expenditure had quadrupled in just over one year to £10,000 million. This is not the whole story, since it does not include regional aid grants and 'disguised' subsidies such as public sector spending by local authorities and public projects such as motorways and arms expenditure. This growing trend of government responsibility for investment is reflected in the fact that between 1962 and 1969 investment in the private sector (as a percentage of total investment) had fallen from 58.8 per cent in 1962 to 53.4 per cent in 1969.[10] In 1974–5 government investment included £300 million to British Rail, £375 million to the British Steel Corporation and £300 million to the Post Office. In addition the government was committed to giving £1,400 million to British Leyland, £540 million to the Concorde project and to the nationalisation of the failing shipbuilding and aircraft industries, as well as purchasing Burmah Oil at a cost of over £500 million. Further large grants were detailed for the firms of Ferranti, Meriden, Triang Pedigree, Alfred Herbert, Bear Brand, and IPD.[11]

Industrialists who were in receipt of government contracts and credit for investment bid against one another for scarce raw materials and plant (i.e. machine tools, premises and land) This by itself would create inflationary pressure. Second, throughout this period (especially between 1970 and 1973) governments were encouraging banks to lend money, in the hope that industrialists would borrow it to invest and expand. However, industrial investment overall was in relative decline and this was coupled with low industrial growth. While the supply of commodities remained low, the amount of credit available was increasing. This again added to the growth of inflation.

In this situation, one industry which did grow was speculation in land and property as the banks lent money both to the speculator and to ordinary buyers, who were forced to borrow increasing amounts as the price of commodities such as houses increased. The process by which this occurred was adequately summarised in an editorial in the *Investors' Chronicle*. Here it was argued that[12]

> In the summer of 1973, the government was allowing the amount of money for use in the country to expand rapidly in the hope that industry would use it to invest in new plant to produce more goods and earn more foreign exchange by exporting.
>
> It did not work out that way, because industry was not confident that it could sell enough goods profitably enough to cover the money for new plant. So the extra money being pumped into the economy found other uses.
>
> At first some of it found its way into buying shares where it helped to force prices up. More important, vast amounts of money were being lent by the banking system to buy property. Since property is in limited supply, the main effect was to force prices sky high.

The importance of this as an explanation of crisis is that money was directed away from productive capital to finance speculative activities. This provides both a partial explanation of industrial decline (since low investment means that machinery and plant is not being replaced) and also an explanation of the rapid increase in prices. In Britain, from February 1971 to May 1972, borrowing in the finance and personal sectors (including speculation) doubled from £2,176 million to £4,403 million, while investment in manufacturing in 1971 actually fell by 7.7 per cent.[13] The artificial production of price increases extended beyond speculation of land and property. In 1974 The *Guardian* reported that between 30 per cent and 75 per cent of price increases in food and raw materials were the result of speculation.[14] This amounts to financiers or dealers buying a significant stake in the world supply of food, raw materials or semi-produced goods and waiting for the price to increase because of the shortages that have been artificially created.

The key element in explaining inflation for the critical theorists is, then, declining rate of profit throughout the 1950s and 1960s, which produced a relative decline in private investment in the key sectors of industry. In the face of this threat, governments first financed investment and production, and second expanded bank credit. The inflationary effects of this were compounded as much of the money was drawn into the more lucrative areas of property speculation and commodity dealing. Thus the critical theorists offered an explanation both for the decline in the economy and for the growth of inflation in which wages did not contribute significantly. Indeed, according to this theory, inflation can be generated whilst real wages may remain the same or even fall.

The monetarists share certain assumptions with the critical theorists.[15] In particular they also maintain that wage increases are not necessarily the initial cause of inflation. They focus their analysis on the failure of governments to adequately restrict the money supply. For the most part they are anti-Keynesian and oppose the expansion of credit and the pumping of money into the economy to encourage production. They argue that governments must 'balance their books' and spend only what they can raise through taxes and borrowing. Governments must no longer be allowed to engage in deficit financing. It follows that the monetarists reject the responsibility of the government to maintain full employment. Firms that cannot generate sufficient profits to reinvest (the 'lame ducks') must be allowed to fold.

The monetarists therefore root the explanation of inflation firmly in the inadequacy of contemporary government policies. As one Conservative MP, Michael McNair-Wilson, put it: 'When the Chancellor is spending £100 for every £80 he gathers in taxation, I cannot believe our credit worthiness is likely to last.'[16] They are quite clear about the relative unimportance of wages as a source of inflationary pressure. While the cutting of wage rates might be seen as a way of temporarily removing surplus money from the economy, the central problem remains the government expenditure which created and maintains the surplus. This position was at the core of the major economic debate at the Conservative conference of October 1976. The *Guardian* reported that[17]

The first major debate as the conference got underway yesterday was on economic matters and it produced an immediate attack on the social contract as a 'confidence trick'.

The charge was levelled by Mr John Butcher, prospective Tory candidate for Coventry South West, who moved a resolution welcoming co-operation between government and unions on incomes policy as a short term way to reduce wage-cost inflation. But the resolution said there were 'other more important causes of inflation' and therefore called for a fundamental review of public expenditure. . . . Rachel Tingle, of the National Association of Conservative Graduates, was one of several speakers to warn of the pitfalls of the social contract. Scorning any form of incomes policy and calling for pure monetary control, she said 'co-operation between government and trade unions is at best irrelevant, and at worst harmful'. . . . The main motion and the addendum were carried by an overwhelming majority.

This analysis is not a new development in the Conservative party. It has in fact been growing in strength and gathering adherents for a number of years. Thus, Nicholas Ridley, who was Under-Secretary for Trade and Industry in the last Conservative government, wrote in January 1974:[18]

Contrary to the popular view, the cause of inflation is not high wage settlements but the way in which they are financed. In the public sector, wages must be paid for out of taxes, in the private, they must be paid for out of the earnings of the firm. If this is done, no inflation results. It is only when the Government pays for high public sector wage settlements, or rescues bankrupt companies with money that it prints, that inflation results.

The view that the motive force of inflation may not be sought in 'excessive' wage settlements is prominent in other sections of the political and economic spectrum and especially among trade union leaders.

Political and economic opinion is therefore deeply divided as to the nature and cause of the inflationary crisis. What is significant is that across a whole range of opinion, which includes the monetarists of the right wing and the critical theorists of the left, there is an explicit denial that the fundamental cause of the crisis may be sought in 'excessive wage claims'. From some of these perspectives, wage increases are unlikely to be much more than a process of catching up on increases in the cost of living.[19]

Given this range of economic debate, what then were the basic inferential frameworks chosen by television newsproducers to explain the background of economic and industrial reporting in the first months of 1975?

'Explanations' in the television news

In the period of our study, the news reported four broad areas of policy. First, the 'centre' and 'moderate' wings of the Labour party emphasised wage inflation and were the chief proponents of wage restraint. Second, the left of the Labour party and the left in general tended to emphasise the lack of investment as a leading problem. They advocated nationalisation and government planning of the economy and recommended that sources of investment, such as banks, insurance companies and pension funds, should be brought under public control. Third, the monetarists, mainly in the Conservative party, rejected the explanation that wages were the main inflationary force and argued primarily for cuts in government expenditure. A fourth policy recommendation came from some sections of the trade union movement, who advocated a stimulation of demand according to the Keynesian model. There were other positions on policy, of course, which are derived from combinations of these. For example, many unionists, including Jack Jones, then General Secretary of the TGWU, held that although the crisis and inflation were not the result of the actions of working people, a degree of wage restraint would none the less be necessary to help resolve it.

The immediate political context for this study is the Social Contract, and Denis Healey's redefinition of it in January 1975 to mean that in future trade unions would have to accept lower living standards rather than attempt to keep wage rises at the level of price increases. In pressing for this redefinition the Chancellor was making an essentially political stand which was associated with the specific economic view that wages should be held back, and perhaps actually cut. This stance did not express a political consensus on what was wrong with the economy and what ought to be done about it. It was a partisan position probably representative of a majority of the Labour party and at variance with the views of the Conservative monetarists. But it was also being attacked vociferously by the left of the Labour party and by sections of the trade unions. The divisions within the Labour party came to a head with the Budget

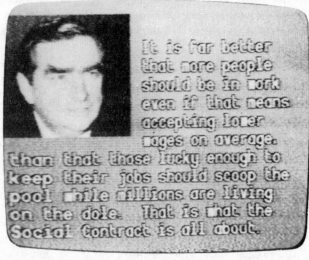

Photo 1a   Denis Healey, *News Review*, BBC2, 12 January 1975

and were referred to in the news bulletins on Budget Day – for example in the item from BBC2 in which the political editor notes

> Mr Healey denied strongly [in the Budget speech] that he will use unemployment as a weapon to fight the country's economic problems, nevertheless, he does accept that some further unemployment must come as an outcome of his Budget. Now it's this part of the speech that is being seized on by a great many Labour MPs, particularly on the left tonight. They are not all the party but they do tend to be the most vocal part of it and the part which has the most influence with the trade unions – and they are bound to express their deep unhappiness about the Budget when the Parliamentary Labour Party meets at the Commons to debate it tomorrow morning. (BBC2, 22.55, 15 March 1975)

The character of government policy in this period was referred to very clearly in a Budget Day bulletin on ITN, in which the Industrial Editor commented that

> The reasoning behind Mr Healey's tough language to the unions

in the absence of an incomes policy is also puzzling to people on both sides of industry. A typical reaction was that, given the current rules of the wage/price game, the government has now entered as a player and is no longer the referee. (ITN, 22.00, 15 April 1975)

The central explanatory theme which underlay the television news coverage of the Social Contract was the position associated with Mr Healey that wage increases were the main cause of inflation and that these should therefore be restrained. In this period the view that inflation was not wages-led was severely under-represented. By contrast, the view that 'excessive' wage settlements were the cause of the crisis was regularly and systematically repeated in both direct and reported statements on all the television channels. Often the argument over whether inflation was in fact caused in this way was pre-empted by simply prefixing references to wage settlements with the word 'inflationary'. In the ITN bulletin of March 1975 relating to an argument within the Labour party between Reg Prentice and Michael Foot, it was noted: 'The row, says our correspondent, illustrates the deep divisions both in the Cabinet and in the Parliamentary Labour Party on whether to take tougher action over inflationary wage settlements' (ITN, 22.30, 1 March 1975). Media personnel sometimes acknowledged, or implied that there were other possible explanations for inflation, but there were comparatively few references to what these might be. Thus in the context of a meeting between the TUC and government ministers in January 1975 we hear from the BBC's correspondent that

While there was an emphatic denial that the wages part of the Social Contract needs rewriting, there is now a considerable pressure on the TUC to try to ensure that the contract is much more strictly adhered to. This reflects the anxiety shared by Mr Healey, the Prime Minister and no doubt other ministers that wages are now a, *if not the*, principal factor in inflation. (BBC1, 21.00, 20 January 1975, our italics)

Later in this bulletin the same correspondent informs us that wages are the main factor in inflation. We are also informed as to what might be done about this situation:

With wages now as the main boost to inflation,
just getting inflation down to a reasonable level seems to imply
tougher pay restraint. A statutory wage policy is still officially
ruled out, but one cannot help thinking, despite Mr Healey's
denials, that between the lines of his speech ten days ago was a
warning to unions that to insist on maintaining living standards
might be asking too much. (BBC1, 21.00, 20 January 1975, our
italics)

It was not clear in this period that real wages were in fact increasing.
On 21 January 1975, Michael Foot referred to the problem pointing
out that the official statistics on wages actually overestimated real
wage increases. However, the television news coverage of this
period simply accepted the argument that real wages were going up.
Foot's comments make possible the view that real wages for most
people might have been stationary or even declining, but this was
ignored in the news. Thus Mr Foot was reported on BBC1 as
follows:

Also in the Commons, the Employment Secretary, Mr Foot, has
been replying to attacks from Conservatives, who claimed that
the 23.5 per cent rise in weekly wage rates last month was a
disaster for Britain. Mr Foot argued that, disregarding threshold
payments and special cases like miners, wage increases averaged
around 14 per cent. (BBC1, 17.45, 21 January 1975)

Yet in other television news commentaries of this period it was
regularly announced that wages were rising faster than prices and
that this was the cause of inflation. In the following bulletin Mr
Foot's statement was reported and was then discussed by the
newscaster and the industrial correspondent:

Newscaster (to industrial correspondent): The problem facing
    the government is dealing with the inflationary pressure of
    the wages, going up for no matter what reason?
Industrial correspondent: Yes indeed, regardless of how this
    figure is made up we still have wage inflation running at a
    rate of 28 per cent, unprecedented, and the Prime Minister
    has made it quite clear, and the Chancellor Mr Healey has
    made it quite clear, that the main inflationary boost just
    now comes from wages. (BBC2, 22.30, 21 January 1975)

Their discussion is remarkable, first because they appear to have failed to understand the implications of Mr Foot's argument and thus refer to wages as 'going up for no matter what reason'; second, this questionable interpretation is linked to comments on the 'inflationary pressure of wages' and this view of inflation is finally reinforced by the two reported statements. A numerical analysis of all such references reveals that there were no direct statements from media personnel that wages might not be the main factor behind inflation. By comparison there were 14 direct statements which suggested that it was. (By direct statements we mean statements made by media personnel as their own and which are not attributed to another source. See 'Media statements' in Appendix B (p. 436) and Table B.1 (p. 439). In addition there were 56 reported statements which blamed inflation on wage increases and 14 interview responses which introduced this as a theme; 12 interview questions indicate a similar emphasis on wage inflation as the key economic problem. The total number of such references is therefore 96. Refutations of this position, when they appeared, came as either reported statements, of which there were 7, or as responses made to interview questions. There were 5 such responses. A complete table giving the numerical frequency of all explanations of the crisis is given below (p. 23) and a more detailed exposition of this, showing both the manner of their appearance and the channel concerned, is given in Appendix B.

One of the five refutations of the view that wages were chiefly to blame for inflation came in an interview with Ian Mikardo, MP, who clearly articulated an alternative view. In this interview the MP initially outlined a possible series of economic policies, including the redistribution of income and the introduction of import controls. This was immediately followed by the interviewer returning to the theme of wage increases. The sequence was as follows:

I. Mikardo: I think we have got to have some really strong
   economic controls . . .
Interviewer: Such as?
I. Mikardo: Such as some import controls and much stronger
   exchange controls than we have got at the moment. I would
   like to see the planning agreement system pushed ahead
   very fast. I would want to see the National Enterprise
   Board set up quickly. I would want to see a rapid extension

of the public sector and I would want to see, above all, a major redistribution of income and wealth, lopping off the top and adding to the bottom.

Interviewer: Ah, but here's the rub, isn't it, because it seems that the CBI and the government are almost agreed that it's the increases in wages at the present rate that is not tolerable?

I. Mikardo: Yes, and of course this is subscribing to a hoary myth, that the only cause of inflation is increase in wages. This is a nonsense.

Interviewer: What would you do . . ?

I. Mikardo: There are no British wages that have caused the increase in the price of oil, no British wages have caused the increase in the price of land, which is one of the great inflationary forces, and no British wages have caused high interest rates. (ITN, 13.00, 13 January 1975)

On both channels, the views that are represented here by Ian Mikardo were heavily outweighed by opinions which linked wage levels to the economic crisis. This imbalance may be seen both in terms of the numerical frequency of certain types of interviews and the internal structure and organisation of them. By the latter we mean primarily the selection of the interviewee, the organisation and content of questions and pursuance or rejection of themes by the interviewer.

The above interview may be compared with one which is more typical of this period. It occurred at the time of the Budget of April 1975 and involves a discussion between a BBC2 newscaster and an economist, who is introduced as working with a firm of stockbrokers on Budget forecasts. In the course of the interview, the economist voiced the opinion on five separate occasions that the economic crisis was the result of current wage levels. At one point he argued that 'After all, it is pay that is causing the massive inflation rate that we have at the moment and without tackling that we are likely to get more Budgets of this sort.' At no point in this interview did the newscaster challenge the explanations or assumptions upon which the economist was making his case. There is no equivalent here to the criticism of the interviewee's analysis, which we saw in the previous example. The dominant framework that wages cause inflation remains unchallenged. Thus the following exchange occurs later in the interview:

Interviewee: Until you fetch the rate of inflation down you cannot expect business confidence to improve. There is only one way to bring the rate of inflation down and that is to stop the very large wage increases that we are seeing at the current time.

Newscaster: Are we going to go on seeing large companies laying off men, shortening their working week?

Interviewee: Very largely, I think that is a very likely prospect and we calculate that the overall impact of the Budget is to put another 50,000 men out of work. Now that is the price that we had to pay for the excessive wage rises that we have seen during this winter. (BBC2, 22.55, 15 April 1975)

The conclusion from this, which is borne out from our findings across the whole of this period, is that statements and explanations which contradict the interpretative framework of the media are much more likely to be challenged than those which do not.

The wage/inflation theme is most commonly embedded in a variety of reported statements. These come consistently and regularly from a number of 'official' sources, including the Bank of England, the Price Commission and from individual members of the government. The following bulletin is from ITN, in April of 1975, and deals with a report from the Price Commission:

Newscaster: And now the economy. Prices in Britain rose at their fastest rate ever between December and February, mainly due to high wage settlements, according to the Price Commission Report published today. In three months up to last December, the Commission approved an average of £350 million in price increases each month, particularly in nationalised industries, but as subsidies started to be phased out and the big pay increases started to push labour costs higher, the Commission were forced to allow an average of £1,105 million in increases each month between December and February. This quarterly figure is about as large as the previous nine months combined. Well here with a report is our industrial correspondent, Giles Smith.

G. Smith: Today's message from the Price Commission is grim and it's no less grim because it's not a new one. Inflation is now rampant and, according to the Commission, wage inflation is almost entirely to blame. Ominously, they say the pace of prices explosion has so far been understated. In the three months covered, the retail prices index went up 5.8 per cent, wholesale prices 6.5 per cent, but the Commission's own index, which should be more up to date, rose 7.5 per cent. For this the Commission firmly blame wage-cost increases. (ITN, 22.00, 24 April 1975)

Such a heavy and unqualified repetition of reported statements is one dimension of the manner in which dominant explanations come to be established. A second dimension is the way in which the official report and its figures are utilised in order to reinforce the dominant conclusions that are drawn by the news media. A careful reading of the Price Commission's report shows that a number of factors apart from wages were cited as contributing to price increases. For example, they included the increased cost of oil. The contribution to price increases that was directly attributable to increased labour costs *was in fact calculated by the Price Commission as only 20 per cent of the total*. This represented a decline in the figures for direct wages in the preceding quarter.

Yet the bulletins of this date refer to much higher figures than this. The main news on BBC1 of this day stated that 'between 60 and

Photo 1b   Sir Arthur Cockfield, Chairman of the Price Commission, *News at Ten*, ITN, 29 April 1975

75 pence in the pound' of the price increases arose through wages. One reason for these high figures was that the Commission and its chairman, Sir Arthur Cockfield, had estimated upwards their own figures for the effect of wage costs. On the next day the *Financial Times* reported that this had apparently been done in two ways.[20] First, by taking away the effects of oil increases, and second by the chairman suggesting that *indirect* wages 'probably' accounted for two to two and a half times as much as *direct* wages. The reference to oil in the Price Commission's report is as follows:[21]

These increases [in oil prices] represented cost increases which had accumulated throughout 1974 and were only passed through to the U.K. consumer in December. As a result, the labour cost element in the figures notified to the Commission in the current period fell to 20%; but excluding oil, the figure would have remained at just over 30%.

The Commission then argued that the effect of 'indirect' wages could be calculated as follows: to arrive at the true contribution of labour cost increases to price increases, we need to multiply the figure for labour cost increases shown in the notifications to the Commission *by something like 2 to 2½ times.*[22] The BBC had presumably arrived at the figure of 75 per cent of price increases coming from wages by multiplying the 30 per cent figure (after the deduction of oil) by the 'probable' two and a half times. Any professional economist or statistician reporting such calculations would feel obliged to note that they are not precise but are really only crude estimates which contrast with a calculated figure which is much lower.

There are two points to be made here about their use in television news. First, that on both the BBC and ITN, the highest possible estimate of the effect of wages was taken as the basis for reporting that wage increases were primarily responsible for inflation. At no point in the bulletins was there any comment on how these high figures had been arrived at, and at no point was the information given that the *proven* figures for the effect of wages was only 20 per cent, which represented a decline on the previous quarter.[23]

The reporting of 'economic facts' thus depends critically upon the interpretative framework which informs which information is given and the manner in which it is presented. This may be further illustrated by two press reports of the Price Commission, which differ markedly from the television news and from each other. The *Morning Star* that day explicitly attacked the Commission's estimates. Citing a recent *Sunday Times* survey on profits in British industry, it argued that 'The Price Commission's report for the three months to the end of February blames wages, and using highly dubious arithmetic and reasoning exonerates profit entirely.'[24] The *Daily Telegraph*, in an editorial on the same day, argued that the focus of the Price Commission on wages detracted from what was, for it, the central point – that wages do not cause inflation:[25]

> Although the Price Commission was correct in pointing out that
> wage increases rather than raw material prices are the cause of
> many price increases, they are not themselves the cause of
> inflation. That occurs only if the government prints money to
> enable consumers to buy the same amount of goods at the
> increased price.

The economic arguments embraced by the *Telegraph* here are essentially monetarist and they thus differ significantly from those embraced and underlined by the television news.

The use made of statistics in television commentaries is a crucial dimension in the establishing of specific and limited ways of understanding how the economy works and the actions of different groups within it. Furthermore, they are frequently linked to descriptions of industrial activity such as the development of wage claims. In a sense, they set the context for the evaluation of these. Thus the ITN bulletin which we quoted above continued with a discussion of current wage negotiations. These are linked quite explicitly to the wage/inflation theme, and this provides a kind of rationale for a negative evaluation of groups of workers who are engaged in wage negotiations. Thus later in the same ITN bulletin we hear:

> Industrial Correspondent: The broad and inescapable
> conclusion drawn by the Commission is that prices are going up,
> quote, 'far too fast'. As the Commission chairman Sir Arthur
> Cockfield states, 'taking industry as a whole, the primary factor
> causing prices to rise is and can only be rising labour costs'. Well
> the sort of wage rises the Commission is thinking about are those
> in the 30 per cent-plus bracket and today there came another: the
> 11,000 London dockers who were on strike for 5 weeks just a
> while ago were today offered and accepted a pay deal which

averages out at well over 30 per cent. On the face of it well outside the social contract guidelines. Tonight, too, a new threat from the electricity power engineers to strike in support of a 33 per cent pay claim. (ITN, 22.00, 29 January 1975)

The move from what are apparently 'factual' explanations to the explicit articulation of values and political prescriptions by media personnel comes very swiftly in this kind of coverage.

The examples which we have given of the development of explanatory themes through direct and reported statements and interviews give some indication of the nature of coverage in the four-month period of our sample. However, they would be inadequate as individual examples, and it is therefore necessary to give a numerical account of their occurrence throughout the coverage. Table 1.1 gives the number of references in the news to different explanations of what had caused inflation and the economic crisis.

Table 1.1 Causes of economic crisis identified on TV news

Problem identified	Number of references
Wages/'excessive wage increases'	96 (+ 12 'negative', i.e. denials of problem)
Lack of investment/decline in industrial investment	33
Increase in oil price (plus some other key commodities)	29
Government borrowing/foreign loans	23
Government expenditure	22
High taxation in industry (corporation tax, etc.)	10
Price control	5
Overmanning in industry	5 (+ 2 'negative')
Speculation	2
'Management'	2
'World recession'	2
Tax evasion	2
High interest rates	1
Foreign import competition	1

Appendix B (p. 439) gives the number of references by channel, and by the manner in which they appeared; i.e. as direct statements from media personnel, or as reported statements, as interview questions or as responses from interviewees.

These figures indicate the degree of emphasis given in the news to wage increases as the central economic problem. There were 94 references of this kind, 14 of which were from media personnel. On only 12 occasions was this position explicitly denied and none of those denials originated from reporters or correspondents.

In one rare piece of coverage the industrial editor of ITN acknowledged quite clearly the importance of another problem – the failure of large sections of private capital to invest adequately in new machinery and in advanced production techniques. In January 1975, while discussing the rise in unemployment and the decline of investment, he noted that

> Of these two developments, the revelation that manufacturing industry has cut its plans to invest this year by between 7 and 10 per cent is by far the most serious. Investment is the new machines, plant and building that firms buy. This new equipment is what literally manufactures a new wealth for a country in the years ahead. Things other countries want to buy. Wealth that is more than a piece of paper. Since the war, Britain's overriding problem, almost universally agreed, has been a failure to invest adequately. Since 1969 the problem has become worse, with investment increasing at nowhere near the rate of production. The result, machines increasingly out of date, working at their limit and uncompetitive. 1975, to cap it all, now looks like being a year of huge investment collapse. (ITN, 22.00, 21 January 1975)

This 'overriding problem' received only 33 references as a cause of industrial crisis compared with 94 references to wage increases as the central problem and the cause of inflation. A further indication of the different priority given to 'wages' as opposed to 'investment' as explanations of the economic crisis is revealed by the relative number of 'media statements' and 'interview questions' which focus on them (see Appendix B, p. 439). The higher frequency of direct statements and interview questions from media personnel which draw attention to the 'problem' of wages, when compared with those on investment, demonstrates a crucial aspect of the control of information by TV news in reporting the British economy.

Another 'problem' referred to on the news was the increase in world commodity prices, notably oil. This explanation of economic crisis received 29 references on the news and 12 of these came as direct statements from media personnel.[26] Yet, although the validity of this explanation was directly acknowledged, it was never used by media personnel to criticise the view that the central cause of inflation was wage increases.

As we have argued, the *numerical* dominance of the wage/inflation explanation is clear. Yet merely to count the appearance of direct and reported statements and interview questions and responses, is to severely underestimate the role of this explanation in news coverage. As we will show, much of the news simply pre-supposed that wages were a 'problem' in the way that wages and prices figures were routinely compared. More crucially, this explanation was systematically taken up and used as the organising principle for coverage. It informed routine coverage of wage claims and settlements and was at the core of Social Contract coverage. By contrast, as we will show, alternative accounts of the economic problem typically appear as disparate fragments and have a quite subsidiary role in the text. News reports were not organised to illustrate the content of these alternative views or to follow their meaning through from their premises to their conclusions. For example, media references to oil costs appear typically as fragments which never challenge the central theme that wages are the critical problem. Thus in the BBC coverage of the Price Commission's report (29 April 1975), which we discussed above, we were told that 'Although oil prices and nationalised industry price increases figured largely in the overall costs, wages were directly or indirectly responsible for between 60 and 75 pence in the pound of final price increases' (BBC1, 21.00, 29 January 1975). As we noted above, the figure of 'between 60 and 70 pence' in the pound could only be arrived at by discounting the effects of oil price increases from the calculations. This information was not given on the news.

Another possible explanation of the economic crisis, referred to on the news, was that of government spending and over-borrowing. References to this when they came were mainly in reports or interviews with Conservative spokesmen. The fragmentary nature of references to this and to some other problems may be illustrated by a report on the Budget of April 1975. Here, Sir Keith Joseph's position is summarised as follows: 'His [Joseph's] main attack over and over again, was on too high Government spending. We were over-spending, over-taxing, over-borrowing and over-manning' (BBC2, 21.00, 21 April 1975). Here four separate causes all appear in one short sentence. Government policy on expenditure, from a monetarist perspective, was not a central or organising theme of the news at that period. However, it must be said that at that time the debate in the country over government expenditure and cuts was at a very early stage. It became a central issue in the period following our study, which, as we will show later, may account for the low number of media references, and the manner in which they appeared.

An examination of all references to all causes of the economic crisis therefore reveals wages as being the most stressed single cause, with all other causes as subordinate. We will turn now to a detailed examination of how this central theme underpinned the organisation of routine coverage.

2 Wages and Prices Figures

One month's figures are an unreliable guide.

BBC1, 21.00, 19 February 1975

The use of official statistics in the development of specific themes is a very common practice in media reporting. In industrial stories, the figures which received most regular attention in the period of our study were the Department of Employment statistics on increases in the levels of prices and wages. These were not only reported but were systematically used on both channels to convey the view that wage inflation was the prime cause of Britain's economic crisis. A typical illustration may be seen in an interview which occurred on ITN between a newspresenter and the General Secretary of ASLEF. Here, the interviewer asked about a contemporary pay claim and in his question made clear his belief that the claim was actually above current price increases:

> Robert Kee: Can we look at your claim you've already got in; you see, I mean, you said to one of my colleagues not long ago on this programme, that this claim was likely then – this was in February – to be in the range of 25 per cent to 30 per cent; now, you see, that is already between 5 per cent and 10 per cent more than the rise in prices and it's just this excessive demand above the price rise that Mr Healey was saying was endangering our whole national economy. (ITN, 13.00, 16 April 1975)

Official figures on the current rises in prices were thus used to underpin a particular view of the crisis. Throughout this period a causal relationship was consistently inferred by media personnel in describing price and wage movements. To draw such a direct relationship between wages and price increases is effectively to pre-empt much of the debate over whether or not inflation *is* largely caused by wage increases. The consistent juxtaposition of wages with prices simply avoids presenting those viewpoints that suggest that wages are not the single crucial determinant of price increases.

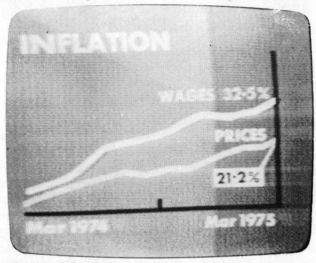

Photo 1c   Inflation – the wages and prices figures, *Nine O'Clock News*, BBC1, 18 April 1975

The following example, from BBC News of April 1975, includes a discussion of the then current retail price index and a comparison of this with the index of basic weekly wage rates. In discussing these figures a graph was used on which two lines appeared – one for prices and one for wages. The spoken commentary from the industrial correspondent linked the movement of the two:

> And there are other prices still to work through and yet as the Chancellor said in his budget speech on Tuesday, the dominant inflationary influence just now is high wage awards. Retail prices [graph is shown] which have risen 21.2 per cent over the past twelve months still lag well behind the movement of basic weekly wage rates, which have risen 32.5 per cent in the same period. (BBC1, 21.00, 18 April 1975)

We may ask what it means to juxtapose two sets of figures in this way. The current level of price increases could have been shown in relation to increases in government spending, or to estimates of the effects of speculation or of price fixing, etc. To have done this would have been to acknowledge that there were other central 'problems' in the economy, apart from wages, which produced inflation. Yet wages alone are consistently presented as if they are in some way 'pulling' prices along behind them. The whole of the coverage of such figures in our four-month sample was organised around this view.

The industrial news presents its discussion and *evaluation* of the activities of management and labour in the context of an apparently factual and objective analysis of the state of the economy. There were two dimensions to this approach. First, as we have indicated, we were informed on the news that wages were the central problem and, on the basis of this, current wage settlements and wage rates in general were evaluated and commented upon. The second dimension of the media's 'factual' analysis was to link this month after month with Department of Employment figures which apparently revealed that wages were actually increasing in excess of prices. However, by a number of other accounts, 'real wages' for the mass of the population were not 'far in advance' of price increases. Indeed, it is probably the case that real wages were falling.

The distinction here between money earnings or wage rates and real wages is critically important. The figures shown in Table 2.1, produced by the Cambridge University Economic Policy Group, indicate some of the startling differences between money earnings

Table 2.1   Average earnings 1970–6 (percentage increase on previous year)

	1970	1971	1972	1973	1974	1975	1976
Pre-tax money earnings	12.8	11.9	12.2	12.5	20.7	30.4	14.8
Post-tax money earnings	11.0	12.0	13.0	11.7	18.0	25.3	12.7
Post-tax real earnings	4.1	3.4	5.3	0.3	2.2	2.0	−2.4

Source: *Economic Policy Review*, no. 3, March 1977, p. 103.

and real earnings in the period 1970–6. These figures are merely adjusted for direct taxation and consumer price inflation. If increases in indirect taxation are taken into account along with other factors, real earnings diminish even further for wage earners receiving the average wage or less. Figure 2.1, taken from the *Department of Employment Gazette* and the *Bulletin of Labour Statistics*, reveals that over the four-month period January–April 1975 the general index of consumer prices (using the same base year) rose 12.6 points compared with a rise of only 9.2 points in the average earnings index. Indeed, if we take six months' figures (January–June 1975) a variety of different measures reveal a similar trend. For example, the percentage rise in average earnings over the period was 7.3 per cent compared with a 14.4 per cent rise in the general index of consumer prices (using 1970 as the base year). The

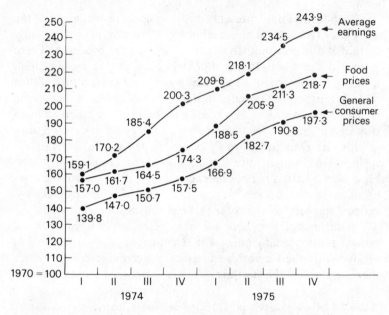

Figure 2.1   Index of average earnings and general index of consumer prices, 1974–5. *Source*: Department of Employment Gazette, December 1976; Bulletin of Labour Statistics, ILO, Geneva, 1977

rise in the food prices index was even greater. Whichever way the relative movement of wages and prices is compared there is no support for the notion that wages were rapidly outstripping price increases. By some measures wages fall, by most measures real wages fall, and by no criteria can there be said to be a 'sharp acceleration of wage inflation'.[1]

The Times reported on 21 August 1975 that average earnings in the first half of the year rose by 6.1 per cent; yet 'Retail prices over the same half year rose by 17.3% implying a drop in the real value of the average pay packet of nearly 10%'. There was also evidence at the time of our sample that the official figures for price increases may have underestimated the rate of inflation that most people experienced. This was because the figures were calculated on the increase in price of a wide range of items, including luxuries. Yet some major necessities, such as food, were rising at a higher rate than the general increase. For example, ITN reported on 18 April 1975 that, while price increases for all goods were rising at 21.2 per cent, food prices were rising at 23.5 per cent.

Of course, some of these calculations are retrospective and not all of the data which they use were available to the broadcasters at the time. Yet at least some of the figures were available, and certainly enough to cast doubt on the possibility of drawing any firm conclusions on the relation between wages, prices and inflation. In addition, it was known that the official figures at this time were an unreliable guide. Yet television news consistently affirmed that wages were rising far ahead of prices and linked this directly to the economic crisis.

As we noted above, average earnings or money wages are not real wages. The Department of Employment figures on wage increases are a very unreliable guide to real spending power. One reason for this is that they give figures for gross pay rather than for what people actually take home. Approximately one-third of all pay is deducted for tax and national insurance, etc. Thus to compare increases in gross pay with price increases gives a very unacceptable estimate of whether people have actually received a pay increase, and the figures have to be qualified to take account of this and other forms of taxation and inflation. On rare occasions this was partially recognised in the television commentaries. In the following example, the industrial editor of ITN compared the wage and price figures for the year up to the beginning of 1975. On this occasion he noted the importance of adjusting the figures to work out what actual take-home pay was:

> Industrial editor: This is the comparison which really counts, the average earnings of 7 million workers: 25.3 per cent up from November to November, the latest month to which the figures are available. Prices from December to December 19.1 per cent up. Now it is usually a reliable guide to look at the gap between the two. In general it has to be 4 per cent or more for actual take home pay to be keeping up with prices. (ITN, 22.00, 20 January 1975)

Another reason why figures for wage increases have to be qualified is that rates of increase are often based on comparisons with earnings in the previous year. The year before our study had included the three-day week and the miners' overtime ban, which had *lowered* many people's wages for that year. Thus in the following year (the period of our study) when industry returned to a more normal situation, according to some calculations it looked as though there had been a large increase in wages. The television news coverage which we recorded acknowledged on a small number of occasions that the figures had been affected in this way. However, it still overwhelmingly concluded that 'wages' were increasing far in excess of prices. There are two central points which should be noted about the television news coverage at this period. First, that even when qualifications were given, the conclusion was that 'wages' were rising faster than prices and this was normally linked to the explanation of inflation and economic crisis. Second, that in a large part of the coverage no qualifications were given at all. This is particularly important since the Department of Employment figures were often used in the evaluation of wage settlements and as the basis for saying whether a pay award was 'inside' or 'outside' the Social Contract. Although the broadcasters were aware of the differences between 'real' and 'money' wages, little attention was paid to this important distinction in routine news coverage. In fact in most of the coverage, this important and crucial feature of wages – namely whether an increase is real or merely monetary – was obscured by the consistent assertion that 'earnings were far outstripping the retail price increases' (BBC1, 21.00, 20 January 1975).

A breakdown of the coverage on this topic reveals the following. In the case of ITN, out of a total of 11 occasions during the four-month period in which the wage/price figures were reported, 6 made no reference to where real wages might have stood in relation to prices. They gave only the gross figures for apparent wage increases. In the BBC bulletins (both BBC1 and BBC2), the gross figures were given without reference to possible 'real wages' in 17 bulletins out of a total of 20 during the same period.

In the reports of the Department of Employment wage/price figures, the BBC never mentioned the probable effects of the three-day week of the previous year. ITN mentioned this upwardly distorting factor in 5 bulletins out of a total of 11 during the months of February, March and April.

The routine accounts – January–April

January 1975

We have already commented on the need to qualify official figures on wages and prices if sense is to be made of them. At different points in the coverage, the ITN industrial editor did make some attempts to do this. As we noted above, in the January coverage he made the references to the difference between gross wages and real take-home pay. In *News at Ten* on 20 January, the general conclusion was that 'wages are now rising a little faster than prices'. The ITN correspondent qualified this further by saying 'this is the first time for more than a year that this has happened'. In addition he quoted evidence compiled by a firm of stockbrokers which suggested that wage settlements were being reduced in the long-term. By comparison BBC news on this day was quite different. The early news made one brief qualification of the figures (a reference to tax and real income) but its general conclusion was that wages were in advance of prices. The newscaster commented:

Meanwhile the nation's wage bill is going up faster than ever before. Official figures today show that average earnings last November were 25 per cent higher than in the same month in 1973, a record increase. Our economics correspondent says that after taxation, the actual rise in spending power is just over 20 per cent. That is still ahead of the increase in retail prices of 18.3 per cent.[2] (BBC1, 17.45, 20 January 1975)

Later, the main news bulletin on BBC1 of that evening was even firmer in its conclusions. It began:

Newscaster: The figures published today by the Department of Employment show that wage-inflation is still accelerating sharply, with earnings keeping well ahead of prices. During 1974 basic weekly wage rates rose by a record 28½ pence in the pound. While in the year up to last November, average earnings, which include overtime and bonus pay, also soared by a record 25.3 per cent, far outstripping the retail price increases of 18 per cent during the same period. (BBC1, 21.00, 20 January 1975)

The linking of the wage/price figures to the 'acceleration of inflation' allowed the statement that wages had 'soared' and that they had 'far outstripped the retail price increases'. This conclusion

Photo 1d   Pay and prices, *Nine O'Clock News*, BBC1, 20 January 1975

was facilitated because the qualifications to the figures which we noted above were left out of the bulletin.

February 1975

One month later, in February, when a new set of Department of Employment figures appeared the conclusion on both channels was the same – that wages were still out-pacing prices. By other accounts, which we noted above, real wages were now declining for the second month running, and there was some evidence to suggest that this view was available at the time of these news bulletins. The increase in basic wage rates for February was extremely small. This was noted by the BBC in both of their bulletins for the day, but at this point they felt obliged to say that the figures for one month were unreliable. The industrial correspondent noted:

> This relatively small increase in basic weekly wage rates brings the annual increase in basic wages down from 28.5 per cent to just under 28 per cent. That must be some consolation to the Government and must make them hope that pay settlements, at

least in the private sector, are moderated. But one swallow doesn't make a summer and one month's figures are an unreliable guide. (BBC1, 21.00, 19 February 1975)

No similar reservations had been made in January when the figures appeared to show a 'record increase' in wages. Therefore the BBC correspondent had minimised the impact of figures which might have qualified his basic conclusion. This was that wages were increasing 'much faster than prices'. His final comments for the early BBC1 bulletin were: 'The way pay rises are out-pacing prices is hard to reconcile with the objective of the Social Contract, which was to try and ensure that wages rise no faster than prices' (BBC1, 17.45, 19 February 1975). Later in the main news, he concluded that: 'Now the fact that pay rises are out-pacing price increases cannot be reconciled with the purpose of the Social Contract – that was to try and make sure that wages rise no faster than prices' (BBC1, 21.00, 19 February 1975).

ITN reports of the wages and prices figures were very brief on that day. They reported the official figures that earnings were 10 per cent ahead of prices but gave two important qualifications. The first of these was that the miners' overtime ban and the three-day week for industry had lowered wages in the previous year. The effect of this was to make the following year's figures for wage increases look extra large. Second, the ITN bulletins reported that recent wage figures had also been made to appear larger by back-dated pay deals. These qualifications were entirely missing from the BBC coverage. Had they been included it would have been more difficult for the BBC correspondent to have reached the conclusions that he did. No such conclusions were drawn in the ITN coverage.

A further qualification which might have been made in these bulletins was that about one-third of gross pay goes in tax and other deductions. There was no mention of this by ITN and the BBC referred to it only to say that 'even net take-home is up on prices' (BBC1, 21.00, 19 February 1975).

Another important qualification of the Department of Employment figures has to do with threshold payments. The basis of this argument is the suggestion that the way in which wage increases are calculated tends to overestimate the value of pay awards because these often involve money in payment for past cost-of-living increases. In this sense, payments of such 'old money' were not pay increases at all. It is this qualification which caused the

Financial Times of 20 February 1975, which appeared on the day after the February figures were published, to argue:

> The latest wage rate and earnings figures showing wages at 27.29% above a year ago are a most doubtful guide to the future rate of wage inflation. For this we would have to have a carefully costed index of new settlements taking account of thresholds, which just does not exist. Indeed it is probable that the average rate of new money in settlements is nearer 20% than 30% and there may have even been a slight decline.

The argument about 'old' and 'new' money did surface in the following television news bulletin on 27 February, in which Hugh Scanlon, the President of the AEUW, was interviewed. However, the presenter set the interview agenda in terms of the economy threatened by wage inflation:

> Presenter (R. Kee): Now in as much as your reappraisal might lead to higher wage settlements, how much do you take into account the warnings Mr Healey, your Chancellor, was giving only at the weekend that it was wage inflation that was now the real danger to Britain's economy?
>
> Mr Scanlon: Well I have never accepted that wages are the root cause of Britain's economic difficulties.
>
> Presenter: He does, though.
>
> Mr Scanlon: He does and I disagree with him and I think the majority of trade unionists disagree with ministers who advance that. (ITN, 13.00, 27 February 1975)

The interview shows how the argument about threshold payments or 'old money' does not fit in with the dominant view. Mr Scanlon suggested that the figures for wages and prices were being calculated in such a way as to give the appearance that the Social Contract was being broken (i.e. that wages were rising much faster than prices):

> Mr Scanlon: I'm saying that the Contract is quite clear. The wage increase should be to the amount that the cost of living has increased. Now that must mean new money to that amount and what I am suggesting is happening in the calculations, in order to try and prove that the Contract has been broken, old money is

being used to assess the total figure and given an appearance that the Contract's been broken, when, in fact, it hasn't. (ITN, 13.00, 27 February 1975)

On the basis of this Mr Scanlon suggested at the time that the TUC should set up new standards to estimate the real relationship between wages and prices.

One feature of news reporting that we have commented on in previous work is that the establishment of a dominant view leads not only to the neglect of alternative views in news coverage, but on occasion to the use of such alternative information to support rather than contradict the dominant view. Mr Scanlon's position was essentially that the Social Contract was not being broken and that proper standards had to be set up by the TUC to show this. The BBC at this time was committed to the opposite view that wages were 'soaring' and the Social Contract was being broken. In one noteworthy piece of coverage, on the day after the above interview, the industrial correspondent of the BBC reported:

> Industrial Correspondent: It might seem to many, however, that Mr Hugh Scanlon of the Engineering Workers has got close to the real truth earlier this week, when he suggested that the TUC should assume the job of saying which pay settlements fell within and which without the Social Contract rather than trying to justify some of the manifestly extra contractual pay deals which are being made. (BBC2, 21.00, 28 February 1975)

This is scarcely the interpretation put forward by Mr Scanlon, that current wage levels were within the Social Contract, and that this would be shown if proper standards were set up by the TUC.

March 1975

In the following month, March, a new set of wages and prices figures was published by the Department of Employment. These were reported on both channels, together with a speech made by the Chancellor, Denis Healey, on the same day. In this speech, Healey argued that wage increases were the main cause of inflation. His comments were made in the context of a vigorous debate within the Labour party on future government policy, in particular on what would be done in the Budget, which was due to appear a few weeks later. As we have already shown, the Chancellor was a key representative of the stream of official thought which sought to resolve the economic crisis by wage restraint. The Chancellor's

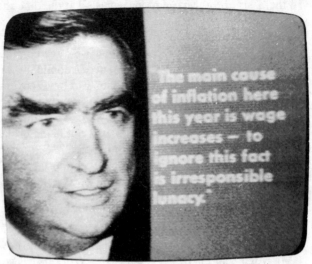

Photo 1e   Denis Healey, *Nine O'Clock News*, BBC1, 19 March 1975

speech on the 'dangers' of 'wage inflation' occurred almost simultaneously with reports from the Department of Employment and from the Bank of England which apparently showed that in the previous year wages had been the major factor influencing price rises.

There is some evidence (see Figure 2.1, for example) to suggest that real wages had increased in the previous year. An analysis of long-term wage trends by Frances Cairncross suggests that wages had gone down at the end of 1973, then went up again in the latter part of 1974, and then down again in 1975. In other words there was a cyclical rise and fall which, taken overall, suggested that real wages were remaining constant over a fairly long period. Thus Cairncross notes that 'the purchasing power of the average male worker's earnings has been virtually unchanged for four years'.[3] Such conclusions did not inform the television news bulletins of the period of our study. The overwhelming theme of these was that a huge wage explosion was taking place. The occasion of the wage and price figures for March was used extensively to develop this theme and to heavily underline the content of the Chancellor's speech on wage inflation and the apparent necessity for wage restraint.

The news on BBC1 on 19 March contained an extensive report of the Healey speech, which was then underlined by the use of official figures which were presented in a completely unqualified way. The early news went as follows:

> From the Chancellor of the Exchequer, Mr Denis Healey, a stern warning on the effect of wage increases on inflation. The Chancellor told a meeting of the Parliamentary Labour Party this morning that to ignore current wage rises was irresponsible lunacy. At the same time official figures were published showing that wages are now about 29 per cent higher than a year ago while prices have risen by 10 per cent less. (BBC1, 17.45, 19 March 1975)

The *Nine O'Clock News* again reported the Healey speech and explicitly linked this with the unqualified Department of Employment figures:

> The Chancellor, Mr Denis Healey, has given another stern warning about the effect of wage increases on inflation. He told a private meeting of the Parliamentary Labour Party in the House of Commons that if one looked to the future there was danger of inflation rising to double the rate of Britain's competitors. Mr Healey said the main cause of inflation here this year was wage increases. To ignore this fact was irresponsible lunacy. Mr Healey's warning was reinforced by figures issued by the Department of Employment. These show that average earnings rose by almost 30 per cent in 1974. It means that earnings are still well ahead of prices, which had risen 19 per cent in the year to January. (BBC1, 21.00, 19 March 1975)

Both of the above reports were followed by extensive discussions of figures from the Bank of England, which again apparently showed that wages had in the past year been a key factor in price increases.

The BBC coverage of 19 March did not suggest that any of these figures or the conclusions that were being drawn from them might be open to several interpretations. No alternative version was given of what might be wrong with the economy.

By contrast, some press reports made heavy qualifications to the

Department of Employment figures. For example, the *Guardian* noted that, while these showed that wages had been ahead of prices in 1974, it none the less suggested that the growing economic recession was beginning to push down average earnings in the current period. More importantly, it suggested that this was being shown by the most recent figures. For although basic wage rates were apparently high, average earnings figures, which are normally a much more reliable guide, were beginning to show a decline. Thus the *Guardian* noted that[4]

> a growing gap is emerging between nationally negotiated wage rates and earnings, which are affected directly by short-time working and reduced overtime. The January figures suggest that the growing recession is pushing earnings down even though nationally negotiated wage rates are still very high.
>
> The earnings index is unlikely to reflect the true trend of pay until it moves away from a yearly comparison with last year's crisis period.

None of these qualifications or points was made in the BBC news presentation of the Department of Employment figures at this time. The crucial distinction between money and real wages was again substantially absent. The only mention of an alternative point of view in the BBC1 coverage of that day came with a brief reference in two bulletins to the Tribune group of the Labour party. Thus we were told that

> Without more modest wage deals and better productivity on the shop floor Mr Healey says our prices will soon be rising twice as fast as those of our competitors. So his message called for belt-tightening and the party meeting rejected a call from the left-wing Tribune group for an opposite, give-away Budget. (BBC1, 21.00, 19 March 1975)

These were the only references in this coverage to the view that if wages were severely cut then the consequence would be heavy unemployment, since if people do not have money to buy commodities then these will not be produced. This view is basic to much modern economics and was held not only by the Tribune group of Labour MPs but also by large sections of the trade union movement. To reduce the Tribune group view to 'a call for an opposite, give-away Budget' is scarcely to offer an adequate account of it. The BBC2 bulletins of that evening omitted any reference at all to the views of the Tribune group. Rather, they engaged in underlining the Chancellor's views on 'wage inflation'. In the late BBC2 bulletin this was accompanied by an interview with a former chairman of the National Economic Development Council. This interview again offers an example of how dominant media themes permeate the organisation of questions and responses. The inferential framework was initially established by the newscaster. He introduced the interview with a reference to the Department of Employment figures. These were used in such a way as to imply that the relation between wages and prices was the key factor in explaining inflation. After an extensive report of the Healey speech, the newscaster said: 'With wages running 10 per cent ahead of prices, what can the government do to keep inflation under control? This was the question Dominic Harrod put to a former chairman of the National Economic Development Council Sir Frederick Catherwood' (BBC2, 23.05, 19 March 1975).

Sir Frederick suggested that if wages went up there would be more unemployment, and he argued that the man on the shop floor would have to choose between these two. The interviewer then asked the following question:

Well now, the Chancellor of the Exchequor of course is preparing his April Budget. Is there anything at all that he can do in terms of taxation or in terms of stiffening up the Social Contract, about which we know so much, or is there anything that he can say? (BBC2, 23.05, 19 March 1975)

Sir Frederick then reiterated his previous point that in his view there would be more unemployment unless wages were restrained, and that this had to be explained to the workforce. The interviewer made no attempt to raise any alternative viewpoints. Rather, in his next question, he asked how the interviewee's viewpoint could be got across to the workforce: 'Well, how in fact can managers get that point across, what can they actually do to convince the workforce of this proposition?' The interviewee replied that the real income of everyone must be 'dampened down' and that the country was borrowing too much from abroad and that this must be explained by managers to the people who work with them. The interviewer did not take up these points, but moved to a remarkable statement on the nature of the economic crisis. His final question was as follows:

> Some recent figures which have been produced by the Bank of England show for instance that in this period where we've had 20 per cent inflation, more than three quarters of that, slightly over 16 per cent has been caused sheerly by increased wage costs. Now what can industry do in fact to slow down the rate of increase in prices, which is what is undermining the country, if in fact it's nearly all wage costs that are causing this increase?

Broadcasters sometimes argue, when justifying vigorous or hostile questioning, that it is the role of the interviewer to play 'Devil's advocate', in the sense of putting oppositional points of view to interviewees in order to produce lively and varied responses. This did not happen in the above sequence. Rather, the interview is an example of the structuring of information around a very narrow range of explanations and political policy prescriptions – which seemed to be shared by the interviewee and the interviewer.

The ITN bulletins of this day followed a similar pattern to those of BBC1. Both the early and late bulletins gave extensive reports of Mr Healey's speech and accompanied these with references to the Department of Employment figures on wage rates. However, while the BBC had argued that wages were 10 per cent ahead of prices, the ITN industrial correspondent stated that they were '7 or 8 per cent ahead'. Again one reason for this lower figure given by ITN was the qualification that the figures had been distorted by the comparison with the three-day week of the previous year. As we have already noted, there were a number of other qualifications, which might have shown that there was little or no gap between real wages and prices. However, such conclusions were absent from both channels and instead we were given the consistent reiteration of Mr Healey's warnings in the period leading up to the April Budget. The connection between the warnings and what was to be done in the Budget was made very explicit in the ITN news of this day, where the industrial correspondent commented:

> This will almost certainly be the last warning from Mr Healey about the scale of wage increases before his Budget next month and it's bound to fuel speculation about just how tough he is going to be. The latest wage figures were published today. In the

year to last month basic wage rates for manual workers rose by
nearly 29 per cent, a figure that doesn't yet reflect the miners' pay
settlement. (ITN, 22.00, 19 March 1975)

There are no alternatives to Mr Healey's view given here, and the
brief references made by the BBC to the Tribune group are absent
from the ITN bulletins on the same day.

April 1975

On 15 April 1975, the Budget appeared. It was essentially
deflationary in that it sought to take money out of the economy by
increasing taxation. This produced vigorous protests from a large
body of trade unionists and Labour MPs, since they believed that
the consequence of doing this would be to seriously increase
unemployment. The Chancellor was accused by the chairman of the
Tribune group of 'blandly accepting unemployment rising to 1
million' (ITN, 22.00, 16 April 1975).

The monthly figures for wage increases appeared two days after
this, in the middle of the highly contentious political debate on the
policies contained in the Budget. The manner in which the figures
were broadcast was thus crucial for how the government's policies
might be understood and evaluated by the public at large. If 'wage
inflation' was indeed rampant then there might be some rationale to
the Chancellor's policy of taking back via taxation what workers
had received through 'excessive' wage increases – even if this had
the unfortunate consequence of increasing unemployment. If,
however, 'wage inflation' was not rampant and real wages were
relatively constant at this time, then the effect of the Budget would
be to push down real wages even further. This, it may be noted,
would be in line with the 'redefinition' of the Social Contract by Mr
Healey that had been reported by the television news in January.
Then he had been quoted as saying that in future the Social Contract
might involve the lowering of living standards. This interpretation
of the April Budget, i.e. that it was putting the 'new definition' of
the Social Contract into effect, was never raised or considered by
the television news. Instead, the Budget was presented as a
necessary response to the way in which wages were apparently 'far
outstripping' prices. In other words, the Budget was presented by
media personnel in news commentaries as if it were in some way
putting 'right' the inflation caused by 'excessive' wages. From this

perspective, a deflationary Budget which would increase unemployment was seen as necessary and in a sense inevitable. This view is expressed very clearly in the following example from a BBC1 news bulletin on the day after the March reports of the Department of Employment figures on wages and prices. The view is not attributed to any outside source and is apparently that of the newsproducers. In a commentary on contemporary unemployment figures, it is stated that:

> Even with 3½ per cent of the working population out of a job, we are still better off than other Common Market countries – where unemployment averages about 5 per cent – and the United States with over 8 per cent. That unemployment is lower here is probably due to the budgetary measures taken by Mr Healey last year. But it seems quite certain that in next month's Budget the Chancellor can't afford to respond to trade union pressure to expand the economy and stimulate demand as an answer to unemployment. (BBC1, 17.45, 20 March 1975)

When the Budget appeared on 15 April it was introduced as a direct response to the crisis that had been 'caused' by wages. The main news of ITN that night began as follows: 'Good evening. In the toughest of budgets, the Chancellor, Mr Healey, has fired a broadside at all those who have taken high pay rises. These, he said, were the main cause of the present rate of inflation' (ITN, 22.00, 15 April 1975). We may well ask here who were 'all those who have taken high pay rises'? In the previous month ITN had reported that according to the government 75 per cent of all pay rises were being settled within the Social Contract (ITN, 13.00, 3 March 1975). By other accounts a higher proportion than even 75 per cent were within the Social Contract, because the figures on which pay claims were assessed were being wrongly calculated. In these accounts, inflation was not caused by wage increases but by government spending or by speculation in land or commodities, oil imports or a variety of other causes. Whatever the cause of the inflation initially, one of the most crudely effective ways of reducing it would be to cut real wages, and thus to take money out of the economy. It is certainly possible to argue that this was a central purpose underlying the government's Budget of April 1975. As we have already suggested above, the crucial question in terms of policy is how the 'necessity' of such cuts in living standards is understood by the

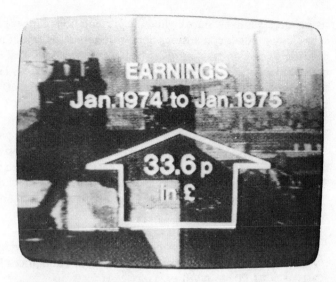

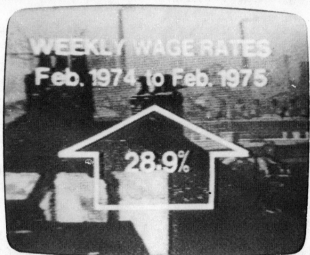

Photos 1f and 1g Wages: gross earnings and weekly rates, *News at Ten*, ITN, 19 March 1975

public at large. It might be easier for politicians to introduce wage restraint if wages are thought to have been 'excessive' in the past. While we are not suggesting direct collusion or conspiracy to deliberately give a false picture, there is no doubt that the television news focused on the theme that wages were 'far outstripping' prices in this period. This interpretation and the policies with which it was associated massively outweighed the presentation of other points of view. The media's conclusions here were reinforced by the systematic use of the official figures, which were directly linked in news commentaries to the Budget and to what were termed Mr Healey's 'warnings' within it. On the day after the Budget, the BBC main news went as follows:

> After Mr Healey's tough Budget warning about recent pay rises being too big, Government figures have disclosed that wage rates have jumped up nearly a third in the past year and that's a record. The increase between February and March alone was close on 4 per cent, the second highest monthly rise ever. Here's our industrial correspondent, Ian Ross:
> 'Well, these figures rub in Mr Healey's warnings about wage-led inflation and pay rises well in excess of the cost of living. And they reveal a widening disparity between pay and prices.'
> (BBC1, 21.00, 16 April 1975)

It should be clear by now that the conclusions that are drawn from such figures depend upon the qualifications and context of their presentation. The figures for basic weekly wage rates were showing the increase that the BBC newscaster mentions here, and the 4 per cent increase over one month was indeed extraordinary. But the industrial correspondent, along with other commentators, had previously noted that the best measure was *not* the index of basic weekly wage rates, but the more usual index which measured *average earnings*. This in general gave a much better indication of how much people were actually earning. In fact on 19 February the same BBC correspondent had said of the average earnings index that 'it is the best guide that there is to the relationship between pay and prices' (BBC1, 17.45, 19 February 1975).[5]

But in April this index received little attention in the BBC news bulletin. This is particularly odd when according to other sources this index showed that actual earnings were beginning to be held back. For instance, *The Times* commented on 17 April: 'there is accumulating evidence that falling industrial output and the increase in short-time working is beginning to hold back the rise in actual earnings, which include payments for overtime and bonuses.' This is very much the conclusion that the *Guardian* had reached in the previous month – that, although basic rates appeared high, real earnings were being pushed down.

No such conclusions informed either the BBC or the ITN bulletins which discussed these figures at the time of the April Budget. Of the six BBC bulletins which discussed them (on 16, 18 and 20 April), only two mentioned briefly the index of average earnings. The main focus was on the index of basic weekly wage rates, which apparently showed a large gap between wages and prices. On the two occasions when the BBC acknowledged the difference between the two indexes, there were no conclusions drawn which challenged the dominant view. Rather, as in the next example, the message that pay was ahead of prices was reiterated at the end of the reference to average earnings. This was then followed directly by an accusation from the correspondent that the trade unions were thus not adhering to their commitment to the Social Contract. The BBC1 main news the day after the Budget, which we quoted above, continued directly as follows:

> a widening disparity between pay and prices. The percentage increase in basic weekly wage rates for the year to March is 32.5 per cent against an increase of 19.9 per cent in the latest retail price index in the twelve months to February. This latest monthly increase in wage rates of 3.9 per cent is attributable in the main to pay rises for two groups of workers. In engineering, which is a big group which always influences the index heavily, and in coal mining. *Now when it comes to average earnings, that is gross pay, the picture looks different and not so bad.* The government estimates here that earnings are up something like 29 per cent on the year and there are two reasons for this being lower than the rise in wage rates. The earnings index is a month behind and short-time working is having an effect on total pay. *Pay has moved well in advance of prices and this clearly questions the trade unions' adherence to their commitment to the Social Contract.* (BBC1, 21.00, 16 April 1975; our italics)

In the ITN bulletins at this time, there was no distinction made between the two indices, and the focus was again very largely on the index of basic weekly rates. Out of four bulletins (on 16 and 18 March) only one uses a comparison which is based on the average earnings index. It must be said of the ITN coverage, however, that, unlike that of the BBC, on two occasions (ITN, 17.50 and 22.00, 18 March 1975) it did suggest that the figures were distorted. None the less the overall conclusion of ITN was the same as that of the BBC. This was that

> the gap between earnings and prices is now so great that real incomes after all tax deductions are increasing while the central guideline of the Social Contract is that Britain can afford only to maintain them. These are the figures that persuaded the Chancellor to be so tough and today's news from the railways won't have altered his convictions that the wage price spiral needs drastic treatment. (ITN, 22.00, 18 April 1975)

At this time, the yearly increase in average earnings was calculated by the Department of Employment as being 'about 29 per cent'. However, *The Times* had suggested the day before the above news bulletins that even this might be an overestimate. It argued that for the months from December 1974 to February 1975 earnings were increasing at a rate of only 19.4 per cent. Thus in a discussion of the *average earnings* index it noted on 17 April 1975 that

> This index rose 1.9% in February (the information for earnings lags a month behind that for wages), after actually showing a fall in January. The three-day week last year makes it difficult to estimate how much earnings have risen in the past 12 months but the Department calculated this at about 29%.
>
> However, if the December–February rise is expressed at an annual rate, this suggests earnings may be rising at only 19.4% a year.

The figure of 19.4 per cent was in fact below the rate of increase in prices and would have represented a drop in real wages, relative to price increases. No such calculations informed any of the television news bulletins. Rather, as we have indicated, the persistent message was that wages were far in excess of prices.

In conclusion, perhaps the most salient point to make about the use of Department of Employment figures is that these are an uncertain guide to the relation between wages and prices. The conclusions that could be drawn from these figures depend largely upon which months or years were used on the computations and upon what qualifications were made to them. An essential feature of the television news coverage is that the figures were used invariably to suggest that wages were ahead of prices and in the mass of the coverage to suggest that the gap between these was rapidly increasing. This conclusion was reached and heavily emphasised despite what *The Times* and other sources called 'accumulating evidence' that the rise in actual earnings was beginning to be held back.

The predominant feature of this news coverage therefore was the manner in which official figures from which a number of conclusions could have been drawn were used consistently to emphasise only one interpretation. Perhaps most significant were the explicit links made between this conclusion and severe wage restraint as a political policy.

3 From Diagnosis to Prescription

There were essentially four broad areas of opinion reported in the period of our study as to how the economic crisis might be resolved. First, the Conservative monetarists who called principally for cuts in government expenditure. These were aimed at spending on the social services, and against direct government intervention and financing of industrial enterprises. In addition they demanded large reductions in the level of taxation of private industry in order to boost profits.

Second, there was extensive reporting of the section of opinion represented most prominently by Mr Healey. Here, the chief demand was for severe wage restraint and actual cuts in living standards. This policy involved increased personal taxation and cuts in government welfare spending in order to divert money into financing both private and public sector manufacturing industry.

There was another group whose policy demands to some extent crossed these two areas of opinion, namely the CBI, which added its voice to calls for wage restraint as a priority and strongly opposed the government's plans for industrial investment and reorganisation.

A third area of opinion reported was that represented by the TUC and prominent union leaders such as Jack Jones. This group, whilst accepting wage restraint under the Social Contract, insisted that this also involved the defence of living standards. In general they were opposed to wage cuts on the grounds that this would increase unemployment by reducing demand in the economy. They called for limited government intervention in the economy and some use of government spending to create jobs.

The fourth section of opinion was that of the Tribune group of Labour MPs and those trade unionists who rejected the view that the economic crisis was the result of excessive wage increases. The priorities of this group were the reorganisation of the economy through the development of the public sector, with a programme of increased government investment. They were also in favour of using government spending to reduce unemployment radically.

Each of these positions appeared in some form on the news in this period. For example, Sir Keith Joseph, one leading Conservative monetarist, was quoted by the BBC on the final day of the Budget debate in Parliament. His position was summarised as follows:

> His [Joseph's] main attack, over and over again, was on too high government spending. We were overspending, over-taxing, over-borrowing and overmanning. 'Cut out Bennery,' said Sir Keith. 'More control on local government spending, cut misconceived subsidies.' He attacked the government for their abuse and interference with the 'ulcer people', the managers and entrepreneurs who got ulcers doing their best for the country and it was on their success, these ulcer people, that the country's prosperity really depended. (BBC2, 21.00, 21 April 1975)

The most extensively reported position on the economy was that associated with Mr Healey. The Chancellor was one of the most quoted people on television news in the context of the Social Contract. His view that lower living standards were necessary and that this would in some way help to reduce unemployment was frequently expressed on the news. Thus, the following example from ITN news of 10 January, which occurred at the time when the Chancellor was apparently 'rewriting' the Social Contract:

> The Chancellor of the Exchequer suggested tonight that to avoid unemployment people might have to exist on lower wages. In a speech in Leeds defending the Social Contract, Mr Denis Healey said that it was far better that more people were working even if it meant their accepting lower wages on average, rather than those with jobs getting high pay while millions were on the dole. (ITN, 22.00, 10 January 1975)

The Confederation of British Industry was also reported on the news as being in favour of severe wage restraint, as were some Conservative party spokesmen such as Mr Robert Carr. The position of the CBI was clearly summarised in the following BBC bulletin of 15 January 1975:

The CBI has tonight added its support to the view expressed recently by the Chancellor that people must accept lower living standards or face much higher unemployment. The CBI say pay increases should be less than the current rate of inflation. They are proposing a new voluntary pay policy to replace the present guidelines in the Social Contract and it could be much tougher. Here is Ian Ross:

'We are living beyond our means, we are going to suffer a cut in our living standards, anyway, and the present rate of pay increases is pushing up the rate of inflation. That is what the CBI say.' (BBC1, 21.00, 15 January 1975)

There were other positions which related to these. One of the most politically contentious was the demand for statutory control of wages. A pay policy which was backed by law had been last attempted by the Conservative government under Mr Edward Heath and had led directly to its fall from office after the three-day week and the miners' strike of 1974.

Reported statements and interview responses on this area of policy were mainly *against* the introduction of statutory wage controls. These negative statements and responses came predominantly from members of the government (especially Michael Foot, Minister for Employment) and the TUC, totalling twenty for all the three channels. It should be stressed that these rejections of statutory controls were not criticisms of wage restraint as such. Rather, they normally came from speakers who were in favour of wage restraint, but who for obvious political reasons initially ruled out compulsory control, before speaking in favour of voluntary restraint. Demands for a return to the legal control of wages appeared very infrequently on the news. It is noteworthy that, when they did, they were raised predominantly by media personnel. Of a total of eight *positive* references to statutory wage controls, five came as strong statements on the necessity for this policy and appeared within the context of interview questions.[1]

This may be seen if we look briefly at an interview which appeared on ITN in January between the lunchtime newscaster and Robert Carr, who was then the Conservative Shadow Chancellor. Here, the newscaster went beyond merely raising the statutory control of wages as a possibility, and quite clearly advocated its necessity. The questions which he asked thus contained implied statements urging a political position. The sequence of the newscaster's questions on this was as follows:

1   'Now can we look at this proposal of yours for voluntary monitoring of the Social Contract. Surely voluntary monitoring is what we have in the Social Contract. That could be just what's wrong with it?'
2   'But then what in the long-run if there were to be a dispute as to what should be the Social Contract and shouldn't, what in the long-run is going to be the sanction? Don't you need something statutory, really?'
3   'You see you said earlier that you thought if you once had a policy you thought was right, you should stick to it. One wonders if your reluctance to introduce or propose statutory incomes policy isn't due to your unfortunate experience last time rather than that you don't probably think there ought to be such a thing. I mean, we've already heard you saying we're steering for the rocks. Nothing could be worse than that, so what are we waiting for?'
4   'But aren't we driven to it (statutory controls) if we're being driven to the rocks?' (ITN, 13.00, 21 January 1975)

We may certainly ask who it was that the newscaster was speaking for here. He had put himself into a position which was clearly not accepted by Mr Carr, who in this interview appeared to be doing his best to draw back from the prospect of compulsory wage restraint. Thus, Mr Carr's reply to the last of the above questions was as follows:

No, because I want to keep off the rocks and I think it's much better, it always is better in our sort of economy, if we can do these things by voluntary agreement. We only introduced the statutory policy in 1972, very reluctantly. I hate it except as a matter of dire necessity. (ITN, 13.00, 21 January 1975)

The BBC coverage did not contain any emphasis on statutory controls. There was, however, at times a similar emphasis by interviewers on the need for wage restraint. Thus in an interview between the General Secretary of the NUR and a BBC interviewer the following exchange occurred:

> Sidney Weighell (NUR): What would make it very difficult for me and the 200,000 people I represent, is if an important group, miners or anybody else, simply went through the ceiling with a settlement. I would find it almost intolerable from the point of view of our members to ask them to tighten their belts and stick within the limits of the Contract. I would find it absolutely impossible.
>
> BBC interviewer: But some unions have got to make that stand – if others go over the edge the policy isn't going to succeed at all if people, some of them, don't stand fast. (BBC2, 23.00, 12 January 1975)

Later in this same interview, the BBC journalist stated that the trade union movement was 'very much divided over wages'. If it was so divided then it follows that there were different sides and different opinions on economic policy that might have been represented on the news. In this interview and throughout the whole of the coverage of our sample, only one of these opinions was systematically embraced and developed in the organisation of the coverage by media personnel. The questions from the BBC journalist after the above exchange were as follows:

1 'So the General Council of the TUC should be using more muscle in this, you say? They should be in some way disciplining unions who don't observe the Social Contract?'
2 'But the trade union movement was united in its opposition to the Industrial Relations Act and very much divided over wages?'
3 'It's a terrible dilemma for a union leader who wants to pursue a moderate course, seeing all round him that it's tough negotiating policy which produces the goods for his members.' (BBC2, 23.00, 12 February 1975)

The third area of opinion on how the economic crisis might be resolved was held by the dominant section in the TUC and included Mr Jack Jones of the TGWU. They accepted a degree of wage restraint provided that living standards remained constant. In general they were opposed to cuts in living standards in as much as these would produce higher unemployment. Thus, Mr Len Murray, the General Secretary of the TUC, appeared on ITN on the day of the Budget of April 1975 and said: 'We don't take the view that cuts in living standards are the solution to Britain's economic problems, nor yet increasing unemployment' (ITN, 22.00, 15 April 1975). On a number of occasions Mr Murray also spoke against the concentration on wages as the source of economic problems. Thus, on the same day he appeared on the BBC and argued that Mr Healey's Budget had been 'unduly influenced' by the 'oversimple theme' of wages (BBC1, 21.00, 15 April 1975).

The fourth group that featured on the news was that of the trade unionists and Labour MPs of the Tribune group who were severely critical of Mr Healey's policies and were openly opposed to the view that wages were the source of Britain's economic problems. There were thus serious divisions in the trade union movement over the principle of wage restraint. In January 1975 Clive Jenkins of ASTMS attacked Mr Healey's suggestion that wages should be lowered. He was reported on ITN as saying:

> The union leader Mr Clive Jenkins has accused the Chancellor, Mr Healey, of returning to the dangerous language of the 1930s by suggesting that people might have to accept lower wages so that more could keep their jobs. Mr Jenkins, who leads the white collar union ASTMS, said high wages were essential for a healthy economy and that lower pay and living standards would in fact increase unemployment. (ITN, 22.30, 11 January 1975)

Clive Jenkins was representative of the group who were opposed to cuts in public expenditure and sought vigorous government action to reduce unemployment. One consequence of the conflict of opinion in this area was the emergence of a deep division within the Labour party, which came to a head at the time of the Budget. In April 1975 ITN reported the hostile reception which Mr Healey's Budget speech had received from many Labour MPs:

> What visible opposition there was during Mr Healey's speech was certainly not confined to the Opposition parties. When the Chancellor said he wasn't able to reflate to get unemployment down, many left wing MPs were in clear disagreement, with Mr Eric Heffer prominent on the back-benches again, shaking his head sadly. (ITN, 22.00, 15 April 1975)

The solutions to the economic crisis proposed by this section of the Labour party were radical. They focused largely on the redistribution of income and the regeneration of the economy through increased state investment. In fact all of the four areas of opinion which we have so far mentioned agreed that more investment in some form or other was necessary if Britain's economy was to recover. They differed sharply, however, on whether this investment should come with the encouragement of free enterprise and development of the private sector or whether it should come from the state with the development of public ownership.

The four groups that we have discussed all appeared in some form in the coverage. It was the case, however, that some of the explanations and viewpoints were given a much greater priority in the organisation of the television news. The emphasis given to these explanations is in part shown by enormous differences in the numerical frequency of references to the different viewpoints.

In total we identified and counted references to sixteen different proposals for the resolution of the economic crisis in the period of our study. In general all these solutions related to the four major political positions which we have outlined above. The numerical frequency of all references was as shown in Table 3.1. There were a small number of occasions where individuals were reported or themselves made statements (in public speeches shown on film or video-tape), *against* a specific proposal. These are recorded after the main figure for references from those who *supported* the proposed solution.

The most obvious point to be drawn from these figures is the massive emphasis on wage restraint in the news coverage, with 287 references in favour of it in four months. By comparison, there were 17 reported statements and comments against wage restraint. It will be remembered that for those trade unionists who supported the Social Contract, there were essentially two 'sides' to it. The first was the acceptance of limited pay restraint and the second was the condition that living standards would be defended, in order to prevent the increase in unemployment. There is no doubt which 'side' of the Social Contract received the most attention in the news, since there were only 79 references to the defence of living standards against the 287 to wage restraint.

These figures illustrate the low priority which was given to alternative views of the economy and how its problems might be resolved. There were many trade unionists and politicians who saw the history of declining investment in Britain as a far greater problem than the allegedly 'excessive' wage increases. One

Table 3.1   Policies or 'solutions' to economic crisis identified on TV news

Proposed solution	Number of references
Wage restraint/lower wages	287 (+17 negative)
Defence of living standards (including maintaining wage levels and government intervention to protect jobs)	79 (+15 negative)
Expansion of the public sector, the need for a government investment programme, including National Enterprise Board and proposals to reverse decline in industrial investment	47 (+50 negative)
Cuts in government expenditure	21 (+1 negative)
Reduction of company taxation (corporation tax, etc.)	15
Better communications in industry (including informing workers of company plans)	14 (+6 negative)
Increased direct personal taxation, to cut 'spending power'	13 (+2 negative)
More progressive taxation ('cuts at the top', 'tax the rich', etc.)	12 (+4 negative)
Abolition of price control	11 (+6 negative)
Increased profits for industry	10
Statutory wage control	8 (+20 negative)
Increased investment in private industry (including government aid to private companies)	9
Import controls	7
Reduction of 'complex' VAT rates	6
A ban on the export of capital (exchange controls, etc.)	2
Lower interest rates	1

Appendix B (p. 440) gives the number of references by channel, and by the manner in which they appeared, i.e. as direct statements from media personnel, or as reported statements, as interview questions or as responses from interviewees.

proposal which they put forward to remedy this was the development of the public sector and the setting up of the National Enterprise Board (to promote government investment in industry). There were only forty-seven references to this as a solution, compared with the large number in favour of wage restraint. One difference between these policies was that wage restraint was supported by the Confederation of British Industry, while the setting up of the National Enterprise Board was vigorously opposed by it. As the above figures show, even the forty-seven references in favour of the National Enterprise Board and the expansion of the public sector were outweighed numerically by reports which were critical of this solution, there being fifty references against it. It should also be noted in relation to these figures, that there were a low number of references to some Conservative solutions to the crisis, notably those formulated by monetarists such as Sir Keith Joseph. These solutions included calls for cuts in government expenditure of which there were twenty-one reported in the period of our study. One factor which possibly contributed to this low level of reportage was that the Conservative party at this time was not yet totally committed to monetarism. There were other Conservative spokesmen such as Mr Carr and Mr Prior who were quoted as advocating wage restraint as a solution to the economic problem. Thus a number of Conservative party spokesmen did in fact appear in the news but not to speak in favour of what is now the dominant Conservative philosophy.

The numerical frequency of different themes which we have outlined above goes some way to illustrating the dominance of some of these in the news. However, the analysis of news coverage must go beyond this to examine the *manner* in which these references appear. Our research was essentially directed towards the identification of the explanatory themes which underlay the production and organisation of television news coverage. Our argument is that descriptions and accounts on the news are predicated on assumptions as to the nature of the social and industrial world, on how it works and on how its problems may be solved. The selection and organisation of information is crucially affected by such assumptions. They determine not only the number of times certain viewpoints are referenced, but also the *manner* in which explanations are treated. In a very real sense, the process of news production which we have documented represents the organisation of a flow of information within a specific and very limited picture of the industrial world. Thus, although a variety of different opinions may appear in some form, and the illusion of balance is created, it is the case that some views and explanations have a different status in the coverage. These dominant explanations occur more frequently, but in addition are highlighted and underlined in the coverage. Only some explanations are embraced by media personnel in that they use them directly without attribution. In the case of the wage inflation limit these are also systematically underlined by linking them with other reported information, such as figures on wages and prices and with official reports such as those for the Price Commission. The structuring of interviews and the organisation of questions similarly reflects the development and emphasis of certain economic and political themes. Information and reporting is thus generated and organised within specific and limiting assumptions on the nature of social life. A picture of the world and of what can and ought to be done in it is contained within news accounts which may on the surface appear as merely factual.

There is a further dimension to this process of producing descriptions and reports from within a particular world view. We have shown that explanations exist numerically at different levels in the coverage and that some are embraced and underlined in the development of the dominant framework. These dominant explanations have a further status in that their content is described exhaustively in the coverage – indeed a large part of the coverage has the function of illustrating them: In a real sense news coverage is organised from within the logic and premises of these explanations. By contrast, alternative accounts appear as fragments. Although, as we have shown, alternative explanations appear, the news reports are not organised in such a fashion as to illustrate the content of these or to follow through their meaning from their premises to their conclusions. This is more than saying that alternative explanations are not embraced, underlined or emphasised. It is to say that when they appear, they occur in such a fragmented and disparate form, that their sense and rationality is normally lost.

We noted above, for example, how the views of the Tribune group were at one point in the BBC coverage reduced to a call for 'an opposite, give-away Budget' (BBC1, 21.00, 19 March 1975). We argued that the view that the government should expand the economy to reduce unemployment was held not only by the Tribune MPs, but by a large section of the trade union movement, and that to summarise it in this fashion was scarcely adequate. The coverage given to the Budget when it appeared in April 1975 provides further evidence of the different levels at which explanations appear and are integrated into the text. In the following example one explanation of the economic crisis and what might be done about it is articulated very clearly. It contrasts sharply with the fragmented and disparate references to the views which contradicted it. The example is from the weekly news summary given each Sunday evening on BBC2. This news appeared five days after the April Budget. It is notable for the remarkable synthesis which it made between a narrow and restricted economic explanation and the political policies which apparently flowed from this. Official figures were used here to underline and legitimate these themes. The item thus began:

> Now home, and as you know this week there's been a lot of heavy news on the country's economic front. Two figures from the week give the real story. Everything else in one way or another is reaction to those figures. One: prices rose in the last twelve months by the biggest ever increase, 21 per cent. Two: wages rose in the last twelve months by a far greater figure: 32 per cent. The Chancellor, Denis Healey, for one regards that extra 11 per cent on wages as the main cause of inflation. His answer, as we saw in the Budget on Tuesday, is to take the extra money away in taxes. (BBC2, 18.15, 20 April 1975)

There are very notable differences here between the presentation of the views of the Chancellor and of those who oppose him. What distinguishes the account given of Mr Healey's views is that in essence they were carefully explained by the newscaster as well as being underlined by the use of the apparently incontrovertible figures (all the more so since the figures were used here without any comment that they might be in any way unreliable as they stood). There is a logic and sense given to Mr Healey's arguments in that they are carefully followed through from the premise that wages cause inflation to the conclusion that therefore money must be taken away in taxes. This cannot be said of the reports in the same news of the position represented by Mr Len Murray:

> Newscaster: Len Murray, General Secretary of the TUC, liked some of the long-term measures of the Budget but disliked the fact that Mr Healey in his view seems to accept high prices and unemployment.
> Len Murray: I am disappointed. There's a far too high prospect of unemployment to make me happy and so these price increases that are going to come through are going to make life very much harder for a lot of people. (BBC2,18.15, 20 April 1975)

There were no figures or calculations used here by media personnel to support alternative views. There was no explanation here of the alternative view that wages might not be the cause of inflation and no explanation of why the Budget would cause more unemployment, or of what other policies might have been followed. What there *is* here, is an illusion of balance, whereby statements are included for what appear as different sides. But these statements have a totally different status, legitimacy and meaning in the text. In a very real way, only one set of statements makes 'sense', in that we are given the information necessary to understand the explanations and policies which they represent.

Rationality and hard 'realism' are transformed into the prerogative of those who are in favour of wage restraint and of allowing unemployment to rise. The alternative accounts of those who were opposed to this were at times reported on the news, but they remained at the level of emotional appeals against the apparently 'inevitable', since the logic and rationale of these alternative viewpoints was substantially absent. The difference in the manner in which the two sides were made to appear was clearly summarised in a BBC bulletin of the day after the Budget. The item began:

> The Chancellor had to face his own Parliamentary colleagues today with explanations about his Budget which, as he had admitted yesterday, could increase both the cost of living and unemployment. One of our Westminster staff said criticism and praise were evenly matched. Right-wingers said the Budget was realistic, left-wingers said it wasn't socialist. (BBC1, 21.00, 16 April 1975)

The same may be said of even the most outright condemnations of the Budget which were reported. The news was never organised to develop the rationale of the alternative positions. For example, Mr Hugh Scanlon appeared on BBC news six days after the Budget. Film of his speech to a union conference at Blackpool was shown. The text was as follows:

> Mr Scanlon: There can be no doubt in my view, whatever else we say was welcome in the Budget, and there were certain aspects that were, the overall position was an almost disdainful ignoring of the proposals of the TUC and an almost absolute compliance with the proposals of the CBI and the City. Now it is not pleasant to say these things but the cost of the Chancellor's proposals in the coming months is going to be catastrophic on many working-

class families throughout Britain. And, unfortunately, we all
know that the effect on the families will be on those families
which are at the lower end of the wages and salaries bracket. And
this makes the whole situation the complete reverse of what the
TUC were proposing in its economic review and in the points
that we made quite specifically to the Chancellor. (BBC1, 21.00,
21 April 1975)

Why Mr Scanlon believed the Budget to be in the interest of the CBI
and the City, was not explained or developed in the television
account. In the absence of such an account, Mr Scanlon's attack has
the status only of an emotional appeal by a left-wing trade unionist.

The most politically contentious issue at this time was, of course,
wage restraint. One of the key premises of those who were out-
rightly opposed to this policy was that the economic crisis had not
been caused by working people and that therefore they should not
be made to pay for it either by cuts in wages or by cuts in
government expenditure which would cause unemployment. To
understand this premise, it would be necessary to have an alternative view of what had caused inflation and economic decline. As
we have already indicated, one dimension to this alternative view
was the failure of private industry over a long period to engage in
adequate investment programmes. The effect of this had been to
make a large section of British industry inefficient relative to foreign
competitors. With this increasing decline, a large number of firms
had been 'bailed out' by the state using public funds. Both the
critical theorists on the left and the monetarists on the right were
agreed that the government policy of providing money to rescue
bankrupt industry was a major cause of inflation. There were other
causes which were linked to this, such as the large-scale movement
of funds away from investment in productive industry into
profitable forms of speculation, mainly in land, property and
commodities. Some groups of opinion argued that this added to the
decline of industry and at the same time fuelled inflation. It was
partly because of the failure of private investment to produce
growth and stability in the economy that many members of the
Labour party and the trade unions were demanding that investment
should be organised and controlled by the government. This might
have included, for example, the nationalisation of insurance
companies, which were key sources of investment, and the
expansion of publicly owned industries. The understanding of

factors such as the decline in investment is thus crucial for those explanations of the economy which do not focus merely on 'excessive wages' as the source of all problems.

But when references to the decline in investment did appear, there was no sense in which this problem was consistently related to a whole way of understanding the nature of the economy and how its problems might be solved. For example, the following report appeared on ITN in January 1975:

> Bad economic news for the government on two fronts today – investment by companies is now expected to be as much as 10 per cent down this year compared with 1974 and unemployment is still accelerating upwards. The investment forecast comes from a survey of firms' intentions published by the Department of Trade and Industry. The Department says the money that firms spend on new plant and equipment is expected to be between 7 per cent and 10 per cent down this year. That compares with the original forecast which showed it would in fact rise slightly. And today's survey says that the forecast for next year is that investment will be even lower. On unemployment there haven't been any government figures for two months because of an internal staffing dispute. However, Sir Dennis Barnes, chairman of the Manpower Services Commission, warns that the forecast of higher unemployment appears to be coming true. He said more firms will sooner or later be forced into announcing redundancies. (ITN, 17.50, 21 January 1975)

The only causal link that appears to be made here is between investment and unemployment. There is no explanation of what factors are responsible for this decline. Perhaps more significantly, the figures are not related to contemporary political policies. For example, the Industry Bill, which was designed to increase public investment and to expand public ownership, was to be introduced into the Commons by Mr Anthony Wedgwood Benn ten days after these figures appeared. There is no sense in which the inclusion of such fragmented references to the decline of investment could be compared with the consistent monitoring of wages and prices figures and the use of these by the media to underline the political policies of wage restraint. We were not told, for example, by the news of either channel that these figures on investment 'rub in' Mr Benn's warning on the decline of private industry and the need to expand the public sector. The wages and prices figures, however, were used consistently to underline the necessity of the measures contained in Mr Healey's Budget. Although the official figures on investment were never used to underline the policies of the Industry Bill, there were occasions when the figures and other reports on investment were used in the context of statements by those who were *opposed* to the Industry Bill. The following example is a report of a CBI survey on the investment plans of its members:

> Our industrial editor says this survey bears out the dismal picture painted by official government figures, namely that investment on new machines and buildings by private firms is expected to fall this year by up to 10 per cent. The president of the CBI, Mr Ralph Bateman, said that the government's industrial policy could mean the end of the private sector as we know it. (ITN, 22.00, 4 February 1975)

There were, then, substantial differences in the treatment of the two themes of wages and investment as problems. In addition to the greater numerical frequency of references to wage increases and the fact that only wage and prices figures were used to underline this 'problem', there was also a more systematic explanation of the 'logic' and apparent 'necessity' of the political policies of wage restraint and higher taxation. By comparison, the rationale of the policy of increasing investment through the provisions of the Industry Bill was not explored or analysed at anything like the same level. Such exploration as there was of the policies and provisions of the Industry Bill amounted to a small number of reports and statements mentioning that there had been a decline in investment, that it was essential to reverse it and that the Industry Bill was trying to achieve this. On the day in which the Bill had its first reading in the Commons, ITN reported as follows:

> Industrial editor: The Bill is neither long nor complicated yet within it are set out some of the most fundamental changes ever envisaged in the relationship between industry, government and workers. The main justification for some radical new measures is, of course, industry's poor investment record since the war, culminating in a rapid deterioration between 1969 and 1973. Clearly, if industry by itself couldn't finance the investment the nation needs, then government would have to become further

involved, and this it has decided to do on an unprecedented scale. (ITN, 22.00, 31 January 1975)

There were only two bulletins in which a television journalist spoke in this way of the need for state intervention in the economy through the provisions of the Industry Bill because of the failure of industry to adequately reinvest. In both cases these reports came from ITN's industrial editor. The first such report came in *News at Ten* shown above, and the other occasion was ITN's *First Report* on the same day. Here he said of the Industry Bill: 'Its purpose is to regenerate industry which is now facing one of its worst-ever recessions in private manufacturing investment' (ITN, 13.00, 31 January 1975).

The only other such references appeared later in this same programme, in two interview questions put by the industrial editor to a Conservative opponent of the Bill, Michael Heseltine, MP. The questions were:

1   'What the country needs more than anything else is investment. The investment intentions for the current year and next year are abysmally low and they indicate a collapse during this period. Now if what the government has proposed will help investors, will finance investment, surely this is only to the good?'
2   'But manufacturing investment fell in real terms in 1971 and 1972 when you were in power. Industry was not investing then. Surely a new approach is needed, and must be found?'

Overall, then, there were only four references in which a news journalist drew a link between what the Industry Bill was trying to achieve and gave the reason for it as industry's failure to invest adequately.[1] These four links between *solution* and *cause* in the case of public sector investment were exclusive to ITN. No such direct references appeared on the BBC.

On both channels there was a relatively small number of reported references to the 'problem of investment', the 'need for investment' and to 'a spiral of decline'. In these cases there was no specific cause given for the decline, and no explanation of who or what was responsible. As the tables show, overall there were more reported statements and references which opposed the Industry Bill than there were in favour of it. By comparison the Budget and its policies were introduced and systematically explained on the news as a necessary response to the actions of those trade unionists and working people who had received 'high' wage awards. There was no comparable investigation or systematic analysis of the problem of how or why sections of private industry had declined so drastically in the years since the war. Some trade unionists and Labour politicians blamed the export of capital and the movement of capital away from productive industry into speculation, but these accounts were hardly central in the organisation of the news and indeed they were barely referenced. (See Table 3.1 above and Appendix B, p. 439.)

The Industry Bill was, thus, on a small number of occasions, interpreted as a response to the past decline of industry. What was never explained was how or why this decline in private investment had come about, or who or what was responsible. This was so even of the most detailed account given in the four references, by the industrial editor of ITN, for while he stated that it was industry's 'poor investment record' that had necessitated government intervention, there was no explanation or analysis of the nature or underlying causes of this failure. In fact most of the television news coverage of this area, especially that of the BBC, did not examine the decline of investment as the failure of anyone or anything at all.

While this decline was acknowledged as a serious problem, it was normally treated rather as a natural disaster. For example, the following report from the BBC in February 1975 gave the information that investment was expected to decline according to a CBI survey. There is no explanation of *why* this process was occurring and no link to possible solutions. The only causal link made was to unemployment:

> Newscaster: But in the City confidence is at a low ebb, said our economics correspondent, Dominic Harrod. This afternoon a CBI survey based on information from more than 1,300 firms mostly in manufacturing industry, forecasts a gloomy future for Britain.
> Dominic Harrod: Longer queues for unemployment pay this spring, as industry fires more people than it hires. That is the most disquieting message from the CBI's fifty-fifth survey of more than 1,300 companies. Nearly half the companies, or 43 per cent, expect to employ fewer people than now in four months' time. Only 10 per cent are looking for new workers. Nor does industry expect to be investing

heavily to create new jobs in the future. The number expecting to invest less in new equipment is a record. This is not surprising, since every man out of work means an empty place in the factory or on the shift. All in all, this is the most depressing and demoralised survey of the CBI members, with one exception: that taken this time last year, on the eve of the three-day week and power rationing. (BBC1, 17.45, 4 February 1975)

Because there was so little analysis of what might be wrong with the system of private investment, a crucial dimension was missing from the arguments of those who sought to change it, through, for example, the Industry Bill. There was no routine examination of who or what was to blame. As we show later, this is in sharp contrast to the way in which the 'wage problem' was identified and the wage claims of individual trade unions were consistently evaluated on the news.

The overwhelming emphasis on the news was on a diagnosis of the economic problem and inflation as resulting from higher wage increases. The solution embraced by the television news was severe wage restraint. The political conflict around this position was summarised very clearly in a news item in January 1975 on BBC2:

BBC industrial correspondent: Mr Healey and his Treasury team, supported by the Prime Minister, appear to believe that the Social Contract's target of maintaining living standards, insisting that take home pay keeps pace with rising prices, may not be realistic, and that there may have to be a reduction in living standards despite what the Social Contract and the trade unions say. (BBC2, 22.35, 13 January 1975)

Throughout the period of our study there were alternative views available both of the nature of the economic crisis and of how it might be resolved. On very rare occasions, they appeared on the news with some clarity, though again as fragments rather than being emphasised and explored in the organisation of news coverage. For example, in January, Anthony Wedgwood Benn was quoted on the BBC as follows:

The Industry Secretary, Mr Benn, today gave his explanation for the country's industrial failure, for which he said working people had become the most popular scapegoats. The real cause was lack of investment and he said inflation was the result of overpriced goods produced with outdated equipment by underpaid workers. (BBC2, 21.00, 25 March 1975)

In this example, a link was made between investment, economic crisis and inflation. There were only three occasions in the whole four-month period in which such a causal link appeared in the news, and only then as reported speech. These were on BBC bulletins of the same day, 25 January. Wage inflation as a theme dominated the explanations of the economic crisis on television news. Yet this was at a time when the industrial correspondent of ITN had noted that 'Since the war, Britain's overriding problem, almost universally agreed, has been a failure to invest adequately' (ITN, 22.00, 22 January 1975, quoted above). In total, the references to wages as a problem and wage restraint as a solution numbered 383 in the four-month period. By comparison, the number of references to investment as a problem and the need to increase it as a solution, totalled 89 (taking both public and private sector solutions together). This figure actually overemphasises the role of investment as an explanation in the news. References to this, when they came, occurred usually in a fragmented and disparate fashion, and were very rarely part of a coherent alternative view of the economy and the nature of its problems. As we have indicated, the important dimension in the analysis of news coverage is not merely the numerical frequency of references but the manner in which coverage is organised to give credence and coherence to specific explanations. The rationality of alternative views was rarely explored or even referenced.

4 Pointing the Finger: Evaluations and Judgments

Broadcasts do not represent adequately the industrial and commercial life of the country.

Report of the Committee on the Future of Broadcasting[1]

A further dimension to the organisation of the industrial and economic coverage remains. This was the systematic evaluation of individuals and organisations such as trade unions from within the partial and limited viewpoint that the television news had established. This process of evaluation follows from what we have said about the media's control of explanation. It may be implicit only because whether people's actions appear rational or reasonable will depend very much upon how the world in which the actions are occurring is portrayed and understood. If wage increases are thought to be the source of economic problems then the demands for these may be seen as irrational. The control which the media exercise over the flow of information and explanation grants them an enormous power over how individual and group action is evaluated and judged. In the following example from ITN in February the reported statements of two trade unionists were juxtaposed. The first is Arthur Scargill, who is reported as having spoken at a rally in London:

It was addressed by the Yorkshire miners' leader, Mr Arthur Scargill, who said that the Social Contract had been smashed by the latest miners' pay settlement, and, he added, my advice to the trade unions is to press through the breach. But another union leader, Lord Allen, speaking at another conference in London, said that the worst thing the unions could do was to endanger the Social Contract by taking a 'go it alone' attitude on pay claims. (ITN, 18.05, 23 February 1975)

The apparent neutrality of the news is sustained by the formal 'balance' of the two speakers, which is a familiar feature of news coverage. But such an apparent balance appears within an already established context of social and economic explanations. This taken-for-granted background context influences how each statement is 'heard' and 'understood' and how the alternatives proposed by each speaker are to be evaluated.

The language used in the description and assessment of pay claims was often quite explicitly critical. The following example is taken from an interview between a trade unionist and an ITN newscaster. Here, the newscaster argues consistently from within the economic assumptions of the television news. In two of his questions, he equates 'rational' and 'reasonable' behaviour quite explicitly with the acceptance of wage restraint. The first of these follows the introduction to the item:

> Newscaster: Bank employees, who've just had a 30 per cent pay rise, have put in a claim for 20 per cent more. Their leader, Mr Leif Mills, in fact said, 'we broke the contract last year and we intend to break it again'. Of course it's possible – reasonable – for him to say that because the bank employees' union is not in the TUC, whose Social Contract this is meant to be. However, I now say, turning to the Assistant Secretary of the National Union of Bank Employees, Mr David Dines, who's in the studio with me now, you can opt out of your responsibilities to the TUC all right, but can you really opt out of your responsibilities to the national economy as a whole? (ITN, 13.00, 24 February 1975)

Later in a follow-up question, the theme is made even more explicit:

> Interviewee: Our job as a trade union is to maintain the purchasing power of our members' salaries and that's all we're trying to do with the pay claim we've now formulated.
> Newscaster: But as reasonable men and responsible citizens can you say that's all you are trying to do and all you are interested in when you hear warnings from the Chancellor to the effect that increases of this sort are going to wreck the national economy? (ITN, 13.00, 24 February 1975)

Throughout this period the news consistently spoke on behalf of the values and beliefs which followed from its analysis of the nature of the economic crisis. It appealed to a restricted system of values about the common good and the benefit of everyone in the society. It then established by its limited account of the workings of the economy what people ought to do to produce this common good. This view of how society works and of what ought to be done was assumed to characterise the beliefs of a vast majority, except, of course, those who were creating problems, such as the coalminers. Thus in the following description from ITN of the miners' pay negotiations of February 1975, we were told that there were 'fears' about what the miners would do. The 'fears' at this point were presented as general and were not related to any specific group:

> It is almost certain that they [the miners' leaders] will then formally tell the Coal Board that the offer is unacceptable – probably it will be on Tuesday afternoon. The Board's offer was within the framework of the Social Contract, but there are now fears that the miners' pay target will force a breach in the Social Contract. (ITN, 22.00, 6 February 1975)

The miners as an industrial group have, of course, in recent years attracted a huge amount of media coverage. In the period of our study, they were treated by the television news as perhaps the most significant trade union in the success or failure of the Social Contract. It is therefore important to assess how their pay negotiations and eventual settlement were covered by the newsrooms. A detailed account of this now follows.

The miners' pay negotiations and the Social Contract

The miners' pay deal in February 1975 was followed closely by both BBC and ITN, mainly from 5 to 16 February. The sequence in its simplest outline was as shown in Table 4.1. The whole of this sequence is framed against the relevance or supposed relevance to the Social Contract of the miners' pay claim and how this was perceived by various participants or media commentators.

5 February 1975

In the two BBC1 bulletins where the subject was raised on 5 February there was a brief newscaster introduction followed by an

Table 4.1   The miners' pay deal, 1975

Date	BBC1	BBC2	ITN
5 February	NUM receive NCB offer		
6 February	NUM reject NCB offer		NUM reject NCB offer
9 February		News Review résumé	
10 February	Threats of industrial action from Yorkshire and Scotland		
11 February	NCB increase offer		NCB increase offer Inter-union conflict
12 February	NUM pay and the railwaymen		NUM reject new offer
13 February	NUM accept latest offer		NUM and railwaymen CBI views Miners accept latest offer
14 February	Reactions to pay deal: Foot and railwaymen		
16 February		News Review résumé	

extended comment from Ian Ross, the industrial correspondent. In the first newscast (17 April 1975) the point was made by the newscaster and the correspondent that the offer was within the terms of the Social Contract but that dissatisfaction with the offer was to be expected:

> Newscaster: Miners' leaders got details today of the Coal Board's full pay offer. The proposals, which conform with the terms of the Social Contract, seem certain to cause a row among the union's left-wing when its full negotiating committee meets tomorrow morning. Here is our industrial correspondent, Ian Ross.
>
> Ian Ross: The Board is offering increases of between £7 and £10 on basic rates, about 22 per cent, which is rather more than prices have risen in the past year. But, as the Social Contract stipulates, the offer does take account of what the miners have been getting under threshold cost-of-living payments and that is £4.40 per week per man.

The correspondent then gave some information, saying that the effect of the deal would be to raise the basic wage of face workers from £45 to £55; of other underground workers from £36 to £44; and of surface workers from £32 to £39. He also indicated that this had the effect of widening differentials between face workers and surface workers and that there was also a new production bonus related to quarterly output figures. He concluded:

Some of the union's negotiators won't regard this offer as a satisfactory answer to a pay claim which demanded substantial pay increases, and there is bound to be a move to reject it, but the union is still likely to go along and see the Coal Board as arranged tomorrow afternoon.

So, here was an offer within the terms of the Social Contract and even a little generous, since the 22 per cent was 'rather more than prices have risen in the past year', although as we showed above, this was in fact a very dubious conclusion. The 22 per cent, had it been accepted, would have, it could be argued, represented a cut in real income. The *Nine O'clock News* item contained similar information and comment to that of the early bulletin, with a slightly different gloss. The 22 per cent was now in the newscaster's introduction: 'Miners' leaders got details today of the Coal Board's full pay offer. The offer will mean increases of between £7 and £10 on basic rates, or about 22 per cent.' The correspondent then adjusted his earlier piece at the beginning and the end. He began:

> The wages side of the Social Contract is all about making sure that wages rise no more than prices and the Coal Board, faithful to the government's dictate, has offered 22 per cent, which, in fact, is rather more than retail prices have risen in the past year.

Here, then, was the Coal Board keeping to the wages side of the Social Contract. What other side was there to the Social Contract? The bulletin was silent on the matter, but referred to union negotiators who would not see this as a substantial increase, adding, 'especially those who not long ago were talking about only being satisfied with an extra £30.00 per week: the same people who have no time for the Social Contract'. The scene was set whereby the rejection of this award, already presented as slightly generous in Social Contract terms, would be interpreted as a threat to the Contract by those who wanted to breach it anyway.

6 February 1975

On this day the NUM rejected the NCB's pay offer and this was reported on BBC1, BBC2, and ITN. With the exception of BBC, 21.00, the rejection of the offer referred to the 22 per cent in the opening sentence:

BBC1, 17.45:   'Miners' leaders have rejected the Coal Board's pay offer which would give them a 22 per cent increase in basic rates.'

BBC2, 23.05:   'Miners' leaders have rejected a 22 per cent pay increase offered by the Coal Board: instead they want an increase of around 40 per cent on basic rates.'

ITN, 17.50:   'Leaders of the miners' union have recommended that a 22 per cent pay package offer should be turned down.'

ITN, 22.00:   'The miners' leaders have unanimously decided to recommend that their members should reject a 22 per cent pay offer made by the Coal Board.'

In each case this is followed by the information that the union had called off its arranged meeting with the NCB.

The BBC's treatment of the NUM's attitude on the preceding day had been to distinguish between the left-wing of the NUM and the rest of the negotiating committee and to make specific reference to those 'who have no time for the Social Contract'. In the light of the unanimous rejection of the pay offer by the negotiating committee some adjustment was called for. On BBC1, 17.45, the industrial correspondent commented as follows:

Even moderates among the miners' leaders are unhappy about the offer and the left is positively contemptuous. The militant Mr Arthur Scargill, the Yorkshire miners' leader, likened the offer to a 'bag of crisps'. We should serve notice of industrial action on the Coal Board right now, he said. Well, they won't, because the offer is still negotiable. The Board is prepared to look again at the question of pay differentials, widening the gap between the surface worker and the man right down at the coal face, who could end up getting more than the basic £55 per week that is on offer now. That would be permissible under a clause in the Social Contract which refers to reforming outdated pay structures. But what is really at issue here is the miners' attitude to the Social Contract. Although the union was the first to speak in its support at the Trades Union Congress last September, to many of its leaders it no longer matters and they are now looking for the kind of pay rises which could in no way be reconciled with the Contract. (BBC1, 17.45, 6 February 1975)

A distinction was made here between moderates and militants on the NUM. The latter are 'left-wing'. To juxtapose 'moderates' and 'militants' in this way in the context of an analysis of the economy which was organised around 'wage inflation' and the necessity of wage restraint carried with it an implicit judgment. The force of this stereotyping came through with the opening phrase: 'Even moderates . . . are unhappy'. Second, Ross, in saying that the NCB was still negotiating and was still looking at pay differentials, recognised that this was permissible under a clause in the Social Contract which relates to the reform of outdated pay structures. This was, however, immediately followed by a *but*. The correspondent was concerned to tell us 'what is really at issue'. He then compared the attitude of the union, which was 'the very first to speak' in support of the Social Contract at the September TUC Congress, with the assertion 'and they are now looking for the kind of pay rises which could in no way be reconciled with the Contract'. Given the subtleties of the Social Contract taken as a whole and given that negotiations were still in progress at the time of the assertion, this was an imputation that pre-judged the outcome. This may be a point of view, but it was scarcely a 'fact' which the correspondent had conclusively demonstrated was the case.

The BBC's *Nine O'Clock News* was organised on similar lines. The contrast between the Board's 'offer' and the miners' 'demands' was developed in two consecutive sentences:

> The Board's offer was for a 22 per cent pay increase on basic rates; that is, between £7 and £10 a week more excluding a production bonus, an improved sick pay scheme and free working clothes. The miners are demanding between 37½ per cent and 41 per cent increases on their basic rates and improvements in the bonus for productivity. (BBC1, 21.00, 6 February 1975)

The picture now drawn was of a generous offer spurned as 'a bag of crisps'. The continuing reference to Mr Scargill was surprising, for he was not the spokesman for the NUM negotiating committee. Ian Ross in his comments supplied us with an answer: 'Mr Scargill and the left . . . have highlighted the real issue here, and that is the credibility of the Social Contract, which may stand or fall according to what the miners settle for.' He went on to say: 'Certainly it is impossible to reconcile a claim for increases of 40 per cent with even the very flexible terms of the Social Contract.' This general point was reiterated when Ross acknowledged again that reforming an outdated pay structure was compatible with the Social Contract and that Mr Foot might have recognised a special case for pay rises but not to the tune of 40 per cent. The miners' pay claim was, says Ross, 'the acid test of the Contract'.

The BBC2 *News Extra* report followed closely *The Nine O'Clock News*. In addition to concluding that this was the acid test of the contract, Ross's opening comment assured us that another miners' strike was not likely, despite left-wing pressure: 'No, it is a battle between the miners and the Social Contract, with the Coal Board and the government waiting in the wings. What the miners finally accept as a pay settlement will, to a very large extent, make or break the Social Contract' (BBC2, 23.05, 6 February 1975).

If we turn now to ITN's coverage on the same day there was a reference to the 22 per cent and the newscaster said on the early evening bulletin that the miners' pay target would 'impose a serious threat to the government's Social Contract' and in *News at Ten*, that 'there are now fears that the miners' pay target will form a breach in the Contract'. Michael Green, the industrial correspondent, agreed with the BBC's correspondent when he began by saying: 'There is no doubt that the miners' pay negotiations can make or break the Social Contract as it stands.' However, there were some noticeable differences in tone and content. For example, apart from the newscaster's mention of a '22 per cent pay package offer', there was only one further reference to the 22 per cent by Green on the 17.50 bulletin and none at 22.00. There was no reference to the miners' 'demands' for 37.5–40 per cent increases. In fact it was easy to set the NCB's offer against the miners' claim with the information we were given (see Table 4.2). Green also calculated that the difference in the total wage bill between these two positions was £70 million for the NCB and a further £80 million for the NUM. The fact

Table 4.2 The miners' claim and the NCB offer (in £)

	NCB offer basic weekly rate	Increase on present rate	NUM target basic weekly rate	Increase on present rate
Face workers	55	10	63	18
Other under-ground workers	44	8	50	14
Surface workers	39	7	44	12

that the negotiations of their nature had to do with offers and counter-claims and that first offers and replies are the beginning of the bargaining process was clearly presented by Green:

> The negotiating committee which met this morning turned down the Coal Board's offer without so much as a vote, and, to be frank, that won't surprise the employers a bit. They have been criticised in the past for offering too much too soon, and this time they were determined to keep something in reserve. (ITN, 22.00, 6 February 1975)

Another significant difference in presentation was this. While BBC reported the language of Mr Scargill in his attitude to the offer – 'a bag of crisps' and 'disgusting' – no reason for this was advanced other than the implication that he was opposed to the Social Contract. But since the rejection by the NUM was unanimous, there was surely more to be said? Green made a crucial point which the BBC report ignores:

> Part of the dissatisfaction with the current offer is that it includes the consolidation of threshold payments of £4.40 which all the miners already get. So in new money terms the men would only get between £2.60 and £5.60 more on basic rates. (ITN, 22.00, 6 February 1975)

9 February 1975

The Scargill words 'disgusting' and 'a bag of crisps' were given a further airing on BBC2's Sunday *News Review*. In fact the interview with the Chancellor of the Exchequer, Denis Healey, was structured around them:

> Newscaster: A new pay offer from the Coal Board to the miners this week. 22 per cent extra, which means a weekly increase of £7 and £10. It was rejected and described by Arthur Scargill, leader of the Yorkshire miners, as 'disgusting' – 'a bag of crisps'. This prompted a question to the Chancellor, Denis Healey – are the miners seeking a fight with the government?
>
> Healey: I don't think so – I don't think there are many miners and certainly very few people outside mining who would regard

£10 a week as a bag of crisps, certainly none of the nurses that I know, or the postmen, or the farm workers who produce our food, would take the view and I think the miners appreciate what the present government has done for them in increasing the social wage, which has gone up, you know, 10 or 12 per cent in the last year after you've taken prices off.

Interviewer: But the miners and other groups of workers are still wanting to settle outside the TUC guidelines. Does this worry you?

Healey: I'm very concerned. In recent weeks a quarter of the people who've had settlements have had them outside the guidelines. That's far too many. If we go on like that we shall price the country out of jobs and that could mean mass unemployment. (BBC2, 18.50, 9 February 1975)

The reference to the pay offer was followed by the phrase: 'It was rejected and described by Arthur Scargill, leader of the Yorkshire miners, as "disgusting" – "a bag of crisps".' Not only was the phrase repeated on several bulletins on BBC, but the drafting of the sentence could convey the impression that it was Arthur Scargill who has rejected the pay offer, whereas the reference should properly be to the miners' political standpoint. It is, however, relevant to comment that Healey's statement is not easy to understand: 'I think the miners appreciate what the present government has done for them in increasing the social wage, which has gone up, you know, 10 or 12 per cent in the last year after you've taken prices off'. It certainly depends on understanding the concept of 'social wage'. Obviously one cannot assume that everyone who watches television news has read the Social Contract.

10 February 1975

This was the day before negotiations were to be resumed between the miners and the NCB, and BBC1 gave further coverage on the theme of calls for industrial action from Yorkshire and Scotland in support of higher wages. The item was once more introduced with another comment from Arthur Scargill, who described the NCB's offer as 'bloody daft'. Scargill then in interview said:

It appears to me that there are far too many people intent on a collision course with the miners and many people in this industry have been accused of being saboteurs. Well, if there are any saboteurs on this occasion it's certainly not on the National Union of Mineworkers' negotiation table. It must be on the negotiation table of the National Coal Board. And I would ask the question why they're sticking so rigidly to a ridiculous offer of 8 per cent, which after all is a net reduction in real terms on the inflation rate of about 20 per cent. (BBC1, 17.45, 10 February 1975)

The 8 per cent was a new figure to appear and no discussion or comment flowed from it.

The news had already established what the 'facts' and 'figures' of current wage claims were. The firm link had been made between wage increases, inflation and the economic crisis. To have seriously considered Scargill's new figure of 8 per cent at this juncture in the coverage would have made a severe dent in this dominant framework. In the event, and this is not untypical of such alternative frameworks, it passed without comment. Subsequently, in the same bulletin, the industrial correspondent stressed the dominant frame: 'Scotland and Yorkshire are merely banging the drum without any real hope of attracting much support. The £30 demand from Scotland would mean increases of up to 94 per cent, alongside which Yorkshire's £20 seems almost moderate' (BBC1, 17.45, 10 February 1975). The BBC's correspondent went on to speak of the NUM's 41 per cent claim and the NCB's 22 per cent offer. Having stated that there was a big gap between their two positions his prediction was that

> where the Coal Board might go further tomorrow without bending the Social Contract too much, is in widening differentials to the advantage of the man working at the coal face and improving the terms of the production bonus. Beyond that, and anything approaching the union claim, would be right outside the Social Contract.

This kind of media judgment is not a matter of unadorned factual information. It is a mixture of prediction and opinion which takes its evaluative strength from the systematic trading upon limited frameworks of analysis.

11 February 1975

The report on negotiations between the NUM and the NCB was organised in BBC1's main news around a speech by Chancellor Healey on 'excessive wage increases':

> The Chancellor of the Exchequer, Mr Healey, has warned again of excessive wage increases as the miners start negotiating on their claim for up to 43 per cent. Mr Healey said in London tonight that Britain could be bankrupt if the national wage bill were too high this year – but it needn't happen if the workers stuck strictly to the Social Contract. During the day the Coal Board twice increased their offer to the miners, mainly to the benefit of those working underground. (BBC1, 21.00, 11 February 1975)

This report was very clearly organised to link the themes of wage inflation as a problem, with the miners' pay negotiations. There was no question of this being a random juxtaposition in the news, since the two themes were presented in the form of a 'double sandwich': i.e. references to them followed alternately in quick succession. The miners' claim was effectively defined as excessive and was linked with a threat of national bankruptcy should it succeed.

If one collates the percentages that have now been given an airing on this claim it amounts to quite a list: 8 per cent, 22 per cent, 25–30 per cent, 37.5–41 per cent, 43 per cent, 94 per cent. References to 25 per cent and 30 per cent which also came in the passage quoted above were somewhat ambiguous. They presumably related to an increase on the present basic wage. In his ensuing comments the BBC's correspondent stated that the Coal Board's offer was 'certainly not the strict interpretation of the Social Contract that Mr Healey is insisting on'. He organised his commentary on a Healey versus Scargill basis:

> In his speech tonight Mr Healey took a swipe at the militant Yorkshire miners' leader, Arthur Scargill, over his philosophy of damn the Social Contract. The contract, said the Chancellor, has two sides: the government's ability to avoid mass unemployment, improve social services and the like depended on keeping wage settlements within the spirit not just the letter of the Social Contract. Mr Healey, whose Department has kept in

close touch with the miners' pay talks today, can't be pleased that there is likely to be a miners' settlement, without a strike, when that settlement looks like being without and not within the spirit of the Social Contract. (BBC1, 21.00, 11 February 1975)

Our concern here is not with the Healey position, but with the media presentation. Throughout Mr Scargill was portrayed more and more like a devil in a morality play, a man who exclaims, 'disgusting', 'ridiculous', 'bloody daft', and 'damn the Social Contract' and who by implication was bringing the country to the verge of national bankruptcy. The bulletins gave Mr Scargill's *attitude* to the Social Contract, but never the rationale which underlay it. His statements were not explained as being linked to an alternative position on the nature of the economy and inflation, which might make more sense of them. His appearances had the status of token references to the 'extremes' of political opinion – in reality they amounted to little more than downgrading a position by isolating it, and indicating by absence that it did not fit the economic model assumed as correct by the broadcasters.

ITN's treatment of the negotiations on this day was differently organised. On *First Report* an account was given of the NUM's meeting prior to its negotiation with the NCB. The Yorkshire miners' claim for a £30 increase on the basic rate (including the threshold payments) was 'narrowly rejected'. Michael Green reported: 'There were only 4 votes in it, in fact.' The vote was 15 against, 11 in favour, and 1 abstention. In an exchange of questions with the newscaster Robert Kee, there was a discussion of the significance of the 'militant noises' and of the possibilities of unofficial strike action. Green stated that the hands of Scargill and the Scottish miners are tied by this executive decision. The closeness of the vote did not accord very well with the dismissive comment of BBC's industrial correspondent the day before: 'Scotland and Yorkshire are merely banging the drum without any real hope of attracting much support' (BBC1, 17.45). As with BBC coverage, the terms 'moderate' and 'militant' were used as descriptive categories for groupings within the NUM – the militants being 'left-wingers' and personified in Arthur Scargill.

Both ITN's early evening bulletin and *News at Ten* began with a presentation of the NCB's new pay offer in relation to miners' current wages and the NUM's claim. This was done for the three main groupings noted before and can be clearly itemised (see

Table 4.3). There was far less emphasis on percentages in ITN's coverage. An ITN correspondent concentrated on the actual wage figures and only once employed percentages – at the close of his

Table 4.3   NCB offer for relation to miners' current wages and the NUM claim (in £)

	Present wages†	NCB's old offer*	NCB's new offer	NUM's claim
Face workers	49.40	55	58.50	63
Other underground workers	40.40	44	46	50
Surface workers	36.40	39	40	44

* Information in this column was given only in the early evening bulletin.
† This column includes £4.40 threshold payments.

News at Ten report: 'The offer, the Coal Board maintains stoutly, is still within the Social Contract, even though it adds between 25 and 30 per cent to basic rates' (ITN, 22.00, 11 February 1975).

12 February 1975

The on-going negotiations continued to be reported on both channels. The main evening bulletins on BBC1 and BBC2 both consisted of a newscaster reporting that the Coal Board had 'again narrowed the gap between what they're prepared to offer and what the Union want'. This was specifically linked to face workers – 'this time a rise of 33 per cent, putting the men in the £3,000 a year bracket' – together with an improved production bonus. There was then a comment from the BBC's correspondent incorporating a brief interview with Joe Gormley, the NUM President. The main negotiating problem was now said to be the pay of surface workers. On both bulletins Ross asked Gormley: 'Do you claim you are still working within the Social Contract?' Gormley replied:

> We always work within the laws of society, within the TUC's figures. We will do that all the time and feel we came out with a good settlement which will still be able to be portrayed as being within the Social Contract.

The industrial correspondent was prepared to contradict this: 'Despite what Mr Gormley says, the offer is already well outside the Social Contract' (BBC1, 21.00, 12 February 1975).

ITN's coverage, while briefer, covered similar ground to the BBC's. Both the newscaster and the industrial correspondent refer to the £3,000 a year offer. On this occasion ITN made more play with percentages. Peter Sissons said,

> What is being scrutinised with some unease in Whitehall are the percentages: 33 per cent for miners at the coal face, taking them to £60; 28 per cent for other underground workers, making their basic pay £46; and 25 per cent for surface workers – a deal which would give them a basic £40.

He then pointed out that the remaining negotiating point centred on surface workers and said that this was relevant to pay negotiations in other industries such as electricity supply and the railways. There then followed a question from Giles Smith to Joe Gormley as to whether these percentages were compatible with the Social Contract – to which Gormley's answer was yes. As with the BBC report the industrial correspondent permitted himself some scepticism on this topic. Here, attention was drawn to what was claimed as the scant regard which the miners were paying to the Social Contract and the principle of wage restraint:

> Without doubt the Social Contract has some fairly vague provisions, but for this key economic policy to succeed, as Mr Healey insisted last night, everything depends on keeping wage settlements within the spirit and not just the letter of the TUC guidelines. What the Contract's supporters will find disturbing is that there's little evidence during these negotiations to suggest that it ever figured seriously in the miners' thinking. (ITN, 22.00, 12 February 1975)

The content and manner in which the news is organised sets the context for the understanding and evaluation of the social world. It may well have been 'true' that some of the miners' leaders did not give much thought to keeping within the Social Contract, but what gave this piece of news its significance was the previously established context from which the evaluation follows, that the miners *ought* to have been thinking about wage restraint. This context was set by consistent references on the news to the limited body of social and economic explanations which it favoured. The significant absence is any explanation of why they should want to reject the Contract.

13 February 1975

This was the day the miners agreed upon a wage settlement to recommend to their members. Matters had not been agreed by the time of ITN's *First Report* and the industrial editor began his piece in an informal style: 'Well, the National Union of Mineworkers are still shaking the gravy train here at the Coal Board. So far this morning nothing really substantial has yet fallen out' (ITN, 13.00, 13 February 1975). He went on to predict that the offer to surface workers, who were now defined as the difficult category, would move from £40 to £41. By early evening the settlement was concluded. What was it?

ITN, 17.50 and 22.00
1 £185 million offer
2 Increase of between 28 and 35 per cent
3 New basic rates between £41 and £61
4 32 per cent to basic wage bill
5 Coal face workers go from £49.50 including threshold of £4.40 to £61; i.e. 35 per cent increase
6 Other underground workers £40.40 to £47; i.e. 30 per cent increase
7 Surface workers £36.40 to £41; i.e. 28 per cent increase
8 Productivity deal – extra pay for all once an average weekly target reached

BBC1, 17.45
1 Face workers basic £61 per week
2 Other underground workers £47
3 Surface workers £41
4 Increase in basic rates up to 35 per cent

BBC2, 22.35
1 Increase up to 30 per cent
2 Cost of £190 million in a full year
3 Face workers £61 per week
4 Other underground workers up to £47
5 Surface workers up to £41

These were the 'hard facts'. There is a difference of £5 million between ITN's and BBC's costing of the offer. Further, the use of percentages is deployed with different degrees of generality. The BBC generally reported increases of up to 35 per cent, whereas ITN related percentages to particular categories of workers. It was also the case that whereas BBC simply announced what the new basic rates would be, ITN said what the old basic rate was.

In both presentations, however, there was an important and significant omission. The settlement could have been portrayed in standard negotiating terms relating the NCB's original offer, the NUM's claim and the final outcome (see Table 4.4). In the case of

Table 4.4   The NCB's offer, the NUM's claim and the agreed settlement (in £)

	Basic weekly rate NCB's original offer	NUM's claim	Agreed settlement
Face workers	55	63	61
Other underground workers	44	50	47
Surface workers	39	44	41

other underground workers and surface workers these were typical 'split-the-difference settlements', familiar to wage bargainers and arbitrators, with the surface workers pegged down somewhat. The shape of the overall settlement did widen the differentials to the advantage of face workers. Despite constant reporting on television news the character of the settlement was not precisely stated within such an explicit frame of reference.

ITN, 17.50 and 22.00
Industrial editor (Peter Sissons): So, is the settlement within the spirit of the Social Contract? Have the miners shown restraint?
Gormley: We've shown tremendous restraint I think in the last two and a half days. I think we've been very patient with one another and there has been real restraint in the way we have tried to negotiate.
Sissons: But what if others,

BBC1, 17.45
Newscaster: The agreement would increase basic rates by up to 35 per cent but Joe Gormley, the miners' President, says it's not damaging to the Social Contract. Here's our industrial correspondent, Ian Ross.
Ross: Well, it must damage the Social Contract and it must put into question what relevance the Social Contract has now to controlling inflation. . . .

ITN, 17.50 and 22.00

other groups of workers, got between 28 per cent and 35 per cent – the Social Contract would mean nothing?

Gormley: Well, I remember what you said at another meeting that nowhere within the Social Contract does it lay down that you can only get this percentage or that percentage. And if as a result of the whole exercise that we have been involved in, it comes up to a certain percentage I don't think anybody can then just say – well, that drives a coach and horses though the Social Contract. If you view the Social Contract as we know it correctly, in order to put some of these injustices that were apparent in the – in any industry – which would have to be dealt with whatever the government policy, then I don't think you can be criticised.

Sissons: Mr Siddell, in these negotiations did you detect any element of restraint by the National Union of Mineworkers?

Siddell: Well, I think restraint is a peculiar term to apply to the National Union of Mineworkers, but if one can look at that in the context of

BBC1, 17.45

The miners' leader, Mr Gormley, when claiming that the deal fell within the spirit of the Social Contract justified this on the grounds that they had reorganised the pay structure which the Contract allows for.

BBC1, 21.00

Ross: Both sides deny that throughout the talks they were under any kind of pressure from the TUC or government ministers to settle at a particular level and both claim that they had been influenced by the terms of the Social Contract, or at least the escape clause in it which makes a special case of a pay deal that reorganises the wage structure and widens differentials. The very flexibility of the Social Contract was their ally. I suggested to the Coal Board's chief negotiator that their original pay offer had been in line with the Social Contract and then they'd thrown the Contract away.

Siddell: No, we didn't throw it away. In fact, I've been reciting it right throughout and right up to today.

Ross: Can you claim then that this agreement falls

ITN, 17.50 and 22.00

a talk about a £30 increase, and indeed when we came to negotiating around the table a minimum claim of £44 on the surface was settled at £41, I think one could detect restraint.

BBC1, 21.00

anywhere within it?

Siddell: Well, we've done a restructuring exercise which was particularly vital in my view to this industry because of the events of the past few years, when we've had settlements virtually imposed upon us, and the differentials between grades that really eliminated the incentive for men to work through the surface, underground, right up to the producing category, which is our important place of course. And therefore we have restored that within this agreement. The difficulty has been the minimum surface rate, which is, I suppose, a place where people can mostly point the finger against us. We have discussed the Social Contract. As I say, I have read it out many times. I can recite it by heart almost now. In terms of percentages it is quite difficult to reconcile what the strict interpretation is. But having regard to other settlements that have been made in the public sector even, the amounts of increases on the basic rate aren't very far outside the sort of settlements that have been made.

While the negotiators are here given a chance to explain the pay deal, this must be seen in the context of the continuous coverage analysed above, which had emphasised in turn the NCB's concession and a sequence of new offers to the NUM, as well as the size and scale of the eventual offer and an expressed scepticism that the deal was within the Social Contract. The BBC's correspondent was prepared to contradict flatly any assertion that it was within the Contract. His opening question to Mr Siddell contained his own judgment on the matter, which he had continuously reiterated from 5 February. Even his references to the restructuring element in the pay deal he described as 'the escape clause' in the Contract, which was only one way of looking at it. Either such an arrangement was within the framework of the Contract or it was not. It was incorrect to call it an 'escape clause'. By the same token, in his comment 'the very flexibility of the Contract was their ally' the BBC manages to imply that negotiators were acting together to take advantage of a 'flexible' Contract.

While both channels clearly used the Social Contract as an organising device in presenting the miners' pay deal, some differences in tone and content have already been indicated. Comments after the settlement also reflected some differences:

Sissons: Britain's most crucial wage claim, the pursuit of which has previously brought down a government and led to damaging strikes, is all but settled and settled quite amicably (ITN, 17.45, 13 February 1975)

Newscaster: The miners through their negotiators put the Coal Board out of its misery this week by accepting a large pay offer. After some haggling the offer crept pound by pound closer to the miners' own demands. (BBC2, 18.50, 16 March 1975)

14 February 1975

The day after the miners' negotiations were settled, the Secretary of State for Employment, Michael Foot, gave a speech in his constituency at Ebbw Vale. Compare the opening of BBC1's main evening news with ITN's *News at Ten*:

ITN, 22.00

Newscaster: Good evening.
The Employment Secretary
Mr Michael Foot tonight
justified the miners' pay
offer, but he warned that
other workers mustn't
expect similar treatment.

BBC1, 21.00

Newscaster: The Employment
Secretary Mr Foot has
admitted that the miners'
settlement goes well beyond
the Social Contract's
guidelines on compensating
for rises in the cost of living.

Whereas ITN's announcement suggests that the settlement was a one-off, the BBC's version was simply that the Contract was broken. The BBC's interpretation continued strongly:

> Throughout today no single Cabinet minister has attempted to claim that the miners' 32 per cent settlement is within the Social Contract. What they've been intent on doing is warning that other groups of workers shouldn't fall behind the miners. Mr Foot in his speech tonight denied that the Social Contract had now vanished into thin air. With what many will dismiss as verbal gymnastics, he attempted to justify the miners' pay deal as a much-needed and long-overdue reform of an outdated pay structure which was consistent with the terms of the Social Contract. And yet in the next breath he said it is undeniable that a settlement of over 30 per cent goes well beyond the figure required to compensate the rise in the cost of living, and if other settlements followed this pattern, he went on, Mr Denis Healey's warning on the economic consequences would come true.
> (BBC1, 21.00, 14 February 1975)

This commentary contained the following features: First there was the argument from silence: 'No single Cabinet Minister has attempted to claim that the miners' 32 per cent settlement is within the Social Contract'. This was a factually doubtful form of argumentation as Mr Foot (a 'single' senior Cabinet minister) was justifying the settlement as *within* the Contract. Second, the crude depiction of the deal as a 32 per cent wage settlement was inadequate. There was by now enough information available to do better than that, as ITN had done the day before. Third, there was the appeal to a multitude of unnamed critics of Mr Foot, linked with the inference that he had not succeeded in what he was claiming: 'With what many will dismiss as verbal gymnastics, he attempted to justify the miners' pay deal as a much-needed and long-overdue reform of an outdated pay structure which was consistent with the terms of the Social Contract . . .' All of this came *before* any interview with Mr Foot and therefore established a framework for viewing such an interview. Whatever else it was, this was not neutral news. It was not for that matter 'balanced' news in the sense of fairly listing the pros and cons. It was a particular and partial perspective on industrial relations and wage policy. For the record, rightly or wrongly, Mr Foot did say in his interview with Roy Roberts on the BBC bulletins that the settlement was within the Social Contract:

> The settlement's taken into account the need to get coal, it's taken into account the need to get miners, who are the only people who can get us to the coal, *it's taken into account also the fact that the National Coal Board's offers were made within the Social Contract*. All these factors have been taken into account in reaching this settlement and all in all I think it's a settlement that is beneficial for the country. Of course it's true that the figures go beyond the figures that would be required to keep up with the cost of living, and that is due to the factors I've mentioned – those have got to be taken into account. If this pattern was followed generally in other settlements then it would be damaging to the Social Contract and that is why we want people to take into account these factors. (BBC1, 21.00, 14 February 1975; our italics)

In this respect, then, the introduction to the ITN main bulletin would seem to be a more accurate description of Mr Foot's views than that of the BBC bulletin. However, this only reflected the more extreme and idiosyncratic stance of the BBC with regard to this pay claim and settlement.

Overall, the story of the miners' pay deal as presented by the media was told in the language of a 'battle' and an 'acid test' for the Social Contract. It was spiced with a bewildering array of percentages; with threats of industrial action and 'militant noises'; with fears of national bankruptcy. It saw in very truth the advent of some £3,000-a-year basic rate miners and a £41-a-week surface worker. The negotiations were under journalistic scrutiny but they were reported in a way which revealed more about the journalists' assumptions than the texture of the negotiations. While some of the participants to the negotiations were able to comment, explain and justify what was happening, this was typically within the highly structured conventions of interviewing and accommodated within the more general dominant framework provided by the television coverage.

'Inside' – 'outside'

The link between the explanation of the economic crisis and the evaluation of the miners' claim was at times generalised to warn of the actions of other groups of workers. In the following example, the BBC industrial correspondent gave his view of the final settlement which the coal miners reached:

> Well, it must damage the Social Contract and it must put in question what relevance the Social Contract now has to controlling inflation. Particularly when other groups of workers like the men in the power stations and the railways, use the 28 per cent increase for the surface workers as the target for their pay negotiations. (BBC2, 17.45, 13 February 1975)

There was no comparable monitoring of the activities of employers. On only one occasion in this whole four-month period did a news journalist suggest directly that the Confederation of British Industry had some responsibility for the resolution of the crisis. This was in a BBC2 bulletin of January, which dealt with proposed talks between the Prime Minister and the CBI:

> They [the CBI] said that with prolonged high inflation on top of price controls and high corporation tax, many more companies are, and will continue to be, forced to seek financial aid from the government. They accepted that management have some responsibility for reducing inflation but they needed union and government help. Without it, they said, unemployment would rise very fast. (BBC2, 22.25, 7 January 1975)

What the responsibility was and how well it was being discharged was not expanded upon. There was no sense in which the news coverage was organised systematically to give this information, or in which it routinely examined the managerial workings of private industry. Rather, the news relayed in great detail exactly what unfortunate consequences could follow from the 'demands' and 'claims' of trade unions, while the 'offers' of the 'other side' of industry remained largely ignored or were left in large part unexamined. Often the concentration moved away from 'negotiations' to the probable effects if agreements were not reached. For example, at the time of the coalminers' pay settlement we were informed of the effect it would have upon coal prices:

> The deal gives them new basic rates of between £41 and £61 and was accepted 15 votes to 11, by the union's executive. It will mean increases in the price of coal to consumers. The Coal Board's deputy chairman, Mr Norman Siddell, said they would have to be fairly substantial and fairly soon, but he wouldn't suggest whether the main burden would be on private consumers or on industry. (ITN, 17.50, 13 February 1975)

We are not suggesting that such news should not be reported. What we are highlighting is that only some actions and their consequences are systematically explored and critically examined in this fashion. The actions of other groups in our society were not balanced by such routinely critical coverage. For example, there was no similar detailed examination or reporting on the news of what many saw as the key problem facing British industry; namely, the failure of substantial sections of private industry over a thirty-year period to mount adequate investment programmes. As we have noted, references to the causes of this problem did occasionally appear in the news, but it is significant that they came normally as interview responses rather than from media personnel. Thus both Ray Buckton (General Secretary of ASLEF) and Ian Mikardo, MP, appeared in interviews and called for exchange controls to stop the movement of capital from Britain (Buckton, ITN, 13.00, 16 April 1976). At other times, there were fragmented references to the movement of capital into speculative areas such as land and property, with its consequent effects on price inflation (Ian Mikardo, MP, quoted above, ITN, 13.00, 13 April 1975).

However, the overwhelming emphasis of news bulletins dealing with the economic crisis during this period related to the activities of the trade unions. This included the evaluation of wage negotiations and settlements, which was a major theme in news coverage.

Individual pay claims, offers and settlements were routinely monitored to an extent quite unlike any other phenomena in this period. In addition, this reporting was organised principally in terms of the supposed effects on the Social Contract. In the period of our study the pay negotiations of doctors, power workers, railway workers, Civil Service staff, engineers and miners were all reported – often simply in terms of whether the sums in question were 'inside' or 'outside' the Social Contract. This concern to point out the significance of pay claims and settlements to the 'wages side' of the Social Contract (itself a significant one-sided view of the Contract) is indicated by the inclusion in each case of reported statements, interview questions and responses directly relating to the question of whether the Social Contract could be said to have been broken. Moreover, in a significant number of cases the media institutions took it upon themselves to judge the issue in the form of direct media statements irrespective of the number of interview responses or reported statements that may have contradicted this. Often, however, the reported statements chosen for inclusion in the bulletins were of the view that the pay in question was 'outside' the Social Contract (see Table 4.5).

Table 4.5   Pay settlements and the Social Contract: direct media judgments

| | Number of media statements | |
	Within the Social Contract	Outside the Social Contract
Miners	—	8
Railway workers	—	5
Dockers	—	4
Power workers	—	2
Civil Service staff	—	1
Engineers	1	1
Building workers	2	—

The interpretation of the Social Contract as being primarily about wages was criticised at this time by both trade unionists and members of the government. Mr Michael Foot, for example, spoke at the Scottish Trade Union Congress in April 1975 against the limited view that some people had of the Social Contract. His speech was reported on BBC1 as follows:

Mr Michael Foot: However some people, of course, when they talk of the Social Contract wish to disguise the fact that it's not only a question that deals with wages at all; the Social Contract was an understanding reached between the political leadership of the Labour Party, and the representatives of the trade union movement – an understanding reached about common economic and political objectives covering a much wider field than anything that is solely concerned with incomes or wages. It is for that reason, first of all, that I say as clearly as I possibly can to this Congress and to anybody else who might be overhearing what we have to say, that we deny that the Social Contract is dead and destroyed for the very first reason that we've got a lot of unfinished business to deal with under that Social Contract. (BBC1, 22.00, 17 April 1975)

One of the groups which focused largely on the 'wages' part of the Contract at this time was the television news personnel. The report of this speech which criticised the exclusive focus on wages was actually linked twice on the BBC news with references to a current wage claim. The above bulletin continued:

The unfinished business Mr Foot went on to list included the repeal of the Conservatives' Industrial Relations Act, putting into law the Employment Protection Bill and moves like the setting up of the National Enterprise Board and for dealing with North Sea Oil.

As Mr Foot was making his speech leaders of 100,000 workers in the shipbuilding industry were accepting pay rises of over 30 per cent to their members. The deal follows the recent rise for engineering workers and it affects basic rates. (BBC1, 21.00, 17 April 1975)

The late-night BBC2 bulletin that day actually sandwiched a reference to the pay rises into the middle of its report of the speech:

Speaking at the Scottish TUC, where the Budget is being fiercely attacked, Mr Foot said the government remained determined not to reintroduce wage controls, the alternative to the Social Contract. As Mr Foot was speaking leaders of 100,000 shipbuilders were accepting a pay rise of over 30 per cent for their members. Mr Foot also spoke on the Common Market. He believed that Britain's dependence on the bankers of Europe was a humiliating state of affairs. (BBC2, 22.00, 17 April 1975)

The news reporting of the wages side of the Social Contract was reduced substantially to the question of whether it was being 'broken'. The implication was frequently made that wage settlements were in advance of price rises.

In the following example from ITN in April, the pay settlements of the power workers and the railwaymen were discussed in this fashion. An agreement had just been reached for the power workers.

> The damage now is the size of the settlement, which deals yet another blow to the government's hope of keeping wage increases on a par with rising prices. It's bound to increase the aspirations of other workers with pay claims in the pipeline, and it seems difficult for the government to avoid allowing a similar-sized pay rise to the country's railwaymen; and if the railwaymen get around 30 per cent too, the credibility of the Social Contract, already under severe strain as a result of tonight's settlement, may be damaged beyond repair. (ITN, 22.00, 3 January 1975)

From the trade union point of view, the 'other side' of the Social Contract at this time was the defence of living standards. This was referred to quite clearly by news journalists on a number of occasions as in the following example from the BBC news of January 1975.

> Industrial correspondent: Well, as the trade unions see it, the Social Contract is all about making sure that wages don't fall beneath the rise in the cost of living and that there is no cut in the amount of money they have to spend. The TUC insists on maintaining living standards and even on increasing wage demands, if unemployment rises. (BBC1, 21.00, 10 January 1975)

If there had been any serious attempt in the television news to consider the point of view of these trade unions, then we might have expected some media personnel to evaluate wage settlements in terms of how they affected living standards. But, as we have indicated, the focus in the news within this area was on the 'breaking' of the Contract in the sense that some settlements were allegedly 'excessive'. There was no comparable focus or even comment on wage negotiations and settlements which were the opposite of this in the sense that they represented cuts in the living standard. They were merely reported as being 'inside' the Social Contract. At no point have we found an evaluation or even a comment from media personnel to suggest that any of the settlements or wage offers from employers were below the rate of inflation or were 'too low' to be inside the Social Contract from the trade union point of view. There were no 'fears' expressed by media personnel on such occasions. A clearer expression of value commitment would be difficult to unearth. The inferential framework of reporting sees wage negotiations as 'threatening' or 'demanding', never as part of continuing process in which both sides sometimes gain and sometimes lose. No union ever 'accepts' too little – but some managements or boards are judged to 'offer' too much.

5 'Who Gets On?': Conclusion

In the discussion surrounding important issues central to our economy, the range of views and opinions included in television news is highly restricted. From a potential cast of thousands the television news has the power to decide who are to be the principal actors on the stage. Restricted access to debate in the media in terms of who is quoted or interviewed must also be seen in terms of the differing status awarded to their contributions in the overall organisation of news bulletins. The manner of appearance and the context of appearance can thus be a more crucial determinant of 'balance' than formal equality of numbers.

The sample for this investigation is all the news items from the national television news reporting of the Social Contract during the four-month period 1 January–30 April 1975. These news items were identified by their explicit reference to 'the Social Contract' and 'the TUC guidelines'. We examined the two main evening bulletins, BBC's *Nine O'Clock News* and ITN's *News at Ten*, from this period. These bulletins were chosen because of their pre-eminence both in terms of audience ratings and the organisational priorities of the newsrooms.

The manner in which the different 'actors on the stage' are identified is as follows: named groups or individuals appear in the news variously in interviews (Interviewees), by directly quoted or attributed statements (Reported statements), named in news reports (Named actor in media statements, not quoted) and lastly those actors merely mentioned by *other* actors within interviews or reported statements (Actors' significant others). A complete list of the 'actors on the stage' is provided in Table 5.1.

Within the hierarchy of access to television news there is a corresponding range of mediation in the level of control that can be exercised over the communication process. In terms of the ability to

Table 5.1 The actors on the stage

Actor	Interview BBC	Interview ITN	Reported statements BBC	Reported statements ITN	Named actor in media statements BBC	Named actor in media statements ITN	Actors' significant others BBC	Actors' significant others ITN
James Wellbeloved, MP	1	—	1	2	—	—	—	—
Harold Wilson, PM	1	2	5	2	5	6	1	1
Denis Healey	2	—	13	13	4	5	1	1
Michael Foot	4	2	2	5	2	2	2	—
Barbara Castle	1	1	—	1	—	—	—	—
Len Murray	3	3	3	2	1	2	2	—
Jack Jones	2	1	—	2	2	—	1	—
Joe Gormley	1	2	1	2	1	1	—	—
Hugh Scanlon	1	1	1	1	—	—	—	—
Sidney Weighell	2	2	3	3	—	—	—	—
Ray Buckton	—	2	—	2	—	—	—	—
Tom Jackson	1	—	—	—	—	—	—	—
John Lyons	1	—	1	—	—	—	—	—
Ernest Knowell	1	—	—	—	—	—	—	—
Frank Chappell	1	—	—	—	—	—	—	—
Arthur Scargill	1	—	1	—	1	1	1	—
J. McLean	1	—	—	—	—	—	—	—
Campbell Adamson	3	3	1	—	—	—	—	—
Sir Ralph Bateman	1	1	—	—	—	—	—	—
Director General, National Chamber of Trade	—	1	—	—	—	—	—	—
Norman Siddell, NCB	1	1	—	—	—	—	—	—
Richard Marsh, British Rail	1	2	—	—	—	—	—	—
Vox pop., Budget	—	1	—	—	—	—	—	—
Wine and spirits retailer	1	—	—	—	—	—	—	—
Deputy chairman, Wine and Spirits Association	—	1	—	—	—	—	—	—
Geoffrey Finsbury, MP	1	—	—	—	—	—	—	—
Harold Hassall, surgeon	1	—	—	—	—	—	—	—
The government	—	—	4	1	13	9	12	10
The Cabinet	—	—	1	1	9	6	—	1
Shirley Williams, minister	—	—	2	—	—	—	—	—
Anthony Wedgwood Benn	—	—	—	1	—	1	2	—
Reg Prentice	—	—	3	4	—	—	—	—
Parliamentary Labour Party/Labour MPs	—	—	1	1	3	6	—	—
Philip Whitehead, MP	—	—	—	1	—	—	—	—
Sid Bidwell, MP	—	—	—	2	—	—	—	—
Michael Stewart, MP	—	—	1	1	—	—	—	—
Willy Hamilton, MP	—	—	1	2	—	—	—	—
Andrew Faulds, MP	—	—	1	1	—	—	—	—
Harold Lever, minister	—	—	1	—	—	—	—	—
Moderate Labour MPs	—	—	1	—	1	—	—	—

Table 5.1 continued

Actor	Interview BBC	ITN	Reported statements BBC	ITN	Named actor in media statements BBC	ITN	Actors' significant others BBC	ITN
Supporters of Mr Prentice	—	—	1	—	—	—	—	—
Left-wing MPs of Labour Party	—	—	1	—	1	1	—	—
The Tribune group	—	—	1	—	1	—	—	—
Edward Short, minister	—	—	1	—	—	—	—	—
The TUC	—	—	1	1	4	5	5	5
Union leaders/TUC leaders	—	—	—	2	4	5	1	1
Mary Paterson, Chairman TUC	—	—	1	—	—	—	—	—
Clive Jenkins, ASTMS	—	—	1	1	—	—	—	—
Lord Allen, USDAW	—	—	—	1	—	—	—	—
Jim Hughes, USDAW	—	—	1	—	—	—	—	—
Mick McGahey	—	—	1	—	—	—	1	—
The unions	—	—	1	—	10	6	7	8
NUM executive	—	—	1	1	7	5	—	—
The rail unions	—	—	1	1	2	3	—	—
Rail unions' leaders	—	—	1	—	—	1	—	—
NUR executive	—	—	1	1	—	—	—	—
Rail union negotiators	—	—	—	1	—	—	—	—
The AUEW	—	—	—	1	—	—	1	—
The power workers' union	—	—	1	—	—	—	—	—
Hospital consultants and Specialists Association	—	—	—	1	1	—	—	—
Left-wing miners	—	—	—	1	1	—	—	—
Moderate miners	—	—	—	1	—	—	—	—
Shopkeepers	—	—	—	1	—	—	—	—
Department of Employment	—	—	3	3	1	1	—	1
The Treasury	—	—	1	—	1	1	—	—
Whitehall	—	—	—	1	—	1	—	—
The Ministry of Defence	—	—	1	—	—	—	—	—
The Price Commission	—	—	1	1	1	—	—	—
Sir Arthur Cockfield, chairman, Price Commission	—	—	—	1	—	—	—	—
The Royal Trustees	—	—	1	1	1	—	—	—
The National Coal Board	—	—	—	2	8	3	—	—
The chairman, Electricity Generating Board	—	—	1	—	—	—	—	—
British Rail	—	—	1	—	3	3	—	—
The GPO	—	—	1	—	—	—	—	—
NHS Pay Review Body	—	—	—	1	1	—	—	—

Table 5.1 continued

Actor	Interview BBC	ITN	Reported statements BBC	ITN	Named actor in media statements BBC	ITN	Actors' significant others BBC	ITN
Joel Barnett, Secretary of Treasury	—	—	1	—	—	—	—	—
Industry/firms	—	—	—	1	3	3	1	3
Industrialists/employers	—	—	—	1	3	—	1	3
The CBI	—	—	4	2	1	4	1	1
British Leyland	—	—	—	1	—	—	—	—
Road Haulage Association	—	—	—	1	—	—	—	—
Wine and Spirits Association	—	—	—	1	—	—	—	—
Margaret Thatcher, MP	—	—	2	3	—	—	—	—
Sir Keith Joseph, MP	—	—	1	1	—	—	—	—
Sir Geoffrey Howe, MP	—	—	1	2	—	—	—	—
Robert Carr, MP	—	—	2	2	—	1	—	—
John Peyton, MP	—	—	—	1	—	—	—	—
Paul Deane, MP	—	—	—	1	—	—	—	—
Geoffrey Gardener, MP	—	—	1	—	—	—	—	—
Jeremy Thorpe, Liberal leader	—	—	2	2	—	—	—	—
John Pardoe, MP	—	—	—	1	—	—	—	—
Buters Crawford, SNP, MP	—	—	—	1	—	—	—	—
The Automobile Association	—	—	—	1	—	—	—	—
Phillips & Drew, stockbrokers	—	—	—	1	—	—	—	—
Financial and political observers	—	—	1	—	—	—	—	—
Anthony Crosland, MP	—	—	—	—	—	1	—	—
The Labour party	—	—	—	—	1	—	1	1
Labour party NEC	—	—	—	—	1	—	1	—
Acting chief whip, Labour	—	—	—	—	1	—	—	—
Deputy chief whip, Labour	—	—	—	—	—	1	—	—
Eric Heffer, MP	—	—	—	—	—	1	—	—
The Manifesto group/moderate Labour MPs	—	—	—	—	1	1	—	—
The trade union group of Labour MPs	—	—	—	—	1	1	—	—
Some Labour MPs	—	—	—	—	2	—	—	—
MPs	—	—	—	—	4	7	—	—
Parliament	—	—	—	—	3	2	1	—
The Commons	—	—	—	—	—	2	—	1
Parliamentary secretaries	—	—	—	—	—	1	—	—
Some junior ministers	—	—	—	—	—	1	—	—

Table 5.1 continued

Actor	Interview BBC	ITN	Reported statements BBC	ITN	Named actor in media statements BBC	ITN	Actors' significant others BBC	ITN
The TUC/Labour party liaison committee	—	—	—	—	3	2	—	—
The Welsh TUC annual conference	—	—	—	—	1	—	—	—
The STUC	—	—	—	—	1	2	—	—
NUM executive moderates	—	—	—	—	—	1	—	—
NUM executive members against the Social Contract	—	—	—	—	2	—	—	—
The engineering union's executive	—	—	—	—	1	1	—	—
ASLEF	—	—	—	—	1	—	—	—
Railway Salaried Staffs association	—	—	—	—	1	—	—	—
UCATT	—	—	—	—	1	—	—	—
Other building unions	—	—	—	—	1	—	—	—
Leaders of shipbuilding workers	—	—	—	—	1	—	—	—
The Seamen's Union	—	—	—	—	—	1	—	—
USDAW annual conference	—	—	—	—	2	—	—	—
Unions who had breached the Social Contract	—	—	—	—	1	—	—	—
The BMA	—	—	—	—	1	—	—	—
Power unions leaders/ executive	—	—	—	—	2	1	—	—
Trade unionists	—	—	—	—	1	—	—	1
Miners	—	—	—	—	12	11	5	3
Scottish miners	—	—	—	—	1	—	—	—
Yorkshire miners	—	—	—	—	1	—	—	—
Railwaymen	—	—	—	—	6	4	2	1
Power workers	—	—	—	—	5	6	1	1
ASLEF members	—	—	—	—	—	1	—	—
Engineering workers	—	—	—	—	3	2	—	—
Power engineers	—	—	—	—	1	—	—	—
Postal workers	—	—	—	—	1	—	3	—
London dockers	—	—	—	—	1	1	—	—
Building workers	—	—	—	—	1	1	—	—
Shop workers	—	—	—	—	—	1	—	—
Merchant Navy officers	—	—	—	—	1	1	—	—
Doctors	—	—	—	—	1	1	—	—
Dentists	—	—	—	—	1	1	—	—
Consultants	—	—	—	—	1	2	—	—

Table 5.1 continued

Actor	Interview BBC	ITN	Reported statements BBC	ITN	Named actor in media statements BBC	ITN	Actors' significant others BBC	ITN
16 stagehands at the London Coliseum	—	—	—	—	1	—	—	—
Shipbuilding workers	—	—	—	—	1	—	—	—
The Queen/royal family	—	—	—	—	2	2	—	1
Civil Service staff	—	—	—	—	1	—	1	1
Workers/ordinary working people	—	—	—	—	1	—	3	6
Workers on short time/redundant	—	—	—	—	1	2	—	—
Thousands of other workers	—	—	—	—	4	4	—	—
'The Lump'	—	—	—	—	1	—	—	—
Temps	—	—	—	—	1	—	—	—
The Bank of England	—	—	—	—	1	2	1	—
Chairmen of nationalised industries	—	—	—	—	—	1	—	—
Sir Derek Ezra, NCB	—	—	—	—	1	—	—	—
The Electricity Generating Board	—	—	—	—	1	—	—	—
Electricity Council/management	—	—	—	—	4	1	—	—
The railway three-man arbitration committee	—	—	—	—	1	—	—	1
The working party on police pay	—	—	—	—	1	—	—	—
The National Enterprise Board	—	—	—	—	—	1	—	—
Motor manufacturers	—	—	—	—	1	—	—	—
The Cowley car factory	—	—	—	—	1	—	—	—
The Aston Martin car plant	—	—	—	—	1	—	—	—
Building industry/employers	—	—	—	—	1	—	—	—
Shipowners	—	—	—	—	—	1	—	—
The City	—	—	—	—	1	2	1	1
A Canadian industrialist	—	—	—	—	1	—	—	—
International companies	—	—	—	—	1	—	—	—
The Opposition	—	—	—	—	—	1	—	—
Friends of Harold Wilson	—	—	—	—	—	1	—	—
People at the top	—	—	—	—	—	1	—	—
Commuters	—	—	—	—	1	1	—	—
The little girl who gave the Queen 10p.	—	—	—	—	1	—	—	—
The teacher of the little girl who . . .	—	—	—	—	1	—	—	—
Denis Healey's wife	—	—	—	—	—	1	—	—

Table 5.1 continued

Actor	Interview BBC	Interview ITN	Reported statements BBC	Reported statements ITN	Named actor in media statements BBC	Named actor in media statements ITN	Actors' significant others BBC	Actors' significant others ITN
The country/the nation/ the public	—	—	—	—	2	3	12	90
The economy	—	—	—	—	1	—	—	—
The consumer	—	—	—	—	—	2	—	—
The pound	—	—	—	—	—	2	—	—
Supporters of the Social Contract	—	—	—	—	—	1	—	—
Foreign creditors	—	—	—	—	1	—	1	—
Germany	—	—	—	—	—	2	—	—
Concorde	—	—	—	—	1	—	—	—
The taxpayer	—	—	—	—	1	—	1	—
All those who have taken high pay rises	—	—	—	—	—	1	—	—
Power engineers' leaders	—	—	—	—	1	—	—	—
Whitehall and Westminster maintenance staff	—	—	—	—	1	2	—	—
Conservative MPs	—	—	—	—	3	2	—	—
Edward Heath	—	—	—	—	—	1	1	—
Politicians	—	—	—	—	—	—	1	—
The Prime Minister's colleagues	—	—	—	—	—	—	—	1
The General Council of the TUC	—	—	—	—	—	—	—	1
One union leader	—	—	—	—	—	—	—	1
Trade union officials	—	—	—	—	—	—	1	—
The Labour movement	—	—	—	—	—	—	—	1
Shop Stewards	—	—	—	—	—	—	1	—
Motor car workers	—	—	—	—	—	—	1	—
Ford workers	—	—	—	—	—	—	1	—
Scottish lorry drivers	—	—	—	—	—	—	1	—
Nurses	—	—	—	—	—	—	2	1
Radiographers	—	—	—	—	—	—	—	1
Low-paid workers in the royal household	—	—	—	—	—	—	1	—
Judges	—	—	—	—	—	—	—	1
Top civil servants	—	—	—	—	—	—	—	1
Old-age pensioners	—	—	—	—	—	—	—	1
Working-class families throughout Britain	—	—	—	—	—	—	1	1
Workers who have stuck to Social Contract	—	—	—	—	—	—	1	—
The minority who have not stuck to Social Contract	—	—	—	—	—	—	1	1

Table 5.1 continued

Actor	Interview		Reported statements		Named actor in media statements		Actors' significant others	
	BBC	ITN	BBC	ITN	BBC	ITN	BBC	ITN
Those with jobs	—	—	—	—	—	—	—	1
The low-paid	—	—	—	—	—	—	1	—
The public sector	—	—	—	—	—	—	1	—
The coal industry	—	—	—	—	—	—	1	—
Export industries	—	—	—	—	—	—	—	1
Management	—	—	—	—	—	—	2	1
Entrepreneurs	—	—	—	—	—	—	1	—
Enoch Powell, MP	—	—	—	—	—	—	1	—
The wealthy	—	—	—	—	—	—	—	1
Those without militant power in the community	—	—	—	—	—	—	—	1
Both sides of industry	—	—	—	—	—	—	1	—
Scotland	—	—	—	—	—	—	—	1
The authors of the Social Contract	—	—	—	—	—	—	—	1
German workers	—	—	—	—	—	—	1	—
Britain's competitors/other countries	—	—	—	—	—	—	1	2
The needy	—	—	—	—	—	—	—	1
The middle classes	—	—	—	—	—	—	1	—
Businessmen	—	—	—	—	—	—	—	1
Farmworkers	—	—	—	—	—	—	1	—

directly intervene in the industrial, political and economic debate as reported on television, interviewees, for example, may be subject to less control than those simply quoted.[1] Obviously, interviews and film of conference speeches are also subject to the process of mediation in that the media retains the power to set the questions and to select the sections of the speech or interview to be shown. Those actors merely mentioned by journalists in news reports have even less influence over the process of mediation and occupy a low position in the hierarchy of access. In order to highlight the range of mediation within the hierarchy of access the actors are only recorded within one category per bulletin.

Although it is often the case that an actor appearing in interview will be introduced by name and quoted by the newscaster as an introduction to the filmed interview or speech, we have only noted the actor's appearance as interviewee. Reported statements are only recorded where an actor is not interviewed. Similarly, actors mentioned in media statements are only recorded where they are neither interviewed nor quoted in the same bulletin. Only the appearance or absence of actors is recorded, not the numerical frequency of interview appearances, reported statements or mentions within any one bulletin. With this method we best illustrate the kind of access an actor achieves within each bulletin.

1 Interviewees

Interviewees are drawn from an extremely narrow section of the social and political spectrum. In addition there is a close degree of similarity between channels in this selection. On Social Contract stories, in the four months of our sample, there were 23 different interviewees on BBC1. ITN had 15 interviewees, plus 1 *vox pop.* sequence (as part of its Budget coverage). BBC1 interviewed 6 trade union leaders exclusively and thus achieved a wider range of interviews than either BBC2 or ITN. ITN had one exclusive interview with a union leader which they used in two bulletins.

In general, there were marked similarities in the selection of interviewees by both channels. Although BBC1 screened 11 interviewees exclusively to ITN's 4 exclusives (including the *vox pop.* Budget sequence) in the sample, 12 of ITN's total of 16 interviewees also appeared on BBC1. In addition, in 11 cases out of 12 this parallel selection of interviewees occurred on the same days. These were Michael Foot, Len Murray, Barbara Castle, Jack Jones, Joe Gormley, Hugh Scanlon, Sidney Weighell, Campbell Adamson, Sir Ralph Bateman, Norman Siddell, and Richard Marsh. In 3 of these cases the interviewees appeared on the same evening on both channels on two separate occasions each: they were Michael Foot, Len Murray and Campbell Adamson. Thus not only was there close consensual agreement between BBC and ITN as to who were the newsworthy people, but there was also agreement as to the days and issues on which they were to appear in the news.

Almost half of the total number of interviews shown appeared on both channels' main news on the same evening. For example, the BBC interviewed Len Murray 3 times, the ITN interviewed him twice and filmed him addressing a meeting on 1 further occasion. Both of the ITN interviews appeared during evenings when he was also interviewed on the BBC1's *Nine O'Clock News.* Similarly, on the 2 occasions Michael Foot appeared on ITN (once as interviewee, once addressing a conference) the BBC also carried an interview and filmed speech on the same evenings. The BBC carried

2 further interviews with Foot exclusively, and on 1 of these occasions 1 statement from Foot was quoted on the ITN bulletin. On the 2 days that Campbell Adamson was interviewed on ITN, BBC also carried interviews with him. Similarly, Sir Ralph Bateman and Norman Siddell are interviewed on both channels on the same day. Parallel coverage was also marked in the case of trade union leaders Jack Jones, Joe Gormley, Sidney Weighell and Hugh Scanlon.

This parallel interviewing of the same persons by both channels on the same evening is reinforced by the occasions when a statement is quoted on one channel from an interviewee who appears the same day on the other channel. In fact interviewees were drawn from a narrow section of the social and political spectrum. In the sample there were: the Prime Minister, 3 government ministers, the General Secretary of the TUC, 11 leaders from 8 trade unions, the President and the General Secretary of the CBI, the heads of 2 nationalised industries, and 2 MPs (1 Labour and 1 Conservative). On Budget Day this group was widened to include the director of the National Chamber of Trade, the deputy chairman of the Wine and Spirits Association and 1 wine and spirits retailer. ITN completed their package with some 'instant reaction' from aggrieved consumers shocked at the increased cost of smoking, drinking and motoring.[2] The remaining interviewee stands out as the only member of an occupational group whose actions were seen by the TV newsrooms as affecting the Social Contract – Mr Harold Hassall, senior consultant surgeon at Leyton Hospital, Crewe.[3] In contrast, no miner, railwayman, power engineer, electrician, docker, postman, shop assistant, building worker or nurse were asked to give an account of his or her views concerning the working of the Social Contract.

2 Reported statements

The frequency with which reported statements are utilised in the news bulletins and the range of areas from which they are drawn further illustrates a restricted structure of access to the news channels.

A large number of the statements quoted and referenced come from the same individuals in the narrow group that were interviewed most frequently. In fact, for both BBC and ITN 35 per cent of all the reported statements carried by BBC1 bulletins came from those also interviewed in the sample. Most notably within this narrow group of interviewees, the Chancellor of the Exchequer received 41 per cent of the statements quoted on the BBC and 37 per cent of those on ITN. Of *all* reported statements, the Chancellor received 14 per cent on BBC1 and 13 per cent on ITN.

Those interviewees who do not receive subsequent reported statements are, not surprisingly, those who appear least in interviews and those appearing once on one channel only: five of the trade union leaders who were exclusive to BBC1, the consultant surgeon, 1 Conservative MP, the Budget Day interviewees, Sir Ralph Bateman, Richard Marsh and Norman Siddell. In the case of the last 2, reported statements which may well have come from them were attributed in the bulletins to the 'Rail Board' and the 'Coal Board'. Similarly, for Sir Ralph Bateman, there are 6 reported statements from the CBI.

The majority of the remaining reported statements, from those not also interviewed elsewhere in the sample, with few exceptions are taken from further members of the same narrow group.

Reported statements came from the following:

   12 from 5 government ministers (only 1, Prentice, quoted on
      both channels)
   11 from 6 named Labour MPs (2 of them, Whitehead and
      Biddell, exclusive to ITN)
   13 from other Labour parliamentary groups and sources (only 2
      of these on ITN)
   18 from 8 named Conservative MPs (only Thatcher, Joseph and
      Carr common to both BBC and ITN)
   7 from other political (parliamentary) parties and groups (not
      including Labour)
   6 from 5 other named trade union leaders (only Clive Jenkins on
      both channels)
   16 from other official trade union bodies and executives
   21 from government bodies and nationalised industry
      managements (2 of these attributed to 2 named heads of
      government bodies)
   5 from employers' groups (all ITN) plus 6 from 'the CBI' (on
      both channels)
   3 statements (1 each) from the AA, a firm of stockbrokers, and
      'financial observers'

3 from 'unofficial' categories of working people ('left-wing miners', 'moderate miners' and 'shopkeepers')[4]

It can be seen that the government and the Parliamentary Labour Party in general receive more coverage in terms of attributed quotes than the Opposition and other parliamentary parties.[5]

Employer's groups and 'industry' (referring always in bulletins to managements and employers) receive less attention than union leaders and trade union bodies. Taking the Social Contract as a document drawn up between the Labour government and the TUC, it may seem logical that the news coverage concentrates upon the actors central to the debate in a clearly defined arena.

However, as with the appearance of interviewees, the apparent numerical bias towards labour representatives must be seen in the light of the inferential frames used in the coverage. The overwhelming majority of all reported statements and references were for supporting the Social Contract. As we showed in the analysis of explanatory themes, there were 289 references in favour of wage restraint and lower living standards, and only 17 which opposed policies of wage restraint. The statements of powerful groups pressing for wage restraint, particularly those from the government, gained extensive coverage. Moreover, these tended to gain even greater prominence as they were situated within a framework of interpretation which favoured their definitions of the economic crisis and their priorities for its resolution. It is within this context that trade union officials were focused upon in the news. Typically, trade union leaders appeared on the news only to be questioned about their union pay claim. By virtue of the established framework of reporting, they were required to justify the actions of their members in asking for more money against an established background of an analysis that blamed inflation and the crisis in general almost exclusively on wages (see especially chapter 4 'Pointing the finger' above). As our analysis shows, a large number of the trade union leaders appear in this manner only as interviewees, and are not elsewhere quoted or mentioned in any other context.

Access to the news is thus related to the interpretative framework which the media persistently establish and reinforce. Our detailed case study of the news coverage of the economy in the first months of 1975 shows the emphasis and priorities given to the themes of wage inflation and the need for pay restraint and the lowering of living standards. The stage for debate and discussion of the economic crisis is set by the framework of interpretation established by the television newsrooms – namely that wage inflation was the main problem. This is reflected in the order of appearance of various actors at different levels of access inside the news coverage. As we have shown, pay claims and settlements were routinely monitored not simply in terms of the progress of the claim, but crucially framed against the established background of emphasis on the supposed problem of wage inflation and in terms of the success of the Social Contract in holding down 'excessive' wage claims. Significantly in this context, the Social Contract was overwhelmingly reported in terms of wage restraint and little else. The high number of interviews given to small number of trade union leaders in the absence of a significant number of reported statements or mentions elsewhere in the coverage must be seen in this light. This is further illustrated by the predominance within both interviews and reported statements of government ministers and parliamentary groups, and within reported statements of government ministers, politicians and official government bodies. In this way the television news had 'framed the debate' within the confines of one dominant interpretation of the economic crisis.

3 Named actor in media statements

These are 'actors' in news reports in those instances where they are neither quoted nor interviewed:

Those interviewed elsewhere

Prime Minister   11 mentions
Healey   9
Foot   4
Murray   3
Jones   2
Gormley   2
Arthur Scargill   1 (although he receives only 1 reported statement and 1 interview elsewhere in the sample)

Those quoted but not interviewed elsewhere

27 actors: all from the government, trade union bodies, and

employers' organisations, or heads of nationalised industries:

'the government'	22 mentions
'the Cabinet'	15
other Labour MPs	9
'the TUC'	9
'TUC leaders'/'union leaders'	9

Many of these instances are merely an extension of the same groupings who are predominant in reported statements and interviews elsewhere in the coverage that establishes the priorities of wage restraint and organises the flow of information around this restricted framework of analysis. This is further highlighted by the last category of 'actors': that of 'significant others'.

4 Actors' significant others

These are groups and individuals who only appear within a news bulletin when mentioned by non-media personnel. There are 38 actors here not elsewhere mentioned by the media, not interviewed or quoted. Very few receive more than 1 reference and only 2 receive as many as 3 mentions. Although some groups of workers, such as miners, railwaymen and powerworkers, were mentioned in media statements, most of the workers' groups which were referenced only appeared in the news when they (or their case) were briefly touched on by others who were interviewed or quoted. Significant amongst such groups in this category for example:

1	shop stewards
1	motor car workers
1	Scottish lorry drivers
3	nurses
1	radiographers
1	low paid workers in the royal household
1	judges
1	top civil servants
1	old-age pensioners
2	working-class families throughout Britain
1	workers who have stuck to the Social Contract
2	the minority who have not stuck to the Social Contract
1	those with jobs
1	the low-paid

3   management
1   entrepreneurs
1   the wealthy
1   those without militant power in the community
1   the middle classes
1   businessmen
1   farmworkers

The opinions of these groups were evidently not seen by news-producers as important in the continuing development of the Social Contract within the period of our analysis. Their 'access' to the news was confined to a small number of occasions when they were mentioned in passing by interviewees such as Jack Jones. Their opinions were not sought directly. Such absences cannot be dismissed simply as an oversight or by the constraints of time available in news bulletins. Rather, their absence is accounted for by the priorities which are set by the established framework of interpretation.

Conclusion

In the period of our study, the news was organised and produced substantially around the views of the dominant political group in our society. We have shown how the views of those who disagree fundamentally with this position, or who offered alternative approaches, were downgraded and underrepresented in the news coverage. This is in stark comparison with the careful explanation and heavy emphasis given to the dominant analysis and the political policies which flowed from it.

The content of news and the manner in which it was organised embodied a specific way of understanding the social and industrial world. In essence our case is that the numerical repetition of certain themes and explanations, together with the embracing and under-lining of them by media personnel, are parts of a general process by which the news is produced from within a limited and partial world view. This is reflected in the choice of material, the themes that are emphasised, the links that are made between these, and the final conclusions that are drawn. At times, as we have shown, fragments of alternative information appear which could be linked, developed and emphasised to produce a quite different body of explanations and policy conclusions. It is a measure of the strength of the dominant social and economic interpretation of the news that this was never done in the whole four-month period covered by our analysis.

At its most basic, the organising principle of this interpretation is that the normal workings of the particular economic system are never treated as if they might themselves generate serious problems. Rather, the causes of economic problems are sought largely in the activities of trade unionists who reject the priorities and purposes of the dominant group. The logic and priorities of the social and economic order thus remain unchallenged. Instead, what we have in the news is a partial diagnosis of what social problems are, and how they may be solved, which is facilitated by a highly selective account of the nature and workings of that economic order.

The importance of this 'world view', which is implicit in journalistic practices, is that it prestructures what the news is to consist of and in a sense what the journalists themselves actually see as existing, or as being significant in the world. Thus information about the decline in investment, which would be a critical part of an alternative world view, is either not treated at all by news journalists, or occurs as a disparate fragment because it has no part in the 'normal' descriptions which they offer of the industrial crisis. The journalists themselves often reply to this with arguments couched in terms of 'relevance' or audience-interest – as if investment figures are somehow intrinsically boring while other figures, for example on the amount of car production lost through a dispute, are somehow intrinsically interesting and therefore newsworthy. Yet such appeals to news value are in reality no more than appeals to the validity of their own world view. In the context of a different world view, figures on investment take on a completely different significance and meaning. Suppose, for example, that investment was low in an industry in part because of a management policy of distributing all profits as dividends.[6] Within the framework of *this* explanation of the economic crisis new and dramatic headlines might suddenly suggest themselves, for example, 'A Million Jobs Threatened by Huge Dividends Payouts'.

The problem with the exclusive appeal to news values which journalists make in their own defence is that it assumes that everyone lives in the same world and sees it in the same way. Therefore newsworthiness is presented as being somehow 'natural' and 'obvious', an intrinsic property which the news journalist recognises instinctively and noses out. Thus a recent BBC pamphlet on the news argues as follows:[7]

> The news value of a story is something immediately recognisable, intuitively sensed by a journalist who has been schooled in the provincial or national newsrooms. . . . The graduates of this school soon learn to spot the significant news point, the relevant detail, the interesting human touch which distinguishes the newsworthy story – the material with news value or news merits – from the candidate for the sub-editors' spike.

This journalistic argument is circular. In fact, the 'significant', the 'relevant', and the merely 'interesting' are all embodied within this view of news values. The same pamphlet comments:

> In a sense the phrase 'news values' is to be used cautiously because it implies that there is an unchanging standard by which news can be measured and that is not true. The news value of a story is what a journalist recognises when he has been brought up in the tradition [editorial] of a particular newsroom or office. The BBC tradition is to tell people accurately and honestly about the most important things going on in the world; then, if there is room, to tell them the things which are very interesting even though they may not be significant, like the winner of the Derby, and in doing so to engage the attention of as many people as possible without lowering standards of judgement.

Of course, significance, relevance, and importance can only be judged and are recognisable only by reference to the world view that these news values express. Our argument, then, is that the world view of journalists will prestructure what is taken to be important or significant. It will do this in two ways. First it will affect the character and content of specific inferential frames used in the news, as we showed above in relation to the definition of what industrial problems are. Second, it will set general boundaries on where news is looked for, and on who are the significant individuals, the 'important' people to be interviewed, etc. There are, of course, other news angles (other inferential frames) which are not so closely related to the articulation of the social and political ideologies that we have so far discussed. For example, the fascination with the 'dramatic' aspects of sex or violence.[8] However, it is not enough to characterise the attention to the dramatic, as such, as the prime determinant of what is produced as news. One effect of the political and economic world view of television journalism will be to pre-structure the areas in which these dramatic news angles are sought. For example, a news story of an industrial dispute might also feature a commentary on a leading militant getting divorced.[9] There are thus different sources of significance for news angles within the general framework of what is being examined and who is being reported. While some relate to more general social fascination (e.g. sex or violence) others will relate more directly to the social and political explanations which lead journalists to initially focus on an area and specific topics within it. The latter set of frames will take their significance from the explanation of what is wrong with industry, for example, the case of news coverage of production losses 'caused' by strikes. At all times, then, the organisation of news is constrained by the limits of the world view within which it is produced. This applies not only to the specific content of news stories and the generation of frames, but also to the organisation and control of who is allowed access to the media. Such access does not exist as an equal opportunity to express an opinion, put forward a viewpoint, or even to provide information. Even less do the media provide an open chance for all to influence the course of public discussion by affecting the terms of debate or the manner in which issues are structured in reporting. Access is structured and hierarchical to the extent that powerful groups and individuals have privileged and routine entry into the news itself and to the manner and means of its production. Our case study of the Glasgow dustcart drivers (in *Bad News*) indicated the relationship between the way in which an industrial news story is reported – the dominant inter-pretative framework – and the ability of the actors involved to appear on the news in order to present their case. That relationship, which reinforces the control over explanation in news reporting, is further illustrated in our evidence above.

It is frequently asserted by some journalists that the limitation of such news could be resolved mainly by having more time or space. Selection and interpretation are thus presented as the necessary result of editing, as there is always 'too much' material available. Such arguments, however, are merely quantitative and tell us nothing about the *quality* of what is produced or why it is that the same interpretations are systematically favoured and why alternative frameworks are routinely discarded. The essential argument which we have made is that a journalism which is rooted in a specific set of explanations about the nature of social reality is unable to encompass or explore the rationale of alternative world views. More time or space would really make little difference to this, for, as we have shown, information which could be used as part of an alternative view, even when it appears, is not used to systematically develop alternative themes and explanations. It appears as fragments in a flow of information organised within the dominant framework.

The day-to-day production of news is based on the inherited wisdom of journalistic routines, assumptions about the audience and about the society that is being reported. This is what enables the journalist in the newsroom to 'recognise' the newsworthy truth with apparent certainty. Against this background, the bland assertion of objectivity and impartiality as a regular professional achievement is little more than the unsupported claim to a unique understanding of events. This serves only to obfuscate what is in fact the reproduction of the dominant assumptions about our society – the assumptions of the powerful about what is important, necessary and possible within it.

PART II

HEAR IT
THIS WAY

For a large class of cases – though not for all – in which we employ
the word 'meaning' it can be defined thus: the meaning of a word
is its use in the Language.

Ludwig Wittgenstein

6 News Ideology: Neutrality and Naturalism

> A simple meaning alters according to the words in which it is expressed. Meanings receive their dignity from words instead of conferring dignity upon them.
>
> Blaise Pascal

Language is one of the most general and taken-for-granted forms of communication. In fact, communication is impossible without some forms of shared language, whether it be a language as formal as Standard English or as apparently unstructured as a shake of the head or the raising of an eyebrow. These latter, when placed in cultural contexts, have their own kinesic meanings. The main issue in looking at language in the news bulletins, 'news talk', is to discover the ways in which its special properties reflect, reveal or can be related to, the structure and ideologies of broadcast communications systems. The study of news talk is a particular case of the analysis of talk in general. Consequently the analysis of the routine structures of news talk turns upon the work that can presently be done on any variety of talk. As a working hypothesis we have assumed that close analysis of the language of the news bulletins should provide evidence of the ideological preferences of broadcasters.

Since a good deal of modern linguistics is dominated by the work of Chomsky, we should make it clear that our approach is located elsewhere in the linguistic spectrum. For Chomsky the intriguing thing about language has been that 'we may discover abstract principles that govern its structure and use, principles that are universal by biological necessity and not mere historical accident, that derive from mental characteristics of the species'.[2] It might be true, although it is by no means established, that there are universals which govern language that are not specific to one language or context. The search for linguistic universals may become so absorbing that questions concerning the relationship between speech and its function or use in the real world are scarcely considered. The focus of our attention, therefore, is not the biological basis of cognition. Rather, given that the human species can and does produce talk, we ask in what ways the talk reflects and refracts forms of social life. Since thought can be transformed into talk and talk is something that most of us can 'do' with varying degrees of competence, the problem becomes one of discovering the rules that govern the use of talk in specific social contexts.

Parallel with the search for linguistic universals, work among anthropologists and linguists in looking at language in use has continued, albeit a little obscured of late by the fashionability of Chomskean concerns.[3] Malinowski considered language to be a 'mode of activity' and that its meaning and use had to be understood not as isolated utterances, but in the context of the situation in which the utterances were spoken and heard. Meaning is thereby articulated from a sensitive appreciation of the culture in which communication takes place.[4] Firth, too, emphasised the social function of language. Thus there may be typical situations in which certain speech styles come to be regarded as appropriate; for example, colloquial, formal or theoretical styles. To look at language in context is to take into account who the participants are and their verbal and non-verbal action. These concerns surface again in current discussions of the 'ethnography of speaking'. Dell Hymes writes:[5]

'Speaking' has been regarded as merely implementation and variation outside the domain of language and linguistics proper. Linguistic theory has mostly developed in abstraction from contexts of use and sources of diversity. But by an ethnography of speaking I shall understand a description that is a theory – a theory of speech as a system of cultural behaviour; a system not necessarily exotic, but necessarily concerned with the organisation of diversity.

As Hymes states, Chomsky and his associates have advanced the development of sociolinguistics by stressing as central to linguistics the concepts of 'competence' and 'performance'. The failure, however, is that[6]

the restriction of competence to the notions of a homogeneous
community, perfect knowledge, and independence of socio-
cultural factors does not seem just a simplifying assumption . . .
nor does the predominant association of performance with
imperfection seem accidental.

Thus, our approach to news talk in the following chapters is to
reveal and analyse the linguistic designs which make for the
production of a *competent* news bulletin and then to analyse the
actual *performances* in terms of the parties and preferences they
reveal within the range of competence which constitutes acceptable
news talk.

Wittgenstein pointed out that there are countless different uses of
what we can call symbols, words and sentences and that new types
of language – or 'language games', as he calls them – continually
come into existence or become obsolete and forgotten. In other
words, Wittgenstein's notion of a language game stresses that
'speaking of language is part of an activity, or of a form of life'.[7] We
share his view that the subtleties of talk relate in some way to the
structure of given forms of life. For instance, at a general level the
choices made by bilingual speakers are determined by the broad
social, political and economic context in which they find themselves. At the other end of the spectrum, the evolution in the use of
the pronouns of address (*thou* and *you* in English, *tu* and *vous* in
French) shows that the dimension of solidarity – the reciprocal use
of 'you' and '*vous*' – has increased with social mobility and the
general development of egalitarian ideologies.[8]

In between the linguistic search for genetic universals and the
demonstration of the historical specificity of modes of address, lies
the cluster of language problems to which we are addressing
ourselves. Our concern is to look at one mode of discourse –
publicly broadcast television news talk – in the attempt to show that
it routinely displays features in its performance which can only be
explained by reference to its tacit trading on a given ideology. To do
this we will have to utilise empirical generalisations generated by
other kinds of linguistic work and in the process we hope to show
that sociolinguistics can begin to open up the study of language
usage and relate this usage to the analysis of ideology. Ideology in
our view is not some set of alien ideas imposed, propaganda-like,
upon willing and unwilling hearers. Rather, it is a representation of
sets of events or facts which consistently favours the perceptual

framework of one group. News talk occurs within a cultural framework which stresses its balance and impartiality. Yet despite this, detailed analysis reveals that it consistently maintains and supports a cultural framework within which viewpoints favourable to the *status quo* are given *preferred* and *privileged* readings.

This representation of events as news is not governed by a conscious attempt to present ideology. The journalists and producers and those they allow to broadcast of course believe that their routines and codes merely serve to fashion the news into intelligible and meaningful bulletins. But, as Goffman observes, that is what a framework does: 'a primary framework is one that is seen as rendering what would otherwise be a meaningless aspect of the scene into something that is meaningful'.[9] This is precisely what the professionals believe themselves to be doing; rendering intelligible to the nation the news of the day. However, the reproduction of ideology need not be, and indeed rarely is, intentional. The cultural framework of our society is complex and subtle. It is this framework which, together with professionalisation, underpins the manufacture of news. Lack of awareness of this framework is no bar to its application, as Goffman points out:[10]

> Primary frameworks vary in degree of organization. Some are neatly presentable as a system of entities, postulates, and rules; others – indeed, most others – appear to have no apparent articulated shape, providing only a lore of understanding an approach, a perspective. Whatever the degree of organization, however, each primary framework allows its user to locate, perceive, identify, and label a seemingly infinite number of concrete occurrences defined in its terms. He is likely to be unaware of such organized features as the framework has and unable to describe the framework with any completeness if asked, yet these handicaps are no bar to his easily and fully applying it.

The cultural routines and codes of our professional practices are difficult to see precisely because they are taken for granted – as is the gender assumption contained in the use of 'he' in Goffman's otherwise perceptive ethnography.[11] Indeed the practice of something as apparently undetermined as 'Standard English' is bound by cultural frameworks. In the case of Standard English we do not have a neutral third-person pronoun in the singular form which can be used to denote 'he' or 'she' without ambiguity. The assumption of male dominance is part of the primary framework of our culture; otherwise there would be many more gender-free terms and descriptions than are available at present. At present, even with the available descriptions, cultural male chauvinism is so institutionalised that workers are generally assumed to be men. It has been pointed out to us on numerous occasions by women observers that this is a frequent assumption in news talk which reflects the nature of our society. Often the terms 'workers' and 'men' are used interchangeably. For instance, Trevor MacDonald reporting on the Meriden co-operative: 'The workers' co-operative at the Triumph motor cycle factory in Meriden was born not out of trade union idealism, but out of the determination of the men to save their jobs and the Triumph name' (ITN, 22.00, 13 May 1975). However, we learn later in the same item that 'men' is being used interchangeably with 'workers' and that some of the workers are women:

with the exception of the managing director and the company secretary, all the workers earn a flat £50 a week. There is no payment for overtime. There are specialist jobs, but the non-specialist ones are shared. Margaret Wright assists in the final assembly of motor-cycle petrol tanks and doubles up as telephone operator and receptionist as well. (ITN, 22.00, 13 May 1975)

In short, the relationship or association between talk and the things it describes is never neutral. All descriptions close off or foreclose on sets of alternatives. The work which follows attempts to show that, although a large variety or range of descriptions is offered up in the industrial news, it is taken for granted that certain key ideological propositions are permanent, immutable, and to be preferred as the code for reporting and reading any story.

For instance: as we are analysing a visual medium, consider the following: imagine a picture representing a striker in a particular stance. This picture can be read as telling someone how they should stand, how they should or should not hold themselves, or how a particular person did stand in such and such a place, and so on. Then any reading of such a picture contains an assumption. Wittgenstein points out that we might call such a picture a 'proposition radical', for there are a number of propositions which could be read off. However, words and things, pictures and propositions are situated in talk and viewing in such a manner that there is nearly always a preferred reading and viewing. It is because words and things, pictures and propositions take on meaning by virtue of being 'keyed' by such preferences that we can use the analysis of routinely given pictures, or repeated given words or phrases, to decode the ideological preferences of the broadcasters.

This is not to suggest that television news is simply ruling-class propaganda. If it were so, the news would quickly lose its credibility and, as Smith has pointed out: 'credibility in the mind of the actual audience is the *sine qua non* of news. All else is either propaganda or entertainment.'[12] Nor are we suggesting that the routine language of the bulletins occurs in such a fashion as to only allow one reading of a situation (although this sometimes happens; e.g. 'Though Britain's trade figures again show a deficit they're better than expected'; BBC1, 21.00, 14 May 1975). Industrial news talk is usually open to a plurality of interpretations but there normally emerges a preferred reading of actions and events which, as we will show, is often inimical to the interests of labour. The broadcasting of talk or messages is not a simple, unidirectional process in which management viewpoints are always given preference over labour's. Instead, there is an attempt to reduce the plurality of meanings inherent in any social conflict to a set of simple formulae or frames of reference which are at base an ideological defence of the legitimacy of the *status quo*.[13] As Hall, Connell and Curti put it:[14]

> In relation to the messages available through television we shall suggest that they never deliver *one* meaning; they are, rather, the site of a plurality of meanings, in which one is preferred and offered to the viewers, over the others, as the most appropriate. This 'preferring' is the site of considerable ideological labour.

However, the problems of using sociolinguistics to refine the analysis of ideology do not simply rest with the problem of whether an ideology exists and is broadcast; but rather in adapting and using the present tools of sociolinguistics to unlock key features of news talk. This latter is highly technical and turns upon the kind of work which has been and is being done by linguists and sociolinguists. It is to a discussion of the relevance and usefulness of this work that we now turn.

Linguistics

To date, the most successful academic studies of language have been made at the micro level. That is, they tend to concentrate on syntax and morphology. Indeed, at present 'linguistics' is still virtually synonymous with the study of phonemes, lexemes and syntax within single sentences. But, as we have indicated, a study of news talk, or rather news stories, which seeks to reveal the ideological features of news must concentrate on the text as a whole rather than discrete sentences. Not that the study of the placing, function or absence of individual words is unimportant. We shall analyse that, too. But rather the focus cannot be on the formal problems of linguistic analysis. As we noted in *Bad News*, Volume 1 of our study, the tools which have been developed for the description and analysis of the basic units of language are often of little direct use in the attempt to explore the relationship between ideology and news stories. It is not simply the fact that our project is different, but that linguistics developed often arbitrarily in the search for universals rather than in the study and explanation of significant presences, absences and variations.

The study of linguistic variation has traditionally been the concern of literary criticism, the sub-branch of linguistics known as stylistics, and the preoccupation of structural linguists (notably de Saussure and the Prague School). This work has increasingly been supplemented by the work of social anthropologists and ethnolinguists (notably Claude Lévi-Strauss, Dell Hymes and Harvey Sacks). The general influence of these and other parallel traditions such as semiotics can be discerned in some of the work which follows.

In England, work which attempts to go beyond the analysis of the sentence is probably best represented by Halliday's studies of language function and cohesion and the beginnings of the analysis of discourse by Sinclair and Coulthard. These authors attempt to analyse the properties which render a text or discourse a meaningful whole rather than a group of unrelated sentences. For instance, Halliday shows how meaningful relationships between sentences are realised semantically, not merely grammatically. For example, the use of a personal pronoun *He* in a sentence following another with an antecedent proper name *John*, semantically allows the assumption that John is still being referred to.[15] Similarly, Sinclair and Coulthard show how the meaningful organisation of sentences in classroom discourse is a function of the relationships between speakers.[16] For example, speaker turns in such conversation vary from 'natural' interaction in that turn-taking is highly controlled by the teacher.[17] The important point about these studies is that researchers from the backgrounds of structuralism, linguistics, education and anthropology have all converged on the methodological problems of analysing units of discourse of a higher order than the sentence.

Sociolinguistics

In one sense the most important development in linguistics for our work has been the emergence of sociolinguistics as a proper field of study. Broadly speaking, this is the study of language as a means of establishing, maintaining and mediating social relationships. At the crudest level, this work involves the correlation of linguistic variations with variations in social and demographic structures. At a more sophisticated level than this, the concept of a 'code' has been widely used to analyse social-class variations in speech. A notable pioneer here is Basil Bernstein.[18] Bernstein intended the concept to refer to linguistic rule systems which manifest themselves in systematic speech differences between the lower and middle classes. Since Bernstein's early attempts in the 1950s to establish a link between varieties of speech and varieties of socialisation there has been an upsurge of research into speech codes. Much of his other work led on to the influencing of educational policies which attempted to rectify the consequences of linguistic 'deficiencies'. But two problems have emerged in the investigation of speech codes. Firstly, restrictions of vocabulary do not necessarily provide instances of communicative deficiency. And, secondly, the notions of 'elaborated' and 'restricted' code do not refer to vocabulary alone. Indeed, as Dittmar has indicated, the difficulty of Bernstein's usage of restricted speech codes is to demonstrate empirically that there is a greater predictability or higher redundancy of meaning and information within such codes.[19] What Bernstein has shown is that social structure intervenes between language and speech. The problem is: how and why? Some further studies in America by Labov demonstrate that even within social classes there are considerable speech variations according to the context. The emphasis in this latter approach is on the description of the varieties of language which speakers from one social class can and do use, and these variations are examined against the notion of a 'standard' language: e.g. Standard English. The normative concept of 'code' does not form part of this concept of variation. The aim, according to Dittmar, is 'to describe and explain the entire social network of speech practice and the complex competence that speakers have at their disposal for communication, in correlation with the social norms and parameters'.[20] The strand of sociolinguistic theory represented by Bernstein proceeds largely from known class differences in the organisation of values and procedures of socialis- ation. However, Dittmar, in his thorough survey of this area, is forced to conclude that 'the discussion of Bernstein's works has yet to arrive at conclusive results or unequivocal empirical judge- ments'.[21] The use of language by various social groups or classes does not necessarily lead to easily identifiable differences of linguistic form.

The problems of utilising existing sociolinguistic work can be characterised as follows: on the one hand social theory has proceeded largely from known differences in the organisation of values and procedures of socialisation, which has meant that the application of the categories to linguistic data has not always led to the predicted results. On the other hand the traditional concerns of linguistics have either meant the automatic restriction of analysis to artificial samples of speech, or the simple extension of categories (syntax, phonology, etc.) by social parameters. Dittmar persuas- ively argues for a new theoretical direction more in keeping with anthropological and interactional linguistics. More specifically it would lead to a consideration of the 'pragmatics' of speech acts, their timing, their placing and the conditions of social and verbal interaction. Dittmar claims that existing grammatical categories are not sufficient to understand these processes. What we require is 'a comprehensive model of speech behaviour that includes the social and psychological configurations of interaction and the rules of interpretation and production specific to speaker-hearers'.[22] This is the direction in which this study of news talk points itself.

Although Dittmar shows that Bernstein fails in the empirical verification of his theory, he does not abandon the concept of 'code'.[23] Instead Dittmar gives a formal definition of speech codes which defines them in terms of their lexical and syntactical predictability. It is in this sense that we can elevate the common observation that the news is a highly stylised, repetitive and predictable form of discourse into an empirically testable proposition. The neutrality and the authority of the news rests to a large extent upon the claim made by the BBC, for instance, that the news conveys the essential, unadorned facts, without interpretation and comment.[24] The language of the news – trimmed of qualifications and explicit evaluative statements – is therefore an important carrier of this supposedly 'neutral' authority. It thus becomes crucial to establish the nature of the 'coding' of news talk, and particularly the appropriateness of calling it a 'restricted code' if one wishes to demonstrate that it is both a highly predictable and an evaluative form.

If we follow Dittmar's formal specification, a speech code can be characterised statistically in a manner which allows the idea of 'greater or lesser predictability'. For instance, Dittmar suggests that empirical tests of Bernstein's theory could be made if one interpreted 'restricted codes' as meaning 'higher redundancy' in the terminology of Information Theory. This means that 'a speech code with n elements, of which some occur very frequently and others very rarely if at all, is more redundant than another speech code with the same elements, but which exhibits a more even distribution.'[25]

Information theory states that the more codified a message is, the less the uncertainty in the receiver. This does not refer only to linguistic messages, of course. It is also a general theory of communication.[26] The English alphabet, for example, has a larger capacity than is required to transmit messages in the English language. Shannon has calculated that the most probable 8,727 words in English need a capacity of only twelve bits (binary digits) and yet the English alphabet has twenty-six letters. This 'extra' capacity is easy to demonstrate. To understand a given word, an English reader or speaker does not necessarily have to receive every letter in that word. If the word is spelt out letter by letter, uncertainty will normally be reduced as each letter is added. In fact the hearer or receiver is likely to make sense of the word before every letter or piece of information is provided. Shannon, one of the founding fathers of Information Theory, uses the term 'redundancy' to refer to those bits of the message that the receiver can do without.[27] Here is an example from English: E is the first letter of a very large number of English words but if it is followed by the letters X and C the chances of predicting the word are somewhat increased. The addition of more letters further reduces the uncertainty. If, after EXC, the next letter is H, the receiver knows by virtue of the structure of English that only one of two letters can come next – A or E. If the next letter is E, the receiver can predict from Standard English that with absolute certainty the remaining letters will be QUER, to form the word EXCHEQUER. In this example, the last four letters are redundant. It has been estimated that as many as 80 per cent of symbols on a page of English are redundant to the transmission of the information of that page. From our own work we now show that in some aspects, the lexicon of industrial news is more redundant in this specialised sense than several other varieties of discourse. For instance, we noted the frequency of terms denoting industrial action on the main evening bulletins over a four-month period (January–April 1975). In the list of words denoting industrial action there were 244 elements on BBC and 292 on ITN (see Table 8.1). We discovered that the two most frequently used terms, namely 'strike' and 'dispute', account for 58 per cent of all industrial action nouns on BBC and 65 per cent on ITN. This shows that lexically industrial news coverage is shaped by a highly restricted code with a massive degree of redundancy in Shannon's terms. So that when the news moves on to some industrial coverage with its common forms of introduction, such as 'And now some industrial news',[28] culturally attuned viewers should know that well over 50 per cent of the time they are about to hear news in which strikes or disputes will figure. Indeed, as the only likely information which follows will be time, location, number involved and place, the industrial stories are a highly redundant form of communication which can be said to be conveying very little that is new or unpredictable.

One way of interpreting this high degree of predictability in news talk is to assume that it refers to a high degree of factuality; that the bare essentials of the news are conveyed by unambiguous, factual categories and vocabulary. But, as we have shown in Volume 1, essential basic facts are frequently not given; information regarding causes, which unions are involved, whether the strike is official or unofficial, amongst other central facts, are rarely given. In many senses, then, the code is restricted and extremely redundant, providing information within a very narrow range. Indeed, as we show later in Table 8.1 we find no instances in the sample period which refer to employers' actions which are the equivalent of strikes, such as lockouts, withholding pay or refusing overtime money.[29] In short, the coding of industrial news is heavily weighted against the trade union and labour point of view; for its lexical and syntactical performance in our sample excluded much of the information that is needed to convey such an interpretation. The ideology of its producers thus far reflects a management and anti-strike bias, and this manifests itself even in its apparently neutral language.

Natural conversation and manufactured news

Although public scrutiny of the news and the continuing debate about its forms and functions might seem to imply that the producers of news are well aware of the principles of discourse involved, in fact the news shares certain properties with other forms of 'restricted code'. Access to its own principles of organisation is effectively blocked. The appeal to neutrality and factuality serves to conceal or bury the properties of news talk as a restricted code. These properties are (1) high context specificity, and (2) high predictability – lexically, syntactically and in discourse structure. We will examine them in turn.

The language of the news is not meaningful simply because its competence consists of English arranged in grammatically accept-able ways and in sentences which cohere. There is a wider context which allows the messages of television news to be received and – in some measure at least – understood by viewers. This context can be regarded as a kind of interpretive competence: a set of expectations and a taken-for-granted knowledge of what 'news' is and how the language of the news differs from other kinds of talk. In theory this competence can be defined in terms of hearers' and viewers' 'maxims'.[30] These are decoding rules which are brought into play when linguistic or visual messages are received. The decoding of English in any context brings into play the basic understanding of grammar and discourse which any native speaker possesses. For example, if we know how to distinguish and decode questions, we can often predict what will constitute a reply. This would not be context specific. In a similar way, familiarity with contemporary cultural phenomena normally entails a certain competence in its decoding. In this sense, the decoding of the news is something the hearer knows how to do even though the news is a special category of language formed in a highly specific context. But just as linguistics make explicit the rules of language which we use automatically, so we can elaborate on the context-bound properties of news talk, in our attempt to unpack its coding.

The news script is unlike either the written word or ordinary speech. Since it is written to be spoken, it relies on some of the properties of both. It is one of the best examples of a 'public' message: neither its origin nor its destination can be closely specified because the newscaster is only a vehicle for articulating a text which has several sources and which is destined for millions whether or not they are construed as 'a few people in a room'.[31] The individual sources (reporter, correspondent, news agency, etc.) which are unknown to the average viewer are usually treated as irrelevant to the comprehension of the message. The text, in part because there is no right of reply and because of its ego-less form, appears to have an autonomous existence independent of its producers, readers or speakers, and hearers. In this it differs from everyday conversation which in performance refers constantly to its own grounding, as for instance in such phrases as 'wouldn't you agree?' or 'I reckon'. The fact that the text is read by a readily identifiable and familiar newscaster does not alter the essential anonymity of the message but simply helps to conceal it. The legitimacy of the news seems to derive more from its immediacy, its claim to neutrality and its appeal to authoritative evidence, than from the newsreaders themselves. Thus, when in September 1976 ITN changed the time and format of the early evening bulletin, neither this nor the much-heralded appearance of Alastair Burnet made any significant impression on audience size or audience appreciation.[32] This British experience need not necessarily be always true. In the United States, ABC's importation of Barbara Walters at $1,000,000 a year was based on the premise that newscasters were 'stars' who of themselves could increase audience size. In the event it seems as if she failed so to do. But if there is little evidence that newscasters will increase audience size, there is even less evidence that they will affect audience appreciation or perceptions and trustworthiness.

How the audience perceives news is of course important. As Collins indicated in his brief assessment of audience surveys in Britain and the United States, if one regards editorialising as perceived by audiences as leading to lack of trust or unreliability, then one believes that any increase in editorialising affects the news' 'trustworthiness rating', as the BBC have called it.[33] In short, from this point of view, a large part of the legitimacy and neutrality of the news turns on the audience not perceiving the editorialising and coding, and not on whether such editorialising or coding exists. In fact, much of the editorialising and selectivity is so deeply embedded in the structure of news broadcasting that the cultural and linguistic codes in use are not readily apparent. Therefore the mass of the audience are probably unaware of the great amount of comment, selectivity and routine handling which packages that which appears on the screen.

In *Bad News*, we noted evidence from the BBC that there had been a long-term decline in the proportion of viewers who thought that BBC news was always impartial.[34] Recent audience research suggests that this may be the case for commercial companies also, although slightly different questions were used. When asked specifically about coverage of industrial disputes (not only in the news), a majority of the sample of viewers claimed that BBC and ITN were 'fair' to both unions and managements. However, the percentage declined from 1975 to 1976, as Table 6.1 shows. And in both surveys between 19 per cent and 28 per cent did not share this view. Whilst about the same proportion claimed that the news showed favour to one or the other side in industrial disputes, in 1976 more people were prepared to say they 'didn't know'.

In view of the fact that the two news services are strikingly similar in every major respect, the finding that the BBC is more likely to be viewed as showing favour towards management and ITV as showing favour towards trade unions cannot derive from any fundamental differences in selection and presentation. The divergence arises from general attitudes towards the BBC and ITV where real differences in output exist rather than from specific differences in news output. As we showed in Volume 1, there is less clear differentiation in the minds of viewers on questions of detail in the news.[35] The audience research findings reveal in these surveys and the 'trustworthiness' survey quoted in Volume 1 that the news is still largely perceived by its audience in relatively neutral and trustworthy terms. But there is a sizeable minority which does not share this view and there is within the surveys some evidence that this minority is growing. However, given Smith's *sine qua non* of news, it would be surprising to find results different from these and they are of course without prejudice to the analysis of the actual examples of cultural skewedness that can be demonstrated by close analysis of the broadcasts themselves.

There are several consequences to the fact that the written-spoken language of the news lies somewhere between the written word and natural conversation and has some of the properties of

Table 6.1 Industrial disputes on TV

Question:
Thinking now about industrial disputes in particular, do you think that ITV/BBC tends to favour trade unions or management, or is it fair to both?

	All adults		Sex		Age						Social class				Voting intention			
Number in sample: all with TV	1975	1976	Male	Female	16–24	25–34	35–44	45–54	55–64	65+	AB	C1	C2	DE	Con.	Lab.	Lib.	Other
	1,000	1,071	507	565	198	209	158	162	155	189	142	245	363	321	428	300	96	39
	%	%	%	%	%	%	%	%	%	%	%	%	%	%	%	%	%	%
ITV																		
Favours trade unions	14	15	15	14	20	15	14	11	14	13	16	15	16	13	20	11	11	21
Favours managements	6	6	7	4	8	7	6	5	3	3	5	5	6	5	3	7	6	9
Is fair to both	81	72	73	71	66	71	71	74	77	76	66	75	70	75	70	76	74	64
Don't know	0	8	5	10	7	8	8	9	6	8	13	6	7	7	7	6	9	6
BBC																		
Favours trade unions	6	7	7	6	7	7	9	4	7	5	6	9	6	6	10	5	2	8
Favours managements	13	14	19	9	20	20	10	10	11	10	15	14	15		12	16	13	21
Is fair to both	81	73	70	76	67	68	72	80	76	79	72	74	72	74	74	73	78	65
Don't know	0	6	4	9	7	5	9	7	6	6	7	3	7	8	4	6	7	6

Source: Broadcasting Attitudes Survey conducted by Social Surveys (Gallup Poll) Ltd for the IBA, 1976.

both. For instance, writing has a measure of economy and cohesion which is lacking in everyday speech or even in most public speaking. This cohesion is reflected in its relatively formal organisation and its apparent autonomy from subjective viewpoints. However, writing also calls for a process of interpretation whereby readers can insert themselves into the communication process. This is the process of 'reading' – the reconstruction of meaning as well as the deciphering of the text's lexical and syntactical components. The fluidity of natural conversation embodies a different structure of communication because the production of language is too immediate for the same kind of decoding. In natural talk, the speakers and hearers orient themselves to culturally available resources which enable them to recognise without reflection what speakers are doing when they construct their talk. News talk obviously makes use of some of these understandings because it is received as speech, not writing. But at the same time, except in the case of interviews and overheard informal talk, it fuses them with a mode of presentation which has more authority than natural talk, for it is underwritten with the permanence and authority of the prepared text. The newspaper readers' task, then, is to 'naturalise' the printed word to restore its functions as spoken communication. One of the priorities of further research must be to explore the cognitive correlates of these processes. There is no reason to assume that the decoding of messages is taken for granted in a fixed fashion. There is always the possibility that the preferred readings and connections could be rejected. But we would deny the assumptions of those critics who suggest that to show that the coding and routine structure of the news demonstrates that output is biased against the trade union and labour point of view is time-wasting because trade unionists already perceive it as such.[36] Although a plurality of receptions is possible, we know from audience survey research that a majority, including therefore many trade unionists, consider BBC and ITN news to be, for instance, more trustworthy than the press.[37] Thus work on 'de-coding' the implicit and routine codes becomes a crucial part of ensuring that the public have ways of knowing what they are seeing.

Paralinguistics

The 'unnaturalness' of the written-spoken mode in the news is matched by a number of paralinguistic features. The impression is of face-to-face talking but the form is primarily a monologue. The news embodies interest, activity and excitement but the news-caster's posture is more stationary and impassive than in almost any other television performance.

Despite this, however, there are subtle kinesic markers which vary stress, emphasis and readings. For instance, the newscaster can read a human interest story with a smile, thus stressing its essential humour. Eyebrows may be used to vary tone and stress. Openings and closings of items can be and often are indicated by looking down, or away from camera. Film or video-tape can be introduced by turning the head to the monitor on which leaders or clocks are running down to the head of the insert, thus not only allowing the performer to accurately cue the input, but also enabling the viewers to be cued as to the input.

Intonation can vary and is a further indicator of how a message should be heard. Further research in this area should be done on the recently developed intonation machines. At present, there seem to be two possibilities. Either stress follows the convention that it occurs on the introduction of new significant pieces of information, as in natural conversation, e.g. 'I'm just going *out*'. Or, as is likely in the sentence given, it occurs on completion of exchanges. As most of the news is written-spoken, it is also plausible to suggest that in many bulletins patterns of stress could be related to the amount of information on each separate line of text as it appears on the autocue. With the exception of 'breakdown and emergencies' and some short weekend bulletins, newscasters read from an autocue in front of the camera lens at eye level. In reading to camera from autocue they can appear to be addressing the audience directly and delivering a face-to-face message. As Chapter 10 will indicate, this allows newsreaders – along with ministers of the Crown and élite entertainers – an unmediated directness to camera which is rarely accorded to the less powerful.

It might be noted that the shifting of papers and the informal signing-off phrases of newsreaders show by contrast the authority with which the rest of the news has been delivered. Having read the news with appropriate *gravitas*, the newsreader may take his cue from the last item to indulge in a pun or a whimsical comment. Thus, in a bulletin which ended with an item on tea-workers in Sri Lanka, the newscaster's closing words before saying goodnight were: 'Something for us all to think about as we sup our evening cuppa'.[38] This shift in key may well reinforce rather than detract from the news just delivered. It is like a ritual divesting of the authority conferred on the newsreader for the duration of the bulletin. It is, in Goffman's terms, a visible breaking out of frame.

The relative absence of regional accents in the national news has probably also helped – albeit unwittingly – to reinforce the ideology of a supposedly classless neutrality. All these encoded features help to make the news unmistakably different from other forms of discourse and prepare the viewers for the preferred ideological reading or decoding of it. They also lead us to expect linguistic features – stylised norms, conventions of composition and a lexical system – which are especially adapted to the stringent conventions of the news and which are functionally related to its ideological make-up.

There are several other ways in which news talk differs from natural conversation. Each can contribute to the legitimacy and authority of the bulletins. They vary in importance and relevance but include such characteristics as the impression of immediacy, factuality and internal coherence. The rapidity and lack of discursiveness in news talk marks its variation from natural talk. For instance, the news is read on average at the rate of about three words per second. (The ability to speak at a regular pace is an essential part of a television performer's professionalism, because otherwise he or she creates problems of general timing and cueing for tape and film inserts.)

Moreover, it is a peculiarity of the news that the topic shifts are rapid and global, often with no apparent connection between the items apart from the cultural convention internalised by the viewers that the news will 'cover the waterfront'.

So we can move from the law on picketing to the royal tour in Japan without any apparent problem.[39] Yet in normal talk to shift topic in such a manner and at such a rate would be highly deviant, and could produce challenges to a speaker's competence. The other expectation which audiences hold of the news, which they do not expect in natural conversation, is a high level of technical and factual accuracy. In practice, in the industrial news, routine attention is paid to certain kinds of factual detail: namely the times, dates, amounts and numbers involved. But on occasion the information varies between channels and bulletins. For example, the miners' pay claim reporting contained quite different percentage figures, depending on bulletin and channel, and in the British Leyland Cowley dispute in 1975 the number of engine tuners on strike was said to be either 250 or 350 depending on the bulletin and channel.[40] In natural conversation ambiguities of detail or contradictions in numbers are allowable and tolerated, whereas the routine use of such detail in the news presupposes no such ambiguities or contradictions.

It has been argued that news differs essentially from current affairs programmes – that the news gives the 'unadorned facts', the basic information, as it were, while current affairs programmes promote balanced explanation, evaluation and comment on this basic information.[41] In our view facts do not exist in isolation and they are part and parcel of encoded messages of which the codes and conventions indicated above turn upon a given ideology. Part of the conventional ideology and claim of newsproducers and broadcasters is that they do not editorialise or deliver a preferred viewpoint. In fact, all of the conventions we have briefly examined above and those which we are about to examine in depth add to the appearance of a natural neutrality in its form and presentation – but this is a spurious, manufactured chimera. Close analysis of the linguistic form reveals that essential assumptions and conventions, coupled with the routine practices of industrial reporting, allow the production of impartiality, which is insisted on as a fetish in the rhetoric of the broadcasters and is embodied in broadcasting law and practice, but which when studied and analysed reveals itself as non-natural and non-neutral.

7 Assembling the News Text

Each sentence, each word, must be made to count.
We must learn to handle words as if they were gold.

BBC News Guide[1]

We now turn to the properties of news talk at the level of the text as a series of more or less meaningfully *related* sentences, since we have previously argued that syntactic and lexical analysis are of themselves insufficient for our purposes. We shall attempt to uncover some of the rules of composition which represent a form of 'competence' (in the linguistic sense described above) in the language of news and also a professional, journalistic competence or expertise.

The codes and rules involved are not necessarily intentional. The features which set the news text apart from other forms of discourse are only partly related to conscious practices and procedures. Those rules which do get articulated are picked up in the course of professional socialisation and are embodied in rules-of-thumb or conventions which journalists adopt when they edit texts for transmission. A crude indication of these professional skills may be found in house style books or in journalistic primers, the rules of which are exemplified in the following extract from ITN's house style book:[2]

A well-written ITN programme sounds clear, intelligent, friendly and authoritative all at once. Though space is limited, good writing is tremendously important. Don't be frightened to be dramatic in your writing, if the story merits it. But try to secure your dramas by facts, not by adjectives. The *fact* that Mrs Kennedy cried out 'No, no!' when Kennedy was shot is of more value than a dozen adjectives. But adjectives can be useful too, provided they are appropriate, and the kind you would use in spoken speech. Sentences should be kept short and simple, and must be completely comprehensible at first hearing. The viewer, unlike the reader, cannot pause to refer back or digest a point. The simple pattern of subject, verb, object usually fits television speech best. Not every sentence needs to be complete, and the verb can be omitted surprisingly often.

Our evidence from observation of newsrooms indicates that style books are used no more than as glossaries of terms which pose difficulties (e.g. the ambiguities surrounding the use of 'freedom fighter', 'terrorist' and 'guerrilla'). They are not normally used as a text on how to write news items. This set of journalistic imperatives begs several questions, the most basic being whether or not journalists regularly follow such advice. In practice it is difficult to conceive of a set of rules which would allow them to achieve the desired effects in terms of clarity, intelligibility and authority. This latter competence is a product of 'experience' rather than instruction.

The majority of the rules of composition remain unarticulated, just as the rules of story classification, placement, duration and presentation remain implicit in the structuring of news bulletins. This structure was described in *Bad News*, and we demonstrated how the content of the news is arranged in predictable ways which vary within narrow limits. The language of the news functions both to uphold the divisions described there and at the same time binds the fragments of 'news' into a coherent whole. Building on Halliday's work on language function, which in turn draws upon the work of the Prague School of linguists, we analyse news talk in terms of language *usage* in an attempt to explain why the text is structured in one way rather than another.[3] One of Halliday's main academic contributions has been to demonstrate that the structure of the clause involves at least three functions. He terms these the 'ideational' function which expresses the content and refers to extralinguistic reality, the 'interpersonal' function which expresses and maintains social relationships between speakers; and finally the 'textual' function which concerns the structuring of the text itself, the delineation of message units and distribution of message units within texts. Any clause may embody one or each of these functions or 'options'. So, for example, to analyse the opening sentence of a news item about a strike by maintenance workers at the Houses of

Parliament would involve identifying the multiple functions of the sentence. In this example (BBC1, 21.00, 10 April 1975) the sentence is as follows:

Strike pickets have been out at the Houses of Parliament.

Here, the content (the ideational function) of the sentence is embodied in three elements which correspond to the classes of noun, verb and adverb or adverbial group. These are the participants, the process and the circumstance respectively. The interpersonal function which defines the roles of participants in the speech situation is expressed in the 'mood', which is declarative; i.e. it is a statement and not a question, response, command or exclamation. The modal subject in our example 'strike pickets', is the same as the subject of the ideational functional. This is generally the case except in the imperative mood. If, for instance, this sentence were cast in the imperative (which is rare in present news talk in part because it supposedly trades on the past and present not the future) then the subject would be the speaker, '[We say] strike pickets out at the Houses of Parliament'. This frequent lack of the newsreader as subject of course helps to reinforce the supposed neutrality and objectivity of news.

The third function, that of structuring the text, can be best illustrated by rearranging the sentence as follows:

At the Houses of Parliament strike pickets have been out.

This cannot be done without altering the emphasis and therefore the meaning of the sentence. In English the theme of a clause is the element which is placed first. The textual function of the original sentence is therefore expressed in 'strike pickets'. Halliday describes this as the peg on which the message is hung. He points out that the actor (the ideational subject), the subject in the interpersonal function and the theme are often identical. Where they are different, as in the passive form, there may be practical or linguistic reasons. In this example as in others if the report were passive the three subjects would be different. Putting the example into the passive we might get: 'The Houses of Parliament have been hit by strike pickets'. Put this way, who are the strikers and related questions immediately arise, but with 'strike pickets' as the modal subject such questions are not necessarily on the agenda because the subjects are all functionally related. None of this detracts from the approach which indicates that the grammarian's notion of 'subject' combines at least three distinct functional elements which can be independent of one another and which are glossed over in a purely grammatical account of sentences. Our own analysis (unlike Halliday's) does not take the clause as the basic unit, but uses that understanding of the ordering and function of elements at this level to apply to discourse units larger than the sentence. It alerts attention to the fact that discourse is not necessarily unitary but may serve more than one function. The news text is not simply a set of discrete sentences. Its assembly and structure carry an ideological meaning of their own which is directly related to its conditions of production and its claim to objectivity.

The sample on which the analysis is based consists of one week's complete news broadcasts between 11 and 17 May 1975, allowing comparisons with the visual analysis presented in Part III below, which is based on the same broadcasts. (We will later use a four-month sample of industrial news – the second sample.) The analytic units are not simply to be regarded as higher levels of grammar but should be seen to lie between the level of grammar and non-linguistic organisation. A unit may consist of a word, a clause or more than one sentence and at the same time it may coincide with a short item, an interview or some other element of extra-linguistic organisation.

Headlines

'Trade figures – some cheering news' (ITN, 22.00, 14 May 1975).
'And there may be some good news for the motor industry . . .' (ITN, 13.00, 16 May 1975).

Headlines are seen as having crucial importance in the language of newspaper reporting.[4] They are one of the most important devices for summarising and drawing attention to a story and, so far as the press is concerned, are also one of the strongest visual indicators of style. In television news they have no exact equivalent because the audience's hearing of the bulletin follows a logic which is pre-determined by news producers and over which the viewers can exercise no discretion (say, over running order) except to switch off – mentally or physically.[5] They cannot turn or jump pages.

The graphological distinctions of the newspaper can have no

precise corresponding variation in loudness, stress, pace, or the kinesics involved in the reading of the news. Instead, the significance of items has to be weighted by the amount of time allocated to them, their placing in the bulletin and the status of those who appear as interviewees. In certain bulletins the most salient stories are underlined, as it were, by repetition – by summaries of the 'main points' at the beginning or end of the bulletins. On ITN's *News at Ten* these points are actually compressed into verbal headlines between the 'bongs', the chimes of Big Ben. In the case of commercial television's *News at Ten*, because of the so-called 'natural break' an item may be underlined by as many as four repetitions.[6] For it could be mentioned in the opening, again as part of the hookers to hold people over the ads (the natural break), until the second half where it could appear as an item; and finally it could be mentioned in the summing-up at the end of the programme, when that is done.

Most television newspersons would agree that the placing of an item in the running order is an indicator of its importance. However, analysis of the headlines reveals that they do not follow the convention slavishly with a direct correspondence between the headline and the running order. See, for instance, the headlines and running order in *News at Ten* on 16 May in Table 7.1. To omit a

Table 7.1   Headline order: ITN, 22.00, 16 May 1975

Headline order	Actual running order
1 Britain's inflation rate a record figure – far worse than expected	1
2 The Dunlop strike is over – 18,000 go back to work	3
3 But Chrysler throw 8,000 out of a job tonight	4
4 The armed forces get a 29 per cent pay rise	5
5 Tennis – Nastase and Taylor in trouble at Bournemouth	14

headline for Item 2 and to include a headline for Item 14 serves as a 'hooking' device. The audience are given some broad notion of attractive stories from the whole bulletin. In effect they are invited to stay tuned and, as in the above example, it is often a key human interest or sports story from the second half of the bulletin that occupies the last 'bong' position. But it is rare that any headline will be taken out of order, as it were. The ranking of the headlines matches the ranking of the stories in the bulletin whatever the omissions in the headline list. One example of this was *News at Ten* on 13 May 1975, which began with the headlines shown in Table 7.2.

Table 7.2   Headline order: ITN, 22.00, 13 May 1975

Headline order	Actual running order
1 Captured cargo boat – American warships and marines stand by	1
2 Work has stopped on printing Britain's banknotes	5
3 Mr Foot tells the Chrysler strikers to go back to work	8
4 CBI forecast a deep recession and rising unemployment	7
5 The once-a-year soccer match fit for a Queen	15

The normal hierarchically related headlines here deviate in that headlines 3 and 4 refer to Items 8 and 7 respectively. There is at least a suspicion of a causal connotation in the headline sequence, as they are presented together, the foreign and human interest stories having no obvious connection in terms of subject matter. The reversing of the actual running order of the economic and industrial items into a new headline order unintentionally or otherwise creates the possibility of the audience causally associating strikes with recession. Sometimes there may be some pragmatic reason for this, for instance it may be necessary to separate two pieces of film or tape by a still photograph or graphic to facilitate cueing the different types of material into the sequence. However, these technical considerations did not seem to apply in the bulletin in question. Instead, what may be illustrated here is the general tendency to associate 'economic' and 'industrial' affairs in preferred ways. In these examples, the selection as well as the ordering of items in the headline sequence is closely consistent with the inferential framework which we found in Part I was used in the coverage of inflation and the Social Contract.[7] The examples tend to reflect the structure and packaging of the bulletins as a whole by bringing together the subject matter of inflation, recession, strikes and pay. The use of headlines in this way is important in establishing, through repetition, the priorities expressed in the bulletin proper.

Here the headlines serve as a signifier of the tone of the bulletin.

We are not only being given the most salient 'facts' of the day's news; we are being invited to take an interest, follow a lead, and ultimately and subtly join in a stance – a stance revealing the basic inferential frameworks used by the broadcasters. In the absence of any imperative form which would immediately reveal the involvement of the newsman with the audience and hence undermine the impression of objectivity, we are asked indirectly to take note of something important, be intrigued, entertained and informed. Amending Halliday, we can apply that analytic to highlight the 'textual' function of the headlines, which are the initial structuring acts of news discourse.[8]

Boundary markers

'More bad news from the car industry' (BBC1, 21.00, 24 February 1975).
'Good news today for one of Britain's major shipbuilders' (BBC1, 21.00, 14 February 1975).

In many bulletins there are no headlines as such and the bulletin has to 'speak for itself' – via the running order of items, the ways in which they are treated and the time allotted. There are a number of linguistic indicators as well as paralinguistic indicators (pauses, head movements, etc.) which demarcate one item from another. These literally mark a boundary in discourse.

In essence boundary markers are phrases which do not contain propositions which are part of the news item's message; rather they serve to specify that a news item is beginning and often they indicate the nature of the item. They refer most frequently to time and places. Often they consist of no more than the simple conjunction and adverb 'And . . .' or 'And now . . .'.

The most common boundary markers separate foreign from domestic news; for example: 'At home . . .', 'Here at home . . .', 'In Britain . . .', or 'In this country . . .'.[9] Details of place are often used to signal a shift from one item to the next. Although the phrases 'In Glasgow . . .', 'On Merseyside . . .' and 'At London's Heathrow Airport . . .' have a content with an 'ideational' function, their position at the very beginning of an item indicates that their function lies in marking the boundary rather than in introducing the theme or in giving an important detail.[10] Sometimes the boundary between items is marked but not specified, as in 'And now some other news . . .'.[11] Less frequently, the boundary markers provide the linguistic context for editorial comment in which the news is defined as 'good' or 'bad' or is otherwise evaluated; as for instance in the above quotations 'More bad news from the car industry . . .', 'Good news today for [shipbuilders]', and 'It's been a critical day for the Health Service' or even 'Very much less glamorously in Glasgow . . .'.[12] These are some of the occasions on which the inferential framework of those who produce the news most obviously comes to the surface. This framework is always there but is usually implicit rather than explicit. We have previously described the inferential framework of industrial reporting. These instances indicate that the framework trades on and assumes a consensus of values. There is no way in which 'good' and 'bad' news can be readily understood if the question 'Good or bad for whom?' is admitted.

Boundary markers not only set one item apart from another; they sometimes take the form of subheads which label as well as delineate the item. This type of specific boundary marker is called a 'catchline' by professional broadcasters. Schlesinger states:[13]

> Thus: 'Industrial News', 'The Commons', 'The Watergate Affair' are all phrases intended to swiftly cue in the audience to the content of the next story, while making the assumption that people are sufficiently familiar with its past developments to comprehend present ones. Catchlines contribute to a news style which both looks and sounds economical.

Industrial stories, once they have become running stories, acquire tags (specific catchlines) such as 'The London dock strike', and 'The railway signalmen's dispute' which are used simply as labels, without being formed into sentences. 'Now rubbish' – a label for the Glasgow dustcart drivers' dispute – is one of the more idiosyncratic examples.[14] Like the paging conventions, headlines and subheadings in a newspaper, these tags (including 'Now some industrial news') give the audience clues to what is to follow. Stories which may have wider implications, or events which occur in industry but which are not reported as 'industrial' news, are usually not included in what follows such catchlines.

One major exception to this is news of pay and pay claims, which is often linked to news of prices. Thus 'After today's pay and prices news, one further item about the economy' and 'Now to news of rising prices and rising pay'.[15] Given the basic inferential framework – that is, that wages were primarily responsible for inflation in this period – these boundary markers are only to be expected. 'Industrial' is in fact generally applied to the employment and industrial relations aspects of industry and not to the financial, administrative, production or consumer aspects.

The process of 'labelling', or in Goffman's terminology 'framing', is well understood in sociology and social psychology and it can be shown that circumstances may be altered, behaviour reinforced and conditioned, attitudes affected and perceptions changed by the consistent application of labels.[16] The use of apparently neutral names to describe stories is therefore not as straightforward as it seems. Indeed, Dengler has argued that a study of something as detailed as film labels or titles provides a basis for tracing the pattern of cultural themes in the history of movie-making. Using the *General Inquirer* and the *Psycho-Sociological Dictionary*, he claims that his work lends[17]

> precision to generalisation gained from a mere perusal of titles and lends support to historians of film who have pointed to the role Hollywood played in reflecting American Society and culture and exploiting it at the box office. The domestic preoccupations of the first decade, its latent work ethic set in a communal tone with highly moral undercurrent, gives way to the blatant enticements and fantasies of the 1920's and 1930's, the incisive and personalised propaganda of the 1940's, and the suggestions of nihilism and degradation in recent times. Movies have shifted their focus from what is publicly most cherished and best reputed in the good life to what is most personal and perverse. In the process of change movies have moved from light entertainment to the convulsive.

Thus a close retrospective analysis of film titles can reveal their connection with broader cultural themes. The simple label 'industrial news' demarcates an area in like fashion. Indeed the labels for industrial disputes, for instance, contain a single act or group of actors – this 'actor' being the labour side of the dispute, as we shall demonstrate in the section on vocabulary (see p. 177 below). The omission of one party in the dispute must give a preferred reading

that the labour side is the active, responsible party, and by implication, the one which precipitates the action.

Boundary markers are not always labels. The use of the adverb
'Meanwhile' is a case of a boundary marker whose function is
almost purely 'textual'.[18] In natural conversation and narrative,
'meanwhile' is generally used to link temporally concurrent activity
which is separated by location – classically, 'Meanwhile, back at the
ranch . . .'. The nature of the news frequently renders the use of
'Meanwhile' redundant, as one can assume that the news is the news
of the day and is *ipso facto* temporally connected. More crucially
perhaps, the word 'Meanwhile' is conventionally used in narrative
to refer to a connection between events if this connection is implied
or hidden. If 'Meanwhile' is used to mark a boundary in television
news its function is chiefly 'textual', but because it carries overtones
of sequentiality and ordering it can function to contribute to the
internal coherence of the news; i.e. give it the quality of narrative
even though discrete news items are not in fact elements in a single
plot.

Boundary markers are crucial to the audience's decoding
process. The news, we have argued, presents a surface confusion in
that disparate events are reported with little or no surface thematic
connections. We have shown that when such connections are made
they carry semantically significant implications for decoding. But in
general the deeper structuring of the bulletins presents a coherent
world picture. Basically the predictability of what sort of events will
be covered, at what length, in what order and with what presentational devices all work towards this coherence. Boundary markers
therefore serve to sequence the surface disorder of the message and
relate that disorder back to the basic inferential frames governing
the production of the bulletins. They thus offer the audience crucial
clues to aid the decoding process.

The structuring of information within items

In general the structure of news stories in television is linear: there is
a single theme established at the outset which is elaborated in a
single direction by additional information, illustration, quotation
and discussion, even if these inputs appear to contradict one
another. The logic of this has to do partly with notions of balance,
partly with presentation and partly with the requirement of editing
both film and news scripts. The formulae of the bulletins allow little

or no time for scene-setting; the first few phrases – the first few seconds – have to attract and hold the interest of the viewer and at the same time give the most important information. To create interest by giving priority to the bizarre, unusual or humorous would be to abandon 'objectivity'. To give salient facts without regard to their presentation would be to ignore the demands of the audience. In theory, each succeeding section after the opening should contain information of decreasing importance. Regardless of the overall length of an item and whether or not it contains a piece of film, the opening phrases delivered by the newscaster in vision are unlikely to vary in any significant way. This is because the opening phrases establish the theme by presenting 'the main facts of the story in an arresting and lucid fashion'.[19] How this works in practice and how the choice of the lead paragraph situates the report and establishes its basic framework is demonstrated in the television's coverage of the Chrysler strike in May 1975 (see Tables 7.3 and 7.4), which was featured in the week chosen for visual and linguistic analysis.

The Chrysler strike story

The pay claim by Chrysler workers and the strike which ensued was a major running story which was reported thirty-one times on ITN and thirty-seven times on BBC1. At a Coventry engine plant 4,000 production workers withdrew their labour on 9 May in support of a pay claim for an increase in basic rates of £15 a week. Work was eventually resumed on 5 June, following acceptance of an interim offer of £8 a week. Interpretations of the dispute were complicated by the fact that Chrysler had simultaneously published proposals for worker participation. Whilst the workers insisted that this was a separate issue, some reports (for example, those in Table 7.4) were quick to imply that the workers' initial response to the proposals showed evidence of their unreasonable attitude. However, it is not our purpose here to provide a detailed case study of the Chrysler strike story but rather to show, with examples, some of the general principles whereby themes are established and elaborated.

In each BBC bulletin on Thursday 15 May the theme of the opening paragraph was the same – the vote to continue the strike. The two-sentence item in the short BBC lunchtime bulletin contained little more than this except for a statement of the workers' demands (not the company's refusal to make an offer, it may be

Table 7.3   The Chrysler strike: reported by the BBC on Thursday 15 May 1975

Lunchtime bulletin	Early evening bulletin	*Nine O'Clock News*
		At home the two big disputes in the car industry.
		A peace formula has been worked out in the Dunlop dispute but the Chrysler strikers have voted to stay out. (Report on Dunlop dispute)
The 4,000 strikers at Chrysler's engine factory in Coventry voted overwhelmingly to continue their stoppage which began on Monday. They want a firm offer of £8 a week more as part of their claim for a £15 a week rise.	But the 4,000 workers at Chrysler's engine factory in Coventry have voted overwhelmingly to continue their strike.	The 4,000 workers at Chrysler's engine factory in Coventry voted overwhelmingly to stay out on strike. They want a firm offer of £8 a week more from July.
	They want a pay rise of £8 a week now and another £7 later. Peter Colbourne's been covering this story too:	
	PC: The strikers were told that Chrysler should get out of Britain if they can't pay a living wage. The workers were being used as cheap labour and have become the poor relations of the car industry.	Peter Colbourne reports on the mass meeting: PC: The strikers were told that Chrysler should get out of Britain if they can't pay a living wage. The workers were being used as cheap labour and have become the poor relations of the car industry.
	MORRIS (shop steward): And I ask you to vote unanimously for this recommendation. The manipulation of the press, the mass media in vision, and the unprecedented intervention of the First Minister of the Land – who spoke about something when we weren't even on strike – Mr Wilson, your platitudes and your attitudes and your	MORRIS (shop steward): And I ask you to vote unanimously for this recommendation. The manipulation of the press, the mass media in vision, and the unprecedented intervention of the First Minister of the Land – who spoke about something when we weren't even on strike – Mr Wilson, your platitudes and your attitudes and your

Table 7.3 continued

Lunchtime bulletin	Early evening bulletin	*Nine O'Clock News*
	political inspiration – you horrify me. (Applause.) SECOND SPEAKER: All in favour of that recommendation please show (cheers) . . . those against . . . (cheers).	political inspiration – you horrify me. (Applause.) SECOND SPEAKER: All in favour of that recommendation please show . . . (cheers) . . . those against . . . (cheers).
	PC: An overwhelming vote to stay out. So tomorrow night all Chrysler car production will have to stop. There's no hope of a speedy end to the strike and the men aren't to meet again for a week. But earlier at the meeting the workers voted in favour of the principle of worker participation at Chrysler's.	PC: An overwhelming vote to stay out. So tomorrow night all Chrysler car production will have to stop. There's no hope of a speedy end to the strike and the men aren't to meet again for a week.

Table 7.4   The Chrysler strike: reported by ITN on Monday 12 May 1975

First Report	Early evening bulletin	*News at Ten*
Well, to add to the general gloom the Chrysler car workers (recently offered, you will remember, part ownership in the company) decided this morning to continue their strike – a strike which Mr Wilson in that TV interview yesterday described as 'deplorable'. Talks over the weekend between the men and the American-owned company management have led to some hopes that the	The Prime Minister also said yesterday that he utterly deplored the prospect of a strike by Chrysler workers. He said he was horrified to feel that the company's proposals for participation had been rejected without full examination. But today Chrysler's shop stewards at the company's engine	In spite of the Prime Minister's warning yesterday that he deplored the stoppage at Chrysler, shop stewards in the engine factory at Coventry have voted to strike.

Table 7.4 continued

First Report	Early evening bulletin	News at Ten
strike might be averted. It's being staged by 4,000 men at the engine-building plant at Stoke in Coventry and it's meant the layoff of 6,000 more workers at other Chrysler factories throughout Britain. But this morning 140 shop stewards having got a report on the weekend-long discussions ended any hopes of an early return to work and from Coventry now Trevor MacDonald sends us this report:	factory in Coventry voted to go ahead with their strike for higher pay. This could put 10,000 men out of work at three Chrysler factories by the weekend. And more than 12,000 British Leyland workers will have to stay off work because strikers at a Dunlop components factory in Coventry are continuing their strike.

Trevor MacDonald reports: | It could put 10,000 men out of work at three Chrysler factories by the weekend. And more than 14,000 British Leyland workers will have to stay off work because 700 clerks at a Dunlop factory in Coventry are continuing their strike.

Trevor MacDonald reports: |
| TM: When the meeting ended a short while ago the mood of the men was in no doubt. The shop stewards remain as firmly as ever on their demand for £8 a week now as part of an eventual £15 a week pay claim to be achieved by July 1st. Paradoxically, if any single factor could be held to have hardened attitudes here about the strike, it's perhaps the Prime Minister's statements on television yesterday, which have been widely interpreted by the men as a condemnation of their dispute. Bob Morris, senior transport workers' union's shop steward at Chrysler's engine plant, who last night said he was 'absolutely stunned by Mr Wilson's outrageous interview', said after his morning's meeting at | TM: There was never any doubt about the mood of the men at Chrysler's, even before today's crucial meeting began. And when it ended the shop stewards' tough line was confirmed. Their spokesman, Bob Morris, was critical not only of the Chrysler management, but also of what some shop stewards saw as the Prime Minister's unhelpful intervention in interviews he gave yesterday.

BM: What they should do – they should sack Harold Wilson. Yes.

TM: But don't you think that his call for some sort of national stand on the question of wages and prices deserves some . . . attention? | TM: There was never any doubt about the mood of the men at Chrysler's, even before today's crucial meeting began. And when it ended the shop stewards' tough line was confirmed. Their spokesman, Bob Morris, was critical not only of the Chrysler management, but also of what some shop stewards saw as the Prime Minister's unhelpful intervention in interviews he gave yesterday.

BM: What they should do – they should sack Harold Wilson. Yes.

TM: But don't you think that his call for some sort of national stand on the question of wages and prices deserves some . . . attention? |

Table 7.4 continued

First Report	Early evening bulletin	News at Ten
the Stoke Plant Social Club that the men will not go back to work unless they get the money they're demanding now. He scornfully dismissed Chrysler's plans for greater worker participation and profit sharing, saying that the unions had not yet fully studied the plan. And when I asked him whether the men should not go back to work until the union's had an opportunity to study the company's proposals, he said there was no chance of that. And as though to reinforce the tough line the unions are taking on this whole question, the shop stewards have decided against bringing forward Thursday's mass meeting. Given the mood of today's ninety-minute session, there is no question now about the sort of recommendation the men will be asked to ratify on Thursday.	BM: Certainly. But Mr Wilson yesterday – his comments and so on – we haven't refused worker participation. We want the details so we can examine the position of worker participation. We haven't refused to do anything. TM: But aren't there any good points at all about the plans for industrial democracy – for more worker participation? BM: When we find out the details it may be a wonderful thing, but we know no details and it's not the basis to call off a strike. TM: But shouldn't you go back to work, until you know the details, and perhaps then consider strike action? BM: No, no. Our strike is on the basic. We are on strike for a living wage, full stop.	BM: Certainly. But Mr Wilson yesterday – his comments and so on – we haven't refused worker participation. We want the details so we can examine the position of worker participation. We haven't refused to do anything. TM: But aren't there any good points at all about the plans for industrial democracy, for more worker participation? BM: When we find out the details it may be a wonderful thing, but we know no details and it's not the basis to call off a strike. TM: But shouldn't you go back to work until you know the details, and perhaps then consider strike action? BM: No, no. Our strike is on the basic. We are on strike for a living wage, full stop.
Trevor MacDonald, *First Report*, Coventry. (Report on Dunlop dispute)	TM: Will you call forward the meeting which you planned for later this week to try to get this thing settled a little earlier? BM: No, no. Wednesday the stewards meet again – we meet all our massed workers on Thursday at 12 o'clock	TM: Will you call forward the meeting which you planned for later this week to try to get this thing settled a little earlier? BM: No, no. Wednesday the stewards meet again. We meet all our mass workers on Thursday at 12 o'clock

Table 7.4 continued

First Report	Early evening bulletin	*News at Ten*
	and that's it and the strike will continue.	and that's it, and the strike will continue.
	TM: (Report on Dunlop dispute)	TM: (Report on Dunlop dispute)
	Trevor MacDonald, ITN, Coventry.	Trevor MacDonald, *News at Ten*, Coventry.

noted). The BBC's early bulletin was prefaced by the boundary marker, 'But', which separated it from a report of the dispute at Dunlop. There were two additional sections in this report: a piece of film of the vote, together with a commentary by an industrial correspondent; and a statement about a previous vote on the issue of worker participation. Appearing as it did at the end of only one of the three items, this report of an earlier vote was clearly the most dispensable piece of information as far as the newsroom was concerned. As such it illustrated the propensity of television news to cover events rather than issues; cases rather than their connections. The item as it appeared in the *Nine O'Clock News* was deliberately 'packaged' with the Dunlop story, so there was a joint headline and boundary marker, 'At home the two big disputes in the car industry' and a subheading '. . . but the Chrysler workers have voted to stay out'. Repetition helped to establish the theme. The first paragraph remained virtually unchanged from the early bulletin except for details of the wage demand (again no details of the company's response and the possible use of the participation offer as a ploy) and the film report of the vote was identical. The theme of the story was the vote and its elaboration through film and commentary. In the two longer items the information was sequenced in such a way as to give space to the 'conflicting possibility' of the labour view.[20] This was presented in the indirect form 'strikers were told . . .' spoken over film indicating speakers at a mass meeting. But viewers were left in the dark as to who the speaker might be.

In even longer industrial stories other points of view (management, government, CBI, etc.) are likely to be presented but even this example shows that alternative possibilities are introduced by virtue of the theme and not in opposition to it. The correspondent's reporting of the speech at the mass meeting introduces a new possibility – the 'living wage', 'cheap labour', and comparative rates in the car industry – but the return to the film report of the vote reasserts the 'strike vote' theme, excluding any development of the alternative view. It actually reinforces the impression that the strike is about a wage demand of £8 a week and a further £7, a 'fact' which was established at the outset. But analysis of the internal evidence of these reports (i.e. the words spoken by the Convenor of Shop Stewards in *sync.*) reveals that the meeting was also concerned with the wider issues of media manipulation, intervention by politicians, the power of multinational corporations and with the worker participation offer. The 'factuality' of the (selective) reporting of the vote is undoubtedly enhanced by the piece of film, which is the key piece of supporting evidence for the theme as presented.

A comparison of the lunchtime bulletin with the corresponding sections of the other two reports illustrates some of the stylistic changes which may occur in the process of editing and updating. These have to do with presentation rather than content but they are not insignificant, as our analysis of vocabulary will show (see next chapter). The reference back in the lunchtime bulletin in the phrase '. . . which began on Monday' was omitted in the subsequent reports. This detail is of some importance since the gravity of a strike is a function of the length of the strike and the numbers directly involved. Reference back – even of this rudimentary kind – is not a regular feature of television news, so it is unsurprising that it was edited out of the later bulletins, possibly in order to make the key opening sentence shorter and simpler. The change of the two nouns 'strikers' and 'stoppage' in the lunchtime bulletin to 'workers' and 'strike' in the later bulletins was especially significant. 'Stoppage' is one of the most frequent nominal forms used to describe industrial action (see below, Table 8.1) and one, we argue, whose agent is consistently assumed to be labour. In this case we see that 'stoppage' and 'strike' were used interchangeably, although 'stoppages of production' have a variety of causes.[21] The change between these reports in a single day may involve recognition of the ambiguity of this use of 'stoppage' but it is more likely to have been prompted by the substitution of 'worker' in place of 'striker'.

ITN's three daily bulletins differed in certain ways from those of the BBC. As we showed in Volume 1, ITN has a greater propensity to report several stories in a single 'package' in the industrial area and there are obvious stylistic differences, particularly in *First Report*. Table 7.4 contains the reporting of the Chrysler story on

ITN on the Monday (12 May) before the Thursday (15 May) which was used in Table 7.3. ITN reported the Chrysler vote story on the Thursday but with less variation between bulletins. Table 7.4 has a number of additional features which show how items are assembled and adjusted in the course of a day's reporting.

The length of the first sentence in the item on *First Report* is the key to the style of this bulletin. The sentence is complex, with a parenthesis and several subsidiary clauses. The essential information is contained in the words 'the Chrysler car workers . . . decided this morning to continue their strike'; the remainder is a gloss on 'workers', 'strike' and the item as a whole. This practice of identifying a piece of news as 'good', 'bad', 'unusual', 'troubling' or even 'big news', together with an informality and flexibility of presentation (compare the 'you will remember . . .' in the first sentence), enhances the presenter's role as an individual personality. It does not, however, affect the framework of the story even though the style is more discursive than in the other bulletins. The gloss on 'strike' in the first sentence legitimated by the phrase – 'described as "deplorable"' by Mr Wilson – is a contextual feature used in the two later bulletins. Its importance in establishing a preferred and 'dominant view' is clear. In *Bad News* we showed that a similar strike by engine tuners at British Leyland was consistently reported by situating the strike as an instance of Mr Wilson's criticism of 'manifestly avoidable stoppages'. As we showed there, such a method is dubious in character, for in the later bulletins the view ascribed changed from stoppages involving both management and labour to stoppages caused solely by workers' action. The Prime Minister's view of the dispute is undeniably newsworthy but the function of the ascribed quote in this item is more ideological than informative. The use of the conjunction 'But' in the third sentence of the early evening bulletin and 'In spite of' to open the *News at Ten* report, show how, at the same time, the information is structured to give a preferred hearing of the strike as an act of obstinacy and against the national interest. The same kind of structuring occurs in an even more open way in the interview with the shop steward, which is an elaboration of this 'dominant view'. Trevor MacDonald uses the union reservations about the Chrysler participation plan to reinforce the 'tough line' view despite Morris's attempts to redefine the strike as separate from the worker participation issue. The news interpretation was shown to be unjustified because the workers later voted to accept in principle the participation proposals while voting at the same time to stay out on strike.

One effect of the frequent 'packaging' of discrete stories on the content of the bulletin is the association of unconnected events in a manner which suggests more than simple juxtapositioning. The inclusion of the Dunlop story between two parts of the Chrysler story in the evening bulletins, linked by the conjunction 'And', effectively places it in the same ideological category as the main Chrysler story. Thus even a simple conjunctive can function ideologically to connect disparate stories, regardless of differences of cause or consequence. The similarity of geographical location is itself merely a function of where the main elements of the motor industry reside. Packaging helps to create artificial coherence by placing 'industrial' stories together and by cementing them linguistically with the use of superficial conjunctions. Table 7.4 provides examples of both artificial coherence and linguistic cementing, additional industrial news being reported at the end of the two evening bulletins.

As the production of *First Report* is basically a separate operation from the production of the early bulletin and *News at Ten*, little can be inferred about the editing process of this bulletin from later bulletins. In the two evening bulletins there is hardly any change, since the interview remains the same. The introduction is slightly shorter in *News at Ten* and this does reflect a priority. In the shorter *News at Ten* version two significant elements have been omitted. In the course of simplifying the Prime Minister's reported statement, the reference to Chrysler's proposals for worker participation is dropped and the phrase 'for higher pay' which gives the one piece of information regarding 'strike' is omitted. Since these pieces of information emerge later in the interview situation, they could possibly be counted as 'dispensable'. But without them both the news item and the action of the Chrysler workers are barely intelligible. The omission of details of the claim and the unelaborated references to the worker participation proposals lead to an image of an action without cause – an explanatory vacuum rapidly filled by the broadcasters' inferential framework which in this area matches popular misconceptions and stereotypes of industrial action; i.e. the 'unreasonable worker' ideology.

If there is a theory which specifies the ways in which the parts function, news items could be said to be bound by a deep structure. We have shown that even within a single sentence language may function in several ways, and that information is likely to be arranged in order of declining importance (according to the value priorities of journalists). Combining these two levels – the functions of language in use and the journalistic value process respectively – we can consider establishing a number of *sequencing rules* which govern the relation of item elements (e.g. boundary markers, interviews, closings) to one another. The term 'sequencing rules' has been employed by Schegloff to describe the pattern of inter-action in telephone conversations and to explain their orderliness.[22] In the study of folk tales, myths and narratives, structural analysis identifies the parts in a sequence and shows how they function to create unity, continuity and resolution.[23] With news talk, as in the above studies, words cannot be considered in isolation but have to be regarded as serving functions in a larger whole, so the elements of a news item are not isolated bits of information whose arrange-ment is unimportant. There is a structure, not necessarily explicit, but deeply embedded, which can be revealed by comparing the relative position of key elements in the narrative. According to its practitioners, television news journalism[24]

> seeks above all to answer the questions WHO, WHAT, WHERE, WHEN and HOW. It is primarily concerned with new facts and the factual background to them. Its interest in the question WHY is confined to the audience's urgent interest in understanding what has just happened within the bounds of immediately available information.

These could be taken as the elements whose regular ordering in certain ways constitutes a structure of thinking and interpretation. But this is a view of news as 'bits' of information – hard 'facts' – supplied through a neutral channel. It pays little but lip-service to the framework which renders any fact or set of facts intelligible. This context, as we explain in Chapter 1, includes the whole range of expectations about 'news' and 'television' to be found among viewers of television news. It also includes the context of the text itself, the other pieces of information which are available.

The second sample, January–April 1975

The regularities which can be observed in the text of industrial action stories – reports of the beginning of a strike for example –

show that the WHO, WHAT, HOW, and WHY elements follow one of several possible sequences according to the story type. Details of time and place are more flexible since their function in the news is to express immediacy and precision and they are, as it were, dependent rather than independent variables. There is a basic sequence of key information corresponding to the WHO, WHAT and WHY question, in that order. The following item illustrates this, in its most commonly occurring form:

> Two thousand dockers at Hull have begun an overtime ban and a series of weekly one-day token strikes over a pay dispute. A docker's spokesman said that they'll continue their action until the employers honour an agreement to offer a pay rise based on the retail price index. And tonight 900 Manchester dockers also stopped work over a pay dispute. (ITN, 22.00, 9 April 1975)

Two-thirds of the reports of industrial action by both ITN and BBC in the four-month sample period (January–April 1975) had this form, the subject of the opening sentence being the labour disputants. Most frequently the subject was placed at the beginning of the sentence, as in this example. The elaboration of the report through indirect speech which occurred in this and other items will be discussed below. Where the subject of the opening sentence is not the labour disputants, a different kind of introduction will be sought. Occasionally, reported statements also contained basic information and could be used to open an item, but only when the framework of the story had been established in earlier bulletins. In the following example, which is part of a running story, the subject of the first sentence is the 'strike'. This opening, which assumes that viewers have prior knowledge of the strike, is only possible in the later stages of a running story:

> Here at home the strike of 250 engine tuners at British Leyland's Cowley works will not be called off when the men meet on Monday, according to Mr Reg Birch of the engineering union. Mr Birch, who attended arbitration talks in London today said any return to work would have to be a union decision, but he said he was prepared to attend further peace talks next week. (ITN, 22.00, 24 January 1975)

Moving from the WHO, WHAT, WHERE and WHEN

questions, the WHY question in the dockers' example is answered in the phrase 'over a pay dispute' even though the information given is very rudimentary. In many items consequences are reported but not the cause, giving a different emphasis as 'strike' becomes the subject of the first sentence and 'production' (rather than the firm, management or the dispute) its predicate. For example:

> A strike by 700 clerical workers at the Dunlop factory in Coventry has brought nearly half British Leyland's car production to a standstill. Dunlop supplies suspension parts for British Leyland and the stoppage, which has made about 8,000 car workers idle, is costing the company £1½ million a day.
> (ITN, 22.00, 30 April 1975)

The vocabulary of this item is revealing. Once again 'stoppage' is used synonymously with 'strike' and the term 'idle' is applied to non-striking workers who have had to stop work. Raymond Williams has traced the usage of this word and its associations both past and the present, showing that there has been a steady 'ideological resistance' to the distinction between unemployment or being laid off (a social situation) and idleness (a personal characteristic).[25]

> The resistance is still active, and in relation to the words is especially evident in the use of *idle*, in news reporting, to describe workers laid off, locked out or on strike. With its strong moral implications, *idle* in this context must have ideological intentions or effects.

Unfortunately, the highly dubious practice of emphasising effects rather than causes and other aspects occurs in as much as 40 per cent of reports of industrial action; that is, in two out of every five reports in our sample. Moreover, as often as not this constitutes the professional defence: these are usually stories which involve large numbers of 'consumers' more or less indirectly. Disputes in transport (railways, ferries and buses) and essential services (the ambulance service, refuse collection) were treated in this way. It was the rail passengers, for example, who were cast in the role of innocent victims – and by implication, they were victims of the 'militant signalmen' rather than victims of the breakdown of 'normal' relations between British Rail management and workers:

Rail passengers today suffered the worst disruption yet in the
series of one-day unofficial strikes by militant signalmen. South
and east of London many commuter services did not run and
important main line services to the west and north were also
affected. But the disruption was patchy depending on where
signalmen joined in the stoppage. There were trains from
London to Devon but not to South Wales; to Scotland but not to
Manchester. Peter Stewart reports. (BBC1, 21.00, 13 February
1975)

In certain areas, especially, when direct inconvenience to the
public looms large in the reporting, the consequences of industrial
action are emphasised, thus serving, ideologically or unwittingly, to
avoid the question WHY. This has been documented by other
observers.[26] There is only one case in the sample period of a cause
providing the main signification of a strike report. It is the exception
that proves the rule since the item occupies the final place in the
running order of the bulletin – the space usually reserved for 'joke'
or human interest stories (see Chapter 8, p. 182). These sequencing
rules which operate to structure the information have little to do
with the 'demands' of the subject matter. They are not merely some
routine way of arriving at an objective account which faithfully
expresses the 'facts'. They represent choices, made more or less
deliberately, and are based in the first instance on journalistic
values and conventions about what is interesting or important. In
favouring events rather than processes, effects rather than causes,
management rather than labour, the structuring and sequencing of
news talk, in spite of its apparent flexibility, is one of the main props
which upholds the rigid definitions and dominant views of strike
activity which, as we have already shown, operate in the categorisation and selection of industrial news. Thus journalistic values work
to buttress the basic inferential framework of the broadcasters,
which has broader ideological components.

Reported speech

On first hearing, the language of the news seems to be in a form
which would allow of fairly simple tests of its truth or falsity. It has
the appearance of being entirely constative (propositional and
capable of being shown either true or false) and not performative.
These terms are Austin's. He distinguishes between constative and

performative utterances, indicating that when a speaker engages in a performative utterance, the speaker is not simply delivering a proposition but is performing an act in the process of speaking. The classic example is the utterance 'I promise . . .' but other examples include commands and greetings. The usual greeting 'Hello' or 'Good evening' is about the only example in the news of an Austinian performative utterance – a statement in which the speaker accomplishes an act in producing the speech.[27] But it has been pointed out that this distinction breaks down on close scrutiny, since the production of any language involves the production of meaning, and meaning is not simply representational. As Halliday describes, every use of language is 'meaningful, contextualised and in the broadest sense social'.[28] We have therefore been describing news language as a form of social behaviour. But a significant proportion of the language of the news is the reporting of someone else's speech; so it is equally a form of social behaviour in a more restricted sense. It follows that although the language appears to be reporting facts, propositions and descriptions, the reworking of these elements into stories involves the creation of ambiguities, contradictions and meanings which may well be absent from some 'ideal' account. A question therefore arises concerning the forms of conventional journalism for handling other people's accounts. A corollary of this is whether the routine violence done to other's accounts occurs systematically along the plane of one ideological viewpoint rather than another. In short, does the transformation from speech to reported speech to news talk simply mediate or does it transform or mediate in a particular direction?

Traditionally there have been two ways of representing speech and they have been labelled direct and indirect. In writing, the former is signalled by quotation marks and is frequently preceded by a verb of saying. A comma or colon may also be used to mark the boundary. Indirect speech is a 'transformation' of direct speech according to grammatical rules which convert the present tense in direct speech to the past tense and which change possessive adjectives from the first and second person in direct speech to the third person in indirect speech. There are in fact other ways in which a writer can represent speech and thought – by using a 'stream of consciousness' technique or by omitting the introductory verb of saying, for example. 'She said' may be dropped in some forms of writing.

For the speaker, especially the television journalist, the problem of representation is rather more difficult since the verbal signal of 'commence quote – end quote' is so cumbersome. The alternative is to modulate voice tones and use pauses to mark the beginning and end of reported speech. There is also greater reliance in written-spoken news talk on the verb of saying than in the written word. In fact, this is a possible source of ambiguity because what is ostensibly the reproduction of meaning can become via transformation the production of new meaning.

In the four-month sample period, the written-spoken parts of the bulletins on BBC and ITN contained 16 per cent and 19 per cent reported speech (both direct and indirect) respectively. The rather higher proportion on ITN is to be expected in the light of that channel's smaller proportion of items with interviews which was noted in Chapter 4 of *Bad News*. For reported speech can be seen as a substitute for interviews. On both channels, however, reported speech occupies a significant proportion of the bulletins. Content analysis of this sample shows that the profile of people quoted has similar characteristics to the profile of the people interviewed: they are selected almost exclusively from high-ranking politicians, trade union officials and senior management. Our analysis of interviewee inputs in *Bad News* showed that in the industrial category (but not in the economic and business categories) there were more inter-viewees speaking for labour. Analysis of attributed speech in this sample shows that 26.5 per cent of quotations were from manage-ment and 31.5 per cent from labour. Formally there is the appearance of balance between these and other 'points of view', but many of the remaining 42 per cent of quotations were from government, judiciary and police sources, with a number from professional associations. Yet, as we noted in *Bad News*, quotations from labour are more likely to include extreme differences of opinion than are quotations from management; as for instance when, in a dispute story, anti-strike workers and officials are used. As with the pattern of interviewees, the lack of expert comment, the absence of unofficial labour spokesmen and the relative promi-nence of political figures is noteworthy. The evidence continues to support our claim that, despite the appearance of balance, the 'hierarchy of access' operates to exclude the systematic represen-tation and quotation of subordinate groups.

News items rarely begin with a quotation. Reported speech is located within a frame which embodies the dominant view of a story, so that reported statements are rarely used as 'facts' in themselves. The occasions on which this does happen are statements and speeches by those of very high status, including the Prime Minister. 'Mr Wilson has said in the Commons that . . .' is newsworthy in itself and may be the opening sentence of an item.[29] Conversely, significant absences are spokesmen for the poorly paid, low status, badly organised or relatively inarticulate groups such as the ambulancemen, the engine tuners and the Glasgow dustcart drivers. Quotations from hospital consultants and from National Graphical Association representatives in the Fleet Street dispute are relatively abundant. These regularities may be formulated as a rule: that the higher the status of the subject the less the mediation. This is not to deny that journalists mediate what is reported, even by those of high status. The editing of a speech for reporting directly or indirectly is a creative process; new sentences may be formed by cutting and new functions may be imported. The use made by television news of a speech by the then Prime Minister to establish the dominant view was described in the case study of the Cowley dispute included in *Bad News*. In the following extracts from two bulletins on the same channel in the same evening the use of what might be called 'free indirect speech' (i.e. the omission of a verb of saying) is part of the process of reduction which operates in favour of the dominant view. The key opening sentences of each item were: 'The Prime Minister in a major speech tonight on the economy appealed to management and unions in the car industry to cut down on what he called manifestly avoidable stoppages' (BBC1, 21.00, 3 January 1975); 'The Prime Minister has appealed to workers in the car industry to cut down on avoidable stoppages' (BBC1, 22.45, 3 January 1975). The obvious difference between the first extract and the second is the ideological reduction of 'management and unions' to 'workers' and the omission of 'what he called'. The verb of saying is one of the first casualties in the editing process in this instance, as one would expect from the inverse relationship between status and mediation. The higher level of mediation involved in using 'He said' may be carried to the opposite extreme of effectively degrading a statement, such as Leslie Huckfield's comment on Mr Wilson's car industry speech: '*He said* the Prime Minister clearly knew very little about the car industry. The real cause of the trouble was the chronic failure of management to invest, *he said*' (ITN, 22.00, 3 January 1975; our italics).

In terms of the constative/performative distinction, many quoted statements – 'threats', 'appeals', 'calls' – can be regarded as performative. The Prime Minister's appeal is one such. But in free indirect reported speech the distinction is frequently blurred as there is no reliable way to tell whose words are being spoken. Compare these two reports of the miners' pay claim which are equivalent in most respects: 'The miners are to use every clause and avenue within the Social Contract to win substantial pay rises, but they still haven't said how much they want' (BBC1, 21.00, 9 January 1975); and 'The mineworkers' leader, Mr Joe Gormley, has said his union will use every clause and avenue within the Social Contract to win substantial pay rises for Britain's 260,000 miners' (ITN, 22.00, 9 January 1975). In the first example the phrase 'every clause and avenue' is broadcast in a constative form; in the second it is clearly attributed as a quotation. The effects of this work in contrary directions: the indirect, unattributed quotation creates a more detached, neutral and factual impression while the attributed quotation gives an impression of immediacy, actuality and possibly directness. These stylistic features and the question of whether they represent consistent styles of presentation on each channel are less important than the fact that reported speech can be used in a variety of intentional or simply functional ways for impression management. Despite the apparent objectivity of 'quoting a point of view', journalists never succeed in removing their presence from the story. The evidence is overwhelming that, in the use of reported speech, the current forms, routines and conventions of television news work unwittingly or otherwise to produce a bias against the understanding of trade union and labour viewpoints.

8 News Talk: Vocabulary and Industrial Action

We also say of some people that they are transparent to us. It is, however, important as regards this observation that one human being can be a complete enigma to another. We learn this when we come into a strange country with entirely strange traditions; and, what is more, even given the mastery of a country's language. We do not *understand* the people. (And not because of not knowing what they are saying to themselves.) We cannot find our feet with them.

Ludwig Wittgenstein[1]

One of the ways in which we are able to identify a person's class, status or beliefs is through their vocabulary – the stock of words which they use to categorise the world. We instinctively recognise the vocabularies of political and cultural discourse used in different institutional settings. The range of words, phrases or descriptions applied to sets of activities are heavy carriers of social meaning. They provide the attuned hearer with ways of locating the preferred descriptions in relation to the larger belief systems of society. As C. Wright Mills observed: 'a vocabulary is not merely a string of words; immanent within it are societal textures – institutional and political co-ordinates.' And 'in studying vocabularies, we detect implicit evaluations and the collective patterns behind them, – "cues" for social behaviour. A thinker's social and political "rationale" is exhibited in his choice and use of words. Vocabularies socially canalise thought.'[2] This generalisation applies to all vocabularies, including the vocabulary of news. Even specialised vocabularies, including those of science and technology, embody ways of looking at the world and have value preferences and judgments built into them.

It may be claimed that the vocabulary of the news is not the outcome of deliberate choice by the news personnel from among a number of alternatives but merely reproduces the vocabulary of the wider society – in the case in hand, the currently available vocabulary of industrial relations. If this were true, there would be inconsistencies, ambiguities and instances of the same terms being applied in a number of different ways. However, our research reveals that this is not the case. For, as we shall show, there are significant absences in the vocabulary of industrial news reporting which, along with the vocabulary which is used, reveal selectivity and value preference for a particular view of the causes and nature of industrial conflict. It is not that this vocabulary is incomprehensible or even unacceptable. Rather, it is simply not what it claims to be. It is not impartial, it is not balanced and it is not merely telling people 'accurately and honestly about the most important things going on in the world'.[3] Nor is it that editorial values and editorial judgments have accidently intruded, for such intrusions would be random or variable.

In fact, the language of industrial reporting contains what C. Wright Mills called a 'vocabulary of motive', by which he meant linguistic behaviour which functions socially to co-ordinate and control systems of action. Motives in this phrase are the acceptable grounds for social action rather than private states within individuals. In this view, 'the research task is the locating of particular types of action within typal frames of normative actions and socially situated clusters of motive'.[4] Our analysis of the particular case of news vocabulary therefore involves a description of the lexical system not simply as a list of denotative and connotative terms, but as the verbalisation in a specific situation of a 'vocabulary of motive'.

As such, the problem of news vocabulary does not concern newsproducers' intentions but reflects a collective value system and choices – a 'strange tradition' of the kind Wittgenstein was referring to in the quotation at the head of this chapter. It centres on those conventions in use which, whether articulated or not, circumscribe and delineate the vocabulary. In our examination of the vocabulary of industrial disputes we shall show that it amounts to a preferred view of industrial disputes which corresponds all too easily with a particular (albeit sophisticated) version of managerial ideology.

The sample

The sample of words used here is the same four-month sample as used in our description of the textual characteristics of news items. We are mainly analysing one mode of news discourse: the written-spoken mode used by the newscaster whether spoken to camera or voiced over film or stills. Initially, this excludes both commentary by correspondents and reporters and interview situations (which are dealt with later). This element is the most concise and formal type of news discourse. It regularly takes up about one-third of the news bulletins. For this analysis we define a lexical item or unit of vocabulary to be either a single word or an idiom like 'industrial action' or 'work to rule'.

The sample size is designed to cover a wide range of industrial reporting and to allow for comparisons between channels. It consists of all industrial dispute, wage claim and wage settlement stories in the main evening bulletins, namely the *Nine O'Clock News* and *News at Ten* for the period 1 January–30 April 1975. A number of other areas of industrial and economic reporting are excluded – industrial accidents, conferences, lobbies and demonstrations (outside the scope of collective wage bargaining) do not appear in this sample. Reports of short-time working, layoffs and redundancies are not included unless they are involved as part of the collective bargaining process, neither are protests by producers against foreign competition (for example the fishermen's blockade and the textile workers' demonstrations). The initial newscaster sample consists of approximately 30,000 words. (The remainder, some 60,000 words, consists of reports and commentaries by broadcasting personnel and accompanying interviews.) The detailed study of the lexicon is based on a third, smaller sample covering the whole of one month's scripted news talk in the area defined above, a total of about 7,000 words (January 1975). The subjects dealt with in the sample are those classically focused upon by industrial reporting, typically those occasions on which 'normal' management and labour relationships break down. In Volume 1 of this study (*Bad News*), we showed how this area of coverage is thrown into sharp relief, so that, for example, reporting of strikes and disputes involving stoppages of work accounts for 20 per cent of the total number of industrial stories but 39 per cent of all industrial coverage by item.[5] Industrial disputes provide topics which in our view best test the application of the norms of impartiality and accuracy in a particularly sensitive area. The choice of bulletins (the main BBC and ITN bulletins) and the four-month span of the coverage in the second sample maximise the possible variations while keeping the data within manageable proportions.

The language used by the news to refer to industrial relations trades on a set of fairly familiar industrial terms and descriptions. For a description to be recognisable, as Sacks has argued, a hearer has to be familiar with the social categories referred to by it, and the cultural associations the category has.[6] In fact, a vast number of descriptions are available in this cultural domain although the siting of their meaning is not without ambiguity. Most terms and descriptions carry a plurality of meanings and therefore the consistent realisation of one set of meanings or connotations is often the result of the routinisation of cultural preferences and practices. For example: 'And now some industrial news' (ITN, 22.00, 21 March 1975) cuts down on the uncertainty of what sort of news is to follow. But only the routine use of the word 'industrial' to describe a very specific set of stories would allow culturally attuned viewers to predict with a high degree of certainty that they are likely to be getting stories about strikes, disputes and disruption. Indeed, industrial accident stories are unlikely to follow such an introduction for they are usually treated as a species of disaster story.[7] Descriptions such as 'industrial', 'economic' or 'business' could denote a multitude of story types. In television practice these categories are restricted by the conventions of use and these conventions work over time to prelocate their meanings. These predefined working conventions seem to orchestrate the particular and preferred meanings of the terms, such that any attentive viewer should be able to make the predictions given above. The categories are also enshrined in the division of labour among correspondents. In short, the conventions and practices of television journalism give specific meaning to general descriptions as a result of the cultural labour of journalists.

The choice of linguistic forms and the practices governing their usage can therefore be seen as a realisation of social meanings and categories. They are, however, realised within a broadcasting and news system which is monologic in character, highly stratified in structure and élitist in its recruitment. These factors combine to produce a vocabulary for industrial news stories which has a bias towards a particular understanding.

News talk has special linguistic and social features which define it as a form of communication. One reason why it should be important for us to reveal some of the rules of news talk is to assess these rules against a notion of 'normal' talk or more 'authentic' talk, to use Blum's term.[8] In the phrase 'the strikers are demanding a pay rise of £10 a week' the strikers are alien to mankind in general – strikers are not you or me, they are somebody else. Thus when it is our strike, we are cut out of the message. It follows from this division, which is a regular feature of industrial news, that the royal, all-inclusive *we* or *us* will be minimised. Other news may stress a notion of communal interest such as the *nation*. In general we would expect less use of first person plurals in industrial news talk than other areas of coverage. Where first person plurals are used or implied they will appeal to commonsense understandings and problems 'about which we would all agree' – for example, 'the cost of just one day's layoff was 1,200 cars worth $1\frac{3}{4}$ million pounds'.[9] 'The cost' is not specified as a cost to anyone in particular. The implication is that it is a cost to *us*, to the community, to Britain. But here the cost is in fact an estimated cost to the firm. Costs to the workers are not counted, neither are market conditions.

Where there is an appeal to communality of interests, such appeals can often be revealed as partisan. As often as not they are concerned with 'production' and this production or accumulation remains sacrosanct. Social relationships are normally treated as matters of secondary importance. Indeed, while almost any breakdown in production is possible in industrial news, changes which do not affect production are unlikely to receive coverage.

The social organisation of values in our present society as interpreted by the broadcasters requires that problems of the social organisation of production take precedence over all other social problems. For example, in the period of our study the report of the Flixborough plant explosion was run mainly as a disaster aftermath story and not as a social issue. The story was presented in terms of the accident and interrupted production. Even the cost to lives was played down. The historical antecedents which raised larger questions were buried or by-passed.

Thus the problems of capital accumulation are presented in such a manner as to assume that they are everybody's problems, while the problems of the workforce are presented as 'failure' – failure to communicate, to resolve, to understand, to wait, or as moral failure by a greedy minority. For capitalism, success is constant and expanding production and all else is failure. So much so that it can even, on occasion, make a strike look a good thing. Reporting on the April 1975 trade figures, Dominic Harrod said:

> I think tomorrow's trade figures will come as a bit of a dis-appointment after the figures published a month ago for March because those figures, because of a dock strike in London which held up more imports than exports going out of the country, were exceptionally good. In fact for the first time in about three years we had a plus in the total balance of payments for the month of March. (BBC2, 23.05, 13 May 1975)

These examples begin to show the directions which a study of 'authenticity' in news talk might take. Sacks's work on conver-sational data already sensitises us to the fact that the social organisation of talk is law-like – and that such laws are, as Wittgenstein would say, part of a form of life. It is clear of course that the discovery of these laws and the purposes and presup-positions of industrial news talk will depend on a close analysis of the output. Our analysis not only demonstrates a restricted vocabulary but will show that, of the very wide range of possible descriptions which could be generated by this vocabulary, only a limited number are consistently presented.

The analysis of language and the analysis of social phenomena converge on the same material. Language analysis must, however, go beyond the simple correlation of linguistic forms with social features. Sociolinguistics has encountered numerous problems arising from the oversimplified notions of language and society which this implies. Instead, linguistic forms must themselves be subjected to close analysis of their construction at the social as well as the grammatical and semantic levels. Here, of course, defined knowledge of the lexical system is a prerequisite for proper work. Speakers' choices cannot be evaluated without an understanding of the range of terms available and how their meanings are presented and actualised by the conventions in use.

Meaning in this view is not purely referential or semantic. Usually it is defined in terms of the relations between linguistic signs, objects or configurations which are non-linguistic and the response which these provoke in a hearer. We would maintain that a sign can only rarely be tied unambiguously to a referent and that a lexico-graphical approach involving the collection of a number of representative contexts in which a word appears does not exhaust its meaning. This meaning can neither be equated with the 'thing' denoted nor with its range of uses in a variety of contexts. The organisation and use of a given vocabulary or linguistic field forms a *Gestalt* which in itself expresses the structure of social relationships. It was one of the earlier insights of scholars of language, including de Saussure and Sapir, that the vocabularies of different languages may divide up particular fields of description in different ways; that semantic distinctions are made in one language which are not made in another.[10] Although comparative work of this kind is beyond our present study, we know that language can be used in more than one way to impose order on the complex subject-matter of industrial relations. Having shown that news language is highly limited, convention-bound, restricted and formal we will demonstrate the manner in which a preferred sense and order are 'constructed' in the sphere of industrial news.

The lexical system: components of industrial action

The description of vocabulary is bound to take account of the frequency with which words are used. However, a narrowly statistical approach would only show the triviality of many of the differences. 'The' is usually the most frequent word in the written-spoken material but its use will rarely yield important clues to style and meaning; neither will uncontextualised statistics of more significant items. In the present sample of news language the context is clearly and unambiguously defined, yet even here differences of frequency are often quite predictable. News stories about a rail strike will include items such as train, railwaymen, station and commuters, simply because news items centrally refer to the subject being reported. Our study therefore makes a selection from the widest possible range of lexical items on the grounds (embedded in news ideology and practice) that people are central to the ordering of industrial affairs and that certain groups of people are clearly definable; that action takes place according to predictable patterns characterised by the people who act; and that explanatory concepts are called into play only when the complexity of the description demands it. Consider the following brief report – some lexical items are more significant than others for our present purposes:

Signalmen are expected to go on strike for twenty-four hours on

Thursday in their pay dispute with British Rail. Disruption is likely to affect the biggest area since the signalmen first started their stoppages three months ago. The main areas likely to be hit include Manchester, Liverpool, Stoke, Crewe, Stafford, Doncaster and Cambridge. The National Union of Railwaymen's executive meet tomorrow to consider British Rail's offer of £3 a week. (ITN, 22.00, 10 February 1975)

According to the above criteria the most significant words are those which refer to the people and organisations involved (signalmen, British Rail, NUR executive) together with any modifiers, if present, and terms which refer to types of action (strike, dispute, stoppage, offer) and their associations (disruption). Other categories (locations, time, etc.) have an important function in the item to the extent that they construct the events described within a temporal and geographical frame. But they do not explain social relationships and to this extent they have a subordinate role in the construction of social reality in the news – a fact reflected in their placing in the text. Consistent with the false and received notion that news mediates reality with the minimum possible intervention, the use of explanatory devices is limited, indeed absent from the above example. But this absence itself is significant. As we will show, the consistent lack of qualification – even the use of 'pay' to qualify 'dispute' is uncommon – can only leave room for the kind of interpretation that suggests that industrial action is unnecessary, non-rational activity, or for the factually incorrect assumption that disputes are always about pay.

Of the industrial relations news read by newsreaders in the course of the smaller sample there were 40 items on BBC and 46 items on ITN. The majority of the 20 stories in this sample were covered on both channels but 3 were exclusive to BBC and 4 were exclusive to ITN. This does not mean that these 'exclusive' stories were never covered by the other channel; only that the stories did not appear in the main evening bulletins. The presence of exclusive stories is of course likely to entail greater linguistic variety than if the range of topics were identical. But the stories appearing on only one channel, such as the farm workers' pay settlement (ITN) and the dispute involving electricians in Glasgow (BBC), were almost invariably single reports. The main areas of reporting in January were the National Health Service (including consultants, junior hospital doctors, general practitioners and dentists as well as the paramedical professions); the dispute between British Leyland and engine tuners at Cowley; two disputes in Fleet Street; strikes by dustcart drivers and ambulance officers; and wage negotiations involving miners, building workers and teachers. The range of stories included the full cycle of collective bargaining from claims through disputes to settlements and the full range of occupations from unskilled manual workers to the professions.

The close similarities of category content profile on all channels reported in Volume 1 of this study led us to expect further similarities of language between channels. The number of words transmitted in the January sample by ITN was slightly more than for BBC: 3,630 compared with 3,460.[11] This can be accounted for by the larger number of items on ITN. The average speech rate on each channel is about three words per second. From the average for the month of January it appears that ITN regularly has a smaller number of words per item (an average of 79 compared with BBC's 86). In view of ITN's greater propensity to 'package' items this implies that complex industrial stories and packages are introduced more briefly and crisply than on BBC, although industrial news items as a whole tend to be longer. This is consistent with other stylistic features noted in Chapter 4 of *Bad News*. However, the differences are not big enough to allow great linguistic variety between channels.

In fact the vocabulary is limited in the ways that would be anticipated from the structural properties discussed above. The clear finding emerges that the vocabulary is a tightly closed system in the sense that in practice it constitutes a peculiar and restricted use of even its own limited range of words which does not convey the openendedness of the actual situation to which it refers. Of course there is a constant inflow of 'new' words, but these are nearly all context-specific. However, there is a basic core of categories and concepts which are not context-bound, which *constantly* recur and which guarantee the system's closure. Even longer items do not necessarily alter this picture. They contain more information, more names and words but they do not modify the key concepts and key words. Our definition of 'keying' here follows Goffman. We 'refer here to the set of conventions by which a given activity, one already meaningful in terms of some primary framework, is transformed into something patterned on this activity but seen by the participants to be something quite else.'[12] Indeed our argument would be that, although the key terms of the industrial vocabulary are comprehensible in terms of the primary framework of any English-language culture, their manner of orchestration and restricted usage creates a situation where many workers would not recognise the accounts of their own disputes as in any way adequate.

Although it is hazardous to define vocabulary size since the criteria for what constitutes a 'word' may be refined to a greater or a lesser degree, there are certain general features of the stock of lexical items used in the industrial news which can be stated without encountering these difficulties. The figures used below are approximations to the nearest 5 per cent as greater precision would be fruitless with a sample of this size. The 7,000 lexical items in the sample (names, titles and numerals are included in this count) are drawn from a range of just over 1,000 discrete items. As we have shown in Chapter 6, this is a highly restricted use of the vocabulary involving little use of most words and frequent use of a few ideologically key words.

The Type-Token Ratio (the relation between the total number of items in a text and the number of separate items from which this total is made up), which is one clear measure of linguistic diversity, is therefore 0.14. As would be expected of a formal, even stereotyped, mode of discourse, this is low compared with the TTR measured for several other varieties of discourse. The Type-Token Ratio is a measure of diversification which[13]

is the ratio of the number of different words (types) to the total number of words (tokens) in the passage. In the count of newspaper English, for example, there were 44,000 tokens and 6,000 types, and so the TTR is 6/44 or 0.136. One difficulty with the type-token ratio is that it gets smaller as the size of the sample gets bigger. If the passage contains only one word, this one word is one type and one token and so the TTR must equal 1.00. If the passage consists of two word tokens, these two tokens will probably be different types. We must take a passage of about 10 tokens before one type occurs more than once. As the length of the passage is increased it becomes more likely that words will be repeated and less likely that new, unused words will occur.

If we compare the size of our sample with the number of tokens in the newspaper sample, it is clear that for a sample of 7,000 words, the TTR for newspapers' English would be considerably higher. That is, according to this rather rudimentary measure of diversification, television news is a highly restricted form compared with another major branch of journalism.

Restrictedness need not necessarily make for greater clarity of expression or understanding of news messages. In fact we will show that it tends towards obscurity. It might be argued that use of a constant basic vocabulary which avoids specialised terms is a requirement imposed by the mass audience. But according to the rule-of-thumb known as the Clarity Index, industrial news on television is not particularly clear.[14] The Clarity Index, like the Type-Token Ratio, is an arbitrary measure useful only for comparisons. It is based on the assumption that longer sentences and words are generally more difficult to read and understand than shorter sentences and words. It is calculated by adding the average number of words per sentence to the percentage of words with more than two syllables. Thus the higher the index number the more 'complex' the text. The tabloid newspapers write to an index number of about 30, which is assumed to be within the reading skills of the average sixteen-year-old school leaver. As one would expect, the number for *The Times* is considerably higher, in the order of 50 or more. The Clarity Index for the sample of industrial reporting both on BBC and ITN varies between 35 and 40. It is therefore unlikely that the restrictedness of the vocabulary can be explained simply as a result of deliberate efforts to achieve clarity and reduce complexity. But these measures are at best only rough indicators. Other measures can show the way in which the vocabulary is restricted in its application as well as in its range.

One perhaps more familiar method of assessing the vocabulary is to analyse the distribution of the well-known elements of the text such as nouns, verbs or prepositions.

Nouns in use: industrial action

In our sample the 'structural' words – adverbs, articles, auxiliary verbs, conjunctions, prepositions and pronouns – accounted for about 15 per cent of the basic stock of 7,000 words. Semantically speaking, we would expect these to have little importance; they modify and relate and tend not to carry the central meaning of the text. For instance, in the following sentence the structural words can be omitted without total loss of meaning: 'The engine tuners on strike at British Leyland's plant at Cowley, Oxford, are seeking official union backing' (BBC1, 22.00, 11 January 1975). In fact newspaper headlines consistently omit such words. If this were to happen in ordinary news talk we would get the following string of words which still carries meaning but with less precision and more ambiguity – rather like a telegram: '—— engine tuners —— strike —— British Leyland's plant —— Cowley, Oxford —— seeking official union backing'. In short, the 'structural' words are not the heaviest carriers of denotative or connotative meaning.

Names, placenames and titles account for, on average, another 10 per cent of the stock of words. Obviously the more very long items there are the lower this proportion tends to be. Names, placenames and titles situate and concretely designate events, people and actions. From many points of view this may be the least important part of a news message. After all, cause and consequence rather than where are the key elements to be examined when analysing the neutrality of reporting, for cause and consequence, involving who and what, depend upon explanations. A Swedish study has revealed that most viewers' recall of news items is such that where recall occurs it concerns place more than persons or things involved and these more than causes and consequences.[15] The point is made in this study that broadcasters are perhaps paying too little attention to this 'unbalanced recall' factor. However, it is upon the crucial explanatory elements of the text that we have decided to concentrate. Excluding the structural words, names, placenames and titles which together involve 25 per cent of the stock of words, the remaining 75 per cent includes both words which are exclusive to one channel and words which are used in common. There are about 1,750 words which are used on both channels. They can be said to constitute the basic fund of categories which are used by both newsrooms to organise the reporting of industrial relations. This basic vocabulary is structured consistently around a few key terms. Many linguists are agreed that nouns and their modifiers are particularly significant. Recent research has argued that in terms of opening up the range of linguistic options the role of nouns is central. For instance, Hawkins demonstrates that 'in system-structure terms, the category *noun* is the entry condition to a greater number of systems than the category *pronoun*'.[16] Noun and pronoun usage has in fact proved to be a good predictor of class differences – the middle class using a greater variety of nouns and showing a relatively greater flexibility of linguistic choice than the working class.

The group of nouns which refer to the 'industrial action' domain provides the central element of the coding of the remainder of the coverage. Unfortunately the processes of collective bargaining are rarely deemed newsworthy in their own right. At present for an item to be newsworthy industrial action must be 'threatened', occurring or have recently ended.

Our research reveals that the noun group consists of half a dozen 'key words' used with great frequency. In the one-month sample period the six terms most commonly used to denote industrial action were, in order of frequency: strike; action (usually qualified by the word 'industrial' or 'disruptive'); dispute; disruption; work to contract and stoppage.

Theoretically this list could be arranged other than by frequency. For instance, in Standard English usage 'dispute' need not necessarily imply any form of 'action'. In fact in news talk it is applied almost exclusively to situations in which action is promised or ensuing. So although this vocabulary could in theory have a variety of associations and connotations, in practice this is not so. Moving from the general to the specific in news talk the following order seems to hold: dispute, action, stoppage, strike and work to contract. Although 'disruption' is one of the key words in this list, it would have to come at the end since in this month it was applied exclusively to the dispute of the members of the National Graphical Association with their employers, the Newspaper Publishers Association, which was described in the bulletin as a 'campaign' of 'disruptive practices'.

If these nouns were not key ideological terms but were merely neutral dictionary definitions, then theoretically they could be applied to a range of groups involved in a dispute – unions, management, men, women, workers, etc. In practice, both the terms which are clearly specific to action by labour (strike, work to contract) and those which could theoretically embrace all groups (dispute, disruption) are applied solely to labour. Therefore it should be clear that, far from being neutral descriptions, industrial stories are constructed in practice so that the labels and imagery constantly imply causal action by labour rather than any of the other elements involved. Consider the following examples:

'Dustcart drivers start another pay strike. The dustmen's strike follows another last autumn' (BBC1, 21.00, 13 January 1975).

'In Scotland, where ambulance control officers have begun their strike, Glasgow and the heavily populated Central Belt have been worst affected' (BBC1, 21.00, 13 January 1975).

Even when the range of groups and organisations involved is mentioned the causal denotation is made in the same way:

'In an attempt to resolve the Cowley engine tuners' dispute, British Leyland and the Amalgamated Union of Engineering Workers will tomorrow meet the government's Advisory, Conciliation and Arbitration Service' (BBC1, 21.00, 22 January 1975).

'In the Cowley engine tuners' strike, the unions and British Leyland have agreed tonight that there should be an independent enquiry into the dispute' (ITN, 22.00, 27 January 1975).

The ideological reduction involved in designating a story in terms of a single protagonist when the activity by nature involves at minimum two groups systematically structures the reporting. It diverts the audience's attention from the causes and the material circumstances of the dispute and implies that the breakdown in social relationships is the responsibility of labour. The effect of this is to shift the balance of the story away from the actions and role of the employer (firm, corporation, government) and to minimise circumstantial and causal detail. Thus the labour force is often painted in a manner which gives it the appearance of being a group of people with apparently suspect motives precipitating unnecessary action against organisations whose legitimacy is taken for granted.

These points are not unimportant in terms of the likely effect of such messages on the audience. It is not simply that they routinely reinforce a predominantly managerial view of cause. We know from retention studies that audiences find it easier to recall the where, who and what of an event and have greater difficulty in recalling causes and consequences.[17] British television news is produced in such a manner that the who, where and what of an industrial story are usually given primacy (as are consequences), while the causes – if mentioned at all – are visually ascribed to labour or merely implied by the nature of the language. Lord Annan's Committee reporting on *The Future of Broadcasting* noted that television news coverage of industrial affairs was 'inadequate and unsatisfactory', precisely because of this kind of significant absence.[18]

> The causes why people come out on strike are often extraordinarily complex. No reporter does his job adequately if he interviews only the leading shop steward or union official. The fact that a strike is not backed by the union does not exonerate broadcasters from discovering why the workforce is out.

In short, the structure of news talk often serves to obscure managerial responsibility for the antagonisms in social relationship which at times explode into the disputes reported.

In order to give greater depth to this analysis of nouns and categories we extended the sample to cover the whole four-month period, January–April 1975. We discovered that the general pattern remained unchanged although the number of new words obviously increased with the length of the sample. Table 8.1 shows the frequency by channel of the nouns denoting 'industrial action'. The terms already mentioned remained the most prominent, with similar frequencies on both channels. Despite the larger total of items in the ITN sample, the BBC had slightly more 'exclusive' words, i.e. words which were not used by the other channel in the same period. The number of these items was rather small but it tends to negate the idea that the vocabulary of the commercial company is more emotive or sensational than that of BBC. If anything, the BBC's use of 'row' and 'clash' suggests the opposite. More important, however, was the very high degree of overlap between the categorisation devices on both channels over an extended period.

For example, the term 'disruption' was used with identical frequency by BBC and ITN during the four months. Occasionally the novelty of a particular dispute and the action taken led to slight divergence. This happened in the case of the hospital consultants' action in reducing their hours to those stipulated in their contracts. Assuming that this followed the precedent of 'working to rule' set in other industries, ITN initially used this phrase. BBC, perhaps taking note of the consultants' rather peculiar insistence that they were not taking 'industrial action', adopted the phrase 'work to contract' from the start. This usage was eventually taken up by ITN as well, 'work to rule' being reserved for railway workshop supervisors and other non-professional groups. Thus, the

Table 8.1 Frequency of terms denoting industrial action: main evening news bulletins, January–April 1975

	BBC1	ITN	Total	Percentage of total
Strike	103	138	241	45
Dispute	39	52	91	17
(Industrial) action	29	43	72	13
(Strike) action	4	—	4	1
(Disruptive) action	1	1	2	*
Disruption	15	15	30	6
Stoppage	9	12	21	4
Work to contract	14	5	19	4
Work to rule	5	13	18	3
Campaign	5	1	6	1
Overtime ban	2	4	6	1
Protest	3	3	6	1
Occupation	2	1	3	1
Walkout	1	1	2	*
Sit-in	5	—	5	1
Sanctions	2	—	2	*
Row	2	—	2	*
Tactics	1	—	1	*
Boycott	1	—	1	*
Clash	1	—	1	*
Withdrawal of labour	—	1	1	*
Practices	—	1	1	*
Demonstration	—	1	1	*
	244	292	536	100

* Denotes <0.5 per cent

consultants' dispute, which had all the marks of industrial action taken against an employer, was labelled in such a way as to set it apart from corresponding types of action in other spheres.

This list of noun usage in television news talk revealed that the category 'strike', as we would expect, was by far the most important in terms of frequency, and unfortunately, as we have shown, in defining the organisation of industrial stories. 'Action', 'dispute' and 'stoppage' were used in a very similar way to 'strike'. The exception was the word 'disruption', which is clearly not in the same lexical class since in conventional usage it contains the meaning of forceful separation or breaking apart. It carries more connotations and is not a simple denotative term.

'Dispute' is the one other important term which does not denote, by definition, a practice limited to industrial situations. Normally it implies disagreement or controversy. The word 'disruption' could of course be applied to the rupture of the normal relationships between employers and employees in dispute but this in practice does not happen. The list includes 'disruption' because it is regularly applied in the same way as any other term to describe industrial action. In news talk the way in which the term 'disruption' is used to describe employer-employee relationships seems to entail the preferred view that a break-up is caused by organised labour. For disruption is ascribed – implicitly or explicitly – solely to workers and unions. To return to a procedure previously used, the simple process of substituting terms confirms that there is an equivalence of meaning between 'strike', 'disruption' and 'stoppage' in the language of industrial news talk. Consider this news item:

> Signalmen are expected to go on strike for twenty-four hours on Thursday in their pay dispute with British Rail. Disruption is likely to affect the biggest area since the signalmen first started their stoppages three months ago. The main areas likely to be hit include Manchester, Liverpool, Stoke, Crewe, Stafford, Doncaster and Cambridge. The National Union of Railwaymen's executive meet tomorrow to consider British Rail's offer of £3 a week. (ITN, 22.00, 10 February 1975)

Here, each of the terms used in the first two sentences could replace any other without significantly altering the nature of the report. This example illustrates well the problems of neutrally reporting a story under the current limitations of time and space.

This story contains a sequence of actions with at least three elements: the bargaining process with its demands and offers; the decision to stop work for one day (the strike); and the consequences of this action for rail users (disruption of the usual service). Part of the first element occurs at the end of the item in a sentence about the union executive meeting to consider British Rail's offer. But the background and sequential ordering which would make the event intelligible are telescoped so that effectively the semantic content is reduced to a neat ideological formula which runs as follows:

> Signalmen's action: – causes stoppage = strike = disruption.

A normal professional defence of this kind of report is that the importance of the story turns upon the 'consumer' angle, since the number of people who may be affected is far greater than the number of people likely to be involved in the strike. While this defence might be a case for ordering the sequence in such a way as to give the consequences of the strike priority (although we noted the dubiousness of this earlier), it provides no grounds whatsoever for equating concepts or categories in the above fashion.

In some stories, the *causes* rather than the consequences of the strike may be emphasised. This is very rare, however, and only occurred in two stories during the four-month sample period – the London bus strike and demonstration following the death of a conductor in an assault, and the strike by workers of Avon County Council.[19] Such special treatment tends to square the ideological circle which we have noted in the news coding that strikes are normally about pay. The strike by busmen is an instance which so obviously contradicts this assumption that its cause had to be elaborated. In general, however, industrial action and the breakdown of 'normal' relationships in industry are not seen as needing causal elaboration. The concentration normally tends to be on the consequence, effects and inconvenience of any dispute. Cultural rules and coding are breakable if broadcasters are prepared to challenge the prevailing assumptions and dig deep. The second clear departure from the norm of implicit causes occurred in the reporting of a strike by Avon County Council workers. It provides the exceptional case which 'proves the rule'. Although it was clearly a strike story it was given a special place in the structure of the bulletin as a final, human interest item. This in itself is highly untypical and alerts attention to other features, including the attribution of cause and the use of metaphor. The item, which included a filmed report of a picket, was introduced by the newscaster as follows:

> Finally, a computer in Bristol has gone off the rails and has caused hundreds of people to go on strike. It belongs to Avon County Council and works out wages for council employees. Recently it has been giving thousands of pounds too much into some pay packets and in others nothing at all. (ITN, 22.00, 3 February 1975)

It is noteworthy that even in this example the cause is assigned to the computer itself rather than, as could easily have been done, to the responsible and accountable authorities. Thus it is written within the referential framework of autonomous technology getting out of hand or 'going off the rails'. This treatment of the story in human interest terms provides not so much a counter-example as confirmation of our general conclusion that the language of industrial reporting as structured at present cannot cope with multicausality and, whether by ignorance or default, almost invariably lays responsibility at labour's door.

The interchangeability of the terms 'strike' and 'disruption' is less likely if the news item is long rather than short. In longer items explanations, however culturally unbalanced, are more likely to be spelt out. The causal relationship is made clear in the following sentence from a longer item: 'another unofficial twenty-four-hour strike by signalmen tomorrow will cause widespread disruption to commuter and inter-city services' (ITN, 22.00, 19 February 1975). The frequent, close association of two essentially different terms, even if it does not always amount to the equivalence noted above, can only tend towards ideological glossing or obscurity. The use of 'disruption' is not limited to the suspension or breakdown of services. It is also applied to the production process. Thus Mr Harold Wilson's January speech which referred to car manufacturing was later reported to be 'a warning about avoidable disruption in the car industry' (ITN, 22.00, 6 January 1975) and 'disruption today cost the *Daily Telegraph* and the *Sun* 360,000 and 170,000 copies respectively' (ITN, 22.00, 15 January 1975). The BBC's usage is almost identical – 'last night the group lost 1½ million copies of the *Daily Mirror* because of disruption by members of the union SOGAT' (BBC1, 21.00, 25 March 1975). Although there may be some variation in the ways in which these statements are understood by different social groups and classes the linguistic evidence strongly suggests that they have to be heard or read in terms of a single preferred conceptual category: strike disruption caused by labour.

Nouns in use: collective bargaining

The group of nouns which refers to the collective bargaining domain shares certain structural properties with the 'industrial action' list. There are fewer key words and a larger number of words which occur much less frequently – many of which were 'exclusive' to one channel during the sample period. As in Table 8.1, there are more of these 'exclusives' on BBC than on ITN, suggesting that the BBC uses a slightly larger though structurally similar vocabulary to that of ITN. In some cases the differences can be accounted for in one channel's use of the nominal form and the other's preference for the corresponding verb. ITN, for example, used the form 'to give a warning' on several occasions when BBC used the verb 'to warn'. However, the way in which some of the most frequent items are applied is more important.

Not surprisingly, the most frequently occurring nouns are 'talks', 'meeting' and 'mass meeting'. These are the events around which the shifting social relationships between employers and employees are structured.[20] Unfortunately they are merely the devices which allow other, more newsworthy, statements to be made about the protagonists. Since the mythology of industrial relations in capitalist society is that of the market place, it might be expected that the language of 'free' collective bargaining would embody the idea of equal exchange. In reality this is far from the case, the unequal exchange between labour and capital is heavily one-sided; and involves the language of rights and coercion rather than the language of free exchange. The most commonly occurring words are 'claim', 'threat', 'offer', 'proposal', 'appeal' and 'demand' and they are used with about the same frequency on each channel. Although our discussion is restricted to the use of the noun forms, each term is also used in the verb form and a list of these would have a similar pattern of distribution. The list which is drawn from the January sample may be arranged as follows, showing how the terms are applied in practice to organised labour, to management or to both (Table 8.2). It illustrates the fundamental lack of reciprocity in a vocabulary in which the terms could apply reciprocally to both labour and management.

Table 8.2   Frequency of terms denoting collective bargaining: BBC1 and ITN main evening bulletins, January 1975

		Appeal	Claim	Demand	Offer	Proposal	Threat
As	Labour	2	16	6	—	3	3
applied to	Management	2	—	—	6	5	6

The language of the news is inhibited from using forms like 'labour offer to work harder' or 'management demand higher output', which are perfectly possible. A. J. Liebling, the American journalist and critic of the press, made a similar observation about the press reporting of strikes:

> The employer, in strike stories, always 'offers', and the union 'demands'. A publisher, for example, never 'demands' that the union men agree to work for a four-bit raise; the union never 'offers' to accept more.

Liebling also points out that 'demand' in English is an arrogant word; 'offer', a large, generous one.[21]

The language thus conforms to a logic which is not simply a reflection of the reported events or relationships *per se* but one which pertains to a more general cultural 'code'. The absurdity of applying concepts like 'offer' and 'demand' to the 'wrong' side shows how this code works to legitimate the side which responds and makes concessions rather than the side which makes requests as though of right. The state has somewhat altered the appearance of the 'bargain' by introducing the limits of the Social Contract, but the vocabulary is still serviceable within these limits.

The vocabulary of conflict resolution is small compared with the vocabulary of industrial action and the bargaining process. It is simply an extension of the latter, with the expected terms 'award', 'agreement' and 'settlement' occurring most frequently. The small number of news stories in this category does not provide a good basis for generalisation but the group of words contains the same ambiguity which is found in the other two groups. There is a set of terms which can refer to a bargain struck in a free market situation (agreement, settlement, deal) and another set which implies a different relationship – that of contest, winning 'concessions', getting 'awards'. Like many items in the 'industrial action' vocabulary, this second group is only applied to labour. The use of imagery as such is very limited and circumscribed. The image which does occur with some regularity is that of competition, with overtones of warlike hostilities. Industry is conceived as two 'sides' engaged in a 'conflict' in which labour may win something from management. The progress of the 'fight' is portrayed in war terms – 'tactics', 'truce', 'peace move'. The persistence of these images (which are of course used by the protagonists themselves as well as by newsmen) is significant because they oversimplify generally complex relationships which involve not just two but three or more 'sides'.[22] There is an example of this reduction in the following report of British Leyland's decision to reopen the Cowley works in the hope that the strike by engine tuners would be called off:

> The decision follows talks between *men and management and union officials*. Afterwards, the union agreed to recommend the 250 engine tuners, whose strike led to the shutdown, to go back to work and await further talks. Leyland management are optimistic that the strike will be called off. *Neither side* would say tonight whether there had been any political pressure for a quick settlement after Mr Wilson's warning. (ITN, 22.00, 6 January 1975; our italics)

Here a trinity is reduced to the normal ideological duo. The absence of alternative images of industrial life in its normal aspect (including the routine workings of collective bargaining) contributes further to the lack of causal and functional concepts in the vocabulary of industrial news.

These deficiencies, absences and distortions may best be illustrated via a diagrammatic representation of the conceptual organisation of industrial news (Figure 8.1). The 'tree' or diagram is made up of the most frequently occurring terms in the bargaining, breakdown and resolution stages of the industrial relations process. It is arranged vertically since it represents a temporal as well as a logical sequence. The categories allow only the most simple distinctions to be made. The noun vocabulary does not provide a balanced set of descriptions of the so-called 'free collective bargaining' approach to industrial relations. If such a pluralistic approach were to operate there are a number of key terms which are absent which would have to be present. For example, labour would offer and make concessions and management would make claims and demands. Even less do they allow room for the expression of fundamental differences of values based on class opposition. The language implies a unitary frame of reference skewed towards management, who exercise control as of 'right'. The dominant value assumptions which are entailed by this view limit and qualify the use of causal and interpretative concepts (e.g. concepts which would explain behaviour in terms of 'class' or 'radical opposition' instead of 'militant', with its ambiguous, aggressive connotations). This deficiency is all the more serious because recent work by Moorhouse on political consciousness and beliefs about class in Britain reveals that in fact the mass perception of the class system is

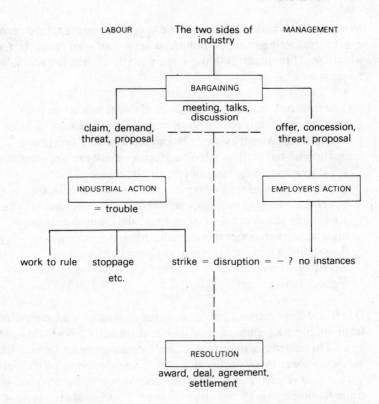

Figure 8.1   The conceptual organisation of industrial news

dichotomous.[23] It is very close to the 'us' versus 'them' view. When asked in a political context whether there is 'class struggle' in Britain most people seem to believe that there is. Gallup showed that in May 1974, 60 per cent of the respondents believed that there was class struggle, while 62 per cent of the *Daily Telegraph* poll in the same year also believed that there was a class struggle.[24] But as the language of news reporting clearly reveals, this does not appear on our screens. It is lost in the process of mediation.

From the point of view of information theory the usage of the noun vocabulary has a high degree of predictability and redundancy. In short, what is present in the vocabulary is used in a constrained fashion, while the significant absences which we have highlighted above mean that industrial news noun vocabulary presents the viewer with a seriously deficient 'vocabulary of motive'. As Hyman and Brough have suggested, this deficiency may exert a real influence upon industrial behaviour – an influence for which the broadcasters are at least partly if not intentionally responsible.[25]

> The manifest absence of socially available justifications for uncompromisingly oppositional behaviour by workers – which would be dismissed as 'sheer bloody-mindedness' and hence irrational – is clearly an inhibiting factor against uncompromising resistance to managerial priorities in the course of the negotiation of order at workplace level. And similarly, the general modesty of wage aspirations is in part attributable to the absence of any vocabulary of motives which would provide a manual worker, for example, with a plausible rationale for demanding a level of income or the associated material advantages conventionally regarded as the prerogative of higher-status groups.

Of critical importance here, as our study reveals, is the dearth of terms on the management 'side' to denote the activities which might be said to constitute 'industrial action' by management. Terms such as 'lockout' are theoretically available. Even the use of 'strike' and 'go slow' in referring to underinvestment is now not uncommon in trade union circles. These, however, were never used in the sample period.[26]

Moreover, as far as television news is concerned, industrial 'trouble' is basically trouble with (labour) strikes and not the difficulties arising from mismanagement or the economic situation as a whole: 'British Leyland's Austin Morris plant at Cowley in Oxford has shut down for the weekend because of industrial trouble' (ITN, 22.00, 4 January 1975); 'Disruption looks like continuing in the national newspapers . . . the trouble is over pay differentials' (BBC1, 21.00, 17 January 1975); 'The industrial troubles that have been affecting Fleet Street papers are temporarily suspended in the dispute which cost the *Daily Mirror* group more than £1 million since Wednesday' (ITN, 22.00, 20 January 1975).

The idea of industry as 'troubled' can only be understood within the value consensus framework. Trouble must mean trouble for someone and in this case it is the 'industry' (the 'two sides' are temporarily forgotten). It is those not on strike or in dispute, who are troubled. There is no equivalent expression for the 'trouble' of those in the subordinate situation. The long-term effect of such underlying values is to continually reinforce a managerially skewed view of industrial relations. The causes ascribed or inferred are rarely given in a balanced manner, so that the workers involved in any dispute can come to be regarded by many viewers as essentially the trouble-makers.

Conclusion

The language of news is highly organised and structured in a number of ways which we have attempted to describe. Some of this description has a commonsense ring about it but the formality and predictability of news talk is something which can be accounted for only in part by the professionals' own understanding of their activities. Many organised features of news talk which appear to be natural or inevitable cannot be neatly described as a system of journalists' lore or rules-of-thumb. However, unspoken assumptions, practices and perspectives are no less important than those which are made explicit, for they help constitute the 'primary framework', in Goffman's phrase, which renders the newstalk meaningful. Industrial relations news relies heavily on a few key ideological propositions which inform everything which falls into the industrial category. They include the identification and labelling of industrial disputes in terms of labour, the attribution of cause to labour and the routine reduction of workers' aspirations to cash 'demands'.

The reporting of industrial news in its encoding effectively conceals the primary assumptions beneath apparent neutrality and naturalistic presentation. We examined the lexical code and found it to be statistically highly predictable over an extended period of time not because of an inherent lack of descriptive terms, but because certain key terms were consistently preferred. In a similar way, we found that industrial news items were structured (by headlines, boundary markers and the use of reported speech) to close off the possibility of multicausality in industrial disputes. Also, there were indications that headlines referring to industrial and other topics were run according to certain preferred connections. This received further strong support in our study of the Social Contract coverage, which showed that the primary framework of industrial news meshed with a larger framework which informed the reporting of economic and political relationships on the large scale.

Ultimately, the present coding of industrial news talk presents its claim to authenticity via its 'neutral' form which patterns all the information which comes within its orbit. When analysed, this 'neutral' form is resolved into an array of routine codes and practices which effectively rest upon a cultural imperative to hear the causes of disputes in one way rather than another.

PART III

SEE IT THIS WAY

Every image embodies a way of seeing. Even a photograph. For photographs are not, as is often assumed, a mechanical record. Every time we look at a photograph, we are aware, however slightly, of the photographer selecting that sight from an infinity of other possible sights.

John Berger, *Ways of Seeing*

9 Measuring the Visuals

> In the photograph . . . the absence of a code clearly reinforces
> the myth of photographic 'naturalness'; the scene is *there*,
> captured mechanically, not humanly – the mechanical is here a
> guarantee of objectivity.
>
> Roland Barthes

Introduction

As was indicated in *Bad News*, Volume 1 of this study,[1] from the
outset the Group had an obvious desire to generate methods for the
analysis of the visual content of the television news bulletin, and
some preliminary indications of the areas to be studied were given.
ITN told the Committee on the Future of Broadcasting that

> the first priority of a television news programme is to present the
> viewer with a plain unvarnished account of happenings, as free as
> humanly possible of bias, and making the maximum possible use
> of television's unique capacity to *show* these happenings.[2]

It is just the examination of how television uses its 'unique capacity'
that we now undertake.

The work of visual analysis is extremely laborious even using the
technology we had available. It was therefore necessary to focus on
one week of transmissions as the sample. Since much attention had
been paid to the structuring of bulletins during the first twelve
weeks of the year,[3] this further analytic task presented us with the
opportunity of cross-checking those basic findings with a further
week's sample. Therefore a week was chosen from the later period
of the data collection phase. The week of Sunday 11 May to
Saturday 17 May was chosen because it was the most complete of all

the weeks available to us, since fewer human and technical mishaps had occurred during that week. Only three of the fifty-one bulletins were unavailable for complete analysis and of these none were totally lost. One bulletin had not been completely recorded at the outset and two other recordings were damaged during the analysis.

It is of course true that in some senses no week's television news is like any other; but the quotidian quality of these broadcasts has already been demonstrated. Thus the sample week was untypical in that it was dominated by a foreign story, yet the percentages of parliamentary, industrial and other categories remain broadly similar to those we had previously documented. The arguments as to the typicality of the visual practice of the newsproducers are limited by the size of this sample, yet we can demonstrate that the week in question matches the twelve weeks we previously documented. Therefore the close description that follows of the visual track in the sample week would include significant general features that could be seen in other weeks. Initially, the creation of this full description of the broadcast visual material involved careful measurement of timings between one change of shot and the next. The shot is thereby conceived of as the basic unit in the visual language of the news and the minimum and maximum times for shots of various types is the most obvious measure of the often taken-for-granted assumptions, by the broadcasters, as to the audience's perceptual capacity and attention-span.

It is also crucial to examine at the outset the various presentational techniques available to the newsproducers. This involves considering the range of such inputs (e.g. graphics, studio, film, etc.) and determining a rough measure in terms of percentage overall bulletin durations of their use. It is with these two tasks that we therefore begin.

Shots and inputs

In comparison with some other audio-visual messages in our culture, such as feature films or television commercials, the television news bulletin is comparatively simple. Nevertheless, the bulletins are complex and present the researcher with a relatively uncharted set of problems. As a first step in attempting to systematically unravel the visual elements of the bulletins we felt that to determine the rate at which the images within the bulletin changed was an important factor in their complexity, especially

Table 9.1 The rate of image change

		No. of shots per minute overall	No. of news-caster shots p.m.	No. of corres-pondent to camera shots p.m.	No. of live interview in studio shots p.m.	No. of voice-over film shots p.m.	No. of sync. film shots p.m.	No. of tape shots p.m.	No. of graphic shots p.m.	No. of portrait photo-graphed shots p.m.	No. of news pictures shots p.m.	No. of map shots p.m.	No. of other photo-graphed shots p.m.	RC caps p.m.
BBC1	Lunchtime bulletin	4.84	3.24	**	**	11.45	2.75	2.45	5.26	5.22	6.89	8.0	8.95*	**
	Early evening bulletin	4.82	2.83	1.52	**	9.45	4.11	8.15	5.22	5.4	8.95	5.55	8.57	1.24
	Nine O'Clock News	4.71	3.31	1.54	**	10.03	5.5	3.97	4.61	5.48	7.5	5.13	5.53	1.49
ITN	*First Report*	3.52	1.89	3.87	3.1	9.95	4.65	2.46	5.55	4.35	6.61	3.79	10.0	1.91
	Early evening bulletin	4.96	3.22	1.64	**	10.03	4.19	6.53	4.72	7.64	8.11	5.02	9.37	0.89
	News at Ten	4.86*	3.37*	2.44	**	9.84	5.04	5.92	4.58	7.14	8.0	5.77	10.43	3.38
BBC2	*Newsday*	4.28	2.94	**	**	**	**	**	5.96	7.1	8.95	7.79	7.27*	**
	News Extra	3.51*	1.35*	0.71	3.5	8.88	5.36	3.05	4.25	3.87	6.98	6.06	8.95	1.77

*Excluding *Chromokey* changes.
**No inputs in this category

Rate per minute = $60'' \div \left(\dfrac{\text{Total duration of inputs}}{\text{Total number of shots per inputs}} \right)$

since many news shots are of news personnel and are static. Taking
the weekdays of the sample week, one finds that the images change
at the rate of approximately five per minute. The BBC1 lunchtime
bulletins, early evening and main bulletins had rates per minute of
4.84, 4.82, and 4.71 respectively (see Table 9.1). ITN's early
evening bulletin and *News at Ten* had slightly faster rates of 4.96 and
4.86. BBC2's bulletin *Newsday* was slightly slower at 4.28 changes
per minute. The two slowest bulletins were those which, as we
established in Volume 1, most approximated a current affairs
presentational formula. *First Report* had a rate of 3.52 and *News
Extra* 3.51. As at other levels the similarities overall in the bulletins,
irrespective of channel or time of transmission, are notable. As
before, the only difference is between the two current affairs style
bulletins and the rest. But these overall rates of image change,
which can also be expressed as the average number of shots per
minute, conceal differences between channels and between
bulletins which can be demonstrated and which *in toto* make up the
different 'texture' of each presentational style.

For instance, it should be noticed that the shot rate per minute on
News at Ten and *News Extra* misses the added dimension of colour
separation overlay (*Chromokey*). This device enables pictures to be
'matted-in' behind the newscasters on a simulated screen. The
pictures on the 'screen' can be changed within a shot. Thus the rates
of 4.86 and 3.51 changes per minute underestimate the speed of
image changing in these bulletins (this will be discussed further in
the chapter on studio presentation below).

The overall rates conceal differences in the way in which each
bulletin uses the standard set of inputs. In essence the bulletins
consist, first, of news personnel talking to camera in the studio. This
category can be divided into newscasters and correspondents or
more rarely reporters. Second, there is film. This can be divided
into various sub-categories, the most important of which is film
without the synchronous sound of speech and film with such speech.
We have described the latter (see *Bad News*, Appendix 2) as *voice-
over* film (that is, film voiced-over with commentary by a broadcaster) or *sync*. (that is, synchronous film). If any film has one or
more synchronous shots in it, it is classed as synchronous in its
entirety, at this stage of analysis. Third, there is tape. With the
closer analysis now available the difficulties described in Volume 1
of distinguishing between film inputs and video tape inputs is
reduced although there are still some ambiguities. Unless it is quite

clear, because of the presence of more than one camera or because it is so announced, all such ambiguities have been classed at this stage as films. Tapes can in theory be as varied as film although, except in the case of sports coverage, there is less chance that commentary will be laid over them. At this stage all video-tapes, positively identified as such, are classed together.

Fourth, there is the possibility of studio interviews. Many bulletins, especially the shorter ones, seldom, if ever, use this input. Conversely it is to be found most in the longer current affairs style bulletins. Where such an interview is recorded and used subsequently (as often happens when *First Report* records a live interview which is then played as videotape in the later ITN bulletins) the first occasion is counted as a live input and subsequent occasions are tape.

The fifth input includes all still photographs and graphics. As has been previously described, these are sub-categorised as 'graphics', 'portraits', 'news photographs', 'maps', 'other photographs' and 'radio circuit captions'. 'News photographs' were more closely defined at this stage as being strictly photographs pertaining to the actual events of the day. Old news pictures were thus categorised as 'portraits' or 'other photographs', as appropriate. Animated graphs were amalgamated in the general 'graphics' index but the animations noted.

These five different inputs have widely varying ranges of shot rates – voice-over film and 'other photos' being the swiftest and correspondents (either to camera or over the radio circuit) being the slowest. In other words correspondents remained on the screen uninterruptedly longer than other types of input. Correspondents on *News Extra* and on ITN's early evening bulletin remained longest. Of the moving inputs (as opposed to stills) voice-over film is cut fastest. Films with synchronous sound shots normally are cut at half their rate per minute. The most extreme example of this is the ratio of 11.45 shots voice-over film per minute to 2.75 shots *sync.* per minute in the early BBC1 lunchtime bulletin. Of those inputs that involve no movement (all the graphics) there are similar discrepancies with radio circuit captions having the slowest rates (since correspondents are more uninterrupted than most other inputs) and photographs of a general nature ('other photos') being the quickest.

These inputs represent the greatest area of individual choice by news personnel, since film and videotape editors can vary the pace of shots and studio directors the pace of graphic inputs. Yet it is noticeable that despite the differences an overall consistency remains in the use of these inputs. This has already been expressed in the overall rate of shot changes (see Table 9.1). It can be further seen by comparing the ranges of these rates. Radio circuit caption shots were always longest in every bulletin. There is, in other words, no bulletin which uses this input quicker than other inputs. Shots with correspondents to camera last longer than shots of newscasters throughout all the bulletins, and so on. Thus the area of individual choice available to the production personnel is artificially circumscribed by very narrow limits of normative professional practices. Each bulletin's range of shot-change rates might differ, but the ranking of inputs from slowest rate to fastest remains the same.

Nevertheless some support can be found in these figures for the perception that ITN offers a livelier bulletin than BBC, a perception noted in various audience surveys. Figure 9.1 compares the BBC *Nine O'Clock* bulletin with ITN's *News at Ten*. Figure 9.2 similarly compares the two early-evening bulletins. ITN allows its

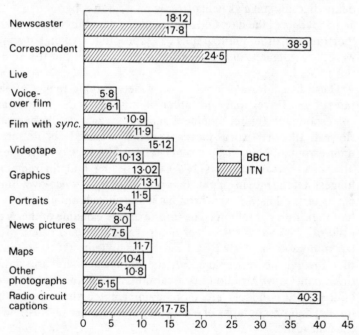

Figure 9.1 BBC1 *Nine O'Clock News* compared with ITN *News At Ten* (average shot durations by input)

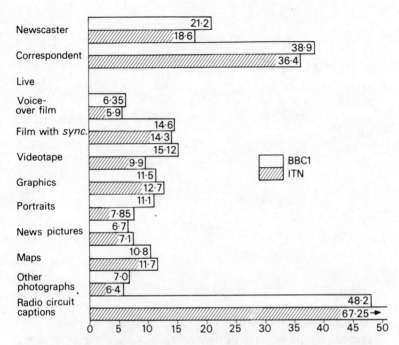

Figure 9.2 BBC1 early evening bulletin compared with ITN early evening bulletin (average shot durations by input)

newscasters and correspondents on average less time to address the camera uninterruptedly than does the BBC. This is also true of the use of correspondents via radio circuit in the main evening bulletins although in the early bulletins the BBC is quicker than ITN. The BBC's main bulletin cut its film faster than did ITN but more slowly in the early evening one. Most graphic inputs were used on average for less time per shot on *News at Ten* than on the *Nine O'Clock News*; however 'graphics', 'news pictures', and 'maps' were held longer on ITN's early evening bulletin than on the BBC's. However, none of these differences amounted to a very wide discrepancy between the average length of shots in any one category – the greatest being in the matter of correspondents. Otherwise the differences in the average lengths of shot within most categories was between one and three seconds per shot from bulletin to bulletin. How much such small divergences in professional practices contribute to audience perception remains to be studied.

The rate of image change and the average length of shots does not measure the utilisation of each of these inputs. Figures 9.3–9.10

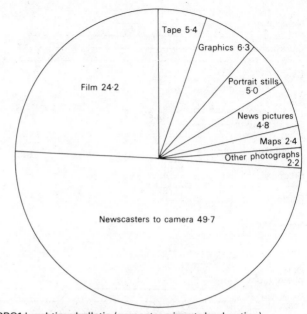

Figure 9.3   BBC1 lunchtime bulletin (percentage inputs by duration)

represent the percentage of time taken by each category of input during the weekdays 12–16 May 1975. Again considerable similarity in the percentages can be discerned especially when the three basic styles of bulletin are distinguished. That is to say, the percentage of time given to each input as between the two short bulletins (BBC1's *Lunchtime*, BBC2's *Newsday*), the two current affairs style bulletins (ITN's *First Report*, BBC2's *News Extra*) and the two early and main bulletins on BBC1 and ITN show considerable similarities.

The main bulletins have an almost equal amount of time utilised by newscasters (26.0 per cent for the BBC and 24.5 per cent for ITN) and for film (42.7 per cent for BBC as against 43.1 per cent for ITN). BBC's main bulletin voiced over graphical material for just over 17 per cent of the total duration of the bulletin, whereas *News at Ten* voiced over just under 10 per cent. (But it should be remembered that *News at Ten* uses further graphical material in its *Chromokey* style of presentation.) ITN spent nearly 13.4 per cent of its time on its correspondents talking to camera and under 1 per cent listening to them on radio circuits. The BBC *Nine O'Clock News* spent nearly 8.5 per cent of its time with correspondents on camera but nearly 3 per cent with them voice only on radio circuit reports.

Further similarities can be found between the two current affairs style bulletins. The newscaster who assumes more of a role of presenter took up 30.7 per cent of *First Report*'s transmission time talking to camera and 29.5 per cent of *News Extra*'s time. *First Report* used little input from correspondents to camera or as interviewees. It utilised them via radio circuits (3.3 per cent), as did *News Extra* (2.7 per cent). But *News Extra* also used correspondents as interviewees, a fact reflected in the increase in tape and live interviews. *First Report* in general used live interviews more, reflecting perhaps its early transmission time. *News Extra* spent 5.9 per cent of its time talking over stills and graphics whereas *First Report* used 9.7 per cent of these inputs, but it should again be noted that this underestimates *News Extra*'s use of graphics since the *Chromokey* element is not here measured. A significant difference is in the amount of film used – nearly twice as much in *News Extra*, again a reflection of the different transmission times. Nearly 50 per cent of the BBC1 lunchtime bulletin is taken up by the newscaster reading to camera and some 65 per cent of the duration of the *Newsday* bulletin is similarly taken up. *Newsday* uses fewer inputs than any other bulletin, eschewing all moving pictures. The BBC

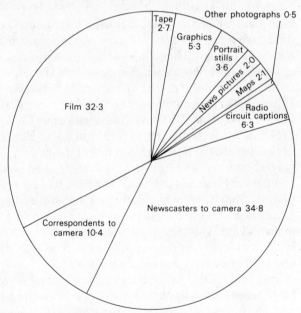

Figure 9.4   BBC1 early evening bulletin (percentage inputs by duration)

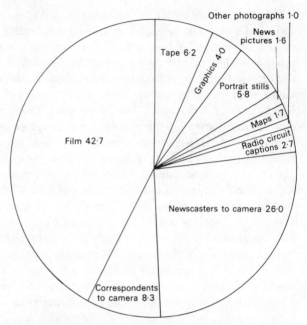

Figure 9.5   BBC1 main bulletin (percentage inputs by duration)

lunchtime bulletin on the other hand had about 30 per cent of its time taken up with film and tape. Graphic inputs are therefore higher on the BBC2 bulletin, especially 'news pictures'. Similarities as between the newscaster, correspondent and correspondents via radio circuits in the two early evening bulletins can also be seen, ITN using 48 per cent of its time in this way, the BBC 51 per cent. On the other hand BBC1 used rather more film (32.3 per cent) than ITN (29.3 per cent). However, within the film category it is noticeable that ITN, in the two sets of major competing bulletins (early evening and main), used more film with voice-over commentary than did the BBC. The BBC had a greater percentage of *sync.* film. There was a decrease on both BBC1 and ITN in the percentage of voice-over film and an increase in *sync.* from early to main bulletin. This reflects the practice of increasing the complexity of the film reports as the day progresses. The overall percentage of film both voice-over and *sync.* also increases.

This basic statistical background is a crucial prerequisite for a more refined analysis of the visual track. As we argue below in our conclusion, we feel it unnecessary at this stage of our work to utilise the total conceptual apparatus made available by semiology. Yet obviously our concerns in documenting and revealing the minutiae of professional practice are parallel. The simple Peircean division of symbolic, indexical and iconic will therefore be used. Before taking each of the basic input categories mentioned above we offer a brief description of the methodologies we employed to generate that analysis.

Methods

Reproducing the complexities of audio visual messages in written form presents an immediate and simple problem. The sound track can be instantly and easily rendered, especially when, as in this case, it almost entirely consists of spoken English. But the pictures that accompany that track are not only of themselves more difficult to describe, but also cannot be easily accommodated on the same page as the spoken text. Scholars have generated various systems to accomplish this basic task but they can be largely characterised as rendering the original visuals unnecessarily complex, not least because they often bear no relation to professional practice.[4]

The problem of representing visuals in print also presents itself to

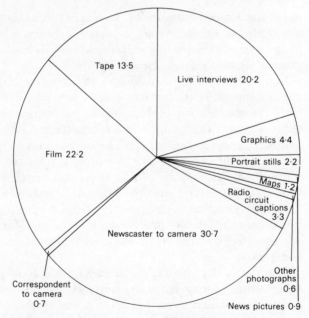

Figure 9.6   ITN *First Report* (percentage inputs by bulletin)

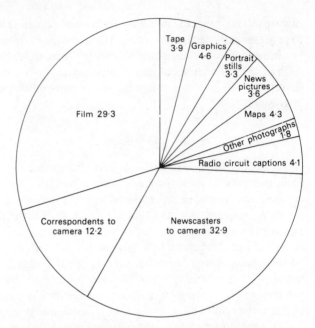

Figure 9.7   ITN early evening bulletin (percentage inputs by duration)

the professional broadcaster or film maker and, as in other areas of this study, we decided to adapt analytic divisions related to their practices rather than to follow academic or quasi-academic models, many of which are simply created *a priori*.

In essence, for the production of all television, including news and current affairs, the text is typed down one side of the page and a clear margin left for instructions to camerapersons and other technicians as to the visuals. In our case the margin was used not before the event as a guide to production, but after it to reconstruct, from a careful examination of the archive tapes, what had been transmitted. Each change of shot in the transmitted news bulletin was marked (/) in the transcript of the spoken text and a line marked from the (/) back across the margin. Then a description of the shot was entered below the line on the margin side. Thus a parallel description of the visual track was created to match the transcribed audio track.

In order to describe the visual track, professional practice was again utilised. For the purposes of intraprofessional communication a simple vocabulary is used to describe the shot. The elements of this vocabulary relate, first, to the distance between camera and subject (i.e. close-up, medium shot, long shot); second, to the movement of camera on tripod (pan, tilt, crab, crane) its speed (whip pan, slow pan, etc.); or to movements created by the lens

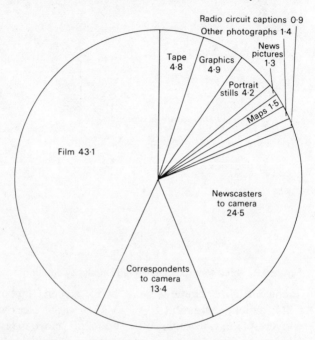

Figure 9.8   ITN main bulletin (percentage inputs by duration)

(zoom in, pull out); third, to the nature of the subject (single shot, two-shot, etc.); fourth, to the nature of the change from one shot to another (cut, dissolve, wipe, etc.). These normative descriptions are used in various combinations but are not entirely precise. Their usage will, within broadly agreed limits, differ from production company to production company and from technician to technician. In using such a system to closely describe material with great visual variety problems can thereby be created. But we were not overly concerned about this in dealing with material such as the news where the visual range is limited. We established a standard notation and used it throughout the work of the project (see Key, and Example 9.1).

Key to abbreviations used in the examples

B/G	background	LFT	left
B & W	black and white	RHT	right

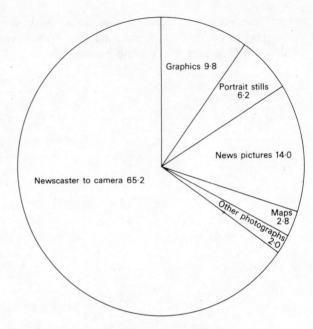

Figure 9.9   BBC2 *Newsday* (percentage inputs by duration)

'Bong' Big Ben chime	SCR screen (right or left)
CSO colour separation overlay, i.e. *Chromokey*	V/O *or* v/o voice over
	zoom in move in fast
CU close-up	zoom out *or* pull back move
F/G foreground	out fast
F/X sound effects	2, 3, 4, etc. number of people
GV general view	in shot (can be used in
LS long shot	conjunction with
matched cut action is	description of size of shot,
continuous	i.e. L2S, long shot with two
MCU medium close-up	people in, *or* W2S, wide shot
MLS medium long shot	with two people in)
MS mid shot	

Example 9.1   ITN, 17.50, 15 May 1975

	/ HONEYCOMBE *(Newscaster) TO CAM*
4 CU Honeycombe (buttonhole) plain B/G	The Cambodian Information Minister has repeated over Phnom Penh radio accusations that the *Mayaguez* was one of a number
Live	of spy ships the Americans had sent to the Gulf

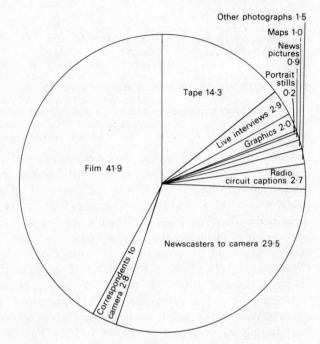

Figure 9.10 BBC2 *News Extra* (percentage inputs by duration)

Example 9.1 continued

		of Thailand. The marines who landed on Ko
CUT 0.15	Tot 0.43½	Tang were from the 1,000-strong force/

5 General view (GV) C5		*HONEYCOMBE VOICE-OVER*
Helicopter moving RHT		airlifted to the American airbase of
slowly full-frame	*Film*	Utapao in Thai/
CUT 0.03	Tot 0.46½	

6 MLS 4 SHOT soldier (2		land. The Thai government have protested
with guns) T-shirts; angle		strongly about the use of the base for action
slightly up	*Film*	against Cambodia despite their official request
FADE 0.10	Tot 0.56½	for the marines' immediate withdrawal./

7 LS single soldier walks
 screen LEFT: zoom in long
 6 shot past wire soldiers
 chatting   *Film*
CUT 0.4½   Tot 1.01 /

Example 9.1 continued

8 CU Honeycombe (button-hole) Plain B/G *Live* CUT 0.02½ Tot 1.03½	*HONEYCOMBE TO CAM* President Ford made th/

9 Ford MCU hands raised *B/W News picture*	*HONEYCOMBE VOICE-OVER* he decision to start the rescue operation at 11.00 our time last night, during a meeting at the National Security Council in the

Thus, after the transcripts had been made up in the way described, indices of the various different technical inputs were made. This involved refinement of the system of technical input categorisation utilised at the early stages of the project which we described in *Bad News*. Eventually eleven indices were created: (1) basic settings including the images matted-in behind the newscasters' heads on the colour separation overlay system (*CSO* or *Chromokey*); (2) opening images for those bulletins without standard opening titles; (3) films; (4) videotapes and outside broadcasts (as previously described, distinctions in certain circumstances between film and tape mean that a certain amount of overlapping was created between the Indexes 3 and 4. The same basic criteria laid down previously however were used to make the distinction between the two at the point of filming or taping, not at the point of transmission). An index (5) of the use of portraits, file photographs was drawn up; and similar indices of (6) maps, (7) news pictures, (8) graphics, (9) miscellaneous photographs and (10) radio circuit captions were also created. Examples from these indices are given in Chapter 12. The basis of the categories used here was largely taken from those previously established. An index was made of all correspondent/reporter appearances in the studio (11). A further index (12) was made of all interviewees and others, apart from news personnel, who were allowed to be heard speaking in interviews or in speeches or press conferences, or were overheard informally. In all of this we were concerned with both the content of the image and, more importantly, with the relationship between visual content and the voice-over commentary (i.e. text and image). To discuss this we made use of a simple tripartite division in the possible range of text/image relationships.[5]

In our terms the possible relationship between news text and news image is threefold: we asked the question To what extent are the words being used to describe pictures iconically (simply descriptive), indexically (partially descriptive), or symbolically (non-descriptive)? Television's 'unique capacity' in our view depends a great deal on this question. If it is the case that news text is largely descriptive (i.e. the text/image relationship is iconic), then the producers are indeed able to fulfil their announced intention 'to *show* these happenings'. But the extent to which the text/image relationship is not iconic is a crucial measure of the extent to which the producers mediate the visual information they are giving.

It will be demonstrated below that the iconic is comparatively rare in news bulletins; that 'happenings' are rare; and that, as we previously suggested, the dominant visual in this area of programming is a man talking to camera about events, people and opinions happening elsewhere.

In order to facilitate the description of the analysis that follows Tables 9.2–9.8 give a brief indication of the contents of each of the bulletins used in the sample. This is expanded in Appendix C, which offers a fuller account of the week as presented by the television newsrooms.

Table 9.2   Bulletin items 11 May 1975*

	Duration**
BBC1 13.50	
The Prime Minister's interview on *Weekend World*	1.27
Shooting of PC Grey in Ulster	0.17
Escape of Rampton patient in Notts	0.21
King Hussein's arrival	0.15
US carrier in Guam with S. Vietnam planes	0.20½
BBC1 18.05	
The Prime Minister's interview	3.45
Bank governor leaves for Basle; exchange rates at airports	1.15
Shore speech (anti-EEC)	0.15
King Hussein's arrival	0.28
Laos Constitution Day	1.34
England v. Cyprus (soccer)	0.10
Monaco Grand Prix	0.12½
BBC1 21.30	
The Prime Minister's interview	3.58½
Heseltine on BLMC redundancies	0.15½
Bank governor to Basle; exchange rates at airports,	
holiday surcharges	1.15
Shore speech (anti-EEC)	0.16½
Laos Constitution Day	1.43½
US carrier in Guam	0.16
Himalaya climbing deaths	0.22

Table 9.2 continued

	Duration**
Sunday League cricket results	0.12½
England v. Cyprus (soccer)	0.12
Monaco Grand Prix	0.27
ITN 18.05	
Prime Minister's interview	3.16
Laos Constitution Day	0.42
King Hussein's arrival	0.18
Shooting of PC Grey in Ulster	0.15
Pro Greek-Cypriot Rally in Hyde Park	0.23
Monaco Grand Prix	0.24
England v. Cyprus (soccer)	0.14½
ITN 22.00	
Prime Minister's interview	5.03
Heseltine on BLMC redundancies	0.23½
Shore speech (anti-EEC)	0.22
'Get Britain Out' cancelled press conference	0.09
Laos Constitution Day	1.21½
Cambodian Radio announces strong links with China	0.26
Himalaya climbing deaths	0.29½
King Hussein's arrival	0.19½
The Queen and Prince Philip last day in Japan (tea ceremony)	1.23½
England v. Cyprus (soccer)	0.21½
Monaco Grand Prix	0.22

* For a fuller discussion of the contents of the sample week's bulletins see Appendix C.
** Excluding headline, hooker and payoff timings unless otherwise noted.

Table 9.3   Bulletin items 12 May 1975

	Duration*
BBC1 12.55	
£ down 24.9 per cent	0.31½
Chrysler/Dunlop strikes go on; Jaguar's MD resigns	0.40
Peart speech (pro-EEC)	0.49½
Jenkins hits press coverage of Benn	0.16
Queen leaves Tokyo	0.19½
BBC1 17.45	
Flixborough disaster report published	2.55
£ down 25 per cent/central bankers meet at Basle	2.07
Chrysler and Dunlop strikes	1.26
Post Office engineers' pay deal	0.18
Bradley criticises unions	0.30
Rail unions reject 21 per cent offer, demand 30 per cent	0.09
Marsh chairs meeting of nationalised industry chiefs	0.26
Jenkins hits press coverage of Benn	0.21
Chester murder trial – juror knows witness	0.28½
Birmingham bombs trial to be held at Chester	0.24½

Table 9.3 continued

	Duration*
Prime Minister's libel action ends	0.21½
Peart speech (pro-EEC)	1.07
Allaun says EEC wants our oil	0.32½
Refugee ships leave Singapore for Saigon	0.24½
Britain out of Davis Cup	0.28
BBC1 21.00	
Mayaguez seized	3.21½
Flixborough disaster report	4.25
£ down 25 per cent/Speaker refuses debate/speculators	
not responsible	2.27
Chrysler and Dunlop strikes	2.21½
Jaguar MD, Geoffrey Robinson, resigns	0.16
Marsh chairs meeting of nationalised industry chiefs	1.35
Commons debates guillotine on Industry Bill	1.46½
Jenkins hits press coverage of Benn	0.19
Bradley criticises unions	0.25½
Post Office engineers' pay deal	0.17
Sir Henry Plumb (NFU) warns against leaving EEC	0.14½
Peart speech (pro-EEC)	1.01
Allaun says EEC wants our oil	0.22½
Heffer accuses Brussels of hushed-up steel cutback plan	0.19½
Drain (NALGO) hits Crosland's 'party's over' speech	0.25
New York's financial troubles	2.46
Queen is on her way home, due in few hours	0.22
Britain out of Davis Cup	0.37½
ITN 13.00	
£ down 24.9 per cent/Kleinwort interviewed	4.20
Chrysler strike goes on	2.19½
Drain (NALGO) hits Crosland's 'party's over' speech +	
feature on ratepayers' revolt in Cardiff	6.10½
Khmer Rouge to accept foreign aid/Lek Hoh Tan interviewed	6.15½
England v. Cyprus (soccer)	2.10
ITN 17.50	
£ down 25 per cent/Speaker refuses debate/Kleinwort	
interviewed/Bank meeting in Basle	3.39
Chrysler strike goes on	2.02
Dunlop strike goes on	0.20
Post Office engineers get 18 per cent rise	0.13
Pathet Lao virtually in control of Laos	0.16½
Khmer Rouge to accept foreign aid	0.11
Refugee ships leave Singapore for Saigon	0.13
Queen and Prince Philip return after farewell to Hirohito	0.12
Flixborough disaster report	2.03
Rees warns releasing detainees could slow up/	
Birmingham bomb trial to be held at Chester	0.53½
Britain out of Davis Cup	0.31½

Table 9.3 continued

	Duration*
ITN 22.00	
Mayaguez seized	2.11
£ down 25 per cent/Speaker refuses debate/Benn defends Industry Bill guillotine	4.52
Chrysler and Dunlop strikes go on	2.11½
Post Office engineers get 18 per cent rise	0.12
Scottish teachers get over 20 per cent rise	0.05
Bradley criticises unions	0.18
Marsh chairs meeting of nationalised industry chiefs	0.23
Drain (NALGO) hits Crosland's 'party's over' speech	0.28
Flixborough disaster report	3.11
Birmingham bomb trial to be held at Lancaster	0.28
(Part 2) Khmer Rouge to accept foreign aid/eyewitness to Phnom Penh evacuation, Tolgarten interviewed	3.38
Gall says Saigon (Ho Chi Minh City) is happy	0.33
Peart speech (pro-EEC)/Jay speech (anti-EEC) + Feature: food price argument, Shirley Williams/Sir John Winnifrith interviewed	5.01½
Britain out of Davis Cup	0.40½
Update – guillotine passed	0.16
BBC2 19.30	
Mayaguez seized	0.22½
Flixborough disaster report	0.51
£ down 25 per cent	0.20
Chrysler, Dunlop strikes go on/Post Office engineers get 25 per cent rise	0.27½
Queen leaves Tokyo, farewell to Hirohito	0.12
BBC2 22.20	
Mayaguez seized	2.11½
Refugee ships leave Singapore for Saigon	0.18
£ down 25 per cent/dealer interviewed: no speculators/*FT* index up, trading in firms with overseas holdings/Basle bankers meeting/Aubrey Jones interviewed/Howe comments from *Newsday* quoted	6.41½
Chrysler strike goes on	0.18
Dunlop strike goes on	0.24
Post Office engineers get 25 per cent rise	0.19
Bradley criticises unions/interviewed	2.18
Industry Bill guillotine motion passed	2.49
Jenkins hits press coverage of Benn	0.25
Callaghan expects Yes to referendum	0.17
Peart speech (pro-EEC)	1.05
Investment gap with EEC say anti-EEC group	0.32
Teng Hsiao Ping visits Paris	1.43
Flixborough disaster report	6.26

*Excluding headline, hooker and payoff timings unless otherwise noted.

Table 9.4   Bulletin items 13 May 1975

	Duration*
BBC1 12.55	
Mayaguez anchored at Ko Tang	1.01
Britain in Europe; first press conference	1.00
Dunlop strike – 1,500 more laid off BLMC	0.14
Cider not to be called champagne – High Court	0.25
Queen and Prince Philip arrive Heathrow	0.24
BBC1 17.45**	
Mayaguez anchored at Ko Tang/Buckley, Humphrey interviewed	
Laos: more army units revolt against right	
Britain recognises South Vietnam	
CBI survey of economic trends/MacDougall interviewed	
£ down 25.2 per cent against December 1971 level; $ down, too	
Dunlop strike – 1,500 more laid off BLMC	
Labour MP demands Finneston's (BSC) sack	
'Britain in Europe'; first press conference	
'Get Britain Out' introduce New Zealanders against EEC/interview	
Sugar price down 20 per cent	
Denning overturns Appeal Court on picketing	
Nypro announce Flixborough to be rebuilt	
Dentists could be liable giving anaesthetics	
Queen and Prince Philip back	
Cider not to be called champagne – High Court	
National Portrait Gallery displays spare paintings at stately home	
BBC1 21.00	
Mayaguez at Ko Tang/Buckley, Humphrey interviewed	3.46½
Britain recognises South Vietnam	0.16
CBI survey of economic trends/MacDougall interviewed/ Short claims economy improving	3.27½
£ down 25.2 per cent on December 1971 level	0.39
'Britain in Europe'; first press conference	2.09½
'Get Britain Out' introduce New Zealanders against EEC/interview	1.03
Feature: How the Referendum Campaigns are working	4.31½
Sugar price down by 20 per cent	0.24
Chrysler strike – Mrs Sheila Willis interviewed	1.42½
Dunlop strike: 1,500 more laid off BLMC	0.14
Steel: Foot sees Finneston/Labour MP demands Finneston's (BSC) sack/EEC Commission deny secret cutback plans	2.16½
Denning overturns Appeal Court on picketing	0.51
Queen and Prince Philip back	0.26
Cider not to be called champagne – High Court	2.25½
ITN 13.00	
Mayaguez at Ko Tang/Kissinger claims Khmer atrocities	2.52½
£ down 25 per cent/foreign exchange market visited	2.25

Table 9.4 continued

	Duration*
Referendum postbag – food prices/Rippon, Buchan interviewed	13.49½
Queen back; visited football, Shinto shrine, pearl divers	3.58½
ITN 17.50	
Mayaguez at Ko Tang; marines to Utapoa/Buckley, Humphrey interviewed	3.08½
Britain recognises South Vietnam	0.28
Israelis kidnap 3 suspects from Lebanon	0.34½
£ down 25.2 per cent/Catherwood predicts pay law	0.54½
Banknote printers suspended	0.22
CBI economic trends/MacDougall interviewed	2.48
Firemen decide emergencies only	0.13
Queen back; visited football, pearl divers	2.34
ITN 22.00	
Mayaguez at Ko Tang; American plane damaged/Javits interviewed/Marines to Utapao/Buckley, Humphrey interviewed	4.26
Britain recognises South Vietnam	0.32
£ down 25.2 per cent/Catherwood predicts pay law/Swiss banking economist interview	3.00
Banknote printers 'stopped work'	1.44½
Bank employees reject 20 per cent offer	0.20
London fares up in November	0.15½
CBI Economic Trends/MacDougall interviewed	2.51½
Chrysler strike – Foot appeals	0.22½
Meriden co-op, after two months' operation/Johnston interviewed	2.33½
(Part 2) 'Britain in Europe'; first press conference/adverse trade balance with EEC feature	5.30½
Montreal strikers riot	0.27
Cider not to be called champagne – High Court	0.24
Scotland beat Portugal (soccer)	0.11½
Queen back/football, pearl divers	2.04½
Prince Abdullah joins bank	0.26
BBC2 19.30	
Mayaguez at Ko Tang	0.32½
Britain recognises South Vietnam	0.15
CBI economic survey	0.12
£ down; $ down	0.19½
Chrysler strike – meeting, wives, Foot	0.26½
Sugar price down 20 per cent	0.20
Cider not to be called champagne – High Court	0.20
BBC2 23.05	
PM economic debate announcement/CBI forecast/ MacDougall interview/tomorrow's trade figures	4.25½
Richards back from Basle	0.13
Dunlop strike – BLMC 1,500 laid off	0.12

Table 9.4 continued

	Duration*
Foot warns on Chrysler; steel – Irlam feature	3.18½
'Britain in Europe', 'Get Britain Out' introduce New Zealanders against the EEC	0.47
Mayaguez at Ko Tang – she's moving	2.16
Britain to open Saigon embassy as soon as possible	0.13
Pay beds out by next month – feature: growth of private hospitals	4.54
Cider not to be called champagne – High Court	3.04½

*Excluding headline, hooker and payoff timings unless otherwise stated.
**Tape destroyed in playback; no timings available

Table 9.5   Bulletin items 14 May 1975

	Duration*
BBC1 12.55	
Chrysler will build new car in UK, wives' poor turnout	1.18
Indexation warning on mortgages by building societies	0.26
Pramoj orders marines out of Utapao	0.30½
Policeman killed in Basque shootout	0.15
Theologians protest exorcism	0.44
BBC1 17.45	
Cambodian gunboats destroyed round *Mayaguez*	2.00½
Laotians seize three US officials	0.14½
April trade figures – £169 million in red	2.24½
TUC economic committee reject new Social Contract initiative	1.22
Chrysler strike – wives	2.17
British Leyland: £43 million loss in six months	0.12
Ferranti – government to aid	0.54½
Commons committee on tea plantations in Sri Lanka	1.02½
PC Grey buried in Belfast	1.01½
Details on referendum counting; Deakins speech (anti-EEC) Heath says 'No' means Bennite socialism	1.00½
Theologians protest exorcism	0.27
BBC1 21.00	
Cambodian gunboats destroyed round *Mayaguez* – Thai protest US action	5.27
Laotians seize three US officials	0.20½
Ferranti – government to aid	3.26½
Chrysler – London meeting, wives, new model	2.58
April trade figures	0.38½
£ finished at 25.1 per cent below December 1971 level	0.14½
TUC economic committee – no new Social Contract initiative Campbell Adamson warns government	2.01½
Indexation warning on mortgages by building societies	0.29
Shirley Williams says ministers must go with vote	
Alf Morris says food up/Deakins says markets exist/vote will be over at 10/new Highland region has polling problems	5.04

Table 9.5 continued

	Duration*
Commons committee on tea plantations in Sri Lanka	2.18½
BBC apologises to Sinatra in High Court	0.20
Theologians protest exorcism	1.28

ITN 17.50

Cambodian boats destroyed round *Mayaguez*	2.28
Laotians seize US officials, destroy aid centre	0.27
April trade figures, Adamson warns government	1.38½
Ferranti – government aid	0.50½
Leyland lose £43 million/talks with Dunlop tomorrow/ Chrysler wives, new model	2.20½
Marsh attacks government; nationalised industries made schizophrenic	0.29½
Referendum vote details	0.30
IRA say weekend slaying of PC in line with policy	0.24
Theologians protest exorcism	0.38
Policeman killed in Basque shootout	0.12½
Bourassa warns Montreal might not be finished for games	0.49

ITN 22.00

Cambodian boats destroyed round *Mayaguez*	7.43
Laotians seize three US officials	0.23½
April trade figures – £169 million in red/£ recovers slightly/ TUC reject new Social Contract	1.45½
Ferranti – government to aid	1.26
British Leyland lose £43 million	0.18½
Chrysler stewards: strike goes on/Jones meets management/wives	2.04½
Marsh attacks government: nationalised industries made schizophrenic	0.21
(Part 2) Referendum vote details	3.08
Brussels claims UK food prices to soar if 'No' vote	
Deakins speech (anti-EEC) – food up more if 'Yes' vote	0.19½
Cambridge rapist – situation report	2.21
Commons committee on tea plantations in Sri Lanka	0.38
Bourassa warns Montreal might not be finished for games	1.53½
MG: fifty years old today	1.47½
Mayaguez update	0.41

BBC2 19.30

Cambodian boats destroyed round *Mayaguez*/Pramoj protests	0.48
Laos: three US officials held	0.13½
Ferranti: government to help	0.21½
Chrysler strike goes on	0.12½
April trade figures	0.29½
Commons committee on Sri Lanka tea plantations	0.46½ (inc p/o)

Table 9.5 continued

	Duration*
BBC2 23.05	
Cambodian boats destroyed round *Mayaguez*/Pramoj protests	5.31½
US ready for Laos withdrawal; three officials seized	0.26
$ down; £ slightly up/trade figures	1.26½
Chrysler: new car/stewards meeting/wives/Hunt and Jones in London interviewed	4.23½
Ferranti: government to help	0.30
Commons committee on Sri Lanka tea plantations	6.15½

*Excluding headline, hooker and payoff timings unless otherwise indicated.

Table 9.6   Bulletin items 15 May 1975

	Duration*
BBC1 12.55	
Mayaguez recovered	1.48½
Chrysler: men vote to stay out	0.14
500 police on Warwick University campus to break up rent-rise protest sit-in	0.47
BBC1 17.45	
Dunlop: peace formula to be put to strikers tomorrow	1.00
BLMC 18,000 idle	
Chrysler: Men vote to stay out	1.19
Mayaguez recovered	3.37
£ up/OECD: Britain is recovering on balance of payments	0.36
Shell profits down £100 million this quarter	0.38
Scottish Tories conference opens	1.10½
Non-nationalised steel says stay in EEC	0.30
Harrier naval jump-jet to go ahead	0.30½
500 police Warwick University to break up rent-rise protest sit-in	0.55
Milan art gallery burgled, same paintings twice in 3 months	0.30½
Sweden: train crash eight dead	0.21
Blind: demonstration to Westminster	0.34½
Locomotion 1 replica runs	0.53
BBC1 21.00	
Mayaguez recovered	8.23
Laos; three US officials released	0.31½
Victory parade in Saigon	0.26
Peace formula in Dunlop dispute/Chrysler men vote	2.00
£ better day/OECD: Britain is recovering on balance of payments	0.37½
Harrier naval jump-jet to go ahead	1.59½
Callaghan pro-EEC speech	1.32½
Scottish Tories conference opens	1.31
Milan art gallery burgled, same paintings twice in three months	0.25

Table 9.6 continued

	Duration*
Sweden: train crash eight dead	0.14½
Graf Zeppelin's niece launches hot-air balloon	0.28
500 police on Warwick University campus to break up rent-rise sit-in	1.05½
Judge: immigrants have transformed peaceful South London	1.00
British shoe industry – situation report	2.05½
Blind: demonstration at Westminster	0.48½
Cricket: Murray sets new record for season's catches	0.17½

ITN 13.00

Mayaguez recovered	7.53½
Chrysler: men vote to continue strike	2.14½
Milan art gallery burgled, same paintings twice in three months	1.04½
Rees meets Fitzgerald/Catholic pub bombed	1.39½
Referendum postbag	4.15½
Feature: French wives shopping in Ramsgate	3.50

ITN 17.50

Mayaguez recovered	3.31½
UK Embassy in Saigon/three US officials held in homes, Laos	0.43½
Chrysler: men vote to stay out	1.46½
£ improves/French wives in Ramsgate	1.52½
Callaghan pro-EEC speech/OECD man: no £ crisis	0.50
Milan art gallery burgled, same paintings twice in three months	0.29½
Catholic pub bombed	0.27
500 police at Warwick University to break up rent-rise protest sit-in	0.27
Blind: demonstration at Westminster	0.26½

ITN 22.00

Mayaguez recovered	9.44
Victory parade in Saigon/UK Embassy occupied	0.54
Harrier naval jump-jet to go ahead	0.57
Chrysler: men vote to go on	1.00½
Dunlop peace formula/BLMC 16,500 idle	0.32
£ stronger/Eire's sterling reserves – situation report	2.53
(Part 2) Wilson quoted from *This Week* interview/ Callaghan pro-EEC speech/anti's claim huge EEC trade deficit/Sedgemore, MP, anti-EEC speech/feature: Parliament at Strasbourg	5.43½
Rees warns on release of detainees/Catholic pub bombed	0.32
500 police on Warwick University campus break up rent-rise sit-in	0.27
Milan art gallery burgled, same paintings twice in three months	0.22
Blind: demonstration to Westminster	0.24
Locomotion 1 replica runs	1.23½

Table 9.6 continued

	Duration*
BBC2 19.30	
Mayaguez recovered	0.41
Dunlop peace formula/Chrysler – strike goes on	0.29
£ improved	0.13
Non-nationalised steel says stay in EEC	0.41
Sweden: train crash eight dead	0.17½
Milan art gallery burgled, same paintings twice in three months	0.19
BBC2 23.05	
Mayaguez recovered/Ford sees Shah/Thais protest demo	6.25 (inc hls)
Dunlop peace formula, BLMC 18,500 idle	0.34½
Callaghan speech (pro-EEC)/non-nationalised steel says stay in EEC	1.49½
British shoe industry – situation report	3.46½
Nestlé annual meeting; feature: baby foods in Africa	5.27½

*Excluding headline, hooker and payoff timings unless otherwise indicated.

Table 9.7   Bulletin items 16 May 1975

	Duration*
BBC1 12.55	
Armed services pay increase	0.39½
Building societies record figures	0.27½
Mayaguez aftermath/official US army film	1.23
US navy visits Leningrad	0.32½
BBC1 17.45	
Record cost-of-living index increase/£ slips/building societies record figures	2.18½
Armed services pay increase	1.52
POWU lift ban against mechanisation	0.54
Steel workers meet for plan to halt job cuts	1.26
Dunlop strike settled	0.22
Mayaguez aftermath/official US army film/Saigon official N. Vietnamese film	2.59½
Michael X hanged in Trinidad	0.16½
Taylor/Nastase rows at hard court championships	2.22½
BBC1 21.00	
Record cost-of-living index increase/Walker, Gormley comment	2.47
Armed services pay increase	1.51½
Building societies record figures	1.17½
Dunlop strike settled/Chrysler goes on	1.42½
Steelworkers meet for plan to halt job cuts	1.37½
POWU lift ban against mechanisation	0.47
Mayaguez aftermath/official US army film	2.31

Table 9.7 continued

	Duration*
Saigon continues celebrations/official N. Vietnamese film	1.36
Kurdistan, quiet now – situation report	4.29
Michael X hanged in Trinidad	0.20
Yugoslavia: train crash, at least thirteen dead	0.20
Ottawa cosmetic plant burns	0.37
Benn attacks Heath's EEC promises/Maudling says 'No' means Bennism at Scottish Tory conference	1.52
Taylor/Nastase rows at hard court championships	3.15

ITN 13.00

Building societies record figures	1.05½
Armed services pay rise	2.21
Dunlop – meeting in progress/Chrysler goes on	1.02½
New Statesman: 'Union Leaders = Gangsters'	4.50
Jackson urges Post Office Workers Union to drop anti-mechanisation ban	0.56
Michael X hanged in Trinidad	1.26
Mayaguez aftermath	1.29½
Yugoslavia: train crash thirteen dead	0.22½
Rippon speech pro-EEC/Jay speech anti-EEC	1.40½
Holiday exchange rate surcharges/£ slipping	2.27½
CAMRA gets Courage to put back real beer	2.36½

ITN 17.45

Cost of living: record increase	2.46
Dunlop strike settled	0.33½
Chrysler dispute goes on	0.31
Armed services pay rise	1.38½
Building societies record figures	0.22½
Mayaguez aftermath/Saigon victory celebration	1.18
Michael X hanged in Trinidad	0.55
Yugoslavia: train crash at least thirteen dead	0.33
Angola council seeks to avoid intercommunal violence	0.24
POWU lift ban against mechanisation	0.31
Nastase row in hard court championships/Taylor, too	0.44½
Mason visits airforce Harrier base	0.29½

ITN 22.00

Cost of living: record increase/Walker, Gormley comment	4.04
Building societies record figures	0.57½
Dunlop strike over	0.34½
Chrysler strike goes on/New York says Chrysler will continue in UK	0.30
Armed services pay rise	0.46
POWU lift ban against mechanisation	0.29½
Independent Television Companies Association threaten lockout if strike goes ahead	0.52
Mayaguez aftermath/South Vietnamese representatives visit Thailand	1.03½
Saigon – official N. Vietnamese film	1.55½

Table 9.7 continued

	Duration*
(Part 2) Michael X hanged in Trinidad	2.16
Yugoslavia: train crash, at least thirteen dead	0.37½
Tel Aviv arms factory explodes; twenty injured	0.13
Benn and Foot attack Heath on Market promises; Heseltine and Rippon speeches pro-EEC; Fitzgerald interview on Eire's position if Britain leaves	4.08
First day of Strathclyde Region	2.44
Taylor/Nastase rows at hard court championships	4.23
BBC2 19.30	
Record cost-of-living increase	0.24
Armed services pay rise	0.30
Mayaguez aftermath	0.50
Building societies record figures	0.27½
Dunlop strike settled	0.13
Nastase/Taylor rows at hard court championships	0.15
BBC 23.05	
Record cost-of-living increase	3.07½
Armed services pay rise	0.21
POWU lift ban against mechanisation	0.28½
Mayaguez aftermath	2.15½
Saigon, official N. Vietnamese film/Provisional Revolutionary Government visit Thailand	2.16½
Kurdistan, quiet now – situation report	6.17½·
Benn attacks Heath's EEC promises/Rippon's speech pro-EEC/feature: the Ulster border if Britain says 'No'	3.11½

*Excluding headline, hooker and payoff timings unless otherwise indicated.

Table 9.8   Bulletin items 17 May 1975

	Duration*
BBC1 17.20	
Mayaguez arrives in Singapore/more Thai demos	2.37
Seven children killed in Lebanon near border	0.21½
Japanese women conquer Everest; more Nuptse deaths	0.27½
Thatcher addresses Scottish Tory conference	0.22½
Jones calls for positive union response to crisis	0.12½
Powell speech anti-EEC/Heffer speech anti-EEC/Crosland speech pro-EEC/Thorpe EEC debate like Weimar	2.00
Flooding in south	0.30
Soccer; home internationals; no trains to Wembley next Saturday; last Rugby League trophy won by Leeds; Ali beats Lyle	2.21
BBC1 21.35	
Mayaguez arrives in Singapore/more Thai demonstrations	2.21
Jones calls for flat-rate wage increase	0.47½

Table 9.8 continued

	Duration*
Thatcher addresses Scottish Tory conference	0.52½
Prentice interviewed on possible education cuts	1.59½
Powell speech anti-EEC/Crosland speech pro-EEC	1.49½
Japanese women conquer Everest; more Nuptse deaths	0.33½
Flooding in south	0.23
Newmarket stable fire	0.15½
Princess Anne and Mark Phillips at army horse trials	0.39½

*ITN 13.10***

Mayaguez arrives Singapore/Thai demands	2.23
Saigon under curfew	0.24½
Healey (in US TV interview) warns AUEW: Scanlon votes for branch voting	1.16½

ITN 17.10

Mayaguez arrives Singapore/more Thai demonstrations	2.06
Jones calls for positive response by unions to crisis	0.25
POWU shelve plans for more Saturday pay	0.17½
Thatcher addresses Scottish Tory conference	0.24½
AUEW: Scanlon votes for branch voting	0.18½
Powell anti-EEC speech/Crosland pro-EEC speech	0.28
Flooding through rain in south	0.22½

*ITN 22.30****

Mayaguez arrives in Singapore/Thai demonstration
Healey (in US TV interview) warns
Jones calls for positive union response to crisis
Thatcher addresses Scottish Tory conference
POWU shelves plans for more Saturday pay
AUEW: Scanlon votes for branch voting
Crosland speech anti-EEC/Thorpe speech pro-EEC/Powell speech anti-EEC/Heffer speech anti-EEC
Sport: home internationals/England rugby in Australia/ cricket: rain hits play/Ali beats Lyle

BBC2 19.30

Mayaguez arrives in Singapore/Thai protests, demonstrations	2.36½
Laos; three US officials still held in homes/More soldiers want communists to take over	1.29½
Seven children killed in Lebanon near border	0.12
Japanese women conquer Everest; more Nuptse deaths	0.29
Thatcher addresses Scottish Tory conference	0.17½
Jones calls for positive union response to crisis	0.13½
Powell speech anti-EEC/Crosland speech pro-EEC	1.44½
Flooding in South	0.21
Newmarket stable fire	0.21½
Sport: home internationals – no trains to Wembley next Saturday – Leeds v. St. Helens (league)/England in Australia; rain stops tennis, cricket; Ali beats Lyle; Princess Anne at army horse trials	5.59

Table 9.8 continued

	Duration*
BBC2 23.20	
Jones calls for flat-rate wage rise	0.37½
Thatcher addresses Scottish Tory conference	0.56½
Mayaguez arrives in Singapore/Thai demonstrations	1.48½
Powell speech anti-EEC/Crosland speech pro-EEC	0.39
Japanese woman conquers Everest	0.16¼
Princess Anne at army horse trials	0.15½ + 0.6 music

*Excluding headline, hooker and payoff timings unless otherwise indicated.
**Rest of bulletin unrecorded.
***Tape destroyed in playback; no timings available.

10   Halting the Flow

Analysis of a distribution of interest or categories in a broad-casting programme, while in its own terms significant, is necessarily abstract and static. In all developed broadcasting systems the characteristic organisation, and therefore the characteristic experience, is one of sequence and flow. This phenomenon, of planned flow, is then perhaps the defining characteristic of broadcasting, simultaneously as a technology and as a cultural form.

Raymond Williams, *Television: Technology and Cultural Form*

Openings

Raymond Williams draws attention to the essential difference in the experience of the television viewer from, say, that of an audience at a play or a football match. The television audience is invited to watch a sequence of miscellaneous 'items' (programmes), often interspersed with plugs for programmes to be shown later, channel announcements, and on commercial television, commercial breaks. The continuousness of this sequence has grown over the years. No more is the programmatic format punctuated by channel continuity icons like the potters' wheel. The sequence now is more of a planned flow designed to keep the viewer 'hooked'. This has little to do with the technical requirements of the medium, but is rather the product of the competition for ratings and channel loyalty.

The viewer does not by and large watch individual programmes but chooses channels. Inheritance of audience from one programme to another is a crucial factor in determining any single programme's audience. The programmes are obviously perceived as separate but the experience of television relies rather on their sequentiality.

In this situation the opening and closing of each programme is important. The different genres of programming, a difference institutionalised by the existence of different departments within the broadcasting organisations, all adopt genres of opening title offering instant clues as to the type of programme that follows. With news and current affairs there are clearly differences governing the styles of titles. Current affairs programmes, at the time of the study, offered as a dominant mode a tapestry of faces, sometimes concentrating on the presenters involved in the programme as well as other newsworthy people. The news bulletins eschew the possibility of using the reporters, correspondents and newscasters in this way. All new titles refer either to the events of the day (which mean that the opening image changes although the superimposed name of the bulletin and the opening music remains the same), or they have standard openings ranging from a simple animated caption (*News Extra*) to a complex film title lasting around fifteen seconds or more as in the case of *First Report*. The images of these standardised openings are all drawn from a narrow range. In the *First Report* title the faces shown are those of the three major political leaders and President Ford. During our period the Heath photograph was substituted by a photograph of Thatcher following her election as leader (Photo 2a). *News at Ten* uses the Parliament building, panning from black (the dark Thames waterfront) on to the House of Commons and then zooming in to the clock face (Photo 2d). Delayed bulletins feature the correct time (although, as Richard Collins points out without theoretic explanation, the weather is unchanging). The pan and zoom last around fifteen seconds in each edition.

During our period the main BBC bulletin featured the newsroom itself via a permanently installed camera (Photo 2b). This gave a general view of the room which could be matted-in to other pictures generated in the news studio some floors below. Thus the opening sequence involved shots of the newsroom with an animated title over, followed by shots of the news studio showing both newscasters and on occasion other correspondents, as in Example 10.1. The system of shots worked except that the relative distances of the newsroom camera from the scene it was photographing and the news studio camera from its scene were different, with the result that on occasion some person in the newsroom could loom giant-like behind the newscaster in the news studio. An example of this can be seen in Photo 2e. The shape behind Kenneth Kendall (who

Example 10.1   BBC1, 21.00, 13 May 1975

---

1   GV newsroom: empty
    desks, etc.
    0.2
    1a *Super Nine O'Clock*
    News cap. (Photo 2b)
    0.5
CUT
	VOICE OVER
	This is the *Nine O'Clock News*
	
	Music

	Music cont.

2   3 shot Baker F/G MS
    profile
    Biddulph B/G MS
    profile (SCR RHT)
    Whitmore B/G MS 7/8
    to CAM (SCR LEFT) +
    BLINDS (Photo 2c)
    0.4
CUT	

	(Fade music) *BAKER (Newscaster) TO CAM* Good Evening.

3   MS Baker (newsroom GV
    Chromokey + *Nine*
    O'Clock Super upper
    SCR LEFT) desk (inc.
    mike and nameplate)	

---

is paying off the bulletin of Wednesday, 15 May) is that of a newsroom worker crossing too close to the newsroom camera. Commenting on the implications of these opening images Collins

Photo 2a   Mrs Thatcher on *First Report*

Photo 2b   *Nine O'Clock News*: newsroom and super

Photo 2c   *Nine O'Clock News*: news studio three – shot

suggests that the use of Parliament by *News at Ten* 'invests the news programme with the authority of Parliament and, reciprocally, constitutes the British Parliament as the centre and source of news'[1] (Photo 2d). Of the ten still photographs that make up the surround in the *First Report* opening title he says, 'the newsworthy world is

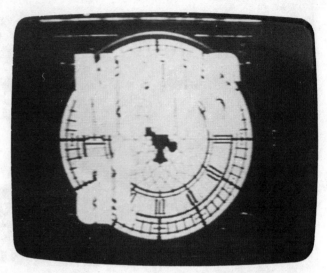

Photo 2d   *News at Ten*: zoom in clock face, animate super

Photo 2e   A 'giant' in the newsroom

constructed as bounded by British parliamentary politics defined in
leaders; the world outside Britain, as represented by the US
President Ford and the EEC; economic activity by images
connoting energy, consumption and exchange'.[2] We would support
these subjective observations of what he calls 'the "ideal" content

Photo 2f   *News Extra*: the straight typographics

of British television news' by noting that his interpretation of this list of images accurately squares with the percentage pattern of story inputs that we have found. There is no image of sport, disaster, science or crime, these being of less importance generally in the running order of the bulletins.

The *Nine O'Clock News* suggested that the news came not from Parliament but from the newsroom, which is perhaps a closer reflection of the reality of mediation. It was nevertheless an odd choice of image (since dropped in favour of a satellite view of the world) because the newsroom during the transmission of the day's final bulletin is not a busy and thriving place. One could compare the nightly levels of inactivity with the early Saturday bulletin inserted at a couple of minutes' length from the newsroom via the same camera. Here, on this 'thin' day, the newscaster sat on the edge of the desk and read a short piece directly to the camera with more activity going on round him than was usual on the *Nine O'Clock News*.

World leaders, centres of political power, newsrooms and the world itself limit the range of changes on which the opening images in this sort of sequence are rung. Apart from the absence of newscasters themselves (a conscious reflection of the British avoidance of making the news personnel stars as they are in the United States)[3] there is now little emphasis on technology – on images of the control room (or gallery as it is called in the BBC), cameras, lights and the rest of television's paraphernalia. The earliest titles (*Roving Report* or *Television Newsreel*) often involved transmitting masts. Perhaps the audience is now presumed to have had its fill of what might be called electronic wonders. In the titles discussed here, titles which reveal a clear social agenda, there is less overt reference to the technology of mediation.

The other standard openings are much simpler, involving plain typographic devices simply announcing the bulletin with music over. And these caption cards are also used to close bulletins. In the use of typography both to open and close bulletins the relationship of the new electronic journalism with the older traditions of print journalism can be seen. The main characteristic of all the typography on the news is that of sans serif type faces, modern and uncluttered. The '2' in the *News Extra* (Photo 2f) is a bastard face specially designed and reflecting the way in which the television picture is constructed line by line. In the *First Report* title the ground on which the inserted images are placed is an abstracted 'degraded' image of hands at a typewriter (Photo 3a), a clear

Photo 3a *First Report*: the inheritance of print journalism

reference back to print. The music, too, often reflects the twin sources of television news practice – journalism and show business. Typewriter rhythms meld into show business trumpet calls.

'Natural fruit juice'

News music is unique in television in that those who commission it require it to be *empty* of myth content. We could paraphrase Barthes and suggest that myth is a kind of music defined by its intention. The clearest use of music-as-myth is that of commercial jingles. It is not for nothing that they have been called 'the folksongs of a consumer society'. For example, the folkiness of the breakfast cereal jingle

> There are two men in my life
> To one I am a mother
> To the other I'm a wife
> And I give them both the best
> With Natural Shredded Wheat.

is an appeal to the powerful mother-provider requirement of our culture, the rustic sun-filled kitchen being a fantasy for millions of city dwellers.

Advertisers go about the business of myth-manipulating with seriousness, and in recent years 'jingle factories' (studios specialising in providing accurate jingles or utility music for advertisers, radio stations, etc.) have proliferated along with specialist independent composers and musicians. That it is a successful and therefore lucrative business is witnessed by the high rates paid to session musicians for jingle recording sessions.

The skills developed by advertising companies in the creation of culturally loaded music themes have been used by television programme producers who look to the specialist to provide themes for new programmes. Retrospectively, since signature tunes pay handsomely in the form of repeat fees, there is always fierce competition for such plums as a series offer.

Looking at specific examples, what precisely is the siren call of the theme of *Coronation Street* (Granada TV) to its particular audience? The theme features a horn melody on a blues scale, seemingly inappropriate to signify the location of the series, a working-class back street in a large Northern industrial town. It is inappropriate until we recall a popular hit of fifteen years ago, *Strangers on the Shore* by Acker Bilk, whose traditional jazz band had been one of the most popular bands of the British traditional jazz revival for years before that. Acker Bilk represents a manifestation of what was most popular with the British working-class youth of the 1950s who are now the middle-aged and still working-class audience that form the faithful viewers of *Coronation Street*.

The theme tune for *Match of the Day* (BBC1) is rich in associations. It is a predominantly brass orchestration over a strong two-beat march rhythm: a martial sound in celebratory mood. It encapsulates the football experience on television – machismo in a fun mood. The Latin-American figure is a reminder of the apogee of football skill and entertainment, the Brazilian national team. There is, too, the possibility that the appeal is to that vast audience who go or hope to go on package tours to the Costa Brava, dancing to the latest cod-Spanish song, 'Viva Espana' or the like: experiencing, as in the World Cup, a vague sense of internationalism.

The use of modern jazz themes to introduce current affairs or interview programmes is interesting since again it would appear, after years of snips from the classical repertoire, to be an inappropriate style. Mozart, Bach *et al.* always registered serious purposes. The switch to modern jazz was probably at first a mimicry of American chat-shows, initially a David Frost innovation. Since then, this kind of music has acquired a cultural familiarity and has become a musical sign that the programme is metropolitan, sophisticated as well as intelligent. The older use of classical borrowings became too sober for programme planners trying to widen their audiences without lowering their emphasis. (Its use is also an indication that jazz has finally been relegated to the cultural élite.)

News music, however, is unique in that those who commission it overtly require that none of the above applies. In that sense it is supposed to be 'empty'. When interviewing some of the composers of news themes, we asked what brief they were given for the commission. The replies suggested that the requirement was that the theme should be emotionally neutral; it should signal the news programme without drawing attention to itself.

The 5.50 ITN news music, 'Non Stop', was written by Malcolm Batt (a television screen writer and lawyer). It was not in fact custom-written but sent by his music publisher in answer to a general request by the ITN for suitable themes. The selection was adjudicated by Sir John Barbirolli. Malcolm Batt claims that its merits as a news theme are that it is 'tuneful, recognisable, difficult to hum. Since musically it is in a circular form it speaks of continuity, constant business, without any further programmatic content. It is without diminuendo or crescendo.' He goes on to describe it as comfortable and predictable.

BBC2's news theme was written by Peter Hope as a response to a general enquiry from the BBC to various music publishers. The idea of the teleprinter and typewriter sound was suggested by them, with the instruction that the piece should indicate immediacy without being over-dramatic and it should have no musical programmatic theme. It should also be serious but not foreboding. Peter Hope describes it as 'neutral fruit juice'.

First Report's search for a theme prefigures the new reliance on specialists. It was commissioned by ITN directly from a company called Emison with much the same brief as we heard of from other composers. Emison provided the music for French ORTF news programmes, as well as six identification packages for local radio stations in this country, and many more throughout Europe.

It is easy to forget that there are very strong precedents for more emotive musical introductions to the news. One has only to remember the stirring signature tune of Pathé Gazette film news; the chimes of Big Ben on BBC radio and the use of Wagner and Beethoven on early television are again reminders that de-mythologised music was not always deemed necessary.

The change in news musical style demonstrates the discomfort with which the news programme itself fits into the flow of television. It is potentially intrusive and contentious. These are qualities that can be of great value in programmes that appear irregularly, but the news is always with us. The music emphasises the image the television companies wish to sustain – that the news is balanced and impartial – in no way are the news personnel personally involved. The news occupies a neutral space in the sequence into which events and facts project themselves almost mechanically. The clackety-clack of the teleprinters, the electronic bleeps that have become the predominant themes of news music draw attention to the *processes* of news collection and presentation, and reflect the typographical origins of 'news'. The news comes, the music suggests, through neutral air waves on to neutral typewriters, a balanced mix of electronic show business and print.

Changing images

The weekend and the two early evening bulletins use music as the unifying factor for their opening because they change their opening image from bulletin to bulletin. The major story of the day is therefore introduced as an image before it is revealed in spoken text. There is a view of television journalism which says that the newsrooms' ability to deliver a full report on the days events is hampered by the need to provide vivid images.[4] We have gone some way to denying this premise by pointing out above that never less than 25 per cent or so of any bulletin is newscaster reading to camera and that the total amount of time spent by newscaster and correspondents reading to camera is far greater. Add to this interviews, speeches and press conferences and our contention that the news largely consists of 'talking heads' must be sustained. In other words, these factors coupled with our analysis, which reveals the predominance of parliamentary, economic and industrial news, means that the newsrooms are not primarily motivated in their daily agenda-setting tasks by what is most visual. Further discussion of this will be found below. But for the moment it is interesting to note that in

Photo 3b   ITN, 18.05, 11 May 1975

those bulletins with a changing-image title, where visual considerations might be expected to be greatest, nevertheless it is still the major story (irrespective of its visual quality) that is placed in the prime lead position.

Thus the opening images of these bulletins are often file

Photo 3c   BBC1, 12.55, 13 May 1975

Photo 3d   BBC1, 17.45, 15 May 1975

photographs, library film, or graphics. The opening images of these
bulletins are listed in Table 10.1. All have the bulletin title (e.g.
'BBC News', 'ITN News') superimposed (*supered*) over them. The
most crucial point about Table 10.1 (in view of the arguments about
the existence of what might be called a 'visual imperative') is how

Photo 3e   BBC1, 12.55, 16 May 1975

Table 10.1   Index of opening images (Index 2): week 11 – 17 May 1975

Date	Channel	T/X time	Description: visual track	Description: sound track
11/5	BBC1	18.05	*Still portrait* Wilson	Mus. + V/O
		21.30	Ditto	Mus.
	ITN	18.05	*Composite still*: Portrait Wilson + Ryton factory sign (Photo 3b)	Mus.
		22.00	*Still portrait*: Wilson	Mus.
12/5	BBC1	12.55	*Graphic* '£'	Mus. + V/O
		17.45	Flixborough *Library* *Film* of fire	2 shot Mus. + 1 shot V/O
	ITN	17.50	*Graphic* '£' declines	Mus. animate V/O
13/5	BBC1	12.55	B&W *Photograph* *Mayaguez* (Photo 3c)	Mus. + V/O
		17.45	Ditto	Mus. + V/O
	ITN	17.50	Ditto	
14/5	BBC1	12.55	*Photograph* Chrysler HQ colour	Mus.
		17.45	*Map*: Cambodia, Gulf of Thailand	Mus. +V/O
	ITN	17.50	*Map*: Utapao, Cambodia, Ko Tang Kompong Som Phnom Penh Gulf of Thailand *Mayaguez*	Mus. +V/O
15/5	BBC	12.55	*Map*: Ko Tang Cambodia Thailand	Mus. + V/O
		17.45	*Graphic*: Dunlop and British Leyland logos (Photo 3d)	Mus. + V/O

Table 10.1 continued

Date	Channel	T/X time	Description: visual track	Description: sound track
	ITN	17.50	*News picture*: B&W: US marines alighting under fire from helicopter GV	Mus. + V/O
16/5	BBC1	12.55	*Film*: British soldiers marching LS/MS	1st shot Mus (Photo 3e) 2nd shot V/O (Photo 3f)
		17.45	*Colour photograph*: Shopping precinct (Photo 3g)	Mus. animate (Photo 3h) V/O
	ITN	17.50	*Film*: (Library?) Track MS down supermarket shelves	Mus. + V/O + super (Photo 3i)
17/5	BBC1	17.20	*News picture*: B&W: *Mayaguez* aerial on tow	Mus. + V/O
		21.35	*Film*: *Mayaguez* docked at Singapore GV bows zoom in CU name	Mus. + V/O
	ITN	13.10	*News picture*: B&W *Mayaguez* at sea + *Film*: Docked at Singapore 4 LS crew + name of ship	Mus. + V/O
		17.10	*Film*: *Mayaguez* docked: GV bows pull back, pan RHT.	Mus. + V/O
		22.30	*Film*: *Mayaguez* docked: 3 LS men on deck, pull back	Mus. + V/O
	BBC2	19.30	*Film*: *Mayaguez* docked: flag + GV bridge	Mus. + V/O
		23.20	*Still portrait*: Jack Jones	Mus. + V/O

few of the images directly and indisputably relate to the day on which they are transmitted. Only the black and white news picture of the American marines on the Thursday and the shots of the *Mayaguez* docked at Singapore on Saturday are in this sense 'news pictures'. The rest range from maps, library film (or film if specially shot that could just as well be from the library – as in the BBC2 lunchtime soldiers footage), still portraits which are on file or graphic designs of various sorts – the most extreme being the Dunlop/British Leyland logos used by the BBC on the same day the ITN used the marines.

There seems to be a general tendency, as exhibited in Table 10.1, for the newsproducers not to worry overmuch about the visual quality of the opening icon. In other words even if the stories of major importance were more accessible, other criteria than the

Photo 3f   BBC1, 12.55, 16 May 1975

Photo 3g   BBC1, 17.45, 16 May 1975

visual would still be used to determine the lead item, and in consequence the lead image. The news, at least in its opening moments, is not the prisoner of sensation-seeking producers thrusting instantaneous, dramatic, but unimportant images at their audience.

The sense of urgency and immediacy that the bulletins have is here conveyed as much by the music and by the typography of the title as it is by the image. In this way the changing image titles match the unchanging ones. The types of title impose via music and typography a sense of urgency independent of the news images of the day. This enables the titles to function as attention-getters but also allows the producers to put visually dull political, economic and industrial affairs in the lead position.

It follows that the majority of the above images are not used iconically. Take for instance the composite still image ITN used for the 18.05 bulletin on Saturday 11 May. Neither element of the composite – the Wilson portrait or the Ryton factory gate (Photo 3b) – was necessarily taken on the day in question. The composite assumes that the audience will read a visual headline – Prime Minister comments or acts on industrial situation at Chrysler. Similarly, when faced with the economy, always difficult to visualise, images of supermarkets or shopping precincts are so used as to give clues to the type of story involved. Here, because supermarkets and shopping precincts are an all-pervasive locale for the inflation story in all its aspects, screen writing is required to make the visual headline clear (e.g. BBC1, 17.45, 16 May 1975; Photos 3g and 3h).

There are thus two extremes in these images. On the one hand there is the image that does express the story iconically. Marines landing on Ko Tang Island are photographed doing so and reported as so doing. The *Mayaguez* at the dock in Singapore is filmed there and is reported as being there. At the other extreme there is a photograph of the Prime Minister, taken at an undetermined time, and a photograph of a factory gate, also taken at an undetermined time, together signifying in some detail an industrial situation. Or there are the two company logos standing symbolically for the companies, as indeed they were designed to do (Photo 3d). In between there are images which are undetermined as to the time they were collected but stand in a midway indexical relationship to the event they represent. The portrait stills of Mr Wilson, not composited with other images (ITN, 22.00, 11 May 1975), the picture of Mr Jones (BBC2, 23.20, 17 May 1975), and above all the only available picture of the *Mayaguez* (until its release) are examples of this. The image of the *Mayaguez* (Photo 3c) is indubitably an icon of the ship; but it is being used to represent the ship in a particular place – Ko Tang. There is no image of the ship in that place available and therefore the iconic image is used indexically. Most of the images in the news, whether stills, film or tape, are indexical in this sense. Only when incorporeal and intangible subjects, such as the economy, are being dealt with does the material become symbolic; and only when events take place in front of the camera, as in the case of sport, does the image become iconic. These last two are rarer.

We have further commented on the overall similarity of the bulletins channel to channel. In Table 10.1 we can see that similar responses are called out for similar stories. In other words after allowing for the fact that the notion of what is important is common to both services, the visual response (as it were) is also common. It would be unfair to cite the *Mayaguez* story under this heading since clearly only one picture of the ship was available for a good part of the week. But the response to the inflation story on the Friday (BBC colour photograph of shopping precinct with information *supered* and ITN film of supermarket, Photos 3h and 3i), or the use of the

Photo 3h   BBC1, 17.45, 16 May 1975

Cambodian map on the Tuesday, are examples of this tendency to find the same solution. Against this has to be placed the failure of the BBC's early bulletin to use the news picture of the marines, one of the only icons to emerge from the *Mayaguez* affair, as the lead on the following day. But the point can nevertheless be maintained.

Competition between these two early evening bulletins does not extend, in practice, into the selection of the opening images.

Table 10.1 reveals the range of possibilities available for this sort of changing-image opening. All the openings we have described have a standard piece of music and a standard superimposed bulletin identification. The images come from an almost full range of the inputs generally available in the bulletins – film, news pictures, file portrait stills, graphics, general ('other') photographs, maps. News personnel, whether live, on film or tape or in the radio circuit caption mode, did not appear. Neither, in this particular week, did live, filmed or taped interview shots.

Photo 3i   ITN, 17.50, 16 May 1975

If the image was a still of any kind then there would be just one used. Animating further written information (that is, other than the bulletin identification) on that still was possible. If there was more than one shot in the opening sequence then the input was always film. In other words only one still image was used per bulletin. The music always covered the opening image and the identification super. Then either the newscaster appeared to camera or he (Angela Rippon not being involved in any of the bulletins using this repertoire of openings) would speak over. If he voiced-over the image a cut would occur as he began to speak on those occasions when film was used. But on one occasion in the week in question the voice-over began four words before the cut. The music never exceeded 10 seconds, running usually between 7 and 8½ seconds. On the BBC the voice-over sections never exceeded 6 seconds if only one image was involved or, in the case of multiple film shots, the total for the two shots was 6½ seconds. The lunchtime bulletin voiced-over every day except Wednesday, the BBC1 early evening bulletin every day.[5] ITN did it every day except Tuesday but did not use the technique on the two Sunday bulletins, when BBC did; or on one of the Saturday bulletins, when both BBC1 and BBC2 did. This is an area of directors' (or general production) choice and the significance is to be found not in the range of differences, but in the similarities involved.

A difference nevertheless is that when ITN does use voice-over, rather than cutting to newscaster-to-camera, it does so for longer than the BBC does: 9 seconds on the Monday, 23 seconds on the Wednesday (which involved a slow zoom into the Cambodian map), 11½ seconds on Thursday and 17 seconds (over the tracking shot, on film, of the supermarket shelves) on Friday. Matching this are the BBC2 bulletins on Sunday, the earlier of which went for three shots of the *Mayaguez* lasting 3½, 5, and 18 seconds following the opening music. In fact the film of the *Mayaguez* at the Singapore dockside was broken by a map and then continued, so it was not until 2 minutes 25 seconds into the bulletin that the newscaster appeared. The later BBC2 bulletin took 55 seconds voice-over before showing the newscaster.

One difference between changing and unchanging image titles is that in the former case, whether voice-over is used or the newscaster appears immediately, there is no greeting – 'Good afternoon', etc. In the unchanging image title there is always a newscaster greeting – Kee's 'Hello' and everybody else's 'Good Evening'. This is true even of *News at Ten* which, as we shall see, combines in the opening 'bongs' sequence a changing image follow-up to one unchanging image opening. Normally, then, with these changing-image openings moving talking heads do not appear, although still portraits do. Images such as maps which have writing on them can be used. Only one still image per opening is preferred, but if film is used up to three shots can appear. The commentary voice-over normally starts after the first cut and follows the shot over which identification of the bulletin is *supered*. Normally, the music does not last for more than ten seconds. If one image is being used there is a tendency to move the camera relative to it after ten static seconds.

It is our contention that these routine practices work with other cultural conventions and codes to establish a set of hidden 'viewers' maxims' by which the audience understands the bulletins. If any of the above are happening on the screen, a bulletin is beginning. With the standard unchanging opening titles the process in terms of viewers' maxims is easier, but we should again note that the longest of these (*First Report*) did not run for more than 17 seconds, *News at Ten* for about 15 seconds, and the three shots at the start of the *Nine O'Clock News* for about 12 seconds. The maxims attached to these are therefore simpler. Since the images never change (except in major revisions from time to time) they can be deemed to be more recognisable than the changing-image openings. The BBC *News Extra* was the most iconic and the simplest of all, a straightforward caption. All the other bulletins were short inserts into other programmes, verbally introduced by other non-newsroom performers. Unchanging-image openings do respond to the events of the day. In such bulletins there is always a summary of upcoming stories. These are anyway the longer bulletins and repetitions are therefore deemed more possible. In the case of *First Report* and the *Nine O'Clock News* this summary or list of headlines was simply read to camera by the newscaster or presenter; in the case of *News Extra* they were read by the newscaster but with changing images on the *Chromokey* screen behind him or her; and, most elaborately, in *News at Ten* they were voiced-over images, punctuated each time by a single chime of Big Ben (the 'bongs').

During the week the *Nine O'Clock News* took on average 33 seconds to read its headlines; *First Report* took 50 seconds. These differences again reflected the more current affairs style pacing of the earlier bulletin. *News Extra* also took 33 seconds on average to read its headlines but the range was greater than the *Nine O'Clock New*'s, where 9½ seconds separated the shortest and the longest headline text; in *News Extra* there was a 23-second spread from the shortest (at 26.5 seconds) to the longest (at 49.5 seconds).

The use of the *Chromokey* for *News Extra*'s headlines was among the more complex uses of this device during our recording period.[6] We will leave detailed discussion of these five opening newscaster shots in *News Extra* until *Chromokey* in general is discussed below. However, it can be here noted that during our period the possibility that *Chromokey* has to allow film, tape or any input to be matted in behind the newscaster's head is eschewed in favour of stills alone. Thus the iconic quality of the images in these headlines is much reduced. For instance, with Aubrey Jones in the studio for an interview the image on the headline was a file still photograph of him. A still colour photograph of a hospital bed indexed a story on private medicine. A general view (colour photograph) of a steel mill at work denoted redundancy in the steel town of Irlam, where the mill had closed. Both of these last were film features and therefore film was available. Similarly Flixborough appeared as a colour photograph in the *News Extra* headline shot and the 'Chrysler Wives' as a black-and-white news picture when footage of these events was available and used later in the bulletin. Thus stills seem to be preferred.

The same is not true of ITN's 'bongs' sequences in the main bulletin. These lasted about 24 seconds and involved the greatest rate of image change. Their spread was from a shortest of 17.5 seconds to a longest of 37 seconds, but the shots within the sequence varied only from 3.5 seconds to 5 seconds, the vast majority lasting a regular 4 or 4.5 seconds. Here every type of input was utilised involving the most complex regular directing operation in any bulletin on any channel during the time of our sample (see Examples 10.2a–10.2e). The director's discretion in this area can be

Example 10.2a   *ews at Ten*, opening headlines 'The Bongs', Monday 12 May 1975

Opening title: pan GV Parliament Sq: zoom in Big Ben *super News at Ten* CUT 0.15 0.15	Music /F/X 'Bong'
GV *Mayaguez* at sea *B&W photograph* CUT 0.5 0.20	BOSANQUET *(Newscaster) VOICE-OVER* The Cambodian navy seizes an American merchant ship. /F/X 'Bong'
President Ford MCU *Portrait still* ease-in (slight) CUT 0.4 0.24	BOSANQUET *VOICE-OVER* President Ford says piracy and demands its immediate release. /F/X 'Bong'
£ in crystal ball *Graphic* CUT 0.4½ 0.28½	BOSANQUET *VOICE-OVER* The pound slides again but not by much. /F/X 'Bong'
GV new fertilizer plant under	BOSANQUET *VOICE-OVER* Flixborough explosion –

Example 10.2a continued

---

construction	*Film*	
CUT 0.2½	0.31	/it was caused by a faulty repair.

CUT GV 2 stacks – pull back		
Aftermath	*Film*	
CUT 0.2½	0.33½	/F/X 'Bong'

		BOSANQUET VOICE-OVER
MLS Orantes serves	*Tape*	Tennis – Spain have beaten us in
CUT 0.2½	0.36	/the Davis Cup.

LS GV down court – balls		
delivered	*Tape*	
CUT 0.1½	0.37½	/*BOSANQUET TO CAM*

Bosanquet MS + CSO insert	Good evening . . .

Example 10.2b   *News at Ten*, Tuesday 13 May 1975

Opening title: pan GV		Music
Parliament Sq: zoom in Big		
Ben: *super News at Ten*		
CUT 0.14	0.14	/F/X 'Bong'

		GARDNER (Newscaster) VOICE-OVER
GV *Mayaguez* at dock		Captured cargo boat; American warships
B&W photograph		and marines stand by.
CUT 0.4½	0.18½	/F/X 'Bong'

		GARDNER VOICE-OVER
Display of £ notes	*Graphic*	Work has stopped on printing Britain's
		banknotes.
CUT 0.4½	0.23	/F/X 'Bong'

		GARDNER VOICE-OVER
CU Foot	*Portrait Still*	Mr Foot tells the Chrysler strikers to go
		back to work.
CUT 0.4	0.27	/F/X 'Bong'

		GARDNER VOICE-OVER
CU Cover CBI report		CBI forecast a deep recession and
	Graphic	rising unemployment.
CUT 0.4½	0.31½	/F/X 'Bong'

		GARDNER VOICE-OVER
GS 6 Japanese (ceremonial		The once-a-year soccer match fit for a
robes) players	*Film*	Queen.
CUT 0.4	0.35½	/*GARDNER TO CAM*

Gardner MS + CSO	Good evening . . .
insert RHT	

Example 10.2c   *News at Ten*, Wednesday 14 May 1975

Opening title: pan GV Parliament Sq: zoom in Big Ben: *super News at Ten* CUT 0.15	Music / F/X 'Bong'
Map: Thailand Cambodia Utapao Gulf of Thailand Phnom Penh Kompong Som Ko Tang *Mayaguez* CUT 0.4½	GARDNER *(Newscaster) VOICE-OVER* The captured cargo boat; America sinks Cambodian warships. / F/X 'Bong'
GV *Mayaguez* at dock *B&W photograph* CUT 0.4	*GARDNER VOICE-OVER* No one knows what's happened to the crew of thirty-nine. / F/X 'Bong'
GV Cranes/Ship dock scene *Colour photograph* CUT 0.4½	*GARDNER VOICE-OVER* Trade figures – some cheering news. / F/X 'Bong'
CU Ballot box, hand dropping in vote *Colour photograph* CUT 0.4	*GARDNER VOICE-OVER* The referendum: we'll know the result by teatime on 6 June. / F/X 'Bong'
CU Rapist – identikit picture B&W *Portrait Still** CUT 0.4½ Gardner MCU plain B/G	*GARDNER VOICE-OVER* The Cambridge rapist – a report from the nervous city. / *GARDNER TO CAM* Good Evening . . .

*So classified.

Example 10.2d   *News at Ten*, Thursday 15 May 1975

Opening title etc. CUT 0.15	Music / F/X 'Bong'
GV *Mayaguez* at dock *B&W Photograph* CUT 0.4½	GARDNER *(Newscaster) VOICE-OVER* After the rescue the *Mayaguez* is heading for Singapore. / F/X 'Bong'
MLS 4 shot marines out of helicopter zoom in CU *B&W News picture* CUT 0.4½	*GARDNER VOICE-OVER* 16 marines are dead or missing. / F/X 'Bong'
GV pan strike crowd *Tape? Film?* CUT 0.4½	*GARDNER VOICE-OVER* Chrysler strikers vote to stay out. / F/X 'Bong'

Example 10.2d continued

CU Dunlop company logo	*GARDNER VOICE-OVER*
Graphic	Settlement is on the cards for Dunlop.
CUT 0.4	*/GARDNER TO CAM*
Gardner MS + CSO	Good Evening . . .
insert RHT	

Example 10.2e   *News at Ten*, Friday 16 May 1975

Opening title etc.	Music
CUT 0.15	/F/X 'Bong'
Shrinking £ effect: *super*	*BOSANQUET (Newscaster) VOICE-OVER*
graphic £ zoom back over GV	Britain's inflation rate a record figure,
top shot shop *colour*	far worse than expected.
photograph + *Graphic*	
CUT 0.4½	/F/X 'Bong'
CU Dunlop company logo –	*BOSANQUET VOICE-OVER*
zoom in *Graphic*	The Dunlop strike is over, 18,000 go
	back to work . . .
CUT 0.3½	/F/X 'Bong'
Chrysler Ryton plant, Stoke:	*BOSANQUET VOICE-OVER*
GV gate zoom back and pan	. . . but Chrysler throw 8,000 out of a job
Colour photograph	tonight.
CUT 0.3½	/F/X 'Bong'
2 MS armed soldiers	*BOSANQUET VOICE-OVER*
Colour photograph	The armed forces get a 29 per cent pay rise.
CUT 0.5	/F/X 'Bong'
Nastase/Taylor montage	*BOSANQUET VOICE-OVER*
2 CU (in whites)	Tennis, Nastase and Taylor in trouble
Portrait stills	at Bournemouth.
CUT 0.4½	/*BOSANQUET TO CAM*
Bosanquet MCU plain B/G	Good Evening . . .

seen in such matters as whether the 'bong' – the single chime of Big Ben – comes before or after or (as on the Friday) over the cut. Otherwise the regularity of the time is again noticeable: 3½ to 5 seconds for stills images and a total of up to 5 seconds for film or tape (which never exceeds two shots). The stills are sometimes subjected to camera movement.

Beyond this one can again see that the range of images is not dictated by the visual quality of the stories. The stories are determined by journalistic criteria, not by a purely visual one. It is however possible to see, as in the case of the Japanese footballers on Tuesday and the Cambridge rapist on Wednesday, a tendency to also headline (as a 'hooker') stories from the second half of the bulletin which follows the commercial break. These two examples were both exclusive but the tendency is not limited to such features. For instance, the sports story which closed the 'bongs' on the Friday was shared by the BBC. It is fair to hypothesise that in this last spot in the headlines the possibility of choice being determined more by the visual excitement of the image than a journalistic sense of the importance of the story was increased.

The tendency to subordinate the visual to the journalistic must again be pointed out. For instance, on the Thursday the most dramatic and iconic image of the week – the news picture of the marines landing on Ko Tang – was second to the indexical image of the *Mayaguez* which had already figured three times as the opening image of the changing-title bulletins as well as having been used every previous night of the week on the 'bongs', as well as on eighteen other occasions in the body of the bulletins for voicing-over and on three occasions in *Chromokey*. Freshness of image is often adduced by critics to be a major newsroom concern and is coupled with the suggestion that it involves trivialisation. But it is not very apparent here. The serious business of agenda setting is too important, as far as we can tell, for the visual imperative to be a major consideration.

The need to visualise the headlines leads to extremely symbolic imagery, especially, as we have previously noted, in the areas of economic and industrial reporting. The '£ in crystal ball' graphic used in Monday's 'bongs' involved a distorted Union Jack which took us a number of viewings to decode.[7] Locked-out banknote printers were signified by a display of pound notes which also served as a backing for the economic correspondent on another occasion; a general picture of the dockside signified trade figures; an industrial settlement was symbolised by the company logo (not, by the way, joined by the union badge). Inflation became a visual pun with a visibly shrinking pound sign, achieved by zooming out from a '£' symbol on the caption. Of the 26 images involved in the week's 'bongs' only 4 were iconic (Orantes serving – 2 shots; the marines on Ko Tang – 1 shot; the Chrysler strike vote – 1 shot) and happened on (or in the case of the marines nearly on) the day they were transmitted. To this must be added the shot of the cover of the CBI economic trends report. And one must also add the iconic image of the Japanese footballers although that did not happen on the day of transmission but some days earlier. Of the rest 11 are indexical and 9 symbolic.

Just as the above title sequences indicate to the audience the particular nature of the broadcast, a news bulletin, so the final images indicate its end and the start of other genres of programming. All the final images with only one exception were straightforward typographic captions naming only the newscasters. The exception was the late Saturday bulletin on BBC2 where a changing image was used, in the week of the sample Princess Anne on horseback. It was the one bulletin that did not have either a mention of later bulletins to come or a 'Good Night' before the final image began. The most significant thing about these final captions was that they routinely only mentioned the newscasters. The news bulletins, together with the weather, commercials and presentation, were the only genres of programmes which had no producers or technical staff as far as public on-screen announcements (credits) are concerned.[8]

It is true that live transmission often means that the closing credits are lost, but even in those current affairs magazines where the credits are not automatically played there is normally one edition a week in which they appear. The only programme emanating from the newsrooms in our period for which this was true was the Sunday news for the deaf. This general lack is significant. We would argue the bulletins must hereby be assumed not to be produced in the sense that other programmes are produced. This is an important expression of the neutrality that is supposed to underpin the bulletins. We might see newsroom personnel in the background of the *Nine O'Clock News*'s presentation but basically it is the faces on screen that are responsible for the bulletins.

Since some bulletins, as we have shown above, use appreciable amounts of time at the outset with repetitive and unchanging opening routines the argument that time alone is responsible for this lacuna in naming producers is not entirely sustainable. Each day *First Report* gave no information about the events of the day for upwards of 20 seconds; the *Nine O'Clock News* did the same for upwards of 12 seconds and *News at Ten* for 15 seconds. Such an allocation of time at the other end could at least be used to add to the names of the newscasters those of the producer and director responsible for the bulletin, as has now happened with ITN. Or is anonymity the BBC's final guarantee of neutrality?

11   'Good Evening'

Whom but a dusk misfeatured messenger
No other than the angel of this life
Whose care is lest men see too much at once

Browning

Television from its beginnings has followed the dominant naturalistic traditions of the early-twentieth-century stage in its settings; a
tradition which has also dominated film design. Thus, rather than
utilise, except for special purposes, alternative non-naturalistic
symbolic or expressionist styles, television has followed the Theatre
of the Fourth Wall and the cinema in making, as it might be, a
constant assumption of reality. All situation comedies and most
dramas are set, like outside broadcasts, in environments that are to
be perceived by the viewer as real. For those programme forms that
are more particular to television (current affairs, 'chat' shows and
the news bulletins) there is no real equivalent of this 'normalcy' to
call upon.

The various responses to this lack are not entirely satisfactory.
Tynan, in describing an appearance by Sir Ralph Richardson on
The Russell Harty Show, draws attention to this:[1]

The setting was the usual mock-up, in this case a semi-circular
arrangement of window draperies with nothing behind it, and a
low window seat and a pair of tulip-shaped chairs (one of them
occupied by Harty) in front of it . . . Sir Ralph enters around one
side of the draperies . . . Sir Ralph; 'You've got a very nice place
here, haven't you . . . You've got a lot more cameras in your
place than I've got in mine.'

The problem of setting can be formulated as a paradox. In those programmes in which television most directly comments on the world, the most obviously non-naturalistic settings are employed. The 'chat' show ranges from Harty's sub-naturalistic drawing room to variants of the airport departure lounge. The most characteristic element in the setting of the 'chat' show is the armchair – the 'easy chair', normally of an extremely expensive modern type.

Studio-based current affairs programmes, although often having an armchair area in the set, create their own even less naturalistic setting. This vision of 'current affairs land', as it were, is characterised not by these expensive leather chairs but by the desk behind which the presenters sit. Desks are authoritative, we would argue, since in our culture for centuries authority has been found behind desks – with its knees covered. The pulpit, the judges' bench, the schoolmaster's table are prime examples of this. Of these three, in current affairs programmes the schoolmaster's is the one most called to mind. This is because, in most settings over the past decade, various devices (back projection, *Chromokey*) have been used to project images on to the wall (i.e. flat) behind the desk. The desk is therefore matched by the blackboard. Since the easy chair element is lacking in the settings for the news bulletins, the school room feel is thereby increased. A naturalistic setting would be the open studio (as used in *That Was the Week That Was*), but this is eschewed, partially because camera crew appearing in vision require, under union agreement, payment for so doing. Further, it would call attention to the electronic making of the news which, as we have argued in the matter of fixed-image main titles, is apparently to be avoided. Thus the main characteristic of the news studio is the desk, accompanied in some bulletins with the inlaid 'blackboard' screen.

Without the *Chromokey* screen, in our period there were three possibilities for backing the newscaster. First there was the plain flat behind the newscaster's head (Photo 4a). This was used by ITN on the Saturday and the Sunday. It is also the effect achieved on *News at Ten* when the *Chromokey* was not being used; that is to say, when we had a medium close-up (MCU). This basic shot could be framed most widely by placing the top of the presenter's pocket at the bottom of the screen and most tightly by placing his buttonhole there, rather than a midshot (MS). Midshots are characterised by either being at the start or end of bulletins or to allow *Chromokey* inserts (Photo 4b) or live interviews (see Chapter 5 above). The plain background was also used by the BBC2 bulletins (with the same *caveat* as to the possibility of a *Chromokey* (CSO) screen to be noted in connection with *News Extra*).

Photo 4a   Studio settings: the plain background. Buttonhole close-up

Photo 4b   Midshot for *Chromokey* screen (CSO)

The second variant used by the BBC1 lunchtime bulletin, and the competing early evening bulletins on BBC1 and ITN, was to texture

Photo 4c Studio settings: patterned background

the flat behind the newscaster with some form of simple pattern. Both BBC and ITN used a similar pattern in our period. The BBC's (which was also used at the weekends) consisted of rows of extruded parallelograms (Photo 4c). ITN used extruded rectangles of the same general size. At the extremes of subtle viewing the rectangles might be considered marginally less 'urgent' than the parallelograms but both illustrate the general point about the non-assumption of reality in this area of programme setting. For where can such wall textures otherwise be seen? ITN's *First Report* also used squares, larger than those in the early evening and lunchtime bulletins, arranged on flats behind the shallow semi-circular desk. These flats gave *First Report* an identification not just in terms of its news presenter, but also in terms of those interviewed in the set. Indeed ITN have on file portrait stills of news personalities clearly taken in this setting. The *First Report* set also had within it a 'screen' on which *Chromokey* could be used in much the same way as *News Extra* for presenter-conducted interviews.

The BBC1 main bulletin, when the newsroom was not matted-in (as happens during the title sequence), backed the newsreaders with a plain venetian blind. But there was also the possibility of suggesting an office with filing cabinets. This was used infrequently (Photo 4d), in fact only once during the week under study (see Example 11.7a, shot 100).

Photo 4d   Studio settings: the 'office' background

Photo 4e   A studio two-shot interview using *Chromokey*

The keynote of these settings is an attempt to achieve a certain neutrality. They are restrained in that they either have no pattern or minimal patterns. They are further restrained as to colour, being for the most part shades of beige or grey. They give no information except that by their unique neutrality they are the material embodiment of those practices that signify the news. Only station announcers are so plainly presented. Within the news settings the *Chromokey* inserts contain information. Otherwise the settings allow the newscaster an absolute dominance of the image. The one exception to this is perhaps the midday Saturday BBC1 bulletin broadcast from the edge of a desk in the newsroom. Here the reality of the setting (it is more iconic than the use of the newsroom via *Chromokey* in the weekday main bulletins) is emphasised by the wide midshot pose which can serve to stress the setting's 'weekend' informality. The informality of this bulletin, inserted into the week's main sports transmission, via the newsroom camera, also allows some of the news studio technical crew to be absent and to come on duty later in the day.

The restraint of the setting is in general pointed up in a number of other ways. First, the range of shots taken in these settings is limited. They are overwhelmingly single shots. In fact in the main BBC and ITN bulletins two or three shots are used only at the start and the finish. Further, only in the BBC main bulletin, in *News Extra* and in *First Report* is there any deviance from the straight-on eye level camera position. In the main BBC1 bulletin angled three shots (Photo 2c) are used only at beginnings and at the end. In the current affairs type bulletins such angled shots are used in interview contexts (shot 36 in Example 11.1; shots 9 and 10 in Example 11.2) (Photo 4e).

Example 11.1   ITN, 13.00, 13 May 1975

33 Kee: CU (bottom of pocket) *First Report* set CUT 1.48	7.48	*KEE (Newspresenter) TO CAM* Anti-marketeers, however, say categorically, that if the vote is 'Yes' your food must cost more. Well, with m (leans back) e in the stud/
34 Rippon: CU (top of pocket) *First Report* set (eyeline SCR, RHT) CUT 0.9	7.57	*KEE VOICE-OVER* io now is Mr Geoffrey Rippon, who as the Conservative Minister with special responsibility for the Common Market negotiated our entry under Mr Heath, two years ago and Mr (scratches chin)/
35 Buchan: CU (top of pocket) *First Report* set (eyeline SCR, LEFT) CUT 0.12	8.9	Norman Buchan who until he resigned last October was Minister of State for Agriculture Fisheries and Food and who is against our continued membership of the EEC. Mr Buchan, why do you/

Example 11.1 continued

36	3 SHOT: Kee (mike-in) + Rippon MS over Buchan's shoulder MCU	*KEE TO CAM* say that a Yes in the referendum will mean dearer food? *BUCHAN*
CUT 0.5	8.14	Well, for/

37	as 35 *super*	*BUCHAN sync.* two reasons principally, and you partly/

- -

37a supercaption: *First Report*, Norman Buchan, MP: Anti-Market lose *super*	explain it in your initial introduction. When you say any cheaper food coming in automatically has a levy placed upon it in order to make the food dear/

- -

and the truth is that the common agricultural policy is a high price policy.

Example 11.2   BBC2, 23.05, 14 May 1975

Videotape

8	Humphrys MS *Colour photo*: day ext White House GV on *CSO* as B/G Full screen (via unilateral satellite ex Washington)	*HUMPHRYS (Correspondent) TO CAM* . . . There will be divisions of opinion and they will continue because there are those people who fear that he is starting on a dangerous trail here but overall he will have the support that he wants. *RIPPON VOICE-OVER*
CUT 0.49	4.11½	Well, I think/

9	Rippon MCU (Top of pocket) ¾ profile Plain B/G	*RIPPON sync.* we have a picture in this country tonight of the might of the United States navy lined
CUT 0.6	4.17½	up with guns pointing at the Cambodi/

10	WIDE 2 SHOT: MS Rippon over shoulder (inc. desk foreground) B/G screen with Humphrys MS & B/G White House (as 8) CSO (Photo 4e)	an Coast. Now what are the chances of those guns being used again?/
CUT 0.4	4.21½	

11 Humphrys MS as 8	*HUMPHRYS TO CAM* I think we have got to consider them fairly strong, diplomatic action hasn't been totally exhausted, that is to say Washington is suggesting it hasn't been totally exhausted.

None of this, however, involves camera movement. The camera in the news studios is virtually always static. The only exception to this across the whole range of bulletins is in the headlines to a medium close-up. By doing so it loses the *Chromokey* screen and gives the MCU with a plain background (Example 11.3). But even

Example 11.3   BBC2, 22.20, 12 May 1975

CUT
1 Rippon MS (½ arm on
desk)SCR RHT *Colour
portrait still* Ford CU
(US flag out of focus as
B/G) on CSO screen left

RIPPON (Newscaster) TO CAM
Good evening/

- - - - - - - - - - - - - - - -

1a *Super* 'Angela Rippon'

Change CSO

President Ford warns the Cambodians of dire
consequences and describes their seizure of
an American merchant ship as an act of piracy.
A report on American reaction in a moment./

1b *Graphic* banknotes
montage
Change CSO

With the pound in your pocket now worth 75
pence, that's since it was floated, I've been
talking to Mr Prices and Incomes/

1c *Colour portrait still*
Aubrey Jones CU
(collar) (Plain B/G)
1a lose *super*

about our econom/

Change CSO

ic crisis.
The Flixbor/

1d *Colour photo* aerial CU
plant day ext. with
smoke
0.30

ough explosion. The official report
blames the management and we ask the
management if they accept it (moves papers)/

Lose CSO screen:
tighten
. . . Hold MCU Rippon
(head & shoulders)
plain B/G

An American merchant ship, the *Mayaguez*
and its crew of 39, all of them American
nationals, has been seized/

- - - - - - - - - - - - - - - -

CUT 0.49½   0.49½

by a Cambodian warship in the Gulf of
Siam. It's not known what the *Mayaguez*'s
cargo is but she's described in the records as
a container ship owned by the Sea Land
Corporation. She was en route from/

---

2 *Map*: Thailand Cambodia
South Vietnam Kompong

RIPPON VOICE-OVER
Hong Kong to Thailand when, say United

Example 11.3 continued

Som Gulf of Thailand	States officials, she was fired on and boarded some 60/
2a *Animate 'X'* CUT 0.12 1.01½	miles off the Cambodian mainland. The *Mayaguez* has been taken to the Port of Kompong Som./
3 Rippon CU plain B/G	*RIPPON TO CAM* President Ford, who was told about the ship's capture at an Intelligence briefing today, called it an act of piracy

here there is an alternative to camera movement. After the *Chromokey* headlines a close-up with plain background can be achieved (Example 11.4) with a straight cut. This involves the newscaster turning to look at a second camera. Again this is the only presentation where this is necessary. *News at Ten*, the only other bulletin to use *Chromokey*, as a general rule moves from midshot with 'screen' to close-ups not on camera but during voice-overs.

Example 11.4   BBC2, 23.05, 13 May 1975

CUT
1 Rippon MS SCR RHT +
    Graphic CBI survey cover
    on CSO screen. SCR LEFT
 	
    Change CSO (0.12)
	RIPPON (Newscaster) TO CAM
	Good evening from *News Extra*. Another voice joins the gloomy chorus. The CBI says we're heading for a deep recession and we ask, as the clouds gather, is there no silver lining anywhere? From the/

1a *Colour photo* GV
     steelworks day ext.
     Change CSO (0.04)
	steel town of Irlam we've a report on what redundancy can mean. We hear what/

1b *Colour photo* GV
     hospital bed day ext.
     Change CSO (0.06)
	private medicine is doing to fill the gap as it's expelled from the Health Service and then how/

1c *Colour photo* pack shot
     Babycham bottle &
     glass
     CUT 0.28   0.28
	champagne protected its name against the interlopers. (Looks off)/

2 Rippon MCU (top of pocket) plain B/G	There'll be a Commons debate on the economy next week, probably Thursday. The Prime Minister announced this soon after the CBI's gloomy forecast of deep industrial depression and more people out of jobs.

Moving the camera

The limitations on the number of persons seen in a single shot and the normal immobility of the camera is further reflected in the movements made by the newscasters themselves.

The range of movement is extremely limited. They never leave their desks. They seldom look anywhere but at the lens. We have already discussed the limited circumstances in which *two shots* or *three shots* occur. It is obviously only possible for glances between personnel to occur in these circumstances. In fact the glance to the other newscaster in the main bulletin is a final kinesic full stop to the bulletin since it never occurs until the last words have been exchanged or spoken. It covers the moments of *supering* closing titles and music. Thus to look at the other caster is to signify the end of the newsreader character – in fact to come out of character, to be seen as human in a more ordinary sense. It is at this point that sometimes the scripts of the bulletin are shuffled – an action which, as Professor Stuart Hood has often pointed out, signifies in our culture a tidying up, the imposition of order on the chaos of information given in the bulletin.

Otherwise, body movement is almost non-existent. There is no turning (the cut to shot 2 in Example 11.4 being the only regular exception to this); the monitors on which the newscaster can see leader material (i.e. film leaders or video-tape clocks, which are put on the front of film and tape inserts to enable the machines – Telecine and videotape recorder (VTR) – to run up to speed and enable the performer to read down to the start of the insert) are placed in the studio to minimise eye movement away from the camera lens. In other words the settings are organised to allow the newscaster to maintain maximum eye contact with the lens and thereby with the audience. All scripts, except for late emendations and additions (which are the exception not the rule), are typed on to an autocue system which enables them to be projected directly in front of the lens so that the performer appears to be speaking rather than reading. Glances down are a form of punctuation, normally serving to paragraph the bulletin. For instance, in the 12.55 bulletin on 12 May Richard Whitmore clearly looked off camera at the end of the first item about the exchange rate. He looked down during the second item between the report of the Chrysler and Leyland strikes and the report of the resignation of the managing director of Jaguar. He looked off camera to a monitor when cueing-in the Peart pro-EEC speech on film. But he also glanced down in the middle of the introductory sentence of the Jenkins defence of Benn story (an unusually short shot for this bulletin – see Example 11.6b).

Robert Kee as a news presenter in the more current affairs format of *First Report* had a greater range of movement than the other performers. He was more often reading from script than autocue. He looked down rather more often and even on occasion, as for instance when introducing interviewees sitting with him, he leaned back. But even he tended to use the glances down as paragraphing. On the morning of 12 May he looked down after his headline on the exchange rate and after the Chrysler strike headline, for instance.

Within this limited repertoire of movement a number of viewers' maxims can be adduced. Although the possibility of late additions to the script, autocue breakdowns and personal predilections render them somewhat tentative, basically it can be said that glances down paragraph reports within a story or distinguish between one story and the next; that looks off camera most often indicate cueing of film or tape inserts; that looks to other newscasters, in the two-presenter shows, are a final punctuation to the bulletin and that their place (as signifiers of the end of 'newscaster' role) is taken by the smile in the single presenter bulletin.

Mention has been made of the framing of these shots. The single shot (with the exception of the BBC Saturday bulletin) is never below waist and never tighter than head and shoulders, cut off at buttonhole level. It should be noted that in portrait stills and in interviews it is possible to frame at the tie-knot and in certain circumstances even tighter – i.e. at the line of the chin. Tighter than that (just below the mouth) has only regularly been used in some current affairs shows, and is seen professionally as a deviant frame.

Gaye Tuchman has pointed out how these tighter shots reflect a closeness to the subject which would only be possible in our society among intimates. It is therefore no surprise that shoulders are normally seen in all news shots. Framing closer is to frame more intimately. The shoulder shots (from MS to MCU in our designation) therefore reflect a cultural norm. They are in fact at the limits of close social space, and the shots do not go over those limits either into the area of far social space or closer intimate space. They are therefore the most appropriate for the newscasters; for the personnel are neither familiars nor strangers.

Thus the dominant image here is of a person at a close social distance, the median point in our culture in the social structuring of interpersonal distances. It is therefore arguable that this again reflects the search on the visual level for a cultural neutrality. The neutral size of the person with the frame (neither intimately close nor distant) matches the neutrality of the bland set colours, the eye level camera and the lack of camera movement.

All of this is without prejudice to the basic fact that between a quarter, in the case of the main bulletins, and over a half, in the short bulletins, of the duration is taken up with the newscaster addressing the lens directly.

Newscaster to camera

But for how long does the newscaster talk in any one shot? The rates of image change in this category (Table 9.1) run from *News Extra* (1.35 changes per minute) to *News at Ten* (3.37 changes per minute). Thus, since these two bulletins use *Chromokey*, it can be said that *Chromokey* does not, *of itself*, affect the length of time the newscasters speak per shot. Basically the distinction remains between current affairs style bulletins and other types.

The current affairs style bulletin allows the performer 44.4 seconds (*News Extra*) and 31.6 seconds (*First Report*) on average per shot (rates of 1.35 and 1.89 respectively). The short bulletin allows 20.4 seconds (*Newsday*) and 18.5 seconds (lunchtime bulletin) (rates of 2.94 and 3.24 respectively). The main bulletins allow 18.2 seconds (BBC *Nine O'Clock News*) and 17.8 seconds (ITN *News at Ten*) (rates of 3.31 and 3.37 respectively). It should be noted that the first part of *News at Ten* allows a longer average shot than the second part, 19.2 seconds as against 16.7 seconds. The early evening bulletins allow 21.2 (BBC) and 18.6 seconds (ITN) – rates of 2.83 and 3.22.

Thus (as was illustrated in Figures 9.1 and 9.2, for the early evening and main bulletins) ITN allows the newscaster to speak uninterruptedly for shorter periods than BBC. This is also true of *First Report* as against *News Extra*, although *News Extra* does use *Chromokey* to increase visual variety.

Therefore the graphs in Figures 9.3–9.10, which show an extraordinary similarity between the bulletins in terms of overall percentage durations of each category of input, must be seen in the light of these further figures. So *News at Ten* spends 24.5 per cent of its time with the newscasters but they talk 0.3 of a second less per shot than the BBC *Nine O'Clock News* casters who have 26 per cent of the total duration of their bulletin. (Again the increased visual interest of the *Chromokey* which is used in *News at Ten* should be borne in mind.) In the early evening ITN's total percentage duration with newscasters is, at 32.9 per cent, less than BBC's at 34.8 per cent. And again ITN allows the newscasters a rather more significant 2.5 seconds or so less per shot on average than does the BBC.

The overall length of the bulletin does not seem to affect the average shot durations. Neither of the two shortest bulletins, BBC1's lunchtime one and BBC2's *Newsday*, allow the newscaster appreciably more or less time than the other main and early evening bulletins. Thus presentational style rather than overall length determines the time newscasters address the screen without interruption. The use of film and tape in the lunchtime bulletin and stills in *Newsday* do not affect the figures either. It is the more expansive current affairs style that conditions the major significant difference in average 'newscaster-to-camera' shot duration.

As can also be noted from Table 9.1, the lengths here are longer than most other inputs except for correspondents, whether they appear to camera or on radio circuit. Film and all graphic inputs are appreciably more quickly cut on the screen. 'Newscaster-to-camera' are in the upper range of shot lengths. We have argued that this implies an assumption on the part of the newsproducers that the audience will watch these talking heads for these uninterrupted lengths of time. This we feel contributes to the authority with which they speak. As will be shown below there is a relationship between social status and this time factor.

The charge of visual sensationalism is again not supported by this willingness to allow the newscasters these shots at these lengths. The newscaster can be used to read a report of an otherwise unillustrated story to camera. These yield the longest shots. In the short bulletins in the week in question the maximum shot was on the Monday lunchtime bulletin, when the newscaster spoke for 62.5 seconds. On *Newsday* that same day 54.5 seconds was the longest shot. For the rest of the week, however, in these two bulletins the longest newscaster shot was under 45 seconds and on four occasions under 30 seconds. For the early evening bulletins the longest was 85 seconds on the BBC on Monday and 75 seconds on ITN on Wednesday. Otherwise the BBC was under 1 minute on every other night of the week and ITN was under on two nights. The longest newscaster shot, however, was never under 30 seconds. The main bulletins offer a contrast. Only once (ITN, Thursday) was the longest shot over 1 minute. Indeed the BBC *Nine O'Clock News* only exceeded 50 seconds once during the week, and (aside from Thursday) ITN exceeded 50 seconds only twice – but it should be noted in their case that of these four long speeches to camera, three were backed with *Chromokey* and, further, they each occurred in the first half of the bulletin. For the second part of *News at Ten*, only once during the week was 40 seconds exceeded.

As would be expected in the current affairs style bulletins, all the longest shots are over 1 minute, except for *First Report* on the Monday. The longest newscaster speech of the week was in *News Extra* on the Monday at 2 minutes and 5 seconds. (But again in *News Extra* every one of these shots was backed by *Chromokey*; see Example 11.5.)

Example 11.5 BBC2, 22.20, 12 May 1975, the longest newscaster to camera piece

CUT	10.15½ /

| 28 Rippon MS + *portrait still* Howe CU (down shot) (blinds B/G) on CSO SCR LFT | *RIPPON (Newscaster) TO CAM* The Conservative Shadow Chancellor, Sir Geoffrey Howe, tonight called for a coalition of understanding between politicians and different parties to fight inflation. Speaking on BBC2's *Newsday* programme, he said there was broad agreement between the Conservatives and a large chunk of the Labour party that there should be big cuts in public spending |
| Change CSO (0.26) | and strict cash limits for wage settlements./ |

. . . .

| 28a *Colour photo* 'Avenger' line GV, nearest car MCU, day, int. | And now some industrial news. The strike at Chryslers in Coventry is to go on. In the absence of any immediate cash offer from the company, shop stewards decided the strike should continue and they made no move to bring forward a mass meeting scheduled for Thursday. 4,000 men could be laid off before |
| Change CSO (0.18) | then./ |

. . . .

| 28b *Colour photo*: Dunlop factory GV day, ext. | And the strike and Dunlops in Coventry is also to continue. After 700 clerical workers turned down a new pay offer. It fell short of their demand for an extra £10 a week. Dunlops themselves have already laid off 2,000 workers and tonight British Leyland laid off another 1,700 men, that makes over 14,000 British Leyland workers laid off because of the |
| Change CSO (0.24) | Dunlop strike./ |

. . . .

Example 11.5 continued

28c	*Colour photo*: 2 shot MS/MCU + Post Office tent over manhole, day, ext.	But Post Office engineers are to get the 25 per cent pay rise in July, a deal which will cost the Post Office about £83 million. It's made up of a flat raise of 18 per cent plus the consolidation of thresholds. A Post Office spokesman said the offer accords fully with
	(0.19)	the guidelines of the Social Contract/
	Lose CSO screen: tighten (200m)	. The head of the railways' white-collar union, Mr Tom Bradley,/
	Hold Rippon MCU + plain B/G	has criticised some unions for not honouring their side of the Social Contract. Mr Bradley, who's a Labour MP on the party's national executive, told his union's annual conference that he found the remarks of some union leaders frightening in their implications for society as a whole. The three rail unions together recently rejected what British Rail say is a 21 per cent offer, claiming around 30 per cent. Mr Bradley argues that in real terms the rises are not as high as that and he told John
	CUT 2.05 12.20½	Burns of his belief in the Social Contract/
29	*Film* Bradley MS, day, ext., arm on rail: seaside cliffs B/G	*BRADLEY (sync.)* I am interested in honouring the Social Contract. My union together with other unions put their hands up in favour of the Social Contract at a special TUC meeting in January 1974 and at the TUC Congress in September 1974.

The newscaster can also be used for shots inserted into stories normally involving a variety of other visual inputs. These yield the shortest values of 'Newscaster to camera' shots. In other words in a sequence which uses film, graphics, etc., the newscaster might appear fleetingly to punctuate items or bridge a visual gap (Example 11.6a, shots 102, 109; see p. 265). Thus in the early evening bulletins and the main bulletins the lowest values are in the 2–3 second range. Since the lowest values are attached to the sophistication of inputs it is not surprising that low values of 3–4 seconds also appear in *First Report* and *News Extra*. And conversely the shortest bulletins might be expected, and indeed have, longer minima – 5 seconds for *Newsday* for instance. The lunchtime bulletin on Monday does have a 2-second shot but it is sandwiched between film and a portrait still and can therefore be accounted for in terms of sophistication of input (Example 11.6b). Also, since

Whitmore looks down throughout, it could be an error. In other words the cut should have been from film to still, and he should not have been seen.

Example 11.6a   ITN, 22.00, 15 May 1975, bridging the visual gap – shot 102, shot 109.

Film		*CHANCELLOR VOICE-OVER*
		They don't mind lending the Europeans our
		Westminster stewards but that's as far as
		it goes. Alexander Chancellor, *News At Ten*,
CUT	5.43½	Luxembourg./

102 Gardner MCU plain B/G		*GARDNER (Newscaster) TO CAM*
		In the commons, the Northern Ireland
CUT 0.3	5.46½	Secretary, Mr Rees,/

103 Rees CU (bottom of tie)		*GARDNER VOICE-OVER*
plain B/G *portrait still*		said the murder of a policeman in
		Londonderry last weekend could only slow
		down progress towards peace and security in
CUT 0.7	5.53½	the province/

104 Gardner MCU plain B/G		*GARDNER TO CAM*
		A girl of nineteen had her right foot amputated
		after being injured in a pub explosion on the
		outskirts of Belfast last night. Six other
CUT 0.9½	6.03	people were hurt. Ma/

105 GV pub day ext. *Film*		*GARDNER VOICE-OVER*
		ny more customers in the Catholic-owned
		Hill tavern, probably escaped injury because
CUT 0.5	6.08	of quick thinking/

106 MS oildrum + rubble		by a security guard. Moments after two armed
day ext. *Film*		youths placed the cylinder bomb inside
		the pub, the guard kicked it back through the
zoom in		door and it exploded while it was rolling/

- -

CU rubble		on to the footpath. Shortly after the explosion
		a newspaper received a phone call claiming
CUT 0.15	6.23	that the bomb was the work/

107 CU wall + stain (blood)		of the Protestant Action force./
day ext.		
CUT 0.2½ *Film* 6.25½		

108 GV 2 cars + pub B/G		
CUT 0.1 *Film* 6.26½		

109 Bosanquet MCU plain		*BOSANQUET (Newscaster) TO CAM*
B/G		Five hundred policemen moved on to the/
CUT 0.2½ 6.29		

Example 11.6a continued

110 GV building: LS students leaving CUT 0.3 *Film*	6.32	*BOSANQUET VOICE-OVER* Warwick University campus at Coventry th/
111 LS police: administra- tion building B/G *Film*		is morning to clear a sit-in by

Example 11.6b   BBC1, 12.55, 12 May 1975, bridging the visual gap – shot 6: an error

 Film CUT	 2.03	*PEART (sync.)* . . . and of the relationship that now exists between the developed and developing countries of the world./
6 Whitmore MCU (above breast pocket) + EEB backing – looking down CUT 0.2	 2.05	*WHITMORE (Newscaster) TO CAM* The union leader Mr Clive Jenkins has/
7 Jenkins CU (out of focus blinds B/G) *Colour portrait still*		*WHITMORE VOICE-OVER* sharply criticised the press for its alleged character assassination of the Industry Secretary, Mr Wedgwood Benn.

Example 11.7a   BBC1, 21.00, 15 May 1975, the comparatively unillustrated story

CUT	19.51½ /	
97 Baker MCU + blinds B/G CUT 0.15	 20.06½	*BAKER (Newscaster) TO CAM* An Old Bailey judge claimed today that parts of South London, once peaceful, had been transformed by immigrants settling there. In sentencing five West Indian teenagers to five years' detention or jail for robberies on unaccompanied women/
98 Morris J. in wig (bottom of pocket) black B/G night ext. *Colour portrait still* CUT 0.15	 20.21½	*BAKER VOICE-OVER* Judge Gwynn Morris said that these attacks were a monotonous feature in Brixton and Clapham, areas which within living memory had been peaceful, safe and agreeable to live in, but immigrant resettlement over the past twenty-five years had radically transformed that environment./
99 Baker MCD + blinds B/G		*BAKER TO CAM* Later Judge Morris said he wanted to emphasise that he was not attacking the great

Example 11.7a continued

		majority of immigrants, who proved themselves to be law-abiding citizens. Tonight the Runnymede Trust said it was high time judges stopped making crudely reactionary statements disguised as objective comments on cases before them. And the Chairman of the Community Relations Commission, Mr Mark Bonham-Carter, said the comments of a highly placed judge would do more to foster racial tension than the offences of five under-
CUT 0.30	20.51½	privileged youngsters./

100	Kendall MCU (top of pocket) + filing cabinets B/G (Photo 4d)	*KENDALL (Newscaster) TO CAM* A major British shoe manufacturer has announced that it's to pay off 750 . . .

Example 11.7b   ITN, 13.00, 15 May 1975, cueing-in

37 Kee MCU (top pocket)		*KEE (Newscaster) TO CAM* However, the continuing violence, it seems, is being evenly applied too, and last night yet another pub on the outskirts of Belfast was
CUT 0.12	12.59	bombed. Ian Sanderson of Ulster Television./

38 GV: ext. pub	*Film*	*SANDERSON (Reporter) VOICE-OVER* It would appear that this was a/

38a	*Super*: *First Report*, Ian Sanderson reporting from Belfast	sectarian . . .

The average length previously noted in the range of 17–20 seconds can be said to reflect a third newscaster function occupying in duration a median position between the two classes of shot just described. It reflects the newscasters' other main task which is, in addition to reading unillustrated, or comparatively unillustrated, stories (Example 11.7a), also to introduce correspondents, films and tapes. In the latter case it should be noted that the Telecine and VTRs require a run-up time (Example 11.7b). Cueing-in these inserts is therefore simplified if the newscaster is reading straight down (as it were) to them. This means an optimum of 10 seconds.

Example 11.8   BBC1, 21.00, 12 May 1975 (Table 11.1, Item 6)

CUT	10.4½ /

46 Harrod SCR RHT mid	*HARROD (Correspondent) TO CAM*
pocket MCU B/G = 5	Indeed one reason for the present nerves in
shot exchange dealers,	dealing is doubt about just when the British
GV room int *colour photo*	government will take firm steps to stop the
'BBC News Economics'	slide. The government view, as the Chancellor
supered	of the Exchequer said on May 1st, is that while
	inflation in Britain is higher than in our
	major trading partners the pound is likely to
	sink against other currencies. And today there
	was more evidence about inflation in this
	country. In the past three months the prices
	charged by industry are up more than 5 per
	cent. Much of that comes from higher wage
	costs but something like a ½ per cent in the last
	month has come from the fall in the pound and
CUT 0.36 10.40½	consequent rise in import costs./

Example 11.9a   BBC1, 17.45, 14 May 1975 (Table 11.1, Item 20)

5.6½ /

14 Ross SCR LEFT (top of	*ROSS (Correspondent) TO CAM*
pocket) MCU B/G =	This is not the first time that the backroom
Congress House,	economists of the TUC, including Mr Murray,
medium GV ext. day,	have tried to stiffen up the unions'
Colour photo	commitment to pay-restraint and had their
	fingers rapped by individual union leaders . . .

Example 11.9b   BBC1, 21.00, 14 May 1975 (Table 11.1, Item 23)

14.12 /

53 Ross SCR LEFT (top of	*ROSS (Correspondent) TO CAM*
pocket) MCU B/G =	No one at Congress House would dispute the
Congress House,	view that gaping holes have been punched in
medium GV ext. day,	the Social Contract.
Colour photo	
'BBC News Industry'	
supered	

It should further be noted that this requirement does not apply to non-synchronous film since that can be started on the first frame as the sound does not have to get up to speed.

The fact that newscasters can take up such a large percentage of the overall durations of the bulletin, and take it up, first, in shots of such lengths, is a prime factor in resisting any visual imperative arguments and defences. It also has the effect of confirming the newscasters' high status, by visually connecting them with those few who are regularly framed in the way illustrated above and who are allowed such durations of uninterrupted speech.

Second, flexibility in shot lengths which allows the newscasters to appear almost fleetingly at times, have further significance. They enable the bulletins to be hung along the line of the newscasters' appearances. The newscasters are the visual final fall-back if other inputs fail. These two modes mean that the image of the newscaster looking neither up nor down, nor right nor left, framed at pocket-top at an impersonal distance, is the typical basic image of the news bulletin.

Here's our correspondent

Correspondents are allowed to address the camera directly for greater lengths of time than newscasters. Correspondents tend to talk for longer uninterruptedly than any other class of speaker on the news, even if one includes interviewees (who anyway address not the lens but the interviewers); only one interviewee, on film, was allowed to give an answer lasting more than 1 minute; otherwise all interview shots lasting more than 1 minute were interrupted by questions. The uninterrupted interviewee was Dr Hans Mast, a Swiss banking economist. As regards filmed speeches, only President Ford and Enoch Powell spoke for more than 70 seconds without shot change. In studio/VTR interviews Mr Wilson and Maurice Edelman gave answers, uninterrupted by questions, of more than 1 minute in length. What characterised all these interviewees and speechmakers was their high status. Correspondents, it can therefore be argued, have the slowest rate of shot change and most closely match the highest status of interviewees and other speakers on the news.

The category of correspondent used here does not refer to the internal status of the news employee but to how he[2] (or she) is presented on the screen. Essentially we have placed every news employee who talks directly to the lens in a studio within this category. In other words, it also includes reporters in studio, and editors, but does not include correspondents, editors or reporters to camera on film or outside broadcasts (live or taped). The correspondent category for our purposes here depends on the studio, on the person being so introduced or in the utilisation of a standard repertoire of presentational forms; not on the persons' actual status in the newsrooms' hierarchy.

Correspondents, thus defined, do not appear in the shorter bulletins nor are they much seen in the current affairs style bulletins. *First Report* tended not to use them and *News Extra* treated them often as interviewees (in which capacity they are not counted here). It is in the competing early evening and main bulletins that they are most likely to appear. In the early evening bulletins, ITN used them 12.2 per cent of the time as against the BBC's 10.4 per cent; and in the main bulletins ITN used them 13.4 per cent as against the BBC's 8.3 per cent. But this seeming discrepancy wherein ITN appear to be more 'talking head' orientated than the BBC, must be read against the other main correspondent input category – that is, their use via radio circuit. This is a cheaper way of having correspondent input, if the person concerned cannot be brought to the studio. Here we find that in the early evening bulletins the BBC used radio circuit captions 6.3 per cent of the time as against ITN's 4.1 per cent. This gives a total for correspondent inputs as a whole of 16.7 per cent for the BBC and of 16.3 per cent for ITN (with ITN relying less on the use of radio captions and more on the correspondent as 'talking head' – a significant utilisation of resources since the radio caption is the slowest and least changing of all visual categories, whether moving or still). ITN in *News at Ten* used only 0.9 per cent of radio circuit captions as against the BBC's 2.7 per cent. This means that ITN used its correspondents 14.3 per cent of the time as against the BBC's 11 per cent[3] (Figure 9.5–9.8). These figures do not include further correspondent and reporter input in terms of voice-overs other than radio captions or further to camera appearances on film, tape or live from an outside broadcast (OB).

The average duration of shot in both the correspondent categories now being discussed was longer than for other inputs including newscaster to camera. But (with the exception of ITN's early evening bulletin) the BBC tended to allow correspondents, whether over the radio circuit or in the studio, to talk for longer uninterruptedly than ITN although ITN overall used them more (Figure 9.1–9.2).

The correspondent, in the studio, can be instantly differentiated from the newsreader because he almost always appears with a visual backing. This is normally achieved by the use of *Chromokey*. A

suitable image is matted-in behind the correspondent (Photo 4f).
On only 6 occasions during the week did correspondents appear
without a full *Chromokey* backing: 2 appeared on the BBC against
plain backings; 2 appeared on ITN against a special 'flat' with a map
of Europe with Britain as a missing jigsaw piece in bas-relief; 1
appeared in the *First Report* set and 1 against a *Weekend Sport* flat.
(These appearances can be found in Table 11.1, entries 12, 28, 29,
32, 36 and 43.) In contrast to the use of *Chromokey* behind
newscasters, here it was used not as a screen, but as a complete
backing.

Photo 4f Correspondents: *Chromokey* as backing

As we have already noted in connection with newscasters, British
television is restrained in its use of *Chromokey*. Behind the
newscasters it pretends that it is a projection screen; but there is no
technical limitation on the size of the matted-in picture. On the
other hand, except in the *News Extra* and *First Report* sets, it never
uses moving images on the screen although, again, there is no
technical limitation to so doing. All British television news services
impose upon themselves the identical set of limitations in the use of
Chromokey; just as the *Nine O'Clock News* and *News at Ten* used
Chromokey identically as a mock screen, so both BBC and ITN
used it similarly as mock backing for correspondents. The only
difference between services is that the BBC, in the main bulletin,

adds a written identification to the area the correspondent is covering ('BBC NEWS PARLIAMENT' in Photo 4f) whereas ITN does not (Photo 5d).

The use of these backings requires decoding work on the part of the audience since they are always symbolic of the area being reported on by the correspondent. Photo 4f is perhaps the most obvious. Parliamentary reporting is signified by a colour still photograph of Parliament. If it is a night-time bulletin then a night exterior photograph is used, but if it is day outside, the backing photograph is a day exterior. The relationship between the substance of the report and the backing image can be more attenuated than this. For example, in the BBC main bulletin on the Monday night, Harrod's piece was primarily about the exchange rate (Photo 4g). This is concretised (as we shall see below when we discuss film) by images of the main exchange dealing rooms of the central

Photo 4g   Correspondents: *Chromokey* as backing

clearing banks. For this report the *Chromokey* backing image was a still photograph of dealers. However, it should be noted that there is little in the backing icon itself to tell the viewer what is being talked of. There are two clear and two obscured figures in shirt-sleeves and ties at desks, one with a telephone in his hand. There is a woman back to camera, leaning over an obscured object in the far background. This general view has to be located, first, by the 'BBC

NEWS ECONOMICS' written identification. Then, at a second level what Harrod is saying becomes crucial. But Harrod broadens his remarks from the particularity of the exchange rate story to general comments on the economy (Example 11.8) so that this already generalised icon of white-collar workers becomes a symbolic image of 'inflation in this country'.

Finding icons for intangibles is a major problem in visualising the news. We have previously argued that the search for such icons does not affect the order and importance given to items, except perhaps towards the end of the bulletins. But assumptions are made by the newsproducers as to the audiences' visual vocabulary which are not matched by the assumptions made as to the audiences' overall attention-span or grasp. For instance when reporting the TUC on Wednesday in the BBC's early evening bulletin, Ian Ross, the industrial correspondent, appeared before a medium general view

Photo 5a   Congress House

of the front of Congress House on which there was no written identification at all (Photo 5a). Examples 11.9a and 11.9b reveal that the newsproducers were expecting a considerable level of visual understanding on the part of the audience to decode the icon behind Ross in terms of his verbal statement. The audience had sixty seconds in which to work it out. Is Ross here struggling with a viewers' maxim that might state 'see the background in terms of what is said' in general, and 'see the background building in terms of the first building mentioned' in particular? If this is so, it is possible to adduce the change in Ross's language to a need, at least in part, to make some sense of the visual element in the presentation. This problem is not confined to correspondents. In the areas of industrial and economic life the *Chromokey* screen behind the newscaster presents the same problems. It is at its most extreme when images are juxtaposed graphically to form semantically significant statements without any comment being needed from the news personnel. Perhaps the best example of this during the week was the repeated 'crystal ball' icon used by *News at Ten* (Photo 5b). This is

Photo 5b   The 'crystal ball'

an extremely complex image. The icon of the crystal ball is used symbolically in terms of generally established cultural codes to signify the future and the flag signifies the nation. The written information localises the image a little by referencing the economy (Example 11.10). On the occasion in Photo 5b Parkin was reading a news story about the pound's slippage against other currencies. Since Parkin's text dealt exclusively with past incidents (the day's fall, the Prime Minister's remarks of the previous day) how was the viewer to decode the futuristic implication of the backing image?

On the following night the same image was used to back the CBI report story (see Example 11.11). It is difficult to see how the

Example 11.10   ITN, 22.00,12 May 1975

	2.11 *PARKIN (Newscaster) TO CAM*
8 Parkin MS	At home the pound has fallen to another record
CSO (SCR LFT) *Graphic*:	low. It's now lost a quarter of its value
Union Jack in crystal ball	against the world's major currencies since
CU + 'The British	December 1971. Its fall on the foreign exchange
Economy'	markets came despite support from the Bank of
	England and despite the Prime Minister's
	strong remarks about the economy at the
CUT 0.17	weekend./
9	*PARKIN VOICE-OVER*
	The pound's fall by 25 per cent against its
	1971 value marks the sixth day of successive
	low points for sterling.

Example 11.11   ITN, 22.00, 13 May 1975

	10.18 /
48 Gardner MS	*GARDNER (Newscaster) TO CAM*
CSO (SCR RHT) *Graphic*:	A report from the Confederation of British
Union Jack in crystal ball	Industry shows manufacturing industry
+ 'The British	moving very rapidly into recession, and the
Economy'	report suggests that the recession will be much
	deeper than those we've experienced in recent
	years. The survey, which covers several
	hundred firms and acts as a kind of industrial
	barometer, forecasts rising costs and
	unemployment and a decline in output and
	investment. It blames the recession on pay
	increases and gives a warning that firms will
	be forced to cut back on jobs. . . .

'crystal ball' aids the viewer in either of the two examples.

To return to the correspondents, there is a further problem using *Chromokey* as a whole screen backing. Since the correspondent is the main foreground part of the image, he perforce obscures much of the *Chromokey* picture – which does not occur if the *Chromokey* is used sparingly as an inserted false projection screen. Few pictures lend themself to being thus obscured. Perhaps the image of the Houses of Parliament with Big Ben is among the most convenient for this purpose. But when this basic design constraint is coupled with a desire to make the image as indexical as possible some results are, in design terms at least, awkward. The backing used in reporting the armed services pay increase on BBC has Luton before a photo-montage of members of each service crudely laid across one another and the whole arranged to balance his position in the frame

(Photo 5c). While this icon is admittedly easy to decode, it nevertheless owes little to the aesthetics of the golden mean.

Photo 5c   The armed forces

Another problem with whole-frame *Chromokey* can be seen in the Photos 5d, 5e, 5f sequence. The image of the supermarket, one

Photo 5d   Sissons and the supermarket

Photo 5e   Sissons disappears

Photo 5f   Sissons new backing

of the generalised images of consumerism specifically used to
indicate inflation as it affects the cost of living (as opposed to pound
notes, £ symbols, crystal balls and flags, etc., which related to the
national economy and inflation) is backing Sissons (Photo 5d).
Cutting to the source which has the actual inflation statistic on it

(Photo 5e) and superimposing that on the same image that has been backing Sissons means that Sissons, in effect, disappears. This occurred in the early evening bulletin but it was changed for *News at Ten*. Then Sissons was backed by pound notes (Photo 5f). The image in Photo 5e was cut-in again in this bulletin but this time without any violence to Sissons.

We have suggested that the range of images in the news is restricted and we have, in the course of these chapters, begun to substantiate that claim in some detail. Table 10.1 offers some evidence in this matter. Of the 26 opening images (in changing image bulletins) 4 were still portraits of the then Prime Minister, Harold Wilson, and 1 was a still portrait of Jack Jones. Graphics involving signs were used twice and maps 3 times. Company logos and still photographs of company buildings were used 3 times. Shopping precincts and supermarket interiors were used twice. The aftermath of a factory disaster was used once, marching soldiers were used once and the *Mayaguez* affair took up the rest – the black-and-white image of the ship 3 times, the ship at Singapore 4 times, the ship on tow twice and the marines on Ko Tang once (1 photograph of a company building was in a montage with a photograph of the Prime Minister).

Turning to the 'bongs' (Examples 10.2a–e) we find portrait stills of President Ford, Michael Foot, Ilie Nastase and Roger Taylor (mounted together) and an identikit picture of the Cambridge rapist. For industry we had the Chrysler strikers voting, the Dunlop logo, a still photograph of the Ryton factory gate, a photograph of a dockside, the cover of a CBI report and the crystal ball mentioned above. We had, in addition, British soldiers, American marines on Ko Tang, Flixborough being rebuilt, ancient Japanese football, a ballot box, one map, Orantes in action and four uses of the black-and-white *Mayaguez* photograph.

The icons used as background to correspondents, which are listed in Table 11.1 below, share a number of characteristics with these groups. First, only two are iconic – the news picture of Vice Premier Teng in Paris and the colour picture of Flixborough after the explosion (Entries 11 and 14, Table 11.1). Most are indexical and largely avoid close-ups of particular people. The Ali portrait in the BBC2 sports package on Saturday is the only exception. The buildings are No. 10 Downing Street (with policeman), Chequers, Parliament, the White House, the Pentagon, Congress House, Ferranti's headquarters, the front of a bank and the Capitol building. It should be noted that all of these are exteriors and some are aerial views. In other words, no assumption is being made that the correspondents should be seen by the audience to be physically before these buildings. The parliamentary correspondents would be sited somewhere above the Albert Embankment, for instance, if this were the case. (Yet night reports have a night photograph to back them.) These images are iconic of themselves but indexical of the subject matter of the reports: the American army is the Pentagon, Congress is the Capitol, the Prime Minister is No. 10 Downing Street or Chequers, and so on. This indexical quality is increased with the exchange dealers, the dockside, soldiers, interiors of supermarkets, people on a pavement, children in a classroom. Apart from the images of soldiers, which relate indexically to armed forces pay, and of children, which relate to education, the rest of these all back economic stories. The *Mayaguez* photograph is also in this group. Throughout the week, wherever the ship was (and for some hours it was completely missing), this icon stood indexically for the story. More symbolic were the graphics – splayed notes, the European jigsaw puzzle, the Far East maps. More use was made of the covers of reports to stand indexically for the reports' contents than in the opening image or 'bongs' group. The CBI report and armed forces pay review were both used in this way.

Both TV news services responded to the same problems of visualisation with similar solutions. Parliament was Big Ben on all channels. On the Monday, Harrod had the CBI cover and so did Green. On the Tuesday, Harrod had the dockside and so did Green. Brunson had the White House and so did Humphrys.

The same basic tendencies can be seen in the choice of background images: the majority were indexical, a few were symbolic (although, as in Example 11.8, the report can render an indexical image symbolic), and, surprisingly for a visual news service, an equal few were iconic. The tendency to avoid portrait stills (an image difficult to mesh with the foreground correspondent figure) and the use of report covers, were the only differences between these backgrounds and the other groups of images discussed in the previous chapter.

Correspondent reports

The correspondents appeared in three main modes – long pieces, uninterrupted; pieces interrupted by visuals but not on the sound track because the correspondent talks over the interrupting image (these visuals being either graphics of various sorts and/or *non-sync*. film); pieces interrupted visually and on the sound track, i.e. *sync*. pieces from other speakers.

The correspondents (a category which, it should be remembered, also includes reporters appearing in studio to camera with full *Chromokey* backing) made 43 appearances in these modes. On 11 occasions during the week they delivered uninterrupted pieces to camera (Mode A, Table 11.1). On 15 occasions they delivered their pieces uninterruptedly on the audio track but voiced-over other visual inputs (Mode B, Table 11.1). On 5 occasions they introduced segments from *sync*. film or tape (Mode C). In addition to this, on 7 occasions they appeared in a combined mode both voicing-over other inputs and introducing other *sync*. (Mode D) and on 5 occasions reporters or correspondents read introductions to *sync*. but did not then reappear after the *sync*. was finished (Mode E).

The uninterrupted mode occurs most often, as would be expected, in the economic and parliamentary categories. But what is less expected is that it never occurred on ITN. In other words, ITN, in this sample using its correspondents more than does the BBC, made a greater effort to add visual variety to that use.

All these 11 appearances lasted upwards of 1 minute or more each, the shortest being pieces from Colebourne on the BBC1 early evening bulletin on 15 May at 45 seconds (29, Table 11.1) and from Harrod in the same bulletin the following day at 58 seconds (32, Table 11.1). (These were the only two correspondent appearances in the week with a plain background flat.) The longest appearance was an update from Jones on a Commons debate in *News Extra* on Monday which lasted 1 minute, 40 seconds. Biddulph on the night of the seizure of *Mayaguez*, Curtoise and Ross were the other correspondents allowed these sorts of durations.

In the second mode it is necessary to differentiate between the long piece interrupted visually at most twice (Mode B_1, Table 11.1) and the complex illustrated pieces that characterised, for instance, ITN's coverage of the *Mayaguez* (Mode B_2, Table 11.1). Of the 15 instances in this mode, 5 consisted of piece to camera, voice-over still, piece to camera sequences (B_1). ITN had 3 and BBC 2 of this type (see Example 11.12).

More complicated were sequences which appeared on 10 occasions (Mode B_2) each as that in Example 11.13 (p. 282). These consisted in the sample week of at least 7 shots up to (as in the example) 23 shots. The correspondent could appear either at the beginning and end of the sequence or in the middle as well (as in the example). Of these sequences 7 were on ITN and 3 on the BBC. The example is particularly instructive in that it was the most visual of all the accounts given of the *Mayaguez* affair.

Example 11.12   BBC1, 17.45, 14 May 1975 (Table 11.1, Item 19: Mode B₁)

	3.49½ /	

| 10 Harrod MCU (top of pocket) (SCR CENTRE) B/G = ship unloading at dock *Colour photo* | *HARROD (Correspondent) TO CAM* The London dock strike hit imports in March, producing very good figures and exports in April. But as these figures show there was no/ |

. . . .

| 10a *Super* 'Dominic Harrod, Economics Correspondent' lose super | rebound in imports so the result was a good deal better than expected./ |

. . . .

| | Indeed after allowing for those invisible earnings, from dividends and interest, tourism and the like, which have been running at |
| CUT 0.20   4.9½ | about £120 million a month,/ |

| 11 *Graphic*: Balance of Payments Current Account Nov., Dec., Jan., Feb., Mar., April on black B/G – 169m on red B/G | *HARROD (Correspondent) VOICE-OVER* the current account of the foreign balance has been improving steadily since last year. Even after the April setback the average deficit for the past three months has been about £112 million. Bad, but nothing like the deficit of more than £300 million a month at the end |
| CUT 0.16   4.25½ | of last year./ |

| 12 Harrod as 10 | *HARROD TO CAM* So there's been an improving trend and in recognition of the figures the pound rose on foreign exchange markets this afternoon for the first time since the steep slide began. The slide had brought the pound down by more than 4 per cent in three weeks but this evening it was the dollar that came under strong pressure on the latest news from |
| CUT 0.19   4.44½ | Cambodia./ |

This sequence contains practically every available image in the story[4]. In the following days, only some official film of the raid, the ship being towed and its arrival at Singapore, were added. In fact only three shots were actually taken in the course of the rescue – shot numbers 17, 18, 22 – used for a total of 24.5 seconds out of a report running for 3 minutes, 16.5 seconds. This must be seen as an achievement because Wain, the most readily available image as it were, talked to camera for only 1 minute, 8 seconds. Thus over half the story was illustrated by indexical photographs, library film and maps. Of this material, most had already been seen (the black-and-white footage of the Coral Sea was new but the BBC had colour footage of the ship two days before). The time span of the story (at this point in its fourth day) helped this presentation.

Yet the sequence also points up the visual limitations of the television journalist in such situations. The icon of the shot-down helicopter stands indexically for 'the others crashed into the sea'. The icon of the running marines stands indexically for marines 'pinned down by gunfire' or 'the helicopter evacuation by darkness'. Thus even the 24.5 seconds of imagery actually emanating from the Far East must also be made to work indexically for the journalists' needs to be met.

Example 11.13   ITN, 22.00, 15 May 1975 (Table 11.1, Item 30, Mode B₂)

	1.4½	*WAIN (Correspondent) TO CAM*
2	Wain MCU (top of pocket) (SCR CENTRE) B/G = *Mayaguez* at dock *B&W photo*	So the great rescue has ended successfully but at considerable cost./

- /

2a	*Super* 'Christopher Wain, Defence Correspondent' lose super	/The *Mayaguez* incident had started on
. . . .		
CUT 0.8	1.12½	Monday when the ten/

3	*Map*: Hong Kong Hanoi Laos Thailand Cambodia Settapao Ko Tang Seized here	*WAIN VOICE-OVER* thousand ton container ship was seized by a Cambodian gunboat while steaming through the gulf of Thailand en route to Settapao. It
CUT 0.7½	1.20	was an act of pir/

4	Ford *Portrait still* (bottom of tie) CU flag B/G	acy said President Ford. He ordered a task force from the seventh Fleet to go in and get the prisoners out/
CUT 0.6½	1.26½	

Example 11.13 continued

| 5 Wain as in 2 | WAIN TO CAM |
| CUT 0.5　　　1.31½ | It all took time. On Tuesday two battalions of US Marines, 1,100 men, arrived at/ |

| 6 *Map* Ream Phnom Penh Utapao Bangkok Ko Tang Cambodia Gulf of Thailand | Utapao air-base in Southern Thailand. Meanwhile the aircraft carrier *Coral*/ |
| CUT 0.4½　　　1.36 | |

| 7 *Coral Sea* aerial GV *B&W film* | *Sea*, a 50,000-tonner carrying seventy-five aircraft,/ |
| CUT 0.3½　　　1.39½ | |

| 8 Pan plane GV forward flight deck – takes off (sea to sea) *B&W film* | was moving to a point midway between Utapao and the island of Ko Tang, where the/ |
| CUT 0.4½　　　1.44 | |

| 9 Plane takes off top shot *B&W film* | *Mayaguez* was lying. By Wednesday the battle plan was ready. A US navy Corsair/ |
| CUT 0.5　　　1.49 | |

| 10 Corsair GV on ground *Colour photo* | fighter bomber sank three Cambodian gunboats and immobilised four others. And as darkness fell, the aircraft direct/ |
| CUT 0.7½　　　1.56½ | |

| 11 *USS Holt* (aerial) GV *B&W photo* | ion-destroyer, *Holt*, moved into the area. Her task was to guide the marine assault helicopters into Ko Tang. According to |
| CUT 0.7½　　　2.04 | so/ |

| 12 *Map* as in 6 | me reports the first wave of 135 marines flew into the attack direct from Thailand, but that's not likely. The aircraft almost certainly stopped to refuel on board the *Coral Sea* |
| CUT 0.13　　　2.17 | before the dawn attack. They went in at mid/ |

| 13 Wain as in 2 | WAIN TO CAM |
| CUT 0.3　　　2.20 | night our time last night. They were flying in on CH/ |

| 14 GV chopper turning – track (ground to air) SCR RHT *Film* | WAIN VOICE-OVER 53D heavy assault helicopters/ |
| CUT 0.2　　　2.22 | |

| 15 CU chopper turning – track: (ground to air) SCR LFT *Film* | each one carrying 37 marines and 3 crew. One helicopter apparently landed on the *Mayag*/ |
| CUT 0.6　　　2.28 | |

Example 11.13 continued

---

16 Wain as in 2		*WAIN TO CAM*
		guez. The marines hurriedly searched the
		ship but found she was empty, the others
		stormed ashore and it was here that they
		started taking casualties. According to the
CUT 0.10	2.38	reports from Washington, three heli/

---

17 GV belly flopped chopper		*WAIN VOICE-OVER*
B&W News picture		copters were lost. One was shot down, the
		others crashed into the sea just off shore.
CUT 0.6	2.44	The marines were/

---

18 4 marines LS chopper		pinned down by gunfire from the waiting
B/G *B&W News picture*		Cambodians, but those ordered to search for
		the missing sailors, couldn't find a sign
CUT 0.8	2.52	of them. Meanwhile jets from the *Coral/*

---

19 Wain as in 2		*WAIN TO CAM*
		Sea had attacked the Cambodian airbase at
		Ream. At 10.00 in the morning, four hours
		after the marines had hit the beach at Ko Tang,
		a Thai fishing boat came out from the
		Cambodian mainland flying a white flag and
		according to the reports from Washington all
		39 of the missing crew members were on
CUT 0.19½	3.11½	board the ship. They were transferred/

---

20 GV *Wilson* (ship to ship)		to the Destroyer *Wilson* and President
B&W photo		Ford announced that the operation was over
CUT 0.5½	3.17	and was a success/

---

21 *Map* Ko Tang (large		But the marine task force was still on Ko
scale)		Tang and under heavy Cambodian fire. There
		was no need for them to be there and so orders
		were given to evacuate them. But this was
		much easier said than done. For one thing,
		they had to wait until the *Coral Sea* had
CUT 0.17	3.34	approached close enough for the heli/

---

22 *Coral Sea* aerial GV		copters on board to be sent in. And when
Colour photo		they did attempt to land they were beaten
CUT 0.7	3.41	back by Cambodian ground fire. So it wa/

---

23 LS marines (no chopper)		sn't until 8.00 this evening, local time, that
B/G *B&W News picture*		the marines were pulled out and the helicopter
		evacuation by darkness under fire was even
CUT 0.10½	3.51½	more dangerous than this morning's landing./

---

24 Wain as in 2		*WAIN TO CAM*
		The last known survivor was lifted out at two
		minutes past 8.00 but the destroyers, *Holt* and
		Wilson, stayed close inshore searching for
		other survivors. The known casualties are 2

Example 11.13 continued

| | | dead and 8 wounded but 14 men are missing. Their chances of survival are slender. So it all adds up to about 10 per cent casualties amongst the marines who took part and that's a rough indication of how hazardous a rescue |
| CUT 0.22½ | 4.14 | this was./ |

Key: sea to sea = shot from one boat to another
     aerial = taken from the air
     ground to air = shot from the ground of aircraft

The tendency for correspondents on ITN to break up the reports with other visual material is yet another indicator that we have found which could contribute to the audience's perception of the service as being 'livelier' than the BBC's.

The use of correspondents to introduce other pieces of *sync.* is less likely to contribute to 'liveliness' because each segment of the *sync.* (apart from being by definition 'talking heads') has to be separately cued (i.e. the video-tape or Telecine projection machine, in the case of film, has to run up to and stabilise at the correct speed). Thus the 5- and 3-second shots (shots 5 and 13 in Example 11.13) are not easily possible with *sync.*

Of the 5 entries in this mode (C), 3 are ITN's and 2 BBC's but it should be noted that 4 of the 5 are from America and in each case the report is from the service's Washington correspondent. In other words, in this week of a major United States story the pattern was to have the correspondent introduce *sync.* material gleaned from American television. The shared language is a major factor facilitating this. The odd value out here is the analysis by Haviland, ITN's political editor, of the Prime Minister's interview on the Sunday. This was carried by the BBC but not at such great length – perhaps because it emanated from an ITV source.

Modes D and E account for the rest. These tend to be lengthy inserts and because of the status of the interviewees and the length of their contributions the cutting rate is much slower than in Example 11.13. Mode D can be characterised as having an insert or inserts with an interrupted illustrated introduction or payoff. Item 8, in Table 11.1, introduces the *sync.* and then voices over one shot in the payoff. Item 12, in the same table, has an illustrated introduction followed by a sequence of *sync.* inserts interspersed with to-camera pieces by the correspondent. Item 25 has an illustrated payoff. (On the third day of the *Mayaguez* incident the ITN

Washington correspondent began his report with film of himself standing before the Pentagon. The previous evening he had been suspended above it – because of the combination of his studio seat and the aerial photograph backing him.)

In Item 39 the *sync*. butt-joins the correspondent's voice-over. Item 41 has an illustrated payoff while the two sports packages are too complex to analyse in this way.

The E mode has five entries (1, 11, 16, 18, 28). What distinguishes these from the above is simply that the reporter or correspondent does not reappear after the *sync*.

Only 11 of the total number of correspondents to camera shots (not reports, as above) were under 10 seconds and 27 of them were over 40 seconds. It is therefore likely in the code of television news that once correspondents appear, they will remain on screen for periods that can only be described as lengthy in bulletin terms. Only in complex sequences (Mode B_2) will they normally get less than 10 seconds in any one shot and usually they get much more.

Introducing correspondents

This high-status uninterruptibility of the correspondents is reinforced by the way in which they are supercaptioned. On only five occasions did correspondents or reporters appear in the studio without supercaptions; Jones on *News Extra*, Wain on *First Report* and Colebourne from the Midlands and Delahaye from the North, Luton and Blackie. Thus most of these non-captioned appearances were on the BBC, the one on ITN being of itself a somewhat unusual event; i.e. a correspondent's appearance in *First Report*. It is fair to say that correspondents are more regularly captioned than any other group. In addition, on only nine occasions was this caption not reinforced by a verbal announcement and significantly all these occasions are on the BBC. In other words ITN never failed to verbally introduce the correspondent and, with the one exception (Wain's appearance on *First Report*), also never failed to caption them. This greater care on ITN's part to identify its own personnel is repeated when supercaptions on film or tape are examined (see Chapter 13). Of these verbal announcements only one, again on the BBC, failed to mention the name as well as the status of the person. This was Item 32, Table 11.1, on BBC1, when Harrod was introduced with just a 'Here's our economics correspondent'.

Table 11.1 Correspondents and reporters in studio (Index 11)

	Date	Channel	T/X	Name	Chromakey backing	Pattern & duration of shots	Identification	Mode
1	11/5	BBC1	18.05	Curtoise	No. 10 (door) + policeman *Colour photo*	1'05'' ↑ (Wilson 0.21'')	Political correspondent	E
2		BBC1	21.30	Curtoise		1'22''	Political correspondent	A
3		ITN	22.00	Haviland	GV Chequers *Colour photo*	44'' ↑ (Wilson 44½'') 15'' ↑ (W 35'') 18'' ↑ (W 67'') 20'' ↑ (W 37'') 13''	Political editor	C
4	12/5	BBC1	17.45	Harrod	GV bank building *Colour photo*	1'21''	Economics correspondent	A
5		BBC1	21.00	Biddulph	Cambodia *Map*	1'05''	BBC News/diplomatic	A
6		BBC1	21.00	Harrod	Exchange dealers *Colour photo*	24'' (9'') 36''	BBC News/economics	B₁
7		BBC1	21.00	Jones	Big Ben GV night *Colour photo*	1'23½''	BBC News/parliament	A
8		ITN	17.50	Green	Splayed £s *Graphic*	55½'' ↑ (Kleinwort/Kee 57'') 39'' (6'') 16''	Reporting	D
9		ITN	22.00	Sissons	Splayed £s *Graphic*	44'' (10'') 7½'' (8½'') 27½'' (6½'') 26''	Industrial editor	B₂
10		ITN	22.00	Mathias	Big Ben GV night *Colour photo*	14'' (8'') 23½'' (10'') 20½'' (7'') 10''	Political correspondent	B₂
11		ITN	22.00	Hatfield	GV Flixborough after *Colour photo*	42'' (50''/12 shots) ↑ (Locke/Hatfield 1'13½'')	Keith Hatfield	E
12		ITN	22.00	Lander	Europe jigsaw (flat)	22'' (17'') 4½'' (13'') 51'' (30'') ↑ (Williams 34'') 13'' ↑ (Winnifrith 35'') 27½'' ↑ (Wil + Win 1'7'') 39¼''	European political correspondent	D
13		BBC2	22.20	Jones	Big Ben GV night *Colour photo*	1'48''		A

Table 11.1 continued

	Date	Channel	T/X	Name	Chromokey backing	Pattern & duration of shots	Identification	Mode
14		BBC2	22.20	Biddulph	Teng + Guard	1'02"	Diplomatic correspondent	A
15	13/5	BBC1	21.00	Harrod	CBI report cover *Graphic*	39"↑ (McDougall/Harrod 1'15") 37½"↑	Economics correspondent (used twice, both shots)	C
16		ITN	17.50	Green	CBI report cover *Graphic*	20" (30') 40"↑	Industrial correspondent	E
17		ITN	22.00	Brunson	White House GV Aerial GV Pentagon/White House *bis* *Colour photos*	25"↑ (McDougall/Green 46") (Javits 29") 20"↑ (Pentagon spokesman 20") 26"↑ (Buckley + Humphreys 45") 28½"	Washington correspondent	C
18		ITN	22.00	Green	CBI report cover *Graphic*	24' (36') 8½' (MacDougall/Green 1'12")	Industrial correspondent	E
19	14/5	BBC1	17.45	Harrod	GV dockside unloading *Colour photo*	20" (16") 19"	Economics correspondent	B₁
20		BBC1	17.45	Ross	Congress House ext. *Colour photo*	1'		A
21		BBC1	21.00	Humphrys	White House *Colour photo*	29½"↑ (Laitkin 42") 22"↑ (Goldwater + Clark 1'37") 52½"**	*	C
22		BBC1	21.00	Delahaye	Ferranti HQ GV *Colour photo*	19½" (10") 11" (38½"/7 shots) 22½"	BBC News/Industry	B₂
23		BBC1	21.00	Ross	Congress House ext *Colour photo*	1'17"		A
24		ITN	17.50	Green	GV dockside *Colour photo*	47" (4½") 23"	Industrial correspondent	B₂
25†		ITN	22.00	Brunson	(On film Pentagon GV) White House *Colour photo*	(TO CAM on film 29"↑ (Laitkin 1') (47½"/3 shots) 41" (11½") 10½"	Reporting from Washington	D

Table 11.1 continued

Date	Channel	T/X	Name	Chromokey backing	Pattern & duration of shots	Identification	Mode
26	ITN	22.00	Wain	Map: Thailand Cambodia Bangkok Utapao Phnom Penh	9" (7½") 13½" (44½/7 shots) 12½" (6½") 7½"	Defence correspondent	B₂
27	ITN	22.00	Green	GV dockside / Colour photo	31" (10½") 37½"	Industrial correspondent	B₁
28	ITN	22.00	Mathias	Europe jigsaw (flat)	32" (13½/3 shots) 32" ↑ (Allen/Mathias 1'21")	Political correspondent	E
29	BBC1	17.45	Colebourne	Plain beige B/G	45"		A
30	ITN	22.00	Wain	'Mayaguez' B/W photo at dockside	8" (7½") (6½") 5" (46½/ 8 shots) 3" (8"/2 shots) 10" (14"/2 shots) 19½" (40"/4 shots)	Defence correspondent	B₂
31	ITN	22.00	Brunson	Pentagon aerial GV/ Capitol dome/White House GV / Colour photos	46½" ↑ (40" Ford) 11" ↑ (McGovern/Sparkman 1'7½") 26" ↑ (Schlesinger 46") 44"	Washington correspondent	C
32	BBC1	17.45	Harrod	Plain blue B/G	58"	Dominic Harrod	A
33	BBC1	17.45	Luton	Montage soldiers, etc. / Colour photo	20" (1'0½"/9 shots) 12"		B₂
34	BBC1	21.00	Harrod	£s	1'11½"	BBC News/Economics	A
35	BBC1	21.00	Luton	Montage soliders, etc. / Colour photo	20" (1'0½"/9 shots) 11½"		B₂
36	ITN	13.00	Wain	First Report B/G	14½" (50"/6 shots) 12" (7") 20"		B₂
37	ITN	17.50	Sissons	GV int. Supermarket / Colour photo	48" (8") 1'30"	Industrial editor	B₁
38	ITN	17.50	Wain	Review body cover / Graphic	18" (51"/10 shots) 4"	Defence correspondent	B₂

(Date 15/5 applies to rows 29–30; Date 16/5 applies to rows 32 onwards)

Table 11.1 continued

Date	Channel	T/X	Name	Chromokey backing	Pattern & duration of shots	Identification	Mode
39	15/5	BBC1	21.00	Humphrys	Capitol/White House *Colour photos*	36" ↑ [Dole 27"] (26½")/ 2 shots) 29*	Washington (2) correspondent	D
40	16/5	ITN	22.00	Sissons	GV people on pavement *Colour photo*	45" (13") 6" (9") 41" (31")/ 2 shots) 1'9"	Industrial editor	B₂
41	17/5	BBC1	21.35	Buerke	GV children in class *Colour photo*	34¼" ↑ (Prentice 36") 7½"* (12") 6½"	*Michael Buerke	D
42		ITN		Parker	Saturday sport + /portrait still/ Ali	37½" (16½") ↑ (Moore v/o) 10" (9½") 10" (2½")/ 22½" (39"/6 shots)	Sports correspondent	E
43		BBC2	19.30	Blackie	Sport on 2 (flat)	13" (2'38"/38 shots) 29" ↑ (Waring v/o 33½"/4 shots) (18½"/2 shots) 15½" (20½"/2 shots) 10" (14"/2 shots) 13" (25½"/3 shots)		E

Key
Flat: a piece of setting: a set
Timing Pattern: figures outside brackets refer to camera shot lengths. If followed immediately by () indicates voice-over. () with timing figure/no. shots = voice-over a number of continuous shots. ↑ before () = *sync.* insert. Name within bracket = interviewee, followed by name of interviewer. Two names within such brackets = two *sync.* pieces butt-joined.

All supercaptions (*) include name unless otherwise stated.
Name alone = only the name appeared without title
* = shots where super appeared. If no * then super appeared in first shot. If no name then no super.
A = Uninterrupted pieces to camera
B₁ = Pieces with one single shot interruption voiced-over by correspondent.
B₂ = Pieces with more than one single interruption voice-over by correspondent.
C = Pieces with one or more *sync.* inserts (or inserts with voice-over from other personnel)
D = Pieces combining voice-over shots with *sync.* inserts
E = Uninterrupted pieces leading to *sync.* (correspondent does not reappear after *sync.*)
† Item 25: this introductory shot on film is also listed in the film indices.

Eight forms of introduction can be found in the week's sample (see Table 11.2). The first type in Table 11.2 dominates the verbal hand-over. It was used 16 times during the week. The second, used only on ITN, was employed 3 times to introduce background or feature pieces from the correspondent concerned. The third was used 4 times, on each occasion to hand over to an American report. The fourth was used once by ITN and the fifth once by BBC (to hand over to Jones in the Westminster studio). The sixth was used 3 times to introduce reporters and the seventh twice – once for Colebourne and once for Luton. Only Blackie on Saturday's BBC2 sports package had the details.

Table 11.2 Newscaster to correspondent/reporter hands-over (studio)

1	Here's our X editor/correspondent (Tony Other):
2	Our X editor/correspondent Tony Other has been looking at Y. Here's his report:
3	(And now) from Place Z, Tony Other reports:
4	Our X editor/correspondent Tony Other reports:
5	Over to Tony Other:
6	Here's Tony Other:
7	Tony Other reports:
8	Here with the details, Tony Other:

Reporter is thus not a job which warrants verbal identification. 'Here's our reporter' was not used in the sample week. A further clue as to the status of correspondents can be seen in the combination of name and job description in types 1, 2 and 4 (Table 11.2). Reporters are not so introduced. Further, 'over to' and 'from' seem to mean that the correspondent is in another studio either at home or abroad.

The combination of caption and verbal identification reflects the organisational hierarchy within the newsrooms. Together, they constitute the equivalent of the press by-line and they seem to reflect press practice in that, just as the by-line is a mark of seniority and status, so too is the combination verbal hand-over and caption, providing a job description is used.

In terms of pay-offs, there is a distinction between the services since ITN has adopted the American practice of signing off a story – thus, 'This is Tony Other *First Report/News at Ten* (etc.), Place Z'. The BBC does not do this. Neither does ITN do it in the studio. Therefore in the correspondents' list, only Michael Brunson signed off in this way, from Washington.

All in all, ITN was more systematic in naming its personnel than was the BBC, but both services were thorough about the use of captions in the studio context. This tendency to carefully name the staff and their jobs not only confers high status on them (we would argue), but also of course serves to legitimise what they say. It is in contrast, as we shall see below, to the more haphazard treatment given to others who appear in *sync.* in the bulletins.

The normal point at which the supercaption appears is during the first piece to camera. The latitude is comparatively wide (as can be seen in the examples) but, obviously, if the piece to camera is short then the supercaption must appear closer to the start of the piece than otherwise. On only three occasions during the week did the supercaption appear after the opening piece; twice when John Humphrys was reporting from the United States and once on Saturday with Michael Buerke. This last occasion looks like nothing but oversight: the caption was not used during his opening 34.5 seconds but was inserted into his illustrated payoff in a shot lasting only 7.5 seconds. The Humphrys examples are more complex. In his longest piece on the Thursday he began by voicing-over film. This was covered by a 'John Humphrys reporting' caption. He then appeared in the item numbered 39 in Table 11.1. Each time he appeared to camera he was captioned 'John Humphrys, Washington'. On the Wednesday, despite his two appearances to camera in the item, the caption was saved until this third and last appearance. However, he was verbally introduced on this occasion.

Again, ITN appears to be marginally more regular in its use of these devices than does the BBC. The rule seems to be that supercaptions appear only once, normally at the first opportunity in the first piece to camera of a sequence.

Voice-only

The use of correspondents and reporters appearing in the bulletins in sound only displays the same range of characteristics as those outlined above. We are not here discussing sound tracks of film that might have arrived via radio circuits but only those appearances which combine reporter/correspondent voice with radio circuit captions.

This sort of input is not used by the two short bulletins but it accounts for 2.7 per cent and 3.3 per cent of the total durations of *News Extra* and *First Report* respectively. It accounts for 4.1 per cent of the ITN's and 6.3 per cent of the BBC's early evening bulletins. But it accounts for less than 0.9 per cent of *News at Ten* and 2.7 per cent of the BBC's *Nine O'Clock News*.

Since there is no particular inhibition about the lengths at which this input is used – correspondents are allowed as long to talk over the radio circuit caption still as they are allowed to talk in the flesh – these figures represent comparatively few actual reports during the week. This input was used on seventeen occasions (see Table 11.3). The discrepancy between the main bulletins can be accounted for as the obverse of the previous discrepancy in the use of correspondents in the studio. Specifically, ITN opened the satellite for Brunson to do a piece to camera on the Tuesday whereas the BBC did not do the same for Humphrys. On the other hand the BBC had Humphrys on radio circuit that night but opened the satellite for him to be interviewed by Angela Rippon on the Wednesday. In other words, although the BBC used Humphrys more on the cheaper radio circuit in terms of the *Nine O'Clock News*, over both its services it used satellite as much as ITN did.

The shot durations in these radio circuit inputs last longer than any other group of still images in the visual vocabulary of the news. In terms of the competing early evening bulletins (Figure 9.2) they last longer than do shots of correspondents in the flesh; and in terms of the BBC's *Nine O'Clock News* that remains true. Only *News at Ten* breaks them up to bring down the average duration, but even then it is still true that on average a radio circuit caption will last a full 9.35 seconds longer than a portrait still, the most common of non-moving inputs (Figure 9.1).

The phenomenon here noted is that we are dealing with a class of still images which are treated in the length they can be permitted to remain uninterruptedly on the screen as if they were moving images. Nowhere, therefore, in the bulletins is the visual imperative less in evidence.

Unlike actual studio appearances the radio circuit appearance was not used, during the sample week, to introduce *sync.* inserts. Therefore there are no examples in Table 11.3 of the Modes C, D and E shown in Table 11.1. Otherwise the range of modes distinguished for correspondent studio appearances also exists for radio circuit inputs, with the radio circuit caption taking the place of the to-camera shots.

On this basis, 9 entries in Table 11.3 are uninterrupted pieces (Mode A), 4 are in Mode B_1 and 4 are in Mode B_2. The uninter-

Table 11.3 Correspondents and reporters via radio circuit (Index 10)

No.	Date	Channel	T/X	Name	Radio circuit caption details	Timing pattern	Mode	Overall duration
1	12/5	BBC1	21.00	Humphrys	PS + White House 'JH reporting'	26" (17") 50"	B₁	1'33"
2	12/5	ITN	13.00	MacDonald	PS + Chrysler gate *'First Report: TM reporting'*	1'33"	A	1'33"
3	12/5	BBC1	22.20	Humphrys	PS + White House 'JH reporting'	24" (9½") 52½"	B₁	1'16"
4	12/5	ITN	22.00	Selvin	White House 'DS reporting'	19" (12") 23"	B₁	54"
5	13/5	BBC1	17.45	Humphrys	PS + White House 'JH reporting'	40"	A	40"
6	13/5	BBC1	21.00	Humphrys	PS + White House 'JH reporting'	1'05"	A	1'05"
7	13/5	ITN	17.50	Brunson	Capitol 'MB reporting from Washington'	49½"	A	49½"
8	13/5	BBC2	23.05	Humphrys	PS + White House 'JH reporting'	1'04"	A	1'04"
9	14/5	ITN	17.50	Brunson	Capitol 'MB reporting from Washington'	1'25"	A	1'25"
10	14/5	ITN	22.00	Seymour	PS + Map (Ko Tang/Cambodia/Bangkok/Utapao/Thailand) 'GS reporting from Bangkok'	9" (22½") 11" (13½") 20"	B₂	1'16"
11	15/5	BBC1	21.00	Humphrys	PS + White House 'JH reporting'	48"	A	48"
12	15/5	ITN	13.00	Seymour	PS + Map (Utapao/Gulf of Thailand/Phnom Penh/Kompong Som/Ko Tang/ *Mayaguez* (in box) *First Report:* GS reporting	15" (9") 8½" (4½") 31½" (7½") 16" (4½")	B₂	1'40½"
13	16/5	BBC1	17.45	Humphrys	PS + White House 'JH reporting'	48"	A	48"
14	16/5	BBC1	21.00	Humphrys	PS + White House 'JH reporting'	30" (9") 30½"	B₁	1'09½"
15	16/5	ITN	13.00	Alick	Aerial GV Port of Spain *'First Report:* Vernon Alick reporting from Trinidad'	52"	A	52"
16	16/5	BBC2	23.05	Humphrys	PS + White House 'JH reporting'	16" (40½"/3 shots) 12½"	B₂	1'07"
17	17/5	ITN	13.10	Seymour	PS + Newspic. *Mayaguez* at dockside Singapore 'GS reporting from Singapore'	(32") 35" (18") 11"	B₂	1'36"

Key:
PS = portrait still

rupted (Mode A) pieces last as little as 40 seconds or as long as 1 minute 33 seconds. The 5 appearances for the BBC in this mode all involve Humphrys broadcasting from Washington, 3 times into the early evening bulletin, once into the *Nine O'Clock News* and once into BBC2's *News Extra*. Of the 4 ITN appearances, 2 are reports from Brunson in Washington, both broadcast in the early evening. The other 2 appearances are from *First Report*, 1, the week's longest, coming from MacDonald in Coventry and the other coming from a stringer in Trinidad.

The visually interrupted piece at its simplest involves voicing-over one still. In the radio circuit input category this takes the form of cutting from the radio circuit caption to another still and then back to the radio circuit caption. This happened on 4 occasions during the week (Mode B_1, Table 11.3); 3 of them occurred on the first night of the *Mayaguez* (Monday). Humphrys's initial report from Washington in the *Nine O'Clock News* lasted 1 minute 33 seconds, 17 seconds of which he talked over a photograph of the USS *Pueblo*. The piece he did for *News Extra* that same Monday night lasted for 1 minute 26 seconds and the USS *Pueblo* was seen for 9.5 seconds. ITN took a piece lasting in all 54 seconds from Selvin in Washington, which it illustrated with a map of Cambodia showing Kompong Som and Phnom Penh for 12 seconds. Humphrys's piece into the *Nine O'Clock News* on Friday lasted 1 minute 9.5 seconds and used a portrait still of Kissinger for 9 seconds.

Of the 4 rather more complex pieces, 3 were in ITN bulletins and 1 in the BBC. The pattern previously established was thus repeated. The more visually complex the mode the greater the percentage of ITN pieces in the mode.

In the case of the B_2 values in Table 11.3, 3 were from Seymour reporting from Bangkok. On the Wednesday (10) Seymour's report lasted 1 minute 16 seconds. He talked over six film shots arranged on either side of a portrait still. On the Thursday (12) he talked for 1 minute 40.5 seconds, interspersing still photographs with the radio circuit caption, a pattern repeated rather less elaborately in (17) on Saturday. The Humphrys piece into the *Nine O'Clock News* illustrated by one still of Kissinger became for *News Extra* two colour news pictures plus a map rather than this file portrait still.

The length of these appearances overall varied little whether they were illustrated or not. They averaged out overall at 1 minute 8 seconds. Most of the unillustrated appearances were shorter than this average. A complex hidden assumption about viewers' tolerance levels for unchanging images can perhaps be discerned here. On the one hand, radio circuit captions were not treated as still images at all when the durations on the screen are compared with durations for other still inputs. On the other hand however, given this, an interrupted radio circuit caption could sustain a longer piece from the correspondent than an uninterrupted one. The only exception to this was the 1 minute 33 second unillustrated piece from MacDonald in *First Report*. Otherwise all unillustrated pieces are shorter overall than illustrated pieces, however limited that illustration might be.

This leaves a residual group of inputs with two entries. In one, in the early evening bulletin on Wednesday, the BBC allowed a Pentagon spokesman to talk for 56.5 seconds over an aerial photograph of the Pentagon with the words 'Pentagon spokesman' superimposed throughout. The visual to this audio track caught up with it, as it were, in a *sync.* insert into *News Extra*. In the second entry on the same day ITN used a portrait still of Premier Bourassa of Quebec and his voice over it for 19 seconds in the middle of a film report on the readiness of the Montreal Olympic site.

The radio circuit caption is among the more sophisticated images regularly used on the news. It consists of three distinct elements (Photo 5g). First, there is a background image of the place from which the report comes. Second, there is a portrait still of the person making the report; and, last, there is written identification. In the case of the photograph, the BBC *Nine O'Clock News* identification of service and area is worked into the caption 'BBC NEWS WASHINGTON'. With stringers the portrait still can also be omitted but some written identification of the place is present normally in the form 'Tony Other reporting from Z'.

Thus, we decode the image by reading the name of the man portrayed as being his name (although it is not under his face) and we hear the voice as being his voice (although by definition, in the still portrait, he is not talking); and finally we hear the voice attached to the silent face as coming to us from the place in the background. ITN add to the complexities of this by having their man in the portrait holding a telephone. This clearly signifies how the sound is reaching us – but, often, as in Photo 5h, the correspondent/reporter has been caught by the photographer listening, not talking. Thus we decode a picture of a man listening in terms of his voice being listened to. Could it be that ITN do not want portrait

Photo 5g   Radio circuit caption

Photo 5h   Listener as talker

stills of their staff caught in the act of speech? If this is the case, it is of interest to consider it again when we discuss portrait stills in general below.

This image consists entirely of various indexical elements, the montage of which symbolically signifies reporters/correspondents talking to us from the site of the event they are talking about. It is used to expedite reports into the bulletin in the case of domestic stories or, more generally, to most cheaply obtain foreign reports. Needless to say, there are almost no iconic images of any kind in these reports – the two photographs of Kissinger and the *Mayaguez* at Singapore being the exceptions.

The correspondent, paradoxically, when he is most out in the world appears in the bulletins most symbolically.

Good Night

We have discussed in this chapter and the last the basics of the bulletins – the opening and closing titles, the studio settings and the appearances of news personnel in those settings.

Not only do news personnel dominate the bulletins in terms of overall durations but also they appear uninterruptedly at great length (given average shot durations), and are accorded the maximum status of supercaptions and hand-overs.

Such a dominance must obviously raise questions as to the possibilities of editorialising. The very length at which correspondents appear means that their interpretive role can be allowed to flourish. It also means that reports in the economic and parliamentary areas, which anyway themselves dominate the bulletins, are overwhelmingly illustrated by the talking heads of these correspondents. For television news, the journalist appears to remain as important as he or she is for print journalism. All the visual apparatus available for reporting the world without the overt mediation of the journalist has in the twenty-plus years of broadcast journalism hardly affected the journalist's centrality in the news presentation process. The close analysis laid out above simply documents the extent to which the traditional role of correspondents has been taken over by television; and how the use of correspondents is a major factor in avoiding the visual imperative – in allowing the bulletins to report on intangibles at at least the same lengths they use to report on filmic events.

12 Still Life

Graphics are the voice of God

Tim Hewat

A basic division in television news imagery is between moving and still pictures. We have already discussed the use of stills as backing to newscasters and correspondents in the studio, as part of titling sequences and as radio circuit captions.

There are six further categories of stills, all of which use the image full-frame with voice-over commentary. These are: graphics; animated graphics; portrait stills; news (wire) pictures; maps; other photographs. The definitions of each of these categories, as used by the Group, are to be found on p. 286 of *Bad News*, Volume 1 of this study. The closer work of analysis here being reported has altered the original categorisation system a little. We are now not making a distinction between animated and non-animated images in the graphics category. But we are dividing the initial 'photographs' category into two: file 'portraits' of news personalities and 'other photographs'.

Stills can account for as much as 34.8 per cent of the overall bulletin duration or as little as 8.6 per cent (see Figures 9.9, 9.10). It is possible to argue that in the *Newsday* bulletin (34.8 per cent) they are used as a substitute for film. In all but the current affairs style bulletins, the percentage duration of film relates to the percentage of stills. The greater the amount of film, the less the number of stills (see Table 12.1).

The exception to this is *First Report* which, as we have already seen, allows its presenters longer pieces to camera unillustrated than do most other bulletins. The low stills usage recorded for *News Extra* reflects that bulletin's use of *Chromokey* and ITN's *News at Ten* uses more stills than are here reported for the same reason. The

Table 12.1 Relationship between stills and film

Bulletin	% stills*	% film/tape
BBC1 lunchtime bulletin	20.7	29.6
BBC1 early evening bulletin	19.8	36.0
BBC1 *Nine O'Clock News*	16.8	48.9
ITN *First Report*	12.6	37.7
ITN early evening bulletin	21.7	33.2
ITN *News at Ten*	14.2	47.9
BBC2 *Newsday*	34.8	—
BBC2 *News Extra*	8.6	55.2

*Including radio circuit captions

argument that stills are a substitute for film is offered only in connection with *Newsday* and then less because of the overall percentage of stills than because of the high percentage (14 per cent) (see Figure 9.9) of news pictures. This view is sustained by the fact that the BBC1 lunchtime bulletin, having less film than the other bulletins, has, as expected, more news pictures (4.8 per cent) (see Figure 9.3). It is not, in our opinion, true to say that the other categories of still apart from news pictures operate as a substitute for film at all. Some categories, notably graphics, convey information of an obviously different order from film.

The way in which these various categories of stills are used illustrates this. There is less range in the percentage of stills used in those categories which are least like film. Thus, all the bulletins use graphics and maps over about a 15 per cent range (see Figure 12.1). News photographs, which some bulletins use as film substitutes, spread over about a 40 per cent range. The 'other photographs' category has as wide a range because of one news item only – *News Extra*'s report of the hazards of bottle-feeding babies in the Third World. This was an action stills sequence (as described on p. 286 of *Bad News*) – a current affairs style of presentation using still photographs as if they were shots in a film story. Without this item, *News Extra*'s 'other photographs' use would be within the 2–10 per cent range of the other bulletins. 'Other photographs', as will be seen, are dominated by the black-and-white image of the *Mayaguez*. There were 36 images in this category, used a total of 68 times during the week.[1] Of these 68 uses 25 were of the *Mayaguez* still. Of the 36 images 11 were in the *News Extra* action stills sequence. It is probably fair to say that the particular combination of a rare action stills sequence and a continuing news story with one

dominant image means that the sample is too small to allow one to
draw firm conclusions about the use of 'other photographs' on the

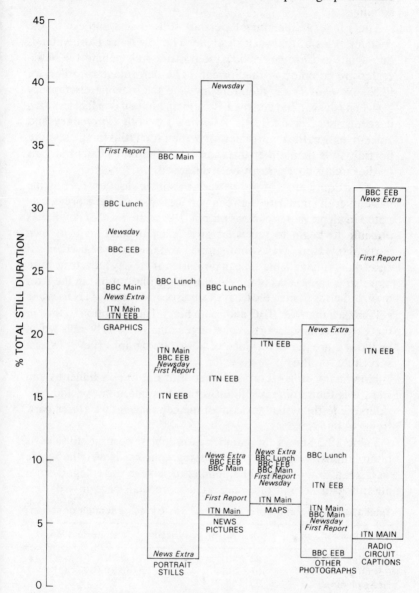

Figure 12.1   Patterns of stills utilisation (% overall stills duration by stills
category)

news in general. A further problem is that both the *Chromokey* bulletins (*News at Ten, News Extra*) use 'other photographs' as backings.

The range in the use of portrait stills is less subject to the particularities of the week's sample. The low *News Extra* value is due again to *Chromokey* because portrait stills behind the newscaster are common in this format. (The percentage recorded for ITN's *News at Ten* is therefore low and the seeming discrepancy between *News at Ten* and the BBC's main bulletin is in fact less than it seems: see Figure 12.1.) Allowing for both *Chromokey* and voice-over use, the main bulletins, in their total stills time, use more portrait stills than either the short or the current affairs bulletins (radio circuits have already been discussed).

This examination of the pattern of stills utilisation reveals the basic overall similarity between services that we have previously noted in all measures of news output. But at this level of detail, it is possible to begin to see what gives each bulletin style its own particular texture. News photographs would seem to be used only if news film is unavailable. The main stories of the day seem to acquire more stills (as well as more moving-image illustration) in the later main bulletins than in the early evening ones. Overall, ITN uses less still images than the BBC and more film. (The exception to this, in the early evening report, is the larger number of ITN stills which includes a greater percentage of news photographs (i.e. stills as a substitute for film).)

How many stills were used overall in the week's bulletins and what was their content? In answering this question, we add considerably to the visual 'lexicon' of the news images we are, in part, trying to build.

Table 12.2 shows the number of graphics, portrait stills, news photographs, maps and other photographs used over the whole week. It also shows the total number of shots in this category since all stills can be and often are used more than once in a day. It

Table 12.2   Total number of still images and their average duration on screen

	No.	No. of times used	Average duration
Graphics	84	137	12"
Portraits	107	165	10.9"
News pictures	50	114	7.8"
Maps	41	71	10.7"
Other photographs	36	68	7.2"

includes uses in the opening title, 'bong' or 'hooker' sequences and the average duration of shots in each category.

The voice of God

We have argued that graphics are used basically for sports results and for economic matters. We have suggested that the lack of graphics in the industrial area, surprising in view of the statistics available, bears out the assumption made by many observers that industrial news is treated less dispassionately than other major areas. For graphics have an incontrovertable quality in contrast to, say, shots of a picket line. In examining the 84 graphics used in the sample week, we find that this contention is amply supported. Of the 137 shots of graphics 63 were in the economic category (designated 40 in *Bad News*). This figure of graphics usage includes the standard *Financial Times* share price index graphic used at the end of *First Report* each day but deals mainly with the trade, currency, and inflation statistics given during the week. The EEC referendum (Category 31) accounted for a further 24 shots. These included 14 shots of postcards and related material in *First Report*'s feature 'EEC Postbag', which was 'opened' twice during the week, on Tuesday and Thursday. But here, 6 of these shots themselves contained economic information relating to Britain's trade balance with the EEC; its trade balance with the rest of the world; and an illustration of where Ireland's sterling holdings had gone. All these occurred in the features done to give background information to the referendum debate.

The remainder in this news story category could be cross-referenced with the Parliament category (Category 10) for they dealt with internal details of the referendum, naming the organisations fighting the campaign and the voting timetable. The last in the group was an advertisement for an English chain of food stores cut from a French Channel port newspaper. Thus, six of these 14 shots in a not obviously economic category contained economic information and were presented in the style of economic graphics.

This use of economic type information in non-economic stories was repeated with the home affairs category. Of the 19 shots in the news story category (60) which used graphics, 8 dealt with the armed forces' pay rise. These could be cross-referenced with the industry category but it should be noted that there were no graphics giving any pay details in the two major disputes of the week, those at

Dunlop and Chrysler. This failure, we would argue from our more general sample, is typical – the factual bases of industrial disputes are not treated in the clear style of graphics. Of the 8 army pay graphics 1 contained the cover of the report of the Review Body. Of the remainder, 2 dealt with the way in which Cardiff spent its ratepayers' money and 1 detailed proposed fare increases on London Transport buses; 5 detailed the building societies story on the Friday. The cover of a report recommending that the birth control pill be available on prescription was used and 2 gave weather details as part of *First Report*'s closing routine. Thus, of these home affairs graphics, 15 presented economic information.

The two foreign graphics (Category 32) were advertisements and quotes from articles on the baby food scandal in the Third World. They were part of the action stills sequence using mainly 'other photographs' presented in *News Extra* on the Thursday. The nine graphics that dealt with disasters all related to the Flixborough explosion report. They were of a different quality from most of the other work in this general visual category, detailing exactly how the explosion had occurred. This was done with animated diagrammatic representations of the reactor tanks and the faulty pipe that blew up. All channels adopted this style.

In the general area of crime there were 4 graphics: 1 dealt with Lord Denning's decision on picketing in non-industrial situations (which could conceivably be cross-referenced to the industrial category). The words of the dictum were printed on the graphic. It was thus typographic in its entirety. This style is necessitated by the restriction on court reporting that exists in the United Kingdom. The remaining 3 graphics dealt with the Michael X case; 1 was a passport page belonging to one of the victims and 2 were of local Trinidad papers carrying details of the murders.

Close to the crime area were the graphics quoting a letter to the Archbishop of Canterbury from a group of leading theologians on the matter of exorcism. This was used twice by the BBC on the Wednesday.

There were 11 sports results captions, 7 of them, not unexpectedly, occurring on the Saturday. (Distinct sports results programmes were not included in the sample.)

Which leaves the industrial area as the only other content area having graphics. There were 3. Each of them was used either in the title or in the 'bong' sequences. The locked-out banknote printers were represented by a fan of banknotes. This abstract and symbolic graphic was the same as those being used in the (42) currency category to illustrate the falling value of the pound. The other two were about Dunlop and BLMC, the BBC putting both company logos together on the early bulletins on Wednesday and ITN restricting themselves to Dunlop's winged wheel in the 'bongs' on the same day. No information of an economic kind was given in any of these. All details of claim and counter-offer, of numbers on strike or laid-off being given verbally by the news personnel. The sample graphically (if we may so call it) illustrates the point that industrial news is not seen as an area from which graphic statements of fact can be culled. It has been suggested to us that our objections on this ground are ill-founded because it is 'natural' that economic stories should have this sort of input.[2] But it remains true that it would be equally 'natural' for pay disputes to be so documented. As it is, and as the week of our sample illustrated, it tends to be pay awards (not pay negotiations) that receive this treatment. There is nowhere a more obvious illustration of the lacunae in the news than in comparing the seeming willingness to document economic trends with the unwillingness to similarly document the history and details of industrial stories. In a week when Shell's quarterly profits were laid out for inspection in a simple graphical form, the Chrysler strikers day after day received no similar presentation. The argument with the management, the history of the negotiations, were never laid out in this way. It must be assumed that the news-producers trade on the commonsense assumption that industrial strife is somehow irrational, sudden, and incomprehensible.

Of course, all of the above makes the assumption that graphics of the dominant economic variety are understandable and do aid comprehension. Occasionally they are subject to studio direction error. But even when they are transmitted as intended there is often an ambiguity as to their meaning. For instance, in detailing the CBI report, Green, in the ITN early evening bulletin on the Tuesday, said 'nine out of every ten firms still report an increase in average costs', while the graphic detailed 'Increase in Costs 90%' (see Example 12.1a). In the later *News at Ten* bulletin, this survey result was simply dropped (see Example 12.1b).

Example 12.1a   ITN, 17.50, 13 May 1975

6.17½ *GREEN (Correspondent) VOICE-OVER*
/More than nine out of every ten firms still

Example 12.1a continued

Graphic: a small engineering factory top shot ext GV as background. *Super*: 'Increase in costs 90%'	report an increase in average costs over the previous four months. Eight out of
0.7 Animate	/ten firms say a lack of sales and a shortage
'Drop in sales & new orders' 80%	of new orders is now the major factor keeping down output. More than 70
0.7 Animate	/per cent of firms say they're working below
'Output below capacity' 71%	capacity, the same cutback as we had during the three-day week and more than during any of the recessions in the 1960s, and omin
0.8 Animate	/ously a record balance of 40 per cent of firms
'Employment cutbacks 40% 0.3 6.47½	foresee a reduction in their labour force./

Example 12.1b   ITN, 22.00, 13 May 1975

	GREEN TO CAM /This is the picture the CBI paints. Eight
49 Green (top of pocket) B/G CSO Cover of CBI trends booklet 0.24 11.13	out of ten/
50 Graphic small engineering factory top shot ext. GV as B/G. *Super*: 'Drop in sales & new orders 80%' 0.6 Animate	GREEN VOICE-OVER firms say a lack of sales and a shortage of orders is now the major factor keeping down output/
'Output below capacity 71%' 0.7 Animate	More than 70 per cent of firms say they're working below capacity, the same cutback as we had during the three-day week/
'Employment cutbacks 40%' 0.36 11.49	A record balance of 38 per cent of firms foresee a reduction in their labour force in the next four months. This follows widespread cutbacks in the last four months, particularly in consumer goods manufacturers and generally among the biggest companies. More than . . ./

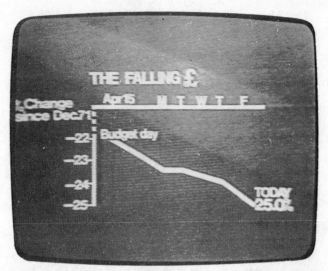

Photo 6a   ITN: the falling £

Even leaving aside these exceptional cases, it is still possible to criticise what has become the standard approach to graphics. Described by some professionals as 'the voice of God' they are difficult to absorb. Take ITN's graphic of the falling pound as used in the early evening bulletin on Monday in the sample week (Photo 6a). First, leaving aside the problems connected with the 'percentage change since 1971', we have an unreferenced base line crossing the top of the graph. Seven percentage points occupy a depth eight times as great as seventeen percentage points. The lateral dimension is equally distorted because of the reference to Budget Day and the details of the preceding few days. The audience had twelve seconds to absorb this and the verbal information (Example 12.2):

Example 12.2   ITN, 17.50, 12 May 1975

---

2 Honeycombe MCU (above   *HONEYCOMBE (Newscaster) TO CAM*
   pocket) EEB Plain backing   Today's figure is the sixth/...
   0.10   19

---

3 *Graphic* 'The falling   *HONEYCOMBE VOICE-OVER*
   pound' % change since   day of successive low points for the
   Dec 1971: Budget Day: pound. It closed on Friday at 24.4 per cent
   April 15: MTWTF: Today   down and on Budget Day four weeks ago it
   25.0%: –22–23–24–25:   stood at 22.1 per cent. In the Commons.../
        (Photo 6b)
   0.12   31

For *News at Ten* that night Budget Day was dropped from the graphic. The BBC adopted what might be called the dramatic 'plunge from nowhere' approach. Although this had the advantage of simplicity, it equally obviously contained little information. This is a difficult area of production and one in which professional opinion is by no means standardised. Since there is little British data on audience perception the exact amount of information per frame per second is subject to crude rule-of-thumb. Either the graphic contains considerable data or it contains very little. That the graphic in Example 12.2 was later amended so that the information 'Budget Day' was removed, clearly indicates that an editorial decision was made subsequent to the first transmission. That graphic therefore perhaps represents the limit of information that professionals currently feel can be conveyed. The BBC's would then represent something of a minimum.

Graphics in news (and for that matter current affairs programmes) are used less iconically than might be expected. In other words, each figure or reference point on the economic graphic is not necessarily explained in the voice-over commentary (as would be the case in, say, an Open University broadcast). For instance, in Photo 6b the figures on the histogram simply legitimise the newscaster's commentary. Not only are they not actually read out; they are not even directly referred to (see Example 12.3).

Photo 6b   Annual inflation rate

Example 12.3   BBC1, 21.00, 16 May 1975

	/WHITMORE (Newscaster) VOICE-OVER
7 *Graphic* (Photo 6b) (Histogram): Britain 21.7% (red bar including Union Jack) Italy (green bar) 20.3% Japan (green bar) 14.2% France (green bar) 13.5% USA (green bar) 10.3% WG (green bar) 5.9%	Britain's annual rate of inflation is at the top of the table of comparable countries, according to the latest figures. Here's our economics correspondent, Dominic Harrod.
0.9 1.1	

The rule could be perhaps best expressed negatively: when using economic graphics, do not refer to each and every aspect of the graphic. This rule then shows the limited iconic nature of the graphic when read against commentary. This non-iconic quality is further reinforced by the failure to reference sources – 'according to the latest figures' being most typical of normal usage. This is important since for all statistical data the base figure for comparison, and the source, affect the way in which the information can be read.

Finally, economic graphics utilise a standard cultural colour code. In Photo 6b, the British bar (containing the unnecessary and redundant flag) is coloured red. All other bars are coloured green. (Although why an annual inflation rate of 20.3 per cent – Italy's – should be 'go' as opposed to one of 21.7 per cent in Britain which is 'stop' is not immediately apparent.) In Photo 6c the trade balance for April is expressed by two thick arrows: one marked 'imports; pointing towards a map of Great Britain, the other marked 'exports' pointing away. The import arrow is coloured red and the export one green.

As we have shown, the vast preponderance of the work of graphics artists in this area involves figures. Aside from mounting other types of printed material for transmission (clippings from newspapers, covers of books and reports, etc.) graphics artists in British television news actually drew little. The use of drawings, schematics and other simplified icons was not allowed by the code of television news for voice-over commentary. Such schematics can be seen on *Chromokey* more as symbolic visual clues as to the nature of an item. Since few bulletins used *Chromokey* it follows that the

Photo 6c   Trade balance

possibilities of visualising the news by this means were not largely taken up.

Compared with North American news broadcasts, where *Chromokey* is a norm, the British bulletins are restrained. Even the use of artists to reconstruct courtroom scenes, a commonplace of the North American bulletin, is eschewed by the British. It would seem that the limited utilisation of the full possibilities of graphics departments is another indicator of the non-primacy of the visual which we have elsewhere argued as a characteristic of the British bulletin.

'As in a map'

Maps are also made by the graphics departments and share much with the category of image we have just discussed. Maps appear for about a second less on average per shot than graphics (10.7 seconds). In the sample week, there were 41 different maps used for 71 shots. With 1 exception (the map of the new region of Strathclyde used by *News at Ten* on the Tuesday) they were all of overseas locations. Two maps, used for 3 shots, were in the disasters story category (90), illustrating the Yugoslav train crash and the deaths on the Nuptse expedition in the Himalayas. There were 2 Middle East maps showing Israel with, respectively, Syria and Lebanon. These were used on 3 occasions. To illustrate the Basque story, ITN used 1 map of Northern Spain on 2 occasions. To illustrate the situation report from Kurdistan the BBC used 1 map of the Iraq/Iran border area twice. All the rest were of Indo-China, 26 of them relating to the *Mayaguez* story. These provided 49 shots in the coverage of that story. The rest dealt with the various other stories from the area during the week. This sample is obviously too small to generalise from in any detail but the clear limitations of maps as an illustrative device are demonstrated. They predominate in the foreign and disaster story categories. It is not insignificant that the one British map during the week actually related to the redrawing of the map of Britain. Maps tend to contain less information than graphics but the same considerations of shot length and commentary seem to apply. In other words, all the names on the map are not referred to, just as all the figures on the economic graphic are not referenced in commentary. Indeed with maps the commentary tends to be even more symbolically related, story details being given in commentary which make the map into a symbolic representation of the event.

The most places marked on any map during the week were in ITN's general *Mayaguez* map used on the Tuesday. Hong Kong, Thailand, S. (sic) Vietnam, Phnom Penh, Saigon, Hanoi, Kompong Som, Ko Tang and the phrase 'Seized here' with an 'X' were all shown. The audience was given 30 seconds on one occasion and 13.5 seconds on another to read this off, each time as the camera zoomed slowly into the 'X'. On another occasion, the map was used, without camera movement, for only 7 seconds.

The symbolic quality of maps can perhaps be best illustrated by comparing Photos 6d and 6e. The main Cambodian town involved in the *Mayaguez* affair had been identified by ITN from the outset as Kompong Som (the BBC preferred Kompongsom). However, on the Wednesday ITN, without any reference in commentary, changed Kompong Som to Sihanoukville (Photo 6d) in the early evening bulletin. By *News at Ten* they had, again without any explanation, altered the name of the town to Ream (Photo 6e). Clearly no geography lessons were being offered. In Friday's *News at Ten*, in reporting the Yugoslav train crash, Bosanquet announced that it had occurred at Vranje, 170 miles south of Zagreb. The map refers to Belgrade, not Zagreb (Photo 6f). What is here illustrated is that the actual details of any particular name are in some way assumed to be below the threshold of the audience's perception. Otherwise surely apologies or explanations would have been

Photo 6d   Sihanoukville

Photo 6e   Ream

offered. Given this, and the fact that not all names are referred to in the voice-over texts, maps, we would argue, are primarily symbolic legitimating devices rather like economic graphics.

Before moving on to those categories of still image that do not contain print, a word should perhaps be said again about the

Photo 6f Zagreb

similarity of the responses of the bulletins. It is true that if a story is shared by both services and uses a graphic or map then both are more likely than not to share the input. Thus, all the economic stories put out by both channels carried economic graphics, although some variation can be seen. The falling pound, the rise in the cost of living, the balance of trade, might show slightly different solutions to the problem of illustration – i.e. more complexity or less – but the basic response would be the same. ITN might favour the United Kingdom map for one graphic, the BBC the Union Jack. But basically it is difficult when examining stills of maps and graphics to instantly identify which service provided them. This similarity is increased by the use of similar typefaces. Although there are differences in style, ITN's being a little more flamboyant and in consequence less comprehensible than the BBC's, the overall effect of bold sans serif faces, normally all capitals, is to diminish the difference. The house styles are thus somewhat attenuated in favour of a general television graphic style. And while, in typographic terms, it cannot be called fussy it probably does not do as much as it might to help the audience identify the bulletin.

'Look on this picture'

The most extensive category of still images is that of portrait stills.

These are normally colour photographs, taken against a plain background, of the head of a news personality. They are kept on file and therefore can be used to illustrate stories indexically. In other words, portraits of politicians are used to illustrate speeches where a news photograph or film of the person actually making the speech is unavailable. They stand then in an indexical relationship to any particular story.

In the sample week, 106 of these stills were used, including 1 identikit portrait of the Cambridge rapist. Only 5 were photographs of women: the tennis player Linda Mottram, the murder victim Gail Benson whose body was found in Michael X's garden, the missing child Jane Taylor and 2 photographs of Mrs Thatcher. In all, there were 28 active politicians and 1 ex-politician, 9 union leaders, 10 figures from the world of industry and finance, 2 judges, 4 figures involved in crime, 15 foreigners (all without exception politicians), 9 sports personalities, 2 climbing accident victims, the Archbishop of Canterbury, Frank Sinatra and Sandy Gall. Some of these figures were represented by more than 1 photograph. Three shots contained 2 portraits mounted in a single frame. Different photographs were used by different channels, none of these images being pooled.

The average duration of shots using portrait stills is 10.9 seconds but this conceals a notable discrepancy between BBC and ITN. In the competing bulletins the BBC tends to have longer shots than ITN; the average duration in the BBC's early evening bulletin is 11.1 seconds as against ITN's 7.85 seconds. The *Nine O'Clock News* has 10.95 seconds as against *News at Ten*'s 8.4 seconds. Leaving aside ITN's use of the *Chromokey* in the later bulletin, this does mean that the BBC uses these perhaps quintessentialy 'Establishment' images more than ITN. This, too, is reflected in Figure 12.1. The *Nine O'Clock News* uses these images for 35 per cent of the time it is using still images. Thus, the texture of the BBC's bulletins, one could argue, would seem to more involve the portrait still and involve it for longer periods per shot than does ITN's texture.

The news story categories covered by this input are, in view of the nature of the people involved, heavily political. This is accented by the restriction on reporting from the House of Commons. The only way the British television was allowed at the time of the study to illustrate debates in the House of Commons was with portrait stills of the MPs. It was also noticeable that reports of speeches (the sample week being in the middle of the referendum campaign) not deemed important enough to warrant a camera crew were also illustrated with portrait stills. Of the union leaders pictured in this way during the week, only one shot of Jack Jones directly related to an industrial dispute story. Tom Jackson was in the midst of a conference of post office workers; Clive Jenkins leapt to the defence of Tony Benn; Geoffrey Drain was attacking Crosland for his 'party's over' speech; Hugh Scanlon was involved in the internal AUEW voting decision; Fred Jarvis commented on training unwanted teachers and Murray, Gormley and Plumb were commenting on the economy or the referendum.

Almost all the foreign figures were involved in the *Mayaguez* affair. Since pictures from the scene of the incident were not available, American reaction to the affair was given heavy play. Thus, in addition to the President and Secretaries Kissinger and Schlessinger, there were also photographs of Senators Sparkman, Javits, Buckley, Humphrey and Goldwater. Pramoj and Chu Havan were used from the Thai side and Lee Duk Toh appeared on the day of the victory parade in Ho Chi Minh City. To cue the Kurdistan situation report, 2 pictures were used, 1 of the Shah and 1 of Barzani. The Irish Foreign Minister appeared in this form once, as did the Premier of Quebec, Bourassa. This last was a deviant use. It was the only occasion in the week where a still photograph of a person other than a news employee was matched to that person's voice; i.e. a sort of radio circuit. This should be compared with the use of the Sandy Gall portrait. Here, Gall's words were reported by the newscaster. He did not himself talk from Saigon. Therefore the form of the picture was that used for standard quotation, not the montage used for normal radio circuit inserts.

The 108 photographs were used for 165 shots. The politicians dominated with 67 shots; the trade union leaders were in 21 shots; finance and industry in 16 shots; foreign figures in 30 shots; sports personalities in 15 shots; crime victims in 6 shots; disaster victims in 4 shots; judges in 3; the Archbishop of Canterbury, Sinatra and Gall in one each. (The discrepancy between this total and the figure of 165 is accounted for by the 3 double-portrait shots.)

The politicians and the trade union leaders appear more frequently – 2.3 times per person – than the foreigners and disaster victims (2 times), the industrial and financial figures and the sports personalities (1.6 times), criminals, their victims and their judges (1.5 times) and the Archbishop, Sinatra and Gall (once).

These portraits bear a great similarity to one another. They range in framing size from top of the jacket pocket to under the chin. The backgrounds are normally as neutral as possible, blue or red drapes (this is especially true of the MPs). Some half a dozen of the 108 broke this rule: Gordon Richardson, the Governor of the Bank of England, Winston Churchill, Jr, and the Archbishop of Canterbury were photographed outside. The two judges, Kukrit Pramoj, Lee Duk Toh and Chu Havan, the Thai Foreign Minister, were also shot outside. Most of the sports portraits were exteriors.

All the figures, except for the 5 females, 3 sportsmen, the 2 judges and Selwyn Lloyd (the last three in wigs), were formally attired in suits and ties. Only Frank Allaun, MP, added a high necked sweater (Orantes, Taylor and cricketer Murray were in whites). Further variations include the possibility that the portrait was in black and white. This sub-category obviously includes the identikit picture of the Cambridge rapist as well as Geoffrey Robinson, the managing director of Jaguar cars, and Sebastian De Ferranti, the head of Ferranti Ltd. The two army officers who died on Nupste were also represented by black-and-white photographs, as were Michael X and Jane Taylor. Kukrit Pramoj and Chu Havan were also in black and white.

Such are the limitations of this set of images that it is possible to plot deviation in terms of expression. On a continuum from laugh to anger everyone of these images falls in the range from smile to talk and most (the standard MP portrait) are passport-like in their neutrality of expression. For the most part, people are looking at the lens in three-quarters profile. There are no complete profiles and few direct 'passport' head-on shots. Of the 108 pictures used, only 8 were of 5 people caught in the act of speech: Margaret Thatcher, Tony Benn, Jack Jones and Geoffrey Drain and Eric Heffer. Thatcher 'speaking' was used just once (and it is possible that this was a colour news photograph taken at the Conservative conference in Scotland) and other 'unspeaking' images were used of her on other occasions. Both Jones and Benn had file portraits 'unspeaking', but the 'speaking' ones were preferred. They were used on all channels in the act of speech. In one of the Drain images (ITN's) the mouth is open only slightly. The BBC's picture of him was definitely in the act of speech, as was that of Heffer. Thus, although it cannot be said that only figures on the Left were on file in the act of speech, it can be said that if a portrait still is shown in which the person is so caught they are more likely to be of the Left than not.

We have previously noticed the strange phenomenon of the radio

Photo 7a   Jones speaking

circuit caption where the audience is invited to see a man in silence but to hear the voice-over as coming from him. A perusal of Photo 7a might perhaps reveal why news personnel themselves are not photographed speaking. And the effect of juxtaposing these 'speaking' portraits to illustrate, say, a parliamentary debate does

Photo 7b   Benn looking up

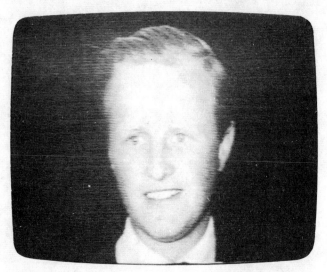

Photo 7c Churchill

reveal the possibilities of extremely subtle editorialising. Comparing Photo 7b with Photo 7c shows that an exchange in the House

Example 12.4   ITN, 22.00, 14 May 1975

	10.29½ / *PARKIN (Newscaster) TO CAM*
49 Parkin (top of pocket) plain B/G CUT 0.10½ 10.40	In the Commons the Conservative spokesman on industry, Mr Michael Heseltine, called the deal unnecessary and expensive. Under further questioning Mr Benn roused the Commons with an answer to a Conservative/

50 Churchill *portrait still*
    colour night ext. (top of
    tie-knot) smiling
    (photo 7c)
CUT 0.6½   10.46½
	MP, Mr Churchill, who asked how many
	redundancies would be required to make
	Ferranti profitable/

51 Benn *portrait still* colour
    int. (between top of
    pocket & tie-knot)
    speaking (Photo 7b) plain
    B/G
CUT 0.10½   10.57
	Mr Benn said this: 'The passion for
	redundancies of secure well-paid people
	like you including cabinet ministers of the
	Conservative party or even present Cabinet
	Ministers, indicates that underlying their
	apparent claim for efficiency lies a hatred
	of working people.'/

of Commons, reported as such in voice-over, is visually reinforced as one man, Benn (7b), literally looking up to the other, Churchill (7c) (see Example 12.4).

As it happens

News pictures, icons of the events of the day, and the category 'other photographs' can be distinguished from graphics, maps and portrait stills because they are on the screen for less time. News pictures' average duration is 7.8 seconds. They can also be distinguished because they are a prime source of black-and-white imagery. As we have seen, few portrait stills are in black and white and they are of lesser-known figures (chairmen of companies, criminals, victims). Colour portraits are thereby associated more with major figures. This is not true of news pictures. Of the 50 images used 114 times during the week, only 3 were in colour and, of them, 1 was old – an aerial view of the aftermath of the Flixborough disaster. The other 2 colour photographs were taken at a Kissinger press conference.

The vast majority of the images came from abroad: 1, used once in *Newsday*, was of the strike vote at Chrysler; of the 18 sport news pictures used, only 2 were domestic, illustrating the Nastase incident at Bournemouth; 11 shots concerned the Queen and Prince Philip leaving the Emperor Hirohito and returning to Britain and, of these uses, 1 image (used twice) was at Heathrow. The most dramatic were of the marines and President Ford's relief at the rescue (Photos 7d and 7e).

Thus, the balance of 109 shots were within the general foreign category although they included illustrations of the Queen (9 shots), foreign industrial stories (Montreal strike – 3 shots), sport (Keegan in Cyprus, heading goal – 2 shots; Japanese lady climbs Everest – 4 shots; Ali boxing victory – 10 shots), 7 shots of the 2 rail crashes, 1 in Sweden, the other in Yugoslavia. The rest came from the Far East or the United States and, of these, 58 were used in the *Mayaguez* coverage. The others dealt with the refugee ships arriving at Guam, the aftermath of the Khmer Rouge takeover of Phnom Penh, Lee Duk Toh's visit to Saigon for the victory parade and the arrival of Provisional Revolutionary Government of South Vietnam representatives in Bangkok (9 shots). Finally, 7 shots illustrated the Italian art theft story.

What distinguishes this group of images from the portrait still

Photo 7d   Marines on Ko Tang

Photo 7e   Ford hears of rescue

category is that they are framed wider. This remains true even when they are portraits of people. Thus, only one shot of President Ford is a single but he is in evening dress, a sartorial deviation from the indexical images of him in the portrait still category. Lee Duk Toh could be in either category except that there is rather more background than would be normally seen in the portrait shot (and Chu Havan was partially obscuring a second figure in his portrait). Lee Duk Toh and, for that matter, one of the images of Kissinger could, following this first iconic transmission, serve as portrait stills. The other Kissinger image is a mid-shot and therefore seemingly too wide for this subsequent use. The other single shots of people include Mrs Yanko standing in triumph atop Everest, Keegan heading and Ali after his fight. All other photographs in this category, if they contain people, are two shots or groups and are framed at least at mid-shot distance.

Other photographs

The last category of still image – other photographs – is similar to that of news pictures. Their average duration is slightly shorter at 7.2 seconds per shot. There were fewer of them, 36 images used a total of 68 times. In some instances it is difficult to determine the difference between news pictures and other photographs. The basic difference, colour, no longer applies so rigidly. Some shots, for instance those of the special counting halls used by ITN for the referendum story on the Wednesday, might well have been specially commissioned and taken that day, making them in fact technically news pictures by our categorisation system. But since the images were too timeless to be iconic they have been classified here. On the other hand, a shot of the Flixborough reactors, originally a clear news picture, is classified here because it was animated. An electronically generated circle appeared on the shot to indicate just where the blow-out had occurred.

The sample week was distorted in this category by the *Mayaguez* affair and the African baby-food scandal story run as an exclusive by *News Extra*.

The *Mayaguez* itself, indexically at dock somewhere, appeared no less than 25 times, the most repeated image of the week aside from newscasters. Various other ships and planes associated with the story accounted for 8 more of the 36 images and 14 of the shots. Thus, no less than 39 of the 68 'other photographs' shots related to the *Mayaguez* affair.

The baby food story was an action stills sequence. This category, we had previously determined, was more characteristic of the current affairs mode than the news. It was therefore not surprising to find it in *News Extra*, a current affairs style bulletin. It was a sequence which was structured like film (and indeed contained 3 film shots) as well as 12 'other photograph' images.

There were 3 shots of counting halls, each used once, and 2 uses of the Flixborough reactor shot. The Russian aircraft 'The Bear' was used to illustrate Roy Mason's explanation of why the navy needed a special version of the Harrier jump-jet. A brochure photograph of the MGB was used to illustrate the *News at Ten* story celebrating the fiftieth anniversary of the *marque*. There were 3 shots of army personnel used in the pay rise story and 4 of various Chrysler plants and buildings, these last being only on ITN. ITN also used a general British dockside view, a close-up of a hand placing a vote in a ballot box and an aerial view of Glasgow. These 3 shots, as well as 1 of the army personnel shots, and 1 view of the Stoke plant, were used exclusively by *News at Ten* in the 'bongs' or 'hooker' sequences.

The shots of the *Mayaguez*, those of the 2 American destroyers involved in the incident, 1 of the shots of the *Coral Sea* and those of the Flixborough reactors were black and white. The rest were colour.

The major difference between this category and news pictures is, that whereas news pictures were overwhelmingly used iconically, 'other photographs' are overwhelmingly indexical. The shot of the *Coral Sea*, the US aircraft carrier from which the 'rescue' of the *Mayaguez* was attempted, perfectly illustrates this point. On Tuesday, *First Report* used the colour aerial photo of the *Coral Sea* to say 'Among the warships ordered towards the scene is the aircraft carrier *Coral Sea*'. And then Kee added: 'There it is' (ITN, 13.00, 13 May 1975). While this statement was clearly nothing but the truth in one sense, for indeed there was an image of the ship on the screen, it is equally true that the aerial (having no point of reference in it) gave little clue as to exactly where the ship was when the photograph was taken. The same image was used the following Thursday to say 'air support and planes from the *Coral Sea* were sent in' (ITN, 17.50, 15 May 1975). Thus, the image had been used indexically to represent the ship on its way to the action and engaged in the action. In *News at Ten* the same night, the image stood indexically for the ship's involvement with the aftermath of the action (see Example 12.5).

What is true of the *Coral Sea* is of course even truer of the *Mayaguez*. Its entire voyage from its first appearance on Monday night's *News at Ten* until it was being towed to Singapore on the

Example 12.5   ITN, 22.00, 15 May 1975

		3.17	/WAIN (Correspondent) VOICE-OVER

21	Large-scale Ko Tang *Map*		But the marine task force was still on Ko Tang and under heavy Cambodian fire. There was no need for them to be there and so orders were given to evacuate them. But this was much easier said than done. For one thing, they had to wait until the *Coral Sea* had approached
CUT 0.17		3.34	close enough for the heli/

22	*Coral Sea* aerial GV at sea		copters on board to be sent in. And when
	Colour photo		they did attempt to land they were beaten back
CUT 0.7		3.41	by Cambodian ground fire. So it was/

---

			n't until 8.00 this evening local time that the marines were pulled out.

Friday (and an iconic news picture became available) was indexically represented by the ship at an unidentified dockside.

When portraits, graphics, maps and other photographs are considered, the dominance of indexical images in the bulletins can again be demonstrated. That this indexical pattern should be repeated with film – potentially the best source of 'as it happens' imagery – is perhaps one of the Group's most surprising conclusions; and it is to film that we now turn. We will include also the last category of graphics, 'supercaptions', used to name people appearing, since this group is almost totally limited to film and tape.

13 'Truth 24 Times a Second' – 25 Times for Television

> Operators filmed new items and soon announced a 'change of program' with local events. The filming of these was done as publically as possible; the idea was to lure people to the shows in the hope of seeing themselves – which they sometimes did. In the event, the local items were often the high spot of the run: in Spain, *Arrival of the Toreadors*; in Russia, *Coronation of Nicholas II*; in Australia, *Melbourne Races* – all 1896 products. To the local audiences they seemed ultimate proof that the *cinématographe* was no 'trick'.
>
> Eric Barnouw

It is film – and increasingly since the period of our study electronic news gathering (ENG) – which gives television news its particular visual impact. Yet we have shown that a high percentage of the bulletins consist of nothing more than a head talking to camera, backed, on a minority of occasions, by still images on *Chromokey*. The stills inputs, news pictures, portraits, maps and the like can be seen just as easily in the newspapers. It is therefore only film, the occasional OB, and latterly ENG, which are unique to television and which afford the producers the opportunity to vary the staple images of the bulletins. The extent to which the television news can really show events as they happen depends, at least basically, on film and ENG cameras.

This perhaps should be stressed since it is a commonplace of professional rhetoric to allow for the effect of the visual imperative. Not only do newsproducers claim this, as in their evidence to the Annan Committee, but academics, too, failing to pay close attention to the output itself, also adopt this myth.[1] Michael Tracey's *The Production of Political Television* concentrates on practice as explained by the practitioners:[2]

A simple example of this within news programmes would be the emphasis on visual stories, the use of familiar images, a focus on conflict, an emphasis on action rather than talking heads, the presentation of stories in a fictional form, with a beginning, middle and end.

The images certainly are familiar and there is evidence, at least in the industrial area, of a focus on conflict. But for the rest the case does not stand up, however often it is repeated. Yet, if the bulletins are to be at all visual in Tracey's sense they must rely on film.

In the week of 11–17 May the bulletins used a total of 193 film inputs. For the purposes of this chapter we have excluded films used in titles, 'bongs' and 'hookers' unless they continued without a break for the newscaster to address camera, and we have classed all dubious videotape inputs as film.[3] We have seen the percentage of overall duration of the weekday bulletins taken up by film (Figures 9.3–9.10). It is now necessary to look at the make-up of this film component in greater detail.

A basic division can be made between those films which have synchronous sound (by which we mean that the audience can hear a person or people talking) and those that do not. The actual technical distinction between synchronous and non-synchronous or mute film does not concern us. Most film these days is shot with sound but we are ignoring all non-speech sound effects and all sounds whether speech or other noises which have commentary spoken over them. In order to make clear the particular way in which we are using the notion of synchronous sound films, we have called all others voice-over films. This means that the main carrier of meaning on the audio level is by commentary, almost always read by news personnel. We have further made the assumption that voice-over films are more visual and less tied to the ubiquitous talking head than are films with *sync*.

On this basis the film inputs for the week under study can be divided up as in Table 13.1. Thus in the all-important input of films, all-important as a way of avoiding talking heads and stills, nearly half the time is nevertheless taken up with talking heads.

Yet obviously this *sync*. element is different in kind from the newscasters and other personnel addressing the studio camera directly. For even in the most formal of interviews and speeches the speakers do not directly address the lens. Only television personnel routinely do this and that tendency holds good when considering

Table 13.1 Commentary and *sync.* speech in film inputs

	Voice-over only	Mixed V/O and *sync.*		*Sync.* only
No. of inputs	85	72		36
% of the total duration of all film inputs	22	62.6		14.4
		V/O 31	*Sync.* 32.6	
	53% Total voice-over element		47% Total *sync.* element	

film; for it is reporters and correspondents on location who directly address the camera in a fashion comparable to their studio-based colleagues. It can be argued that directly addressing the camera is to directly address the audience, without the mediation of the interviewer, without looking off. The dominant convention of all dramatic programme output is that actors do not look at the lens, neither do quiz show participants, sportsplayers, etc. In fact only announcers, news personnel, weather persons, current affairs presenters, people making charity appeals, politicians in Party Political Broadcasts, people selling things in advertisements and a variety of entertainers look towards the lens (although these last routinely endeavour to address both lens and studio audience). What these groups share is a measure of status and authority and therefore it can be argued that to directly address the lens invests the speaker in terms of the code of television production with status and authority (a fact not lost on political demagogues, who will when interviewed answer the questioning reporters by ignoring them and addressing the camera directly).

In terms of overall film duration reporters directly addressing the camera occupy a small percentage of time. In the week in question 19 reporters and correspondents on 21 occasions in the course of 19 stories (9 on BBC and 10 on ITN) took up only 4.16 per cent of the total film duration speaking to camera. It is possible to see this, in contradistinction to studio and North American practice, as a down-playing of the reporter/correspondent role, part of an overall strategy to avoid the creation of personalities and the overall charge that serious and responsible reporting is being sacrificed to entertainment. For it is true that on the majority of occasions reporters will not be seen in vision except when conducting interviews. It is also possible to see in this a tendency on the producers' part not to add unnecessary 'talking heads' to the most visual of all inputs – film.

Interviews comprise the second major category of *sync*. In the week in question they accounted for 26 per cent of the overall duration of film inputs, well over half of the total amount of *sync*. transmitted. There were 67 people interviewed in 90 inputs spread over 40 stories. Both reporter/correspondent pieces to camera and interviews involve the direct intervention of the medium. If the camera were not present the event (interview or piece to camera) would not have occurred. The other classes of *sync*. involve a greater measure of observation, and less intervention.

These other classes involve either formal speech, at meetings, press conferences or rallies, or overheard informal speech. There is very little of the latter and shots with overheard speech are more likely than shots with other types of *sync*. to also have commentary overriding portions of the overheard element.

Thus overheard informal *sync*. took up a maximum of 2.9 per cent of total film time (since much of this was actually voiced-over with commentary). Only 5 stories had this type of sound, the major one being the Chrysler wives' slanging match outside the factory gates. This accounted for 5 of the 9 occasions on which informal *sync*. appeared. The other 4 occasions were taken up with listening to people announce the organisation they worked for on the telephone; overhearing two French shoppers comparing prices in a Ramsgate supermarket; and a street trader telling off a pro-Common Market campaign worker for disturbing the crowd round his stall; and the same campaigners making loud-hailer announcements from a moving car. The last was of Nastase's umpire telling him to play on after a disputed ball call. It is perhaps significant that of the 5 stories involved in this category 3 were feature stories and only 2 directly related to the events of the day of transmission.

This is less true of the last of the four categories of *sync*. we are here determining. Formal speeches and press conferences are more likely to relate to the news of the day but they seem to be more likely to be used as *sync*. at weekends. There were 11 stories which used formal *sync*. and of these 4 were weekend speeches, by Lord Soper, Fred Peart, Enoch Powell and Margaret Thatcher. There were also speeches by two unnamed members of a Cardiff ratepayers' association and one by James Callaghan. We also heard (for 4.5

seconds) a lady formally name the replica of *Locomotion 1*. Two other occasions involved, first, both President Ford and Secretary Kissinger; and, second, Bob Morris, the Chrysler shop stewards' convenor and an unnamed colleague. One Pentagon spokesman and Sir Geoffrey Rippon account for the two last press conferences. All these uses accounted for 9.3 per cent of the total duration of film.

Patterns

A number of basic patterns for sequencing voice-over and *sync.* material can be determined on the basis of this sample.

First there is the plain insert – a sequence of shots with commentary read over them. Of the 193 film inserts used in the week 85 were of this kind. They ranged in number of shots from 1 shot to 28 shots and in length from 7.5 seconds to 3 minutes 23 seconds.

Simple *sync.* – that is, *sync.* film introduced from the studio without any voice-over elements – appeared as 36 inserts (illustrating 19 stories, many of the interviews being repeated from bulletin to bulletin). Of these 9 were interviews, used on 16 occasions; 4 were speeches used on 14 occasions; 3 were press conferences used on 3 occasions – i.e. one each; and 2 were overheard, 1 of these being repeated to give 3 occasions. Although there were as many as 5 shots involved in 1 insert, in 27 of the 36 inserts only 1 shot was used.

The basic combination of the above two patterns might be called 'the intro', where a number of voice-over shots precede a number of *sync.* shots. This is the simplest of the mixed *sync.* and voice-over patterns. There are 13 such inserts relating to 11 stories. The basic voice over – *sync.* pattern involved in the sample was 1 shot v/o–1 shot *sync*. The first element – v/o – extended in the sample week to a maximum of 24 shots v/o introducing 1 *sync.* shot; and in the sample there was a maximum of 5 *sync.* shots (introduced by 1 shot voice-over). However, there was a greater range in the voice-over element than in the *sync.* element in these inserts since of the 13, 10 had only 1 *sync.* shot at the end. The voice-over shots introduced 11 interviews, 1 press conference and 1 speech at a rally. The shortest combination lasted for 20 seconds (15 seconds voice-over followed by 5 seconds *sync.*) and the longest lasted for 3 minutes 21 seconds (2 minutes 16 seconds voice-over followed by 1 minute 5 seconds *sync.*).

Some closely related patterns can be distinguished. There were two occasions in which the voice-over was followed by reporter-to-camera pieces in *sync*. This 'payoff' pattern involved 1 shot of the reporter on each occasion preceded by 12 voice-over shots in one insert and 7 in the second insert. The 13-shot insert lasted for 2 minutes 47.5 seconds and the 8 shot insert lasted for 1 minute 6 seconds. There was one payoff to an overheard piece of *sync*. There were 4 occasions relating to 2 stories in which a 'double interview' pattern could be discerned. Here the voice over intro is followed by interviews with 2 people; e.g. Voice-over, 4 shots – Interview, 1 shot – Interview, 1 shot. The other example (broadcast three times) used Interview, 1 shot – Interview, 2 shots preceded by commentary of different lengths on each occasion spread over 6, 10 or 12 shots. This last insert (12:1:2) ran 2 minutes 2.5 seconds and the shortest mentioned first above (4:1:1) ran for 1 minute 12 seconds.

There was 1 story, inserted into 2 bulletins of a 'reporter to camera intro' type in which 1 shot of the reporter *sync*. was followed by an interview shot. On the first occasion this lasted 55.5 seconds and on the second occasion 1 minute 16 seconds, the interview being extended in the longer, later bulletin.

Finally there were 3 occasions where the basic intro pattern was combined with the basic payoff pattern, i.e. voice-over -*sync*. interview-reporter to camera. On each occasion there was 1 interview shot and 1 reporter to camera shot preceded by a number of voice-over shots ranging from 4 to 16. The shortest of these films lasted 1 minute 15.5 seconds, the longest 2 minutes 33.5 seconds.

This last can also be seen as a variety of the common mixed *sync*. and voice-over pattern which can perhaps be called 'the sandwich'. Here a number of *sync*. shots are placed between a number of voice-over shots to give a basic pattern: Voice-over – *Sync*. – Voice over. There were 13 examples of this pattern related to inserts for 9 different stories. The majority of the *sync*. 'fillings' were interviews; in the sample week 9 of the 13 examples had a single *sync*. interview shot in the middle. Other 'fillings', as it were, included reporters to camera, a snatch of overheard dialogue, and a press conference. There were 2 examples of the reporter and 1 each of the others. On every one of these occasions, as with the interview 'filling', there was 1 *sync*. shot.

This sandwich pattern can be extended to include 'a double filling'. There was 1 example of this where 2 interviews of 1 shot each with different people were joined to make the filling.

The above leaves 30 inserts to be accounted for. Of these only 1 shares the three-element pattern of those films already described. It went voice-over leading to an overheard *sync*. shot and leading to an interview shot. Other three-element combinations do not appear.

Thus, to summarise the film inserts, we find the basic patterns shown in Table 13.2. We have accounted in this way for more than

Table 13.2   Simple film patterns – one, two or three elements

Pattern	Description (*sync*. in capitals)	No. in sample
Plain	Voice-over	85
Simple *sync*.	INTERVIEW	16
	SPEECHES	14
	PRESS CONFERENCES	3
	OVERHEARD	2
Mixed *sync*./voice-over Intros	Voice-over – INTERVIEW	11
	Voice-over – PRESS CONFERENCES	1
	Voice-over – SPEECHES	1
Mixed *sync*./voice-over Payoffs	Overheard – REPORTER TO CAMERA	1
	Voice-over – REPORTER TO CAMERA	2
Mixed *sync*./voice-over Reporter intros	REPORTER TO CAMERA – INTERVIEWS	2
Mixed *sync*./voice-over Double interviews	Voice-over – INTERVIEW/ INTERVIEW	7
Mixed *sync*./voice-over 3-Element payoff	Voice-over – INTERVIEW – REPORTER TO CAMERA	3
Mixed *sync*./voice-over Sandwich	Voice-over – INTERVIEW – Voice-over	9
	Voice-over – OVERHEARD – Voice-over	1
	Voice-over – REPORTER TO CAMERA – Voice-over	2
	Voice-over – PRESS CONFERENCE – Voice-over	1
Mixed *sync*./voice-over Double filling	Voice-over – INTERVIEW/ INTERVIEW – Voice-over	1
Mixed *sync*./voice-over Oddball	Voice-over – OVERHEARD – Voice-over	1

80 per cent of all film inserts used. By their very nature these patterns do not permit sophisticated structuring of film. There are only 29 examples of film inserts using more than 3 elements. These relate to 23 stories. Of them 9 are 4-element patterns, 6 are

5-element patterns, 4 have 6 elements, 3 have 7 elements and there are examples of 1 insert having 8 elements and 1 having 15. The remaining 4 films were all broken by studio links. Three of them related to the *Mayaguez* and one to the ITN feature on the EEC in which Mrs Shirley Williams and Sir John Winifrith debated.

It should be noted that these films illustrated the feature side of the bulletins. The longest of them with 15 elements dealt with the Referendum organisations and the stories on the Referendum in the Highlands and the birth of Strathclyde also appear in this list. Stories on Kurdistan, Irish monetary policy, Cardiff ratepayers, French shoppers in Ramsgate, the state of the shoe industry, the reappearance of real beer, smuggling across the Irish border with the United Kingdom/EEC trade piece, Irlam one year after the steel mill closed, and the Cambridge rapist case, are further examples of the feature quality of these more complex films. However, it would not be true to suggest that multiple elements necessarily mean feature-type items, for there are some news stories in the list as well – Nastase's row with the umpire, a report on the falling pound, the Ceylon tea scandal, the Harrier jump-jet, the champagne cider case, Chrysler wives and the Chrysler vote are also to be found here.

But despite the increased number of elements present it is still possible to claim that these are straightforward and comparatively unsophisticated films. Primarily this is because there is no example within the news of films which are other than linear in terms of time. In other words no news film ever contains flashbacks, flashforwards or any of the other time distortions which are now commonplace in the cinema. Time is, of course, abridged, but it is never warped. This is without prejudice to the reality of actually filming news films. Interviewer questions and reaction shots (noddies) are often filmed after the interviewee has responded. Film is not cut according to the order of the shots in the camera. But the surface effect and the drive of the voice-over commentary is to create a simple one-dimensional timeline. And this is as true of the most complicated feature-type multiple-element inserts as it is of simple voice-over films.

If, then, it is true that films contribute little to making the bulletins overly sophisticated in the visual track, they do nevertheless make them move along. Films are cut faster than any other element and voice-over films, and the voice-over element in mixed voice-over/*sync.* films are cut fastest of all.

Table 9.1 lays out the rate of cutting of various types of film, bulletin by bulletin. We have previously demonstrated that ITN tends to be faster in the rates of its image change than does the BBC overall, but that the current affairs style shows are slower. Also the rate of cutting does not take overt cognisance of the length of the bulletin in that the shortest bulletins match the general pace of cutting in the longer ones.

Apart from the limited range of film structures used perhaps two other major points can be made at this stage. It is noteworthy that a majority of the inserts both voice-over and mixed voice-over/*sync*. use commentary to situate the film. Even in the few cases where overheard (i.e. more observational and less interventionist) film is concerned, there is still the commentator to set up how such shots shall be seen and understood by the audience. That this is so can be seen from the finding laid out below that such commentary does not tend iconically to describe the shots, but rather forces the viewer to see the shots indexically or even symbolically within a framework of understanding thereby established by the professionals.

Second, it is in considering the above figures that we can place the final plank in our argument that the news is more 'talking heads' than anything else. Apart from stills, adding news personnel-to-camera both in the studio and outside to filmed tape and live interviews, press conferences and the like reveals that even the most highly illustrated bulletin (i.e. *News at Ten*) relies for 20 per cent of its time on moving images of things other than people talking in close-up. That the professionals concerned devote a disproportionate amount of time and energy to acquiring this minority element might well be the case. But the theoretical infinitude of the images that could be captured by news cameras is foreclosed on not only by the limited range of what constitutes 'news stories' but also by the limited range of film structures themselves. And this last is further restricted by the predominance of news talk in situating readings and viewings, the dominance of a journalistic rather than a film logic.

Film grammar

The notion that poor journalism (in the sense of being unable to 'cover the waterfront') is the result of television's high dependence upon some visually determined narrative or illustration is not supported by our evidence. A close comparison of the normative grammars of film with the fractured grammar of television newsfilm reveals that the written story, not the visuals, predominates and thereby forecloses on the possible range of visual options.

We have suggested that the determinants of news film usage on television are more closely governed by the conventions and practices of print journalism than by the routine cutting-room practices of the film industry. These film practices are based on a set of rules essentially grounded in the feature film. Feature film production allows for a single camera to take, sequentially, a number of shots of the same action from different angles. These different shots can then be cut together to create a seemingly smooth narrative flow. For documentary to achieve the same effect (using the same single camera) requires that actions be repeated. With repetitive activities (e.g. a worker on an assembly line) it is often possible to obtain various angles of view as the process is, in reality, repeated. These can then be cut together to show the process happening, as it were, only once. But, by definition, news film can seldom allow itself these luxuries. Indeed the presence of *matched cuts* (that is, cuts between two angles of view in which the action appears continuous) where actions are not in reality repeated renders the film suspect. It must have been directed; the news crew must have intervened. (This does not apply only to regular examples of such matched cuts in our period as occurred with tape or live coverage in studios or from OBs. Here the matched cuts occurred because there was more than one electronic camera recording the scene and cuts could be made between them instantaneously.)

More often one can note that a flow of action has been created in the editing by separating similar shots which would not match if cut together. One such instance occurred on Sunday 11 May in the BBC early evening bulletin, which contained a film report from London Airport used to illustrate a story about the slump of sterling. It was pegged to the monthly meeting of the governors of the Central Bank which was to take place the following day in Basle. The fourth shot of this film was a close-up of money being passed under a bank teller's window in the airport. A woman's hands picked up the money and the camera panned as she put it into her wallet. This was followed by a two-shot *establisher* of the interviewee Roger Davis with the reporter facing him back to camera. It was preceded by a *medium long shot* of a different woman obtaining money at the same counter who then (followed with a slight pan) left the frame with a child. Thus Shots 3 and 4 obeyed a basic narrative logic – the wide view showed the audience where they were (at the teller's window) and the subsequent close-up revealed in detail what was happening (getting money). But the logic was fractured since the person in the wide shot was not the person in the close-up.

The week yielded other examples in which the possibility of using matched cuts provided by film crews did not occur. In *First Report* on the Tuesday there was another film seeking to illustrate the sliding pound story. (It is interesting to note that only two possibilities seem to present themselves to the producers when faced with the intangibles of a major financial story – one is to go to the airport; the other is to go to the foreign exchange room of a major clearing bank. The BBC did the airport on Sunday and the exchange room on the Monday. ITN did the exchange room on Tuesday and reached the airport on Friday.) The *First Report* film was as shown in Example 13.1 and Photos 7f and 8a–8g.

Photo 7f   Shot 16

The matched cut avoided here is between Shot 19 and Shot 21. The second of these is simply a reverse (i.e. a camera move through 180 degrees) of the first. The film could be re-ordered in a number of ways which would make it very much less jumpy and allow the viewer to obtain a greater sense of the spatial relationships in the exchange office. For instance the order 22, 18, 19, 21, 17, 16, 20, 23,

Example 13.1   ITN, 13.00, 13 May 1975

3.54 /*HAMILL VOICE-OVER*

---

16 ML 3 Shot-2 dealers on   When the foreign exchange markets opened it
    phone F/G-1 dealer B/G   did seem that yesterday's pres/sure on sterling
    ditto

- -/

ease in slightly   was not going to
    16a Desmond Hamill   be repeated this mor/ning. The dealings soon
      reporting   *Film*
CUT 0.6½   4.0½

17 GV-7 people; 4 F/G (I in   showed that sterling/was not declining any
    MCU-1 in LS waving   - - - - - - -/
    phone) 3 B/G one stan-   /further in
    ding in MS lose cap *Film*/ value against the weighted av/erage but
- - - - - - - - - - - - - -/
CUT 0.5½   4.6

18 GV-6 people; 1 in F/G   remained at 25 per cent
    phone to ear   *Film*   as it closed last night. The main feature
CUT 0.5½   4.11½   this morning was/that the United States

19 M 2 Shot standing at   dollar started losing and dealers are
    Telex   *Film*   selling weak sterling but because of the
        worry over the
CUT 0.8½   4.20   latest Cambodian situation, they're not buy/

20 3 shot on phones (CU to   ing into
    MS)   *Film*   dollars but European currencies. So a weak
        sterling is
CUT 0.4½   4.24½   pulling down the/dollar. This means the pound

21 M 2 Shot at telex (reverse   has improved
    of 19) second man leaves   a bit against the dollar and has therefore
    frame   *Film*   remained over
        all unchanged, but the losses against European
CUT 0.8½   4.33   currencies,/

22 GV as in 17   particularly the Mark and Franc and now
        Film   the Kroner, have continued. So the pound is
CUT 0.5   4.38   worth considerably/less in Europe. For

23 MS man on phone   *Film*   instance, someone taking £50 to
CUT 0.4   4.42   Germany to/day, will find it buys him £1.75

24 3 shot men on phone   less than it
    (CU-MS)   *Film*   would have
CUT 0.4   4.46   la/st week. It's not expected the situation

25 MCU TV monitor   will
CUT 0.3½   4.49½   improve/much and these dealers feel the

Example 13.1 continued

26	2 shot-MS Man standing over telex operator CUT 0.4 4.53½	pound could go on losing until the uncertain/ties of the Common
27	4 shot – 2 F/G at desk MS 1 at desk B/G 1 standing B/G CUT 0.6 4.59½	Market referendum are resolved, and of course everyone is now waiting for tomorrow's trade figures./

24 would isolate first telephones, then the telex and allow the most to be made of the matched cuts the camera person has offered. But the speed at which news film has to be edited means that such refinements are often ignored. The order of these shots is of no particular importance. Shot 16 refers to 'the foreign exchange markets' and while indeed the room does constitute part of that market, the use of the temporal phrase 'when the foreign exchange markets opened' gives this shot a symbolic relationship with the commentary. For actually the shot is not of the room 'opening'; the room is in operation, opened.

This is typical. Film often has sound and picture relating tangentially, i.e. the words symbolically relate to the icons offered. The shot that directly reflects the commentary does so symbolically,

Photo 7g   Shot 17

Photo 8a Shot 19

Photo 8b Shot 20

because of the commentary's time reference. Further general points can be made on the basis of Example 13.1: shots are arranged haphazardly in the sense that such opportunities for improving the narrative logic of the image track are not taken advantage of.

Photo 8c   Shot 21

Photo 8d   Shot 23

Further, the commentary text (pauses, commas and full stops) bears no relationship to the cuts on the image track.

Given the heavy preponderance of 'serious' stories the problems of filming intangibles crop up nearly every day. Film that can be used iconically (that speaks, as it were, for itself) is comparatively

Photo 8e   Shot 24

Photo 8f   Shot 25

rare, especially near the top of the bulletins. In the week in question the few shots of the *Mayaguez* operation released by the United States and the film of Saigon released by the North Vietnamese are among the only examples of such iconic film, apart of course from sports coverage. Iconic sports film, which did not occur in the top

Photo 8g   Shot 26

Photo 9a   Nastase's disputed call

half of the bulletins, offered one particularly good piece of deviant behaviour in Nastase's row with the umpire. (It is perhaps significant that ITN ran this at 4 minutes 23 seconds, the same sort of length that has been devoted to the *Mayaguez*. What is extraordinary is that ITN did not have a shot of the actual ball which

caused the row: they were looking at the spectators (Photo 9a).)
Purely iconic film also occurs in some other minor human interest
stories again towards the end of the bulletins – the daughter of Graf
Zeppelin launching an air balloon, *Locomotion*'s run, and so on.
But these examples prove the point. The major stories will be
covered whatever the availability of visuals. Indeed when faced
with a major running story such as the Common Market referendum routine attempts will be made to cover the issue with film as
well as by studio discussion and straight to-camera exposition. The
results are often essentially written journalistic essays with film
merely added – sometimes in extraordinary ways.

Throughout this period and during the sample week ITN
mounted a sustained effort to explain the issues behind the
referendum as it saw them. Kee in *First Report* devoted considerable time to this on both Tuesday and Thursday and in *News at Ten*
Jon Lander and Alexander Chancellor did a number of features.
Among these, on the Tuesday, Chancellor tackled the question of
United Kingdom/EEC balance of trade. He did this on film. It was
clear that the film had been available for at least twenty-four hours
since one of the shots in it appeared in the 'hooker' sequence ending
Part One of *News at Ten* the previous day (albeit subliminally in
error, since it could only be clearly identified when played back in
slow motion). Therefore it is fair to use this as an example of a
considered piece of film making in that time must have been
available for editing. The film lasted 4 minutes 39.5 seconds,
making it among the longest in the week. It consisted of 35 shots, 4
of which were of Chancellor to camera, 2 of which were animated
graphics and the rest Chancellor voice-over. As would be expected
in a film of this length the pattern was complex: see Example 13.2.

Example 13.2   ITN, 22.00, 13 May 1975

		CHANCELLOR TO CAM
CUT	17.24½ /	
73 GV dock Pan to left to		Before we joined the Common Mar/ket ⌐
MS Chancellor – zoom in		two years ago some optimis/tic pro- ⌐
Super Caption: Alexander Chancellor reporting lose cap		Marketeers were predicting a sharp improvement in our trade balanc/e /

Example 13.2 continued

Hold CU Chancellor top of pocket	with Europe/once tariff barriers started
	— — — — — — — — — — — — — /
CUT 0.17 17.41½	to come down. These barriers have already been cut by more than half but so far exactly the opposite has/happened.
74 *Graphic*: 1970 £84 million Animate 0.13	CHANCELLOR VOICE-OVER In 1970, three years before we joined the market, we actually made a small profit on trade with our present eight European partners, selling them goods worth £84 million more than what we bought from them./ Two
1972 – £530M Animate 0.10	years later this had turned into a loss of £530 million. Then in 1973, our first year in the market,/ this loss more than doubled to
1973 – £1150M Animate 0.5	£1,150 million. Last year/ it reached £2,000
1974 – £2000M Animate 0.10	million. And now according to the Trade Secretary, Mr Peter Shore, it's running at a rate of some/ £2,400 million a
1975 – £2400M CUT 0.41½ 18.23	year./
75 MS Chancellor on ship's bridge foredeck in B/G CUT 0.14½ 18.37½	CHANCELLOR TO CAM The Government points out that we haven't been losing money just to Europe, we've been losing it to the whole world. Last year to the tune of some £5,300 million, but the bulk of this was spent on buying oil at very high prices mainly from the Middle Ea/st. If we leave oil
76 *Graphic*: REST OF WORLD EEC CUT 0.12½ 18.50	CHANCELLOR VOICE-OVER out of the picture we find that our trading losses to the rest of the world were a mere £13 million. To the Common Market countries we lost £1,800 million./
77 MCU Chancellor – LS docks across water in B/G	CHANCELLOR TO CAM On the face of it, therefore, membership of the Common Market looks like a bad deal as far as trade is concerned, but even Mr Shore, a passionate anti-Marketeer admits that there's no way of proving that membership is directly to blame. There are lots of reasons for our bad trading performance which can't be laid at the Common Market's door. One of these is the falling value of the British pound, which means

Example 13.2 continued

	that more and more pounds are needed to buy the same quantity of foreign goods. And there's also been a dramatic rise in the prices of essential commodities we buy
CUT 0.30 19.20	abroad./
78 GV warehouse: working forklift truck in F/G – pan it LEFT	*CHANCELLOR VOICE-OVER* But this doesn't really explain what's happening in the crucial field of manufactured
CUT 0.6 19.26	goods, which includes anything from/ heavy
79 MLS man examines washing machine: clears frame revealing TV: pull back, pan LEFT row stoves, fridges	machinery to German washing machines. What used to be a respectable profit on our trade with Europe in manufactures has lately turned into an enormous loss. One reason is/
CUT 0.10 19.36	
80 Fork lift truck towards CAM: turns SCR LEFT: 'Telefunken' box in F/G	that we haven't been able to produce enough of these things at home, so our imports have soared.
CUT 0.6 19.42	
81 CU 'Krupp' sign CUT 0.3 19.45	Take iron and steel, for example./Last year we
82 GV pan steel mill CUT 0.4 19.49	imported more than four times as much from Europe as we did in/1972. This was due largely
83 MCU blasting 0.4 19.53	to the coal miners' strike/ and the three-day
84 CU blasting CUT 0.2 19.55	week of two wint/ers ago. It was much the
85 MS steel worker (black silhouette) red fire B/G CUT 0.4 19.59	same story with plastics, where a shortage was made worse/by the Flixborough plant
86 CU molten steel pouring CUT 0.2 20.01	disast/er of last June. Foreign manufacturers
87 GU river molten steel – 200min (slightly) CUT 0.6 20.07	have been able to take advantage of our own indust/rial troubles at home and the biggest
88 GV ship-Volkswagens CUT 0.3 20.10	culprit from our point of view/has been
89 GV bows of ship CUT 0.2 20.12	Europe's industrial gi/ant, West Germany,

Example 13.2 continued

---

90 LS car – leaving ship CUT 0.3 20.15	whose profits on trade with Bri/tain increased
91 From hold of ship – GV dock (reverse 90) oil and men (silhouette) car B/G on dock (NB facing CAM, different colour and model from car in 90) CUT 0.6 20.21	nearly eight-fold in three years. European cars have been taking a bigger/and bigger share of
92 LS – rows of cars – ship B/G: pull back pan LEFT CUT 0.10 20.31	Britain's home market, partly because of strikes in the British car industry. However, much the biggest items on our European shopping list a/re food and grain,
93 LS pipes: pan down pipes to grain suction ship hold CUT 0.06 20.37	things we have always had to buy in large quantities abroad. Membership of the E/EC
94 Topshot ML single worker in corner of hold CUT 0.4 20.41	has encouraged us to buy more of our food in Europe/and food alone now accounts for
95 CU suction pipe in grain CUT 0.6½ 20.53½	more than half our total trade losses to the Common Market./In 1972 we spent £652
96 LS dockers in hold with sacks CUT 0.6 20.53½	million on buying food from the Mar/ket.
97 Pan over piles of sacks in hold: tilt to reveal ship's side, water CUT 0.5 20.58½	Last year we spent £1,490 million./That's
98 LS mid ships – ferry CUT 0.2½ 21.01	largely because we've been buying less foo/d
99 GV – Volvo truck (French butter livery) off ferry CUT 0.8 21.09	from the rest of the world. The pro- Marketeers say this is no bad thing, because they claim that food has been cheaper lately in the Common Market than out/side, and regular
100 CU side of Volvo cab 'name: Rouen' CUT 0.2½ 21.11½	supplies are assured./But the antis maintain
101 GV weighing machine plus fruit boxes CUT 0.5 21.16½	that cheaper food would still be available outside Europe

Example 13.2 continued

| 102 MS man tears wrap of apple box
CUT 0.3   21.19½ | if we were allowed to buy it freely, which we aren't under Common/Market rules. According |

| 103 CU apple box
CUT 0.5½   21.25 | to Mr Shore, if we stay in the Community our prospects are appalling./He says our failure to |

| 104 CU Volvo 'Mahe' truck driving pan with it RHT – pull back:
CUT 0.11   21.36 | hold our own in industrial trade will mean the progressive shut-down of British industry and growing unemployment. But the pro-Market Confederation of British Industry points out/ |

| 105 GV customs shed: Volvo 'Mahe' truck parked by second lorry
CUT 0.2½   21.38½ | that British exports to Europe have grown faster th/an to anywhere else, and now account |

| 106 LS lorry park

CUT 0.5   21.43½ | for about one third of our world export.
CHANCELLOR TO CAM |

| 107 CU Chancellor (under tie-knot) docks (not those of 77) B/G

CUT 0.22   22.05½ | The CBI always predicted that adjustment to the Common Market would be difficult for Britain at first, but they say it would be crazy to leave now before reaping the long-term advantages that they are sure will come. On one thing everyone can agree, in or out of the Market our success as a trading nation will continue to depend, as in the past, mainly on our own economic performance at home./ |

The film in question has an opening piece to camera broken by 2 graphics, the first of which was animated. It then goes on with voice-over commentary for 29 shots and concludes with a final piece to camera. The total time taken by the pieces to camera is 1 minute 22 seconds, some 30 per cent of the film's total duration. The graphics last 54 seconds, a further 19 per cent of the total duration. Thus nearly half this film is taken up with reporter talking to camera or graphics. What then of the rest? Each of the points that Chancellor makes in his commentary refers directly to one industry or another. In this film there is a consistent attempt made to match commentary and image. Shots 81, 82, 91 and 93 refer directly in both commentary and image to iron and steel, cars and grain.

But the limitations of this iconic directness should be noted. The steel shots continue (83/84) while the text explains why steel and iron had to be imported in terms of the coal miners' strike. And the steel shots go on when Chancellor turns ('It was much the same story with plastics') to the Flixborough disaster. Obviously footage was available of both the coal miners' strike and the Flixborough disaster (some of the latter had indeed come out of the library for the coverage of the Flixborough Report on the previous day). However, the code does not require that each and every reference be taken up visually. One recalls an effective David Frost sketch in which the tendency of the news to illustrate each point with an image was satirised. It should be restated that the argument here is not one of imperatives. It is simply that the iconic use of material, arguably most possible with film, is extremely limited. It could be said of Shots 81–7 that they leave the audience in less confusion than cutting to footage of striking coal miners and destroyed chemical plants would. Yet on the other hand the work of visually decoding must on commonsense grounds be said to have increased.

The actual juxtapositioning of images in the visual track for the most part remains, by the normative rules of film making, extremely crude. To take two instances from the above example. Shot 90 is a long shot of a car leaving a ship. Shot 91 is a reverse of this general view taken from within the hold with a number of silhouetted dockers in medium long shot. A car is on the dock in the background, stationary. The logic of film would require that it should be moving to match the previous shot, since 91 is a reverse angle of 90. But the car is stationary, and anyway it is a different colour and model from the car in 90. The cut between 104 and 105 illustrates a different aspect of the normative rules and how they are broken. The normative rules say that all camera movement should cease before the cut. In other words pans and tracks should come to a halt. Of course these rules are as much honoured in the breach as in the observance. They are subject to a dynamic, i.e. they are less obeyed now than in the past. But nevertheless a shot such as 104 which both pans and pulls back at the same time would not, even in today's feature film, be cut on those movements. They would normally cease before the cut was made. Yet here the cut is made and, to come back to the continuity faults we have been examining in these examples, the lorry seen moving in 104 is revealed as stationary in 105. This then is not so much a cut as what might be called a hack. Of course the professional defence is that there is insufficient time to either shoot or edit this material as a documentary or even current affairs programme would be edited. But that is why this example is particularly illustrative of the different, and by the norms of film production – lower, standards of news film editing. For this film was to hand for at least twenty-four hours, as the internal evidence of the previous night's bulletin reveals.

While noting the primacy of the texts it is also true that, since film is being used, a film logic is at work. The normative rules of film grammar do, to a certain extent, govern the juxtapositioning of images in news film. This can be seen, for instance, in Example 13.2 in shots 82, 83 and 84 or in shots 102 and 103. In other words the news has not developed an alternative code for this area of production. It has not coherently abandoned traditional editing, but rather uses these rules in a haphazard and inelegant way. There is no finesse in the juxtapositioning.

It is possible to go further. The juxtapositioning often ignores possibilities in the material itself for the smoother editing which, at the level of the images, would better reveal a narrative. This can occasionally be demonstrated from what is transmitted (as in Example 13.1) but must be assumed to be more possible than such examples reveal. The avoidance of the creation of narrative flow on the visual level and the crude use of normative editing rules, both mean that semantic flow and direction must be achieved elsewhere. Obviously this is done at the level of the story via the presences and absences in the commentary. Therefore, since the commentary is subject to print-journalistic logic and ideology, it is only realistic to conclude that alongside the basic inferential frames it is the verbals that act as the dominant carrier of meanings.

This finding is reinforced by our previously verified thesis that the visual element *in toto* does not condition the major selection process. Stories are covered, certainly in the top half of the bulletins, because they are important by journalistic, not visual, criteria. Therefore it should come as no surprise that our evidence reveals that film is used no more iconically than other illustrative (still) inputs. Much film must be read at best indexically against the commentary, just as all the categories of still inputs discussed in the previous chapters must be so read.

Symbolic contradictions

The dominant relationship between text and visual is therefore indexical. It is as comparatively rare to find iconic relationships as it is to find symbolic ones. But in order to establish the limit, as it were, on the possibilities of the symbolic relationship between text and visual, it is valuable to examine those even rarer occasions when the gap between the two becomes so wide as to almost have the text contradict the visual evidence, or vice-versa. The occasions when the commentary claims that the picture reveals something which it does not, stretch the symbolic relationship to the point where it might be called a symbolic contradiction. The examples of such symbolic contradictions during the week in question which are set out in Example 13.3 reveal the absolute limit as to what pictures can

Example 13.3   ITN, 22.00, 11 May 1975

38 B&W *Newspicture* Queen & Prince Philip LS Japanese garden – pool F/G CUT 0.4 9.43	*GARDNER (Newscaster) VOICE-OVER* . . . Earlier in the *GARDNER TO CAM* weekend in Kyo/to the Queen and the Duke
39 MS Gardner + (CSO) *Map* of Japan CUT 0.8 9.51	took part in a tea ceremony at a villa in a seventeenth-century palace. Anthony Carthew reports./
40 MCU Queen: pull back, reveal Queen and Prince Philip sitting *Film* CUT 0.9 10.00	*CARTHEW VOICE-OVER* The tea master waited to explain this extraordinary and quite inscrutable ritual, which was considerably shortened to avoid royal mind-blowing./The brewing went on
41 MS/in F/G Lady obscured by branch. Queen and Prince Philip (in B/G) People seated behind – zoom in tea- master whisking tea *Film* CUT 0.6 10.06	under a near-by tree. The green tea was whisked up to a froth/and presented./ The tea
42 MS Queen takes cup. cap: Anthony Carthew reporting from Kyoto lose cap	is supposed to be consumed/ in exactly three
Film CUT 0.17½ 10.22½	and a half sips. The Queen took sip one and a small grimace escaped.
43 Lady in F/G clears – reveals Prince Philip MS sipping *Film* CUT 0.9 10.31½	The Duke of Edinburgh, who'd been grinning happily, took sip one and the grin fell away like lightning as he registered ugh./The

Example 13.3 continued

44	MS Queen pan to *smiling* teamaster	teamaster's face moved not a muscle, which is training for you.
	Film	
CUT 0.5	10.36½	

45	MCU Prince Philip pan to MCU Queen sipping	At sip two the Queen looked definitely dubious but she ploughed on and did the deed in the correct three and a half sips. It was all rather like someone unwillingly getting down their
	Film	
CUT 0.12	10.48½	medicine.

46	MS Prince Philip holding cup – pull back slightly	But, then, green tea is an acquired taste.
	Film	
CUT 0.3	10.51½	

47	MS Queen gives cup to teamaster – pull back to MLS	Anthony Carthew, ITN, Kyoto.
	Film	
CUT 0.5	10.56½	

go with what words. And this overcomes the fact that for the most part these examples might seem to be at first glance rather minor or trivial. Yet these supposed trivialities not only demonstrate the edge of commentary writing but also trade on deep-seated stereotypes and labelling procedures in our culture. The 'small grimace' in Shot 42 cannot be seen, but Shot 45 does reveal that Their Majesties were not overcome with delight at the green tea (Photo 9b).

Photo 9b The grimace

However, Shot 44 shows a contradiction between image and word. Unfortunately the teamaster was not behaving like the inscrutable Oriental of the racialist stereotype referred to by Carthew. He was actually smiling. To wilfully juxtapose a shot of a smiling man against the sentence 'The teamaster's face moved not a muscle, which is training for you' is extraordinary.

Carthew filed his last piece on the royal tour after the Queen's return. It was transmitted in all ITN bulletins on the Tuesday but at great length in *First Report*: see Example 13.4. One can at best assume that the anxiety of the man in Shot 87, while not readily

Example 13.4 ITN, 13.00, 13 May 1975

CARTHEW VOICE-OVER

84 Boats F/G – LS steps with royal party CUT 0.6½	*Film* 21.38½	Then to the long-awaited lady pearl divers of Tobe. They used to work topless, which
85 CU diver in boat CUT 0.4	*Film* 21.42½	is how they became fam/ous, but today they
86 3 shot divers – 200m. in single – pan boat to 2 shot divers CUT 0.7	*Film* 21.49½	were decorously clad in white overalls. Before the Queen arri/ved workers in a
87 Men in boat LS CUT 0.6½	*Film* 21.56	motor boat anxiously cleaned the ocean. In we/nt the girls, diving without causing a
88 MLS pan/across two boats – divers dive left CUT 0.6	*Film* 22.02	ripple, and showing the correct clean pair of heels./
89 MLS 4 divers in water CUT 0.7	*Film* 22.09	When they surfaced after minutes – they whistled to clear their lungs, and shouted what sounds like HELP,/but actually is the
90 MLS 4 divers – 1 dives CUT 0.6	*Film* 22.15	Japanese for – I've got an oyster./The press
91 GV boat CUT 0.4	*Film* 22.19	boat for Japanese photographers developed a fine list to port,/particularly when the divers
92 Single MLU diver CUT 0.4	*Film* 22.23	started to climb back into the boats./

Example 13.4 continued

93 2 shot GV	*Film*	The trouble with overalls seems that they're
CUT 0.5½	22.28½	not so decorous/when wet. The Queen averted

94 LS Queen/Prince Philip		her eyes and examined the catch of oysters.
+ 3	*Film*	But wet and indecorous or not, the lady
CUT 0.9½	22.37½	divers had enough ene/rgy to wave frantically

95 LS boat – divers drawing		as the boat chugged away.
in pot – pan slight RHT		Anthony Carthew/. . .
waving	*Film*	
CUT 0.6	22.43½	

apparent in the image, was ascertained by the reporter in interview or by other means. Yet the pearl divers in Shot 95 were by no stretch of the imagination waving frantically.

More serious than the above examples is the one shown in Example 13.5, from ITN's 22.00 bulletin on the Sunday. The 'expressionless Communists' in Shot 20 look no different in

Example 13.5 ITN, 22.00, 11 May 1975

SEYMOUR VOICE-OVER

12 GV river and city boat in		That the Communists will eventually take over
F/G	*Film*	in Laos is not in doubt, but the/
Cap: Gerald Seymour		
reporting from		
Vientiane lose cap		
CUT 0.4	6.24½	

13 2 shot CUS soldiers		way the royal troops/and communist Pathet
	Film	
CUT 0.1½	6.26	

14 MLS soldiers on parade		Lao mingle together in Vientiane is an
	Film	indication that when they do there will be no/
CUT 0.5½	6.31½	

15 2 shot BCU soldiers, one		repeat of the blood-bath of Saigon
behind other:	*Film*	
CUT 0.2½	6.34	

16 MLS – track down		and Phnom Penh. The Pathet Lao are already
soldiers on parade		in the Laotian capital in force, allowed there
	Film	under the 1973 ceasefire agreement, and they
Pan to single BCU: Hold		control 75 per cent of the rest of the country.
CUT 0.13½	6.47½	They'd formed up for a Constitution Day/

Example 13.5 continued

		parad/e,

17	LS cars into MS and stop	the twenty-eighth, and almost inevitably the
	Cap: Laos Today lose cap	last./

	Film	His Majesty King Savang Von/g
CUT 0.6	6.53½	

18	MS 5 shot soldiers	arrived to take the salutes in his Russian/
	present arms *Film*	
CUT 0.3	6.56½	

19	Pan RHT along files to	limousine. The King, who once played English
	single BCU soldier	football to league stand/ards, inspected his
	Film	
CUT 0.5	7.1½	

20	MCU King inspecting	own troops, then moved on to the
	troops – track back	expressionless communists, who have
	Film	effectively fought the royal army to a stand-/
CUT 0.8	7.9½	

21	Dignitaries seated GV	still before and after the ceasefire. The
	Film	question that intrigued the perspiring
CUT 0.7	7.16½	diplomats – will the communists make/one

more push or . . . .

Photo 9c   Expressionless communists

expression from any of the other soldiers in the film. Indeed the Laotian forces displayed about as much facial activity during this parade as the Brigade of Guards would on a similar ceremonial occasion in Britain (Photo 9c). All of these adjectival excesses are unimportant except that they all work to confirm stereotypes of various sorts. Yet, although minor, by another token they are extreme examples which further and importantly illustrate the limits of the tangential relationship between word and image. A BBC example from the coverage of the end of the Warwick University student sit-in is shown in Example 13.6. This example illustrates the more common tendency in word/image contradic-

Example 13.6   BBC1, 17.45, 15 May 1975

FRANCIS VOICE-OVER

88 GV six coaches   *Film*   Thirteen coaches of police officers arri/ved
CUT 0.2½   19.10½

89 LS 2 coaches (1 unloaded   shortly after 7 o'clock this morning, 500 men
pan RHT to 14 policemen   designed to discour/age any resistance.
and 2 more coaches
                        Film
CUT 0.5   19.15½

90 MLS 12 police walk past   Within minutes the entire building had been
CAM (1 carrying shield)   surroun/ded and police on the rooftops
pan LEFT with them past
3 more police   *Film*
CUT 0.4   19.14½

91 GV building   *Film*   carri/ed riot shields just in case, but the
CUT 0.3½   19.26½

92 6 police on roof + 1   students, about/500 of them, were
policeman with shield
                        Film
CUT 0.3½   19.23

93 MLS 18 students leaving   prepared for the eviction. They had promised
building   earlier there would be no violence. They
                  Film   trooped out carrying pyjamas and sleeping
                        bags. They had occupied the building for
CUT 0.10   19.36½

94 MLS approx 16 more   twenty-five days in protest at a £2 a week
students leaving   *Film*   rent-rise. The sit-in/has already led to the
CUT 0.4   19.40½

Example 13.6 continued

95 MLS approx 15 more students leaving CUT 0.6	*Film* 19.46½	postponement of all final exams. Today's move, though, was only a short one. The stude/nts transferred to the Arts Centre
96 GV building CUT 0.5	*Film* 19.51½	next door, pledging to continue the fight./

tions where the reporter writes a story without the adjectival excesses previously discussed, as he or she sees it. But these written impressions might not exactly correspond to what the camera team might have seen. The visuals of this film nowhere support the reference to 'riot shields' although perhaps commonsense indicates that the use of the plural is reasonable. Nevertheless in Shot 90 there are twelve policemen without shields and one with. In Shot 92 there is one policeman on the roof with a shield accompanied by 6 policemen without (Photo 9d). Nowhere do we see the 'Thirteen coaches' of Shot 88, nor indeed the 'Five hundred men' of Shot 89. Such symbolisms are a commonplace of 'factual' film.

Photo 9d   Riot shields

These expansions do add up to a degree of editorialising. If there are few examples of iconic relationships between word and image (where the word simply repeats verbally what can be seen in the image), the more usual indexical relationship opens the door, as it were, to these sorts of expansions.

Another point can be made. The example (13.6) illustrates the comparative unimportance of the iconic relationship between word and picture in another way. Example 13.6 is the 17.45 version of the film. This version is 3.5 seconds longer than the one run in the main bulletin. The seconds were saved on Shot 93. The words 'They trooped out carrying pyjamas and sleeping bags' were omitted and the shot shortened. These words relate to the image in question iconically. They are plain description and therefore, as such, seem to be regarded in professional practice as redundant.

This is not insignificant since it is one of only three examples where a later bulletin re-uses a previously transmitted film at a shorter length. Before discussing the other two occasions we shall examine the ways in which all film inserts are repeated.

Repeated use of films

Of the 87 stories during the sample week which used film there is a 1 use to 1 story relationship on 55 occasions; 55 film inserts appeared once in just 1 bulletin; only 7 of the remaining films were used twice unchanged and 1 was used 3 times unchanged. (It should be noted, however, that many of these multiple uses of unchanged (i.e. not re-edited) films occurred at the weekend. Of the 7 films, 3 were on at the weekend and the 1 film used three times was also on at the weekend. The tendency, however, is that if a film is transmitted more than once it is likely to be changed.)

As regards film inserts, 24 were used twice by the same channel (we are here excluding films that were shown by both BBC1 and BBC2 or films that used pooled material exclusively). Of these, 23 illustrate the normal practice in that the later use is longer than the earlier. There is only 1 example of film being used on one channel in two bulletins where the later use is shorter. The expansion from earlier to later bulletins is achieved in various ways. On 12 occasions the commentary was extended and more visual material was added. On 3 occasions the same commentary and the same visuals had an interview added. On 2 occasions interviewees and pieces to camera were substituted for *sync.* overheard material in the first transmission. On 6 occasions the commentary remained virtually the same, and the film therefore was of almost the same length, but it was recut to accommodate more shots within the length.

If the film was transmitted more than twice the possibilities become more complex. The above count includes 2 films used by *First Report* and then again at greater length by the early evening bulletin. Neither of these films was used by *News at Ten*. There are no examples of films being used by *First Report* and *News at Ten*. All 3 bulletins used the same film on 6 occasions during the week. On 3 of these occasions *First Report* had the film in its longest form and the early evening bulletin and *News at Ten* ran the same shortened version of it. On one occasion a straight expansion of duration took place. *First Report* used 16.5 seconds of library film to cover Malcolm X's execution. The early evening bulletin expanded this to 33.5 seconds in 4 shots and *News at Ten* went to 121 seconds in 16 shots. In the report on the state of the Montreal Olympic site *First Report* and the early evening bulletin had library film for 38.5 seconds, while *News at Ten* ran the story for 93.5 seconds with Bourassa, the Quebec Premier, voicing-over his own still photograph (in radio circuit style). On the last occasion *First Report* ran Ford's *Mayaguez* press conference at 70 seconds while the early evening bulletin took 57 seconds of it. *News at Ten* took the same shorter amount of the President but added other *sync.* material to make a 101-second film insert.

There is only one example of a film being used for all three BBC1 bulletins and not then being used for *News Extra* on BBC2. This is the Warwick University sit-in film referred to above. It is therefore an exception to the basic ITN pattern since it expands from the lunchtime bulletin to the early evening one but, as was pointed out, is shortened again for the *Nine O'Clock News*. Apart from this film there are a number of examples of multiple use of films from one bulletin to another on BBC1 and then across to *News Extra*. On three occasions during the week all the BBC bulletins that use film, used the same film. First Fred Peart's speech was played in the lunchtime bulletin at 31.5 seconds. Then the early evening bulletin, the *Nine O'Clock News* and *News Extra* played the speech at 48, 46.5 and 45 seconds respectively. The Chrysler wives were played by the lunchtime bulletin at 37.5 seconds and then both the early evening and main bulletins played it at 99 seconds. *News Extra* recut the material and used only 39.5 seconds and in so doing managed to cut the cheer of support that greeted the pro-striker wife which was heard on all the other BBC bulletins and on ITN's version (which they used unchanged in both the 17.50 and 22.00 bulletins).

Coverage of the *Mayaguez* on the Thursday involved each BBC bulletin using film. Two pooled press statements were available that day, one from Ford and one from Schlesinger. ITN used Ford, cutting him after *First Report* and adding Schlesinger, and some exclusive interview on Capitol Hill. BBC2 ignored Ford and just used Schlesinger. BBC1 at lunchtime used Ford, dropped him in the early evening bulletin and took both Ford and Schlesinger as well as exclusive interviews with relatives of the *Mayaguez* crew for the main bulletin. This led to the following timing pattern: lunchtime bulletin 59 seconds; early evening bulletin 17 seconds; *Nine O'Clock News* 245 seconds; *News Extra* 91 seconds.

A clear pattern can be discerned when films were used by the two evening BBC1 bulletins and *News Extra* but not, as in the above, by the lunchtime bulletin as well. There were three occasions of this sort and each time the usage was longer from bulletin to bulletin. This is irrespective of the initial length of the film insert as used in the early evening bulletin. Thus a 15-second film insert was used with an interview added at 45 seconds in the main bulletin and at 126.5 seconds by *News Extra*. Similarly a film running at 87.5 seconds in the early evening bulletin ran at 201 seconds on the *Nine O'Clock News* and at 293 seconds in *News Extra*. The last example concerns the North Vietnamese film of Saigon, which according to ITN 'arrived'. It was 'released' according to the BBC1 early evening bulletin but the *Nine O'Clock News* 'secured' it. This ran at 27 seconds in the 'released' version, 67.5 seconds in the 'secured' version and at 110.5 seconds in *News Extra* (who 'received' it). ITN ran the same material at 96.5 seconds in *News at Ten*, but, in line with our general finding as to the faster cutting pace of ITN, they used 17 shots of the pooled material in this time as against BBC2's 14 shots in an insert 14 seconds longer.

On 6 occasions the BBC1 main bulletin and *News Extra* shared film. In 4 of these instances the films were used at greater length in *News Extra* and on 2 occasions they were cut shorter by the later programme. The overall tendency remains, however, that later, longer bulletins (if they are replaying a film) replay it recut and at greater length. The instances when this does not occur are all illuminating since they offer an opportunity to examine on the screen what is considered dispensable by the producers. We have already discussed the Warwick University film. We shall now examine those *First Report* and BBC *Nine O'Clock News* films that were cut on subsequent transmissions.

First Report on the Thursday ran a feature story by Angela Thirkettle on French shoppers in Ramsgate. It lasted 3 minutes 1.5 seconds and included *sync.* interviews with two Frenchwomen as well as with a local Ramsgate butcher. In addition there were two snatches of overheard conversation between the women in a supermarket (Photo 9e). The film consisted of 19 shots at an average duration of 9.5 seconds a shot. At 5.50 the film consisted of 11 shots of an average duration of 8.4 seconds each, the overall length being cut to 1 minute and 33 seconds. This early evening version omitted 24 seconds of overheard dialogue, cut the interviews by 12 seconds and generally rewrote the commentary, losing the sequences after the supermarket and the butcher had been visited. Thus the earlier version covered a fuller range of activities by the French, pointing out that clothes and pharmaceuticals were the objects of the shopping trips as well as food. The later bulletin perforce then emphasised just the food aspect of the

Photo 9e   French shoppers

story. The later bulletin also lost 'colour', as exemplified by the snatches of overheard French which played in the *First Report* version. Apart, then, from the general tightening and the resultant limitations on the story one word change can be noted. In *First Report* Thirkettle said 'It takes 45 minutes to get from Calais to

Ramsgate by Hovercraft and the round trip costs just £5; that's peanuts to the French.' In the later bulletin that became: 'It takes 45 minutes to get from Calais to Ramsgate by Hovercraft and the day trip costs just £5. For the French it is a small price to pay.' This supports, in the area of general reporting, what we have discerned in our examination of the industrial area. ITN is often careful and conservative about its language. Clearly the Americanism 'peanuts' is unacceptable in terms of house style and was corrected.

The third example comes from the same day and was found in each of the ITN bulletins (see Examples 13.7a and b).

ITN took film shot by Ulster Television with the local reporter at 1 o'clock but for the later bulletins they removed his voice, recut the images (presumably now on video-tape) and let the newscasters read commentary over. It is perhaps a measure of the difference of emphasis placed on the story by London and Belfast, although the Ulster reporter was writing for ITN. He told us where the blast had taken place by identifying the area by name. ITN placed it on the outskirts of Belfast. He mentioned that the public house was

Example 13.7a   ITN, 13.00, 15 May 1975

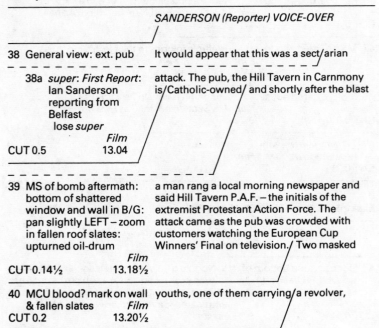

SANDERSON (Reporter) VOICE-OVER

| 38 | General view: ext. pub | It would appear that this was a sectarian |

38a *super*: First Report: Ian Sanderson reporting from Belfast lose *super* *Film*
CUT 0.5   13.04

attack. The pub, the Hill Tavern in Carnmony is Catholic-owned and shortly after the blast

39 MS of bomb aftermath: bottom of shattered window and wall in B/G: pan slightly LEFT – zoom in fallen roof slates: upturned oil-drum *Film*
CUT 0.14½   13.18½

a man rang a local morning newspaper and said Hill Tavern P.A.F. – the initials of the extremist Protestant Action Force. The attack came as the pub was crowded with customers watching the European Cup Winners' Final on television. Two masked

40 MCU blood? mark on wall & fallen slates *Film*
CUT 0.2   13.20½

youths, one of them carrying a revolver,

Example 13.7a continued

41 GV front of car in B/G + 2nd car CU door screen LEFT: upturned oil drums *Film* CUT 0.3 13.23½	placed the beer-keg bomb on the floor/and
42 MLS man seen through window – zoom in broken door *Film* CUT 0.9 13.32½	made off. A security man kicked the device towards the front door, where it exploded seconds later, before any of the occupants could get clear. Seven people/were
43 CU broken window frame *Film* CUT 0.1 13.33½	hurt./Three of them, two women and a
44 CU broken glass in partially boarded frame *Film* CUT 0.1½ 13.35	seventeen-year-old/youth, are still in
45 GV upper story *Film* CUT 0.3 13.38	hospital. One of the wom/en has had a
46 MS boarded window *Film* CUT 0.3½ 13.41½	foot amputated, the other had a piece of metal remo/ved from her thigh. All have
47 MS boarded window *Film* CUT 0.3 13.44½	multiple injuries to their le/gs, but their
48 MS shuttered house *Film* CUT 0.3½ 13.48	condition is said to be comfortable. Ian Sanderson, for/*First Report*,
49 GV bungalow – with new windows *Film* CUT 0.2½ 13.50½	Belfast.

Example 13.7b   ITN, 17.50, 15 May 1975

	HONEYCOMBE (Newscaster) TO CAM
47 Honeycombe bottom of pocket EEB backing CUT 0.12½ 9.39	In Northern Ireland, a nineteen-year-old girl, injured in an explosion at a pub on the outskirts of Belfast last night, has had her right foot amputated. Seven people were hurt by the blast./

Example 13.7b continued

		HONEYCOMBE VOICE-OVER
48 GV exterior pub	*Film*	Many more customers in the Catholic-owned
		Hill tavern of Carmony would have been
CUT 0.5	9.44	injured/ but for the quick thinking of a

49 MS of bomb aftermath:		security guard. Moments after two masked and
bottom of shattered		armed youths had put the cylinder bomb inside
window and wall in B/G:		the front door, the guard kicked it out towards
pan slightly LEFT – zoom		the road and it exploded as it was rolling away
in fallen slates upturned		from the door. A local newspaper was told/in a
oil-drum	*Film*	
CUT 0.14½	9.58½	

50 Blood? mark on wall and		phone call that the bomb was the work of the
fallen slates	*Film*	Protestant/Action Force.
CUT 0.2	10.0½	

51 GU front of car in B/G +	
2nd car CU door screen	
LEFT: upturned oil drums	
	Film/
CUT 0.2½	

Catholic-owned in the first sentence. ITN gave that information in the second. He explained that the customers in the pub were watching television. ITN skipped that. He then said that men came in and the security guard got rid of the bomb as best he could. ITN reversed this, mentioning the quick thinking of the security guard before mentioning the men responsible for the blast. Finally the Ulster reporter gave information on the injuries caused. ITN had led with this – the young girl losing her foot being their lead point. And the telephone call claiming responsibility which the Ulster reporter led with, London left till last. The result of the 'rejig' is to shorten the film from 61.5 seconds in the Ulster TV version to 24.5 seconds in the early evening bulletin. *News at Ten* got a further two seconds out of it by omitting the name of the Belfast suburb and the fact that the terrorists were masked.

The BBC carried a film insert to cover remarks made by Tom Jackson at a special conference of the Post Office Workers Union on 16 May (see Examples 13.8a and b).

Example 13.8a   BBC1, 17.45, 16 May 1975

BAKER (Newscaster) VOICE-OVER

Example 13.8a continued

23 *Portrait still col*: Jackson (flashlight) CU (under chin) CUT 0.8 4.33½	Without mechanisation he/said, the second
24 MLS 5 + workers (in line away from lens) at mechanical keyboard *Film* CUT 0.3 4.36½	delivery in the day would certainly be scrapped/with the immediate loss of 7,000
25 BCU fingers on keyboard F/G: MLS workers in B/G *Film* CUT 0.3 4.39½	jobs and/without a healthy letter service
26 CU letters in sorting machine slipping through frame *Film* CUT 0.5 4.44½	the parcel service might disappear, taking with it another 1/7,000 jobs. Mr Jackson
27 CU letters over rollers (at top of frame) cascading down *Film* CUT 0.5 4.49½	also told the delegates that/the postal service
28 GV cascade *Film* CUT 0.5½ 4.55	had now reached the crunch because inflation had speeded up many of the adverse factors working ag/ainst it and the service was now
29 CU roller (centre frame) letters cascading – zoom out – letters revealed in huge tumbler *Film* CUT 0.9½ 5.04½	not far from the point where price levels would send postal traffic spiralling down./

Example 13.8b   BBC1, 21.00, 16 May 1975

45 BCU fingers on keyboard F/G: MLS worker in B/G *Film* CUT 0.3½ 9.45	Without mechanisation, Mr Jackson said,/the
46 MS over shoulder of worker: letter down through frame *Film* CUT 0.3½ 9.49½	second delivery of the day would disappear and without a healthy letter/service the

Example 13.8b continued

47	CU letters over rollers (at top of frame) cascading down	*Film*	parcel service would probably have to go. Mechanisation was only a partial solution
	CUT 0.5	9.52½	

48	CU letters in sorting machine slipping through frame	*Film*	but to refuse help to an in/dustry in as
	CUT 0.3½	9.56	

49	CU roller (centre frame) letters cascading – zoom out – letters revealed in huge tumbler	*Film*	desperate a state as that facing the Post Office would, said Mr Jackson, be criminal.
	CUT 0.7	10.03	

The main bulletin version of the film is some 9.5 seconds shorter, omitting mention of the number of jobs Jackson claimed would be threatened if mechanisation were not introduced and also the logic of his argument. Shot 29 in Example 13.8a is a rarity – a shot in which the visual acts as an almost literary pun on the spoken commentary for the letters are seen in the shot to be literally 'spiralling down' a huge drum (Photo 9f).

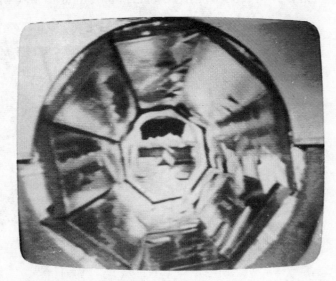

Photo 9f 'Postal traffic spiralling down'

These examples, however, all run counter to the general rule that films get longer as the day progresses. Much production effort is put into this refinement and extension of the film inserts. It is arguable that this tendency is an inhibiting factor on the bulletins in that effort to substitute fresh crude film is eschewed in favour of making crude film more sophisticated. The time that could be taken to bring new material to the screen is in effect taken to recut material already transmitted. The economic constraints obviously work here but it will be interesting to plot the introduction of the new electronic news gathering techniques in these terms. For with the new equipment it should be possible for the bulletins to remake themselves just as newspapers do from edition to edition. If they continue with the new technology as with the old then it would be fair to assume that other forces are conditioning the journalists' response – the need to establish the daily agenda, and to stick with it, perhaps being paramount amongst these.

Mismatches

There is a further minor source of misinformation that can be illustrated from the sample week which offers yet another indicator of the comparative primacy of the words over the images.

Shot 39 in the ITN early evening bulletin on 16 May was of an

Photo 10a   Whose grave?

unmarked grave seen through a wire fence. This was in the Michael X story. The commentary identified the grave as that of Gayle Benson (Photo 10a). Yet the same shot (now numbered 55) in *News at Ten* covers commentary which says 'Skirrett's body might never have been found, but in a search for unlicensed fire-arms police discovered a shallow grave and Skirrett's body. Not far away they found the body of Gayle Benson.' Whose grave is it in the shot, Skirrett's or Benson's? It is clearly less important that the picture be correctly labelled than that the 'facts' be correctly reported in commentary.

There was a minor but interesting example of this mismatching of commentary and image across the two services on the Saturday. Here both BBC and ITN used pooled EBU video-tape of the Monaco Grand Prix. ITN said that the race was won by Niki Lauda over a shot of car number 12 being followed by car number 1. The same shot was used by the BBC to say that the third place was taken by Carlos Pache. There is no way of knowing from the two reports who was in which car but it clearly does not matter much, except that it is part of the national news service.

Lower case is lower class

Supercaptions can be used in contexts other than film but most supercaptions appear over film or video-tape inserts (or in the case of *First Report* and *News Extra* live interviews).

There were 216 supercaptions used during the sample week (excluding the name plates on the desks of the BBC1 *Nine O'Clock News* newscasters; these fulfil the same function as the super-captions but were physically present on the set, not superimposed electronically).

Of the electronically superimposed captions 32 appeared in the weekend bulletins on all channels. BBC1 used 65 captions during the week, ITN 96 and BBC2's *News Extra* (there were none in *Newsday*) used 23.

The vast majority of these identified people; 3 announced a place and a time, i.e. 'Singapore today'; 9 named places, i.e. 'Bangkok'; 3 dated library film and 1 dated a programme originally broadcast on another channel; 2 announced that the picture was 'by satellite'; 6 were used to identify official film; 1 was used to identify a building and another was used to identify a man in a place, i.e. 'Michael X in

London'; 2 were superimposed graphics. The remaining 193 captions identified people. Of these only 1 was not heard. ITN covered a news picture portrait still of the Prime Minister of Thailand with the words 'Kukrit Pramoj'. ITN also used one supercaption to identify the voice of the Premier of Quebec, M. Bourassa, which was being used over a still portrait of the man, radio caption style. Otherwise all these captions related to people talking in *sync*. or in commentary.

It is possible to discern different policies towards the use of supercaptions for identification of persons from bulletin to bulletin. ITN tends to be far more regular in its practice than does the BBC, as we noted in connection with the studio inputs. The three ITN bulletins during weekdays used a total of 96 captions to BBC1's 65 captions. Even if *News Extra* is added (the *Newsday* short bulletin not using any) the BBC total is 88.

To take each weekday bulletin in turn: the BBC1 lunchtime one used 5 captions – identifying the news reader on 3 occasions, 1 interviewee, and a piece of official film. The BBC early evening bulletin identified the newscaster each day by caption as part of a standard closing routine. (The caption on the Tuesday has been lost, however, because of a cassette malfunction and thus only 4 are counted.) In addition the bulletin also identified 3 news personnel other than the newscaster and 8 interviewees. The balance was made up with the place, satellite, and other identifications mentioned above. In contrast the ITN early evening bulletin, which used less captions overall, more consistently identified its personnel and interviewees – 8 reporters and correspondents and 5 interviewees. In the main bulletins BBC1 identified 10 of its personnel, using 2 of these captions twice in the course of long reports. It also named 28 speakers, interviewees or speech makers. *News at Ten* in contrast named 23 of its personnel, which, even allowing for the use by the BBC of some names in the studio set or on the background, is still considerably more than the other channel. It named 27 other speakers.

First Report identified 10 news personnel and 11 interviewees. *News Extra* identified 8 news personnel including the newscaster on 4 occasions of the 5 in the sample and 11 interviewees or speakers. On one occasion it used the same reporter caption twice in the course of one long film (the longest of the week, in fact).

But this account of the captions used must be read against the occasions when people were seen to be speaking, or were heard on the commentary track and not identified in this way. Here the BBC's lesser reliance on captions becomes clearer.

ITN basically identifies everybody whose voice is heard whether in *sync.* or in commentary. The only consistent exception to this appears to be when the *sync.* is of an informal, overheard kind, as with the slanging match between the Chrysler wives, or the policeman answering the telephone in the report on the Cambridge rapist. Aside from this it does appear that the most famous of political leaders do not need supercaptions. Mr Wilson, President Ford, and Mrs Thatcher are the only contributors to the ITN's early evening and main bulletins who are not identified in this way. *First Report*, possibly because its earlier transmission time increases the problems of preparing captions, had three further interviews without visual identification. All told, during the entire week, including the weekend, ITN failed to visually identify 7 interviewees (2 of these inserts appearing in 2 bulletins); 6 speech makers, 2 of these appearing in 3 bulletins each; 5 people in overheard situations, 1 (the Chrysler wives) appearing in 2 bulletins; 3 of their own reporters appearing commentary only; 3 interviewers, and 1 correspondent in *First Report* appearing to camera.

The BBC did not visually identify 25 interviewees, used a total of 27 times; 5 interviewers; 8 speech makers – used a total of 13 times; 8 reporters and correspondents to camera; 15 reporters and correspondents in commentary only; and 7 people in overheard, informal situations. Of all the BBC bulletins only in *News Extra* does there appear to be a deliberate policy not to use supercaptions. This bulletin accounts for much of the discrepancy between ITN and the BBC in general; no less than 15 of the interviewees who were not identified appeared in *News Extra*. Some appeared in other BBC1 bulletins and were identified and conversely some of the captions that appeared in *News Extra* had previously appeared on BBC1. *News Extra* also accounted for 3 of the unidentified interviewers, 5 of the commentators, and 2 of the speech makers.

It can therefore be said that the supercaption appeared to be considered less crucial in the final make-up of a BBC bulletin (especially *News Extra*) than an ITN one.

The supercaption is a legitimating device, the television equivalent of the by-line in a newspaper when it is used for news personnel or to identify places and means of transmission, (i.e. 'via satellite'). The importance of this use is considerable, it being a characteristic of the press to be scrupulously careful in questions of story provenance, and the personal by-line for the reporter being an important factor in career growth. Television seems to be less concerned with this provenance use of supercaptions than it might be. For the BBC reporter it is possible never to be identified via a supercaption. For instance, Mike Mackay filed stories into the main bulletin on Monday, Tuesday, Wednesday and Thursday. In the course of these films, mainly of a softer feature type, he did voice-overs, appeared in vision to camera and conducted interviews, yet on each of those days he had films in the bulletins without his supercaption. ITN reporters do better, if indeed the supercaption can be said to be the equivalent of the press by-line. It can, however, be said that a failure to identify the reporter or correspondent in this way lessens the element of editorial responsibility that can be easily adduced by the watching audience. It increases the tendency of the news to be anonymously produced – although it is normally the case that a verbal identification of reporter will be made by the news-caster in all circumstances except where, in the course of an interview, the interviewer is not heard or heard only for one or more questions in voice-over.

Provenance of the other sort, identification of the sources of film or the method of transmission, is rare. Film obtained via the European Broadcasting Union (EBU) news exchange is not so identified (although by analogy with newspapers this could be

Photo 10b   Film provenance

considered the equivalent of news agency material which in the press would be so identified). It is perhaps significant that when the North Vietnamese film was transmitted, the BBC felt it necessary to twice identify it as 'official North Vietnamese film' in the course of an insert lasting little over a minute (Photo 10b). The only other times the same caption was used for identification twice in the course of a signal transmission was with the Sells film on Kurdistan and in one of Humphrys's extended pieces on the *Mayaguez* from Washington. On each of these occasions, in contrast to the Saigon film, the items were of exceptional length. It is hard to account for the double Saigon caption except to see it as an attempt to indicate to the audience the foreign provenance and consequent lessening of the BBC's editorial control of the material. It is hard to see why television news has not developed more extensive use of captions for this purpose – why foreign television stations are not credited more often, for instance. American practice is much more rigorous in this regard and indeed an American station identification caption ('WGNB newsfilm') appeared in the vox pop of *Mayaguez* crewmen's relatives that the BBC ran as an exclusive on the Thursday.

Particular to television is the use of supercaptions to identify interviewees. As we have previously indicated, the regularity of such uses, even in services such as ITN's which seem to make a point

Photo 10c Chrysler wives

of being regular, extends less to speech makers and even less to people overheard informally. There are no examples in our sample on either service of a person talking informally being identified with a supercaption. Of course such informal *sync.* is itself a comparative rarity and, as we have argued, is seen as being dispensable when films are recut. Only occasionally, as with the Chrysler wives, is it seminal to the insert. But even there, although the piece was being run at some length, no names appeared. It is of course basic to the use of all these captions that the person identified appears in the shot in close-up. If there is more than one figure to be seen then obviously the caption can become ambiguous (Photo 10c). Here British use seems to be stricter than American, where it is sufficient for the caption to relate to whoever is talking, however many people may be seen in the frame.

There does seem to be a tendency to identify certain groups of people more consistently than others. For ITN their own personnel are routinely identified, and this is true also for most BBC bulletins although the 'X reporting' caption is not as regularly used. For non-news personnel the question of whether a caption appears or not seems to depend, first, on the context of the talk. Informal speech does not attract supercaptions. Since most people so heard appear to be of low status this can be described as a preliminary example of the relationship of supercaptions to status. However, in the week in question, amid the shouting Chrysler wives (one of whom did not get a caption even when she was being interviewed by herself, it should be said) and various people on telephones, there was one comparatively extended *sync.* shot which was not captioned. It was in the referendum film transmitted in the main BBC bulletin on the Tuesday. Bob Harrison, the organiser of the Anti-Common Market campaign, was seen for 19 seconds chairing a meeting. Aside from this and the confused Chrysler wives all the other overheard shots were of 2 to 5 seconds' duration.

Formal speech attracts supercaptions less often than interviews but more than informal speech. Two speech makers got super-captions on the BBC and none did on ITN. In fact there were 6 speech makers on ITN and 5 on the BBC who were not given supercaptions. However, many of those whose formal speeches were transmitted were of high status. Clearly, the unmediated quality of the formal speech (unmediated, that is, except by initial selection and editing) confers its own status. High status, which might be seen as giving the figure a certain familiarity to the

Photo 10d   The running interview

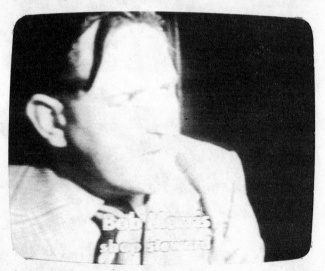

Photo 10e   shop steward

audience in any case, does not require the further support of the supercaption. Therefore it cannot be said that there is a complete isomorphism between the status of the speaker in society and the presence or absence of supercaptions. Against the non-captioned low status of the informal speakers must be set the non-captioned high status of the formal speakers.

The correlation of status to supercaption can be seen most clearly with interviews. The sample is larger than with the above categories of *sync.* and is therefore discussed immediately below. But one last point on supercaptions should be made.[4] Supercaptions reflect the clean sans serif quality of all news graphic work and are either in

Photo 10f   shop steward

Photo 10g   crew member

Photo 11a Butcher

Photo 11b Chief Counting Officer

capitals or in upper and lower case. There was not complete consistency in this (not least because much American material transmitted across the Atlantic had American captions already in place) but in the two main ITN bulletins captions are upper case for names and lower case for function (i.e. in the 'X reporting' caption the name is in capitals but 'reporting' is lower case). *First Report* and the BBC use upper and lower case. However, on two occasions out of the 216 an interviewee had his function entirely described in lower case. Since the functions in the sample that attracted capitals range from Convenor, and Financier to Butcher, as well as Chairmen of Named Companies and the like, it is perhaps not insignificant that both these occasions were low status jobs relating very firmly to the working class – one was 'crew member' and the other 'shop steward'. The 'crew member' acquired capitals in a later bulletin when the man was named. But the shop steward, repeatedly interviewed by both services, never did (Photos 10d–10g, 11a, 11b).

Other voices

To conclude this examination of the visual track we finally turn to the category of *sync.* sound as we have been defining it. As with the previous section on supercaptions this category will now be discussed as a whole, the attempted distinction between film, tape and live inserts being largely abandoned. Therefore we are now dealing with all those people who are not employees of the news services speaking in whatever circumstances and whether recorded on film or tape or live in the studio. (The only exception to this is that interviews with news personnel such as were done three times during the week by Angela Rippon in *News Extra* are here considered – so that statistics that follow do include one appearance by Dominic Harrod and two by John Humphrys as *interviewees*.)

Some further refinement on the system of categorising *sync.* is now possible. Earlier, when discussing film, we suggested that on commonsense grounds *sync.* material could be broken down into informal *sync.*, formal *sync.*, interview (question and answers), and news personnel to camera (this last we are not now considering). It is possible to make a further sub-division of the formal *sync.* category. This category previously contained both speeches at meetings and press conferences. The latter in effect sometimes contained speeches and sometimes contained answers to questions from the floor. Therefore that distinction will now be drawn. Informal talk, overheard talk as it were, and speeches are mediated only by the process of editing the material. The material itself cannot be conditioned at the time of the recording. As we have shown, a crucial part of agenda-setting occurs in the way in which questions are asked and the persistence of the interviewer in following a particular line of questions. With speech, both formal and informal, this crucial function is not possible. The editorial function in these categories can therefore only be performed in physically editing the material. With interviews, too, this can of course be done, but the material is already conditioned.

During the sample there were 120 occasions (film, tape and studio) when voices other than those of news personnel were heard in the bulletins. These occasions were used as inserts 189 times, 45 of them being used in more than one bulletin, 75 of them appearing only once. Not included in this count is the one occasion when the Premier of Quebec was used as a radio caption voice over his own still portrait.

Even in the overheard informal category the vast majority of these occasions involved only one person talking. Only on 4 occasions was a second voice heard which was not that of an interviewer. These were the informal *sync.* and the short interview with the two unnamed Frenchwomen in the Thirkettle report for ITN on French shoppers in Ramsgate (Photo 9e); and the Chrysler wives, where, despite the general shouting, two women were most prominently heard (Photo 10c). In addition there was Robert Kee's long piece with Norman Buchan and Geoffrey Rippon, and Clifford Luton's doorstep interview with Jack Jones and Gilbert Hunt of Chrysler UK (Photo 11c).

Photo 11c   Two-shot interview: Jones and Hunt

Six occasions involved the use of pooled material. Of these 5 were in *Mayaguez* reports and all came from the United States; 2 Senators, President Ford, Secretary of Defence Schlesinger, and the chief Pentagon spokesman Laitkin. The last British pooled example is the interview with the Prime Minister by Peter Jay which was part of *Weekend World* on the Sunday and was picked up by both services for that day's bulletins. On 12 occasions both ITN and the BBC sent their cameras to the same interviewee or event. Both services separately covered speeches by Mr Callaghan and Mrs Thatcher, the Chrysler wives row, the vote of the Chrysler workers on the Thursday, the row between Nastase and the umpire on the Friday. In addition both services separately interviewed Nastase and the chief umpire, Captain Gibson, Roy Mason, Norman Griggs of the Building Societies Association, Sir Donald MacDougall of the CBI and Bob Morris, the Convenor of Stewards at Chrysler. In addition to this interview on the Monday, Morris was again interviewed by both services on the Wednesday and his speech was filmed by the BBC at the voting on the Thursday. No other person appeared on so many separate occasions during the week. In fact the only other interviewee to appear twice (on different days) was the Irish Foreign Minister, interviewed by ITN – at the European Parliament one day, and on Irish policy if the referendum vote should be 'No' on another day. And the chief Pentagon spokesman, Joseph Laitkin, appeared on both Tuesday and Wednesday in press conferences. Geoffrey Rippon appeared twice in *First Report*.

The fact that only 18 of 120 occasions were either shared or duplicated supports the contention that competition between the services is largely in terms of what *sync.* material can be obtained. But the smallness of the shared material must be read against the more general finding that the same events were covered. Therefore the exclusives in the list of the 120 must be reduced on 4 main bases. First, one service, more usually ITN, will not take *sync.* but will do reports in other ways. The pro-EEC organisation's press conference is a good case in point. The BBC ran Roy Jenkins *sync.* in both the early evening and main bulletins, and in the latter also ran Mr Heath and Mr Thorpe. ITN carried none of this but did cover the story with a newscaster piece to camera.

Second, *sync.* can be obtained from different sources on the same day to illustrate the same story. Thus, apart from the pooled inserts mentioned above, the BBC carried interviews with Senators that ITN did not carry (e.g. Robert Dole) but that day (Thursday) ITN carried Senators Sparkman and McGovern and, in addition, in *First Report*, interviewed an American correspondent in London; or BBC interviewed a local Referendum official whereas ITN interviewed the Chief Counting Officer. Third, on running stories, distinctly similar *sync.* material might be obtained on different days. Thus the slipping pound involved a tour operator on the BBC on the Sunday and a spokesman for tour operators on ITN on the Friday.

Finally, it should be said that both *First Report* and *News Extra* carried a significant number of exclusives. Only 1 *First Report* studio interview, with Sir Cyril Kleinwort, was used in a later ITN bulletin. But 14 other interviewees and 2 *sync.* speeches appeared exclusively in *First Report*. Similarly *News Extra* had 20 exclusive *sync.* inserts, including the 3 interviews with BBC personnel, 1 of the two-handers (Photo 11c); and the *sync.* extract from *World in Action* on the tea story.

If we discard these exclusives and the pool of duplicated inserts we have 66 occasions left. Of these the BBC had 43 and ITN had 23. None of them involved *News at Ten* sharing *sync.* with *First Report*. In fact, apart from the interview mentioned above, only twice did *First Report* share and then not with *News at Ten* but with the early evening bulletin. It might be thought, then, that if a *sync.* insert was to appear in all three ITN bulletins it must occur on those occasions when the *sync.* was either pooled with the BBC or obtained by covering the same story. In fact of the 18 possible occasions when this occurred ITN only ran 2 pieces of *sync.* in all its bulletins in any one day. These were the pooled statement by President Ford and the duplicated coverage of the Chrysler vote being taken. Thus is it fair to suggest that ITN tends to re-use its *sync.* less than the BBC does from bulletin to bulletin. Apart from these two instances when it used the same piece of *sync.* three times, ITN only used the same *sync.* twice in any one day on 12 other occasions.

The BBC, in contrast used the same *sync.* twice for 20 items (12 times sharing the double use between BBC1 and BBC2, and on 8 occasions repeating the *sync.* from early evening to main bulletins on BBC1). It used the same *sync.* three times for 4 items, only one of them being used exclusively on BBC1, the other two being shared between the channels. It ran the same *sync.* 4 times on two occasions. Only one interview appeared exclusively in the lunchtime bulletin. Thus ITN repeated about 24 per cent of its *sync.* material, whereas the BBC repeated about one-third. It might seem that the basis of this comparison is a little unfair since the BBC has 4 bulletins to ITN's 3, but the amount of *sync.* in the lunchtime BBC bulletin is quite small (only 3 *sync.* inserts in the week in question). Thus like is being basically compared with like – the two main bulletins, the two early evening bulletins, and the two current affairs style bulletins. As we have previously established, the BBC uses more *sync.* We can now say that it uses the same *sync.* more often than does its rival.

Repetition does not of course mean that the *sync.* is played at exactly the same length each time, although the range of variation in a *sync.* insert appears to be less than in a complete film insert. The *sync.* tends to remain much the same, occasionally being extended. But there are no examples in the sample week of a completely new piece of *sync.* being substituted from the same press conference, interview, meeting or event.

The most common form of *sync.* insert is the most mediated, the interview. Of the 120 uses, only 11 were overheard. Of the 11 uses in the overheard category the majority were in the second half of the bulletins, 4 of the *sync.* shots occurring in the one film, the BBC's round-up of Referendum Organisations. The others were of the French housewives, the woman launching the *Locomotion* replica, a woman heard greeting her friends at the airport, the policeman answering the telephone in the Cambridge rapist story; another policeman in the Canadian fire story, warning people through a loud-hailer to clear the area; and two rather more major uses of informal *sync.* – Chrysler wives and the Nastase row. These last were shared. None of the shots carried supercaptions and, in addition to the *sync.* that could be clearly heard, almost all of them had commentary voice-over. Apart from the 2 duplicated occasions, the BBC had 5 and ITN 4 inserts with this type of *sync.* We have discussed the status of the people appearing in these shots in the preceding section of this chapter. None of them were in any sense well-known, all appeared just on the one occasion, except for Mrs Willis, the Chrysler wife who was interviewed by the BBC the day before her demonstration. Much of this *sync.* was simply of a scene-setting type, a few words caught to establish place or organisation. Thus the two telephones being answered, or the woman arriving at the airport who was heard to say 'I knew they'd be here'. Only the Chrysler wives and the Nastase row contained material which was important to the story. Indeed, without the *sync.*, the story would have been quite different.

In the other inserts the *sync.* can be easily lost, as we demonstrated by comparing the *First Report* version of the film in which the French housewives were overhead with the shorter version transmitted by the early evening bulletin. The shots were for the most part quite short, or if of longer duration then commentary was added. The airport woman, for instance, said her five words in a shot that lasted for 20 seconds, the rest of the time being taken up with commentary. The shortest shot was of the policeman answering the telephone in the Cambridge rapist story – 2.5 seconds. The lady launching the replica of *Locomotion One* got 4.5 seconds.

ITN's coverage of the Nastase row consisted of two shots, one of 4 seconds which had no commentary and one of 35 seconds which had commentary in addition to the *sync*. The BBC's coverage of the same event was in 7 shots (in the earlier version) and in the main bulletin. All had commentary as well as *sync*. and the longest shot lasted for 13 seconds. The BBC's coverage was from the OB at the tournament and thus a number of cameras were available to record the row. ITN seemed more limited, almost certainly because the crew were working with a single film camera and, as has been said, actually did not have footage of the ball that caused the incident.

BBC1 covered the Chrysler wives in two shots 15 seconds and 32 seconds in length with commentary over the first of them. BBC2 used 26 seconds of the second shot without commentary laid over, but omitted the pro-strike cheer at the end of the shot. ITN in covering the same story used three shots of 10, 50 and 10 seconds respectively and each had some commentary as well as the *sync*.

The battle to be able to record events as they happen on film and audio-tape with lightweight equipment was won by the early 1960s. The result of the technological breakthrough achieved then has been a profound revolution in the style of documentary film. Observational cinema (*Cinéma verité*) was designed to 'let the event be more important than the filming', in the words of one of its pioneers. As a result commentary was largely eschewed, long continuous takes were favoured and a whole rhetoric grew up around the problems of intervention and editing. The small amount of news film that takes advantage of these advances is significant. For although there are still considerable problems of mediation even with the most rigorous of observational documentaries, nevertheless this work is less mediated than news film. That news film has not used the lightweight equipment to lessen the mediating effect of filming, that it largely restricts overheard informal sound to semantically unimportant information which can be easily cut, is a

measure of how little technical advances will of themselves move
the newsrooms away from their structured and controlled practices.
The very concept of the story, and the assumed normative rules as
to its length, considerably aid this process. For informal talk is far
less compressed than formal talk and compression is a prime
requirement of the bulletins. These considerations are also likely to
apply to ENG.

Lord Soper, Fred Peart, two unnamed members of the Cardiff
Rates Action Campaign, an unnamed Chrysler steward taking a
strike vote, Bob Morris the Chrysler Convenor, Senator Barry
Goldwater, Jim Callaghan, Enoch Powell and Margaret Thatcher
were all heard making speeches. Of these Peart, Powell, Goldwater, and Morris were exclusive to the BBC, the two Cardiff
speakers and Lord Soper exclusive to ITN. The strike vote,
Thatcher and Callaghan were duplicated. Only Bob Morris and
Barry Goldwater had supercaptions. The shortest of these inserts
was that of Lord Soper, who was heard for about three seconds at
the end of the Cyprus demonstration story on the Sunday. It is fair
to assume that no *sync.* was really intended in that the story stood
quite well without it. In other words it was really more a shot of the
overheard variety than a real speech. The Shop Steward was not in
close-up and each service panned off him to show the hands going
up. All the British politicians were in halls standing at lecterns or

Photo 11d   The political situation

tables (Photo 11d). Goldwater appeared to be addressing an informal gathering at a party. The BBC used the Peart speech 4 times, Powell (on the Saturday) 3 times, and Thatcher (also on the Saturday) twice. ITN used her once. The BBC used Callaghan twice, ITN used him only in the main bulletin. ITN allowed Callaghan 1 minute 9 seconds in a single shot; the BBC cut him about using a long shot from the back of the hall (which was out of *sync.*) for 1.5 seconds and a cutaway of the audience for 2 seconds: the total duration of the film, 1 minute 14.5 seconds. Mrs Thatcher was allowed 34 seconds, Mr Powell 1 minute 10 seconds, in the longest version. The early evening BBC1 bulletin cut him to 49 seconds. Peart, who appeared in every one of the BBC's bulletins that day ran longest at 48 seconds in the early evening one. Goldwater, also broken up by two cutaways, ran 1 minute 3 seconds. Despite the fact that none of the British politicians attracted supercaptions this was a high status input, not least because they were appearing for long periods of time, uninterruptedly. In fact only news correspondents appear for longer uninterruptedly than this sub-group of political speech makers. Bob Morris's speech was played at 28 seconds.

There were 9 inserts from press conferences. These divide into two. First, there were statements given at press conferences – those of President Ford and John Schlesinger (although this last could have been in answer to a question). On both these occasions the man was standing at a podium, as was Laitkin, who was seen stonewalling the press in a 20-second shot on ITN on the Tuesday and in a pooled report making a statement on the Wednesday. The 20-second shot was used by Brunson to illustrate how little information the Pentagon was releasing and therefore was the only shot among these inserts to contain questions. Two were put off camera in voice-over.

On the British side there were 5 responses to unheard questions, 3 of them from the pro-EEC campaign launch conference which the BBC covered. Mr Jenkins had 39 seconds, Mr Heath 37.5 seconds and Mr Thorpe 25 seconds. Mr Deakins and Mr Rippon were given 1 minute 3.5 seconds and 56 seconds by BBC and ITN respectively. It would have been difficult to note these as having a press conference setting except that on the second occasion that the Deakins piece was transmitted it contained a cutaway of journalists and the Rippon piece was introduced as having been at a press conference. The other 3 were not only introduced as being at a press conference but there was a long shot of the room which clearly revealed the setting.

The 3 American statements (but not the Laitkin question-and-answer shot) were all pooled. President Ford appeared in more bulletins in any one day than anybody else – 6 out of the 7 possible. The BBC ran him at 40 seconds at lunchtime and in the early evening bulletin and increased this to 1 minute 11 seconds for the main bulletin. ITN used 1 minute 10.5 seconds in *First Report* but then cut him to 40 seconds for the next two transmissions. Schlesinger was used by both BBC bulletins and *News at Ten* at 46 seconds. Laitkin was used by both BBC bulletins at 40 seconds but *News at Ten* took 1 minute of him.

As with speeches these durations were among the highest un-interrupted ones of the week, matching only the news correspondents to camera pieces. They therefore also have high status. It should be noted that it is custom and practice for the print journalists and the television reporters to deal with press conferences separately wherever possible, so that after the conference is finished the television reporters can then do solo interviews. There must have been other occasions during the week at which this happened but, in the very nature of the case, these would be considered as ordinary interviews.

Having dealt with informal *sync.* speeches and press conferences

Photo 11e Demonstrator

(both statements and answers) we now turn to the balance of 96 interviews. Of these 7 were shared. There were only 3 pooled interviews: 1 with Harold Wilson, 1 with Senator Buckley and 1 with Senator Humphrey.

Some patterns of question and answer can be easily discerned. On 35 occasions the *sync.* insert took the form of a single shot in which the interviewee only spoke. These single-answer shots represent the biggest type of interview insert, and lasted on average 24.5 seconds. Of the 35 interviewees 16 appeared for less than this average – they included 2 of the interviews with Bob Morris; 1 with his colleague McCluskey; 3 with relations of *Mayaguez* crew members; 2 with unnamed footwear workers; 1 with a blind man (also unnamed) on the demonstration (Photo 11e); an unnamed Irish farmer; the bosun of the *Mayaguez*; the butcher, Roger Rook (Photo 11a); tour operator Peter Davis, and three politicians – Senator Hubert Humphrey; Peter Kirk, leader of the British group at Strasbourg; and George Younger, chairman of the Scottish Tory party. It should be further noted that of the 13 non-politicians 7 were filmed outside and 1 (the tour operator) in the airport. Of the remainder, 3 were American interviews conducted in the individuals' homes. The shortest interviews included one with Morris, one with a *Mayaguez* crew member's mother, and those with the blind man (Photo 11e) and with the footwear workers (Photos 11f

Photo 11f   Worker

and 12a). None of these lasted for more than 10 seconds. Of these, only the American one had a supercaption. Of the rest mentioned above only the farmer had no caption.

Of the 19 answers lasting longer than the average, 12 were from politicians (5 American, 5 British and 2 Irish), all of which were supercaptioned, and all of which, with the exception of Senator Buckley, were filmed or taped indoors. The 7 others include the spokesman for the New Zealand farmers and the French champagne industries; the Cambridge professor talking about exorcism (at 50.5 seconds, the longest single answer of the week) (Photo 12b) and the Secretary of the Private Patients Plan, an insurance scheme for private medicine. The captain of the *Mayaguez* and Derroll Castle (who was first identified as 'crew member') are also in this group. Both the New Zealand farming spokesman and the insurance man are uncaptioned; both were BBC exclusives and one, the

Photo 12a   Workers

insurance man, appeared in a *News Extra* feature. A member of the steel union's action committee was allowed 30 seconds and was interviewed inside and captioned.

Thus, although it is not possible to maintain a strict consistency in the matter, it is nevertheless true that broadly speaking the lower the status of the interviewee the less time they are likely to be allowed. It will of course be argued that it is just such people who

Photo 12b   Single-answer interview

lack the articulacy of a Cambridge professor; who, because of their
disadvantaged background, could not necessarily talk in public for
50.5 seconds on anything. It could further be argued that, as in the
case of Bob Morris, there was an obvious reluctance to be interviewed in the first place. But as we shall discuss below, even if these
points are admitted, the fact that the bulletins fairly consistently
reinforce the conditions of the existing social order should not go
unremarked. In North America all who talk, whatever their status,
tend to be named, and currently ITN seem to have come closer to
this practice.

The second stage of interview complexity is reached when the
interviewer is introduced. This can be done in two ways – either the
single shot can be left uncut and the interviewer can put question or
questions in voice-over; or the interviewer can be seen asking the
question. Since most interviews during this period were done with a
single film camera, these questions were normally filmed after the
interview proper was over, often without the interviewee even
being present ('Noddies').

To deal with the simplest form of the voice-over off-camera
question first. This yields a pattern within the shot of Answer-
Question-Answer. There were 23 examples in the week, 15 on the
BBC and 8 on ITN. In all but one the interviewer was unseen. The
exception was the interview with Senator Javits, which was framed

wide enough to include the surrounding journalists. The average duration of these shots was 37 seconds and the breakdown reveals a similar pattern to the single-answer examples discussed above. Those having more than 30 seconds included 2 Government officials, 2 politicians, 2 industrial spokesmen, a banker, a CBI spokesman, a brewer, a spokesman for a Ratepayers' Association, and a Convenor of Shop Stewards. The CBI spokesman had the longest interview at 1 minute 15 seconds (ITN played this 48.5 seconds with the question). Of these only the banker and the shop steward (on one of the two occasions when the interview was transmitted) did not have supercaptions. Below 30 seconds were a sportsman; an industry spokesman; the chairman of the Meriden Co-operative; a politician; a butcher (Photo 11a); a refuse collector (Photo 12c); two members, unnamed, of the Steel Unions Action Committee; and a footwear worker (Photo 12d). The steelmen, the footwear worker, the refuse collector and the sportsman were all without supercaptions and, with the exception of the sportsman, were all filmed outside.

Photo 12c   Refuse collector

If we turn to the rather more complex of these forms we find 13 examples in which more than one question is put off-camera. Of these the commonest is the two-question pattern (Answer-Question-Answer-Question-Answer) which occurred 7 times. One

Photo 12d   Worker

involved the company chairman of Nypro and lasted 1 minute 57.5 seconds, the longest in the group. This was captioned. There was an uncaptioned interview with the chairman of a private hospital, lasting 1 minute 2 seconds. There was an interior interview with Frank Chater of the AUEW which lasted 46 seconds; an uncaptioned exterior interview with Chrysler wife Mrs Willis lasting 57.5 seconds, a 54-second version of the interview with Norman Griggs, the building societies spokesman; and an interview with an unnamed Irish housewife lasting 10.5 seconds (this was an exterior). And finally there was the publican in the real beer story, who got 18.5 seconds inside his pub. (It should be noted that many interviewees will appear more than once in this analysis since different bulletins transmitted different patterns of the same interview.)

There were 3 examples of Question-Answer-Question-Answer. The first of these with the Pentagon spokesman has already been discussed; the other 2 were the ITN and the BBC interviews with Captain Gibson on the Nastase incident. ITN's ran for 31.5 seconds, the BBC's for 18 seconds.

There were 2 examples of three questions being put off camera (Answer-Question-Answer-Question-Answer-Question-Answer). One (1 minute 46 seconds), was with banker Mike Thompson. The other (1 minute 40 seconds), without caption and outside, was with trade unionist and MP Tom Bradley. Both were BBC exclusives.

ITN used 1 interview with Bob Morris twice (see Example 13.9). It consisted of 4 questions and 5 answers and was unique in the week in that it was done at a run (Photo 10d).

There were only 8 examples of Answer-*sync*. Question-Answer.

Example 13.9   ITN, 22.00, 12 May 1975

30 MLS 4 stewards (obscured in bunch)	*MACDONALD (Newscaster) VOICE-OVER* . . . Yesterday/
0.4 7.48	

31 CU Morris + MacDonald at side of frame: track back	*MORRIS* What they should do – they should sack Harold Wilson/. Yes.

Cap: Bob Morris
Chrysler shop steward
B/G factory rails

MACDONALD
But don't you think that his call for some sort of national stand on the question of wages and prices deserves some attention?
MORRIS
Certainly, but Mr Wilson yesterday – his comments – we haven't refused worker

lose caption

participation./We want the details so we

can examine the position of worker partici-
pation. We haven't refused to do anything.
MACDONALD
But aren't there any good points at all about the plans for industrial democracy, for more worker participation?
MORRIS
When we find out the details it may be a wonderful thing, but we know no details and it's not the basis to call off a strike.
MACDONALD
But shouldn't you go back to work until you know the details and perhaps then consider strike action?
MORRIS
No, no. Our strike is on the basic. We are on strike for a living wage, full stop.
MACDONALD
Will you call forward the meeting which you planned for later this week to try to get this thing settled a little earlier?
MORRIS
No, no, no, no. Wednesday the stewards meet again. We meet – all our mass workers on Thursday at 12 o'clock and that's it,

1.5   8.53   and the strike will continue./

Of these 1 was an extract on tape from an interview originally done live in *First Report*. It was with Sir Cyril Kleinwort and lasted 57 seconds, the shot of the interviewer lasting 5.5 seconds. The chairman of the Cardiff Council Finance Committee had 40 seconds, 8 on the interviewer. The Chief Returning Officer had 1 minute 21 seconds, 7.5 on the interviewer. The chief executive of Strathclyde Council had 37 seconds, 7 on the interviewer. The CBI's chief economic advisor had 1 minute 12 seconds, 5 seconds on the interviewer. All of these were on ITN. The BBC gave an out-of-work steelman 30 seconds, 5 on the interviewer (Photo 12e); the Secretary of the London Clinic got 57.5 seconds, 3.5 on the interviewer; and Tom Williams, MP, got 48.5 seconds, 2.5 on the interviewer. Of these last only the MP had a supercaption, the other two being exclusively in *News Extra*. All the ITN examples had

Photo 12e   Unemployed steel worker

supercaptions. The out-of-work steelman was interviewed in a club or pub, the MP in Parliament Square. (The questions both here and subsequently were not necessarily limited to the *sync.* shot of the interviewer. It is common practice to allow either the beginnings or edings of questions to appear as voice-over shots of a listening interviewee.)

Four interviews were split. The policeman in charge of the Cambridge rapist case appeared twice in the film, giving a single answer each time. The feature on the referendum which involved interviews with Shirley Williams and Sir John Winifrith gave them two *sync.* pieces each arranged around studio inserts by Jon Lander. The pattern was: Williams answer; Lander: Winifrith answer; Lander: Williams answer; Winifrith answer, voice-over question from Lander, Winifrith answer. The Prime Minister's interview was also broken up by studio pieces, the BBC taking 2 answers and ITN taking 4. However, the earlier ITN bulletin took a longer complete extract of the original, leaving in 2 of Peter Jay's *sync.* questions and running it at 1 minute 58 seconds. This last is an example of the more complex forms possible in the multi-camera studio situation.

But before discussing the week's other examples it can be said in summary that of the 189 inserts only 22 remain to be accounted for. The range of the patterns of interview is therefore restricted; most inserts can be accounted for in one of four ways: single Answer; Answer – Voice-over Question – Answer; Answer – Voice-over Question – Answer – Voice-over Question – Answer; Answer – *Sync.* Question – Answer. Of the 22 remaining inserts 15 were studio interviews, only 1 of which occurred outside of *First Report* and *News at Ten*. Therefore in the course of the week there were only 12 interviews outside of the studio which did not fit into one of the 4 basic patterns.

There remains one basic pattern of which there are 4 examples in the sample. It is a mixed voice-over and *sync.* question pattern: Answer – Voice-Over Question – Answer – Voice-Over Question – Answer *Sync.* Question – Answer. These involved one of the interviews with the Irish Foreign Minister, one with Nastase, the longest version of the interview with Mrs Long, the footwear industry spokeswoman and one with the Swiss Banker Dr Mast. Three of these appeared on ITN and 1 on the BBC. The Mast interview lasted 1 minute 51.5 seconds, Fitzgerald got 2 minutes 20 seconds, Mrs Long got 1 minute 23.5 seconds, and Nastase 1 minute 10.5 seconds.

There were 2 examples of Answer — *Sync.* Question – Answer – *Sync.* Question followed by Answer with a variable number of Voice-Over Questions. The longest version of the interview with Tom Williams, MP, lasted 1 minute 49.5 seconds. It was patterned as a *Sync.* Answer lasting 24 seconds followed by a *Sync.* Question for 4 seconds, a second Answer for 16.5 seconds, a second *Sync.* Question for 5 seconds and then an Answer, Voice-Over Question, Answer for 1 minute 5 seconds. The interview with Lynda Mottram followed the same pattern: initial *Sync*. Answer for 10 seconds; *Sync*. Question, 3 seconds; second Answer 22 seconds; second *Sync*. Question 2.5 seconds; followed by a 56-second shot containing 5 Answers and 4 Voice-Over Questions.

Dennis Forman was interviewed for the tea story, with the following pattern: Answer – Voice-Over Question – Answer – *Sync*. Question – Second Answer. However, the second answer was in fact two shots jump-cut together without cutaway.

The most interesting variant in the entire week was the BBC's use of the Roy Mason interview. This used cutaways of the aircraft Mr Mason was talking about and (with the only tape interview exclusive to *News at Ten*) was one of the two examples of this happening during the week. The pattern was: a 34-second answer, the last 13 seconds of which cutaway to a still photograph. This was concluded in a 6-second *sync*. shot which also contained a voice-over question. The second answer, which lasted 19 seconds, was covered by two cutaway stills. The still remained on the screen for the second question, after which Mr Mason had 38 further seconds in *sync*.

News Extra had an exclusive in the two-hander interview with Gilbert Hunt and Jack Jones. This was a single shot with voice-over questions lasting 2 minutes 30 seconds. The camera panned from one man to the other as they spoke (Photo 11c).

This last was among the wider shots of the week. Apart from the overheard category, all formal *sync*. and all the interviews were framed in tight close-up. None came closer than the bottom of the chin and most were framed at tie-level or wider. The sizes of the heads therefore matched the sizes in the studio. The possibilities of using location in interviews are somewhat restricted. Occasionally, as with the Cardiff ratepayers activist Mathias or Tom Williams, a long shot established the location. But basically, even when exterior settings were used, the style of camera was to immediately concentrate on the head. All the interviews were with static camera with the one exception quoted in the example. The interviewers' *sync*. questions matched in general terms the size of the interviewee's image. Only in the studio was a marginally greater vocabulary of shots to be seen.

There were 14 studio interviews, 1 in *News at Ten*, 7 in *First Report*, 6 in *News Extra*. Of these 1 was a two-hander (Buchan and Rippon in *First Report*), and 3 were with BBC personnel (Humphrys twice and Harrod). The 2 Humphrys interviews and the Tolgarten interview in *News at Ten* were done down the line; 5 of the interviews were live and introduced as such, 4 of them being in *First Report*: the remaining 4 *First Report* interviews and all of the *News Extra* interviews except the one with Harrod were recorded. The studio shots included in addition to the two heads of interviewer and interviewees, a two-shot relating them together. This is sometimes seen on film as an establisher and is occasionally used in the film interview instead of a *sync.* question. (There were no examples of this during the week – although the Cardiff interview was established in the traditional way.) Because of the multiple cameras in the studio it was possible to use the two-shot during the course of the interview and this was done in every case but one. The exception was the interview in Friday's edition of *News Extra* with Bill Horewood, the financial journalist. This was the only one of the 14 which was not clearly in an electronic studio but was conducted against plain curtains. Yet the interviewer was also the duty newscaster, which would make a setting outside the studio unlikely. So why bring film cameras? The pattern of the interview better matches film than electronic patterns. There was a 37-second shot of Horewood framed to the top of his pocket. This was followed by a 2.5-second shot of Dorling the newscaster/interviewer mute, after which we returned to Horewood. As Dorling started to put a question at the end of this 46-second shot, the camera widened to a mid-shot of Horewood. This is standard film practice. If the frame size is altered as each question is put, the questioner can be cut out without jumps. Each cut will be between frames of sufficiently different size to obey the normative rules. After the question was put voice-over we cut back to Horewood, now in a tight shot framed at the line of his tie-knot for 1 minute 12 seconds. Were it not for Dorling's presence this would have been quite clearly a film and not an electronic interview.

There was no ambiguity about the other 13. They took place quite clearly in the studio and all were announced as such. The vocabulary of shots normally includes a close-up of the interviewee framed around the pocket with the possibility of a tighter close-up framed around the line of the tie-knot. The interviewer will be seen in a similar close-up (with, again, the possibility of tightening it to the tie-knot). There will also be a two-shot across the interviewee's shoulder giving a wider view of the interviewer. Although individual directors can vary the use of these shots their presence is fairly constant and it is possible to see tendencies in the order of their use. Leaving aside the Buchan/Rippon two-hander, which will be discussed below, half the time the *First Report* interviews began with a wide two-shot over the interviewee's shoulder. On the other 3 occasions they began with a tight top-of-pocket close-up of the interviewee. In 4 of the 6 interviews there was a progression in terms of the single close-ups from wider to tighter. In other words on 4 occasions the first shots of the interviewees were around the pocket but, after 2 or 3 answers using this framing, we moved in to a shot framed about the buttonhole, tie-knot line. There were no examples of the opposite happening, for on the 2 interviews in which we did not move in on the interviewee the frame remained static throughout. On 2 occasions when the second close-up was found for the interviewee it was matched by a tighter shot of the interviewer. In fact it is possible that the tight shot of the interviewer will be followed by the tighter shot of the interviewee. In the last interview in this group there were matching top-of-pocket close-ups for both interviewee and interviewer but when the camera went in for a tie-knot shot on the interviewee's sixth answer, the interview's shot widened to a bottom-of-pocket frame.

The two-shot over the shoulder of the interviewee floats. It was used variously for the second question; for the first question; for the first and second questions, for the first, second and fifth questions; and on one occasion it was not used at all. It is not a rule that the interviewer shall be seen whenever a question is put. In other

Photo 12f   Over-shoulder two-shot

words, within interviews with *sync.* questions one can get shots containing answers and voice-over questions. The interview with Paul Johnston on the Friday, which had no two-shots, had 5 questions (out of the 11) put voice-over. Kleinwort's first answer on the Monday was followed by a voice-over second question and a second answer without a cut, as was Schuster's last answer preceded by a voice-over question. And Lee Hon Tung took a question in voice-over which he answered with a 'Yes' at the end of his interview.

But essentially there are 3 basic shots in the *First Report* studio interview, a close-up of each participant and a two-shot over the shoulder of the interviewee.

In *News Extra*, there were 5 interviews apart from the Horewood one discussed above. Only 1 with Dominic Harrod was live and the

Photo 13a   Over-shoulder two-shot to *Chromokey*

2 with John Humphrys were down the line (Photo 12f and Photo 13a). These were similar, using Humphrys in a Washington studio against a background photograph of the White House. In the first of them he was framed wide, to the top of the desk, and the shot did not vary. In the second he was framed initially to the bottom of his jacket breast-pocket and for the third answer this tightened to a top-of-pocket shot. The interviewer was presented in two shots – one was over her shoulder looking towards the *Chromokey* screen

on which the shot of Humphrys was matted. The other, framed at about top-of-pocket level, was a semi-profile shot. For the third question of the first interview both these shots were used. For the third question of the second interview the profile close-up was used, which enabled the shot to be tightened from bottom to top of pocket in the American studio (because Humphrys was not on the screen).

Both these interviews, and the other three yet to be discussed, can be distinguished from the *First Report* group because they all have fewer questions – 3 on 4 occasions and 4 on 1 occasion. This contrasts with *First Report*, where 4 questions was the minimum during the week and 2 interviews had 5 while the last 2 had 10 and 11 respectively.

There is another distinction. Whereas *First Report* reframes the tighter shot off camera (i.e. while the other participant is talking in single close-up), *News Extra* twice zoomed in from a two-shot over the shoulder of the interviewer (a shot which *First Report* did not use) (Photo 12f) to a close-up single of the interviewee. Thus *News Extra* has 4 shots in its vocabulary to *First Report*'s 3 – a close-up of the interviewer, a close up of the interviewee, a two-shot over the interviewer's shoulder and a two-shot over the interviewee's shoulder. In addition, during the interview with Aubrey Jones on the Monday a tape cut was covered by a mute close-up cutaway of the interviewer.

The one interview done in the *News at Ten* set followed the same basic pattern although there was a technical error during the first answer. This was the only interview apart from the BBC's with Roy Mason where still cutaways were used – on this occasion news photographs from Phnom Penh. Instead of cutting to these, for 1.5 seconds there was a big mute three-quarters profile of Parkin, the interviewer. Obviously the lack of a curved desk makes it more difficult to find non-profile shots in the *News at Ten* set. The two-shot of the *Chromokey* screen (for this was a line interview from Stockholm) had the interviewer completely back to camera, and his close-up was more three-quarters than any of the shots in *First Report* or *News Extra*. The two-shot of interviewer's back and *Chromokey* screen was used twice and the interviewer close-up once. The shot coming into the studio of the interviewee did not change.

All of these studio interviews were long; the shortest in *First Report* was 2 minutes 28 seconds and the longest 5 minutes 19.5 seconds. In *News Extra* the shortest was 1 minute 41 seconds and the longest 3 minutes 31 seconds. Even in *News at Ten*, the one example ran for 3 minutes 8.5 seconds, considerably longer than any other interview. Thus the studio setting does mean greatest length of interview, a fact obviously encouraged by its use in the current affairs style bulletins which anyway tend to have longer items than the others.

The longest item of the week lasted 7 minutes 54.5 seconds. It was the debate chaired by Kee between Norman Buchan and Geoffrey Rippon. Here the essential three shots were considerably increased. Obviously, to match the single interview situation, the second interviewee also had a close-up and in this instance both interviewees had two close-ups of varying tightness. There were two over-the-shoulder shots of Kee, one from each side. And these two shots were also widened to give a view, over the shoulder of one participant, of both the interviewer and the opponent. Finally there was an extremely wide shot embracing the whole set taken directly from the front (i.e. Kee's camera pulled back). Kee put only 6 questions and referred to the item later on in the week as 'a lively discussion'. The two participants interrupted each other 3 times and twice spoke together. Kee broke through to put 2 of his 6 questions. This item represents the limits of the bulletin's current form, for in essence it is a current affairs item lacking the strict structure of the news interview, a lack reflected in the wider vocabulary of shots deemed necessary to cover it.

Sync. material on film represents 47 per cent of all film and is an important element in creating the preponderance of 'talking heads' on the bulletins. The people heard come from the whole range of society but, as we have indicated, lower status is reflected in various ways – shorter single answers, more questions put in a shorter time, lack of supercaptions, being overheard, being filmed outside. Yet despite the broadness of the range of interviewees the presence of news personalities – that is, those repeatedly interviewed – is obvious even in this sample (and despite the ubiquitousness of Mr Bob Morris).

During the course of the week 35 politicians were heard, 8 company chairmen (including the private medicine interviewees and the chairman of one nationalised industry), 5 spokespersons for various industries, 5 government officials, 1 local politician and 1 local government official; there were 4 journalists, 1 foreign expert, 2 news personnel, 3 bankers, 1 spokesman for the CBI, 2 professors and 3 doctors; there was 1 ship's captain and there were 3 ratepayers, 4 sportspersons, 5 union officials, 3 shop stewards, 9 workers. There were 13 wives, relatives and the blind demonstrator.

The above included 14 women, 5 knights and 1 lord (as well as President Ford, the Prime Minister, 2 Foreign Secretaries, 1 opposition leader, 2 Secretaries of Defence, and 1 Chancellor of the Exchequer).

Of the 14 women only the two politicians (Mrs Thatcher and Mrs Williams) were heard at length. Only Mrs Williams and the two American *Mayaguez* relatives received a supercaption. Of the 13 workers, none except the *Mayaguez* crew members received supercaptions and the only one filmed inside was filmed inside a pub.

Conclusion

If it is true that the mass-communication research tradition has devoted less attention to the content analysis of messages than to other areas, it is equally true that within content analysis less has been done to grapple with the problems of visual analysis than with other problems. The primary aim of Part III of this book has therefore been to attempt a systematic description of a body of television output. In so doing it has been possible to reach certain conclusions; some of these tentatively concern themselves with what we have called viewers' maxims; others have argued that the visual track exhibits the characteristics in terms of cultural skewedness that we would expect, given our examination of story case studies and language. Thus we have essentially been considering the visual vocabulary and some generalised conclusions that emerge from it. Clearly, the next step must be to use the methodologies here suggested to tackle the visual syntax.

But even at this present level it is in our view essential that the detailed descriptive work be done and presented; although in so presenting it we do not pretend that the descriptions themselves can be made the basis of a comprehensive understanding of the social forces at work in the production of the bulletins, they are nevertheless an essential prerequisite for any such understanding.

Conclusion: Ritual Tasks

> We have an almost ritual task. When I read the news, I am The
> Messenger. I am the Town Crier. I am there to express a
> communal sentiment.
>
> > Richard Baker in Jeremy Bugler, 'Battle of the Bulletins',
> > *Listener*, April 1976

Ideology and news values

The response from both broadcasters and critics to the first volume
of our study, included arguments mounted against the overall
strategy of our work: but, significantly, not against its evidential
detail. The broadcasters tended to respond unacademically and on
occasion almost hysterically from a standpoint which appears to us
to be firmly on the Right. The critics with greater care and a clearer
understanding of our purpose seemed to be largely of the centre or
the Left. It would be possible, but obviously ironic, for us to thereby
claim, as do the manufacturers of news programmes, that this range
of criticism is a testimony to our own objectivity and neutrality. But
of course this is no more true in our case than it is when used as a
professional defence of their output by the broadcasters.

We began Volume 1, *Bad News*, by observing that[1]

> Contrary to the claims, conventions and culture of television
> journalism, the news is not a neutral product. For television news
> is a cultural artifact; it is a sequence of socially manufactured
> messages, which carry many of the culturally dominant
> assumptions of our society. From the accents of the newscasters
> to the vocabulary of camera angles; from who gets on and what
> questions they are asked, via selection of stories to presentation
> of bulletins, the news is a highly mediated product.

In this we were doing nothing more than following a majority opinion among media scholars. Anthony Smith in *The Shadow in the Cave* puts it thus:[2]

> News tends to lay out the order of 'Priorities' among the issues which confront society; it creates some of the doubts and fosters the certainties of that society, placing them all in a context of its own. Yet in every single society which contains broadcasting on any scale the news is under instruction to be 'objective'.

Our justification in stressing the manufactured quality of news broadcasts can best be summed up by a phrase used in an otherwise hostile review of *Bad News*: 'All this is true and cannot be shouted too often into the ears of the broadcasters'.[3] Yet professional opinion still seems to reject this position. As the Annan Committee reported: 'such analyses of the agenda-setting activities of journalists naturally raised resentment, not to say bewilderment, among the journalists in broadcasting with whom we discussed this outlook'.[4] The Committee quoting the Editor of ITN said news 'was dictated primarily by events that had happened that day'.[5] This viewpoint begs considerable questions as to what events and what interpretations are placed on them. We can only endorse Stuart Hall's assessment of Annan's response to what Hall calls 'a well-established conventional wisdom of broadcasting research'. He states:[6]

> But here, at the very centre of the issue, Annan's thinking dissolves into pious platitudes. It raises the critical issue of the power of the media to 'set agendas and define reality' . . . only to find it unproven. What seems to have persuaded Annan against it was the 'bewilderment' with which the very idea was received by professional broadcasters! But the concept of the 'agenda-setting' is a *structural* concept. It deals with the relationship between a highly concentrated system and its professionals (the latter, precisely insulated from larger imperatives of the work they perform by the professional ideologies), which reports on and communicates with, but is not operated by the great mass of the public outside who are 'consumers'. It cannot be reduced to the 'recognition' of this journalist or that.

The refusal of the broadcasters to recognise the basic constraints of their professionalism cannot be taken as a refutation of their power to set agendas defining the perimeters of social issues. Here our evidence is overwhelming.

In Volume 1 we presented a mass of evidence culled from a large sample of recorded news bulletins to illustrate the basic agenda-setting function of the news. We demonstrated that the bulletins of competing services did not really compete as to the stories they were reporting, or the style in which they reported them. We showed a predictability in the ordering of news items and the limited range of presentational devices available to the broadcaster. We further demonstrated that regularities in the area of industrial reporting lead to a consistent failure to cover the area thoroughly; that major factors in industrial life were systematically underreported (e.g. industrial accidents), whilst others which were reported (e.g. strikes) were reported unsystematically.

We further demonstrated in the case studies in that volume how the basic inferential frames regularly used by the newsproducers conditioned the reporting of strikes and did so in ways which were quite clearly skewed against the interest of the working class and organised labour – if only in that the inferential frames accepted uncritically narrow consensus views of the nature of strikes in particular and the realities of industrial life in our economic system in general. And we revealed that these frameworks were, because of their uncritical nature, skewed in this area in favour of the managers of industry. This is without prejudice to the charges laid at the broadcasters' door by those managers. The level and range of industrial reporting on television does not give them access or allow proper explanatory material to be laid before the public as they might wish. But it is our finding that what news there is is based on premises (inferential frames) sympathetic to their point of view.

In the case study in this volume we have again demonstrated that a narrow view, in this instance one based on Treasury policy and interpretation, was used to systematically foreclose on alternative views whatever their source. In detail this meant that as far as the news was concerned wages were the prime source of inflation and wage demands the main cause of the crisis. And that in so presenting the issue media personnel across a wide range of stories throughout the period under study actively embraced these points of view in a way that it would be hard to justify as impartial. The public thereby were never presented, as part of the media institutions' interpretation of these events, with the possibility that other causes than wages and other solutions than the moderation of wage demands could relate to the crisis. And the processes of selection leading to this result include not only the agenda-setting functions we have described, but also a systematic partiality in the reporting and interpretive use of government statistics.

As regards the language of the bulletins we have shown that in many respects it conforms to the restricted and redundant usages of the popular press and that news talk in the area of industrial reporting relies on the assumption that industrial disputes are about 'trouble' – trouble for us as consumers, commuters and members of the public, trouble for the managers of industry, trouble for the nation; but never trouble for the workers involved. In the detailed examination of the vocabulary used we have demonstrated that in disputes the traditional offers of management are inevitably countered by the demands of the workers – to the point where nouns and verbs describing management actions are generally positive while the matching vocabulary for workers' actions is negative. In demonstrating this we have not relied on an examination of what some might consider exotic or provocative terms, but rather the constant repetition of the small stock of descriptive terms which form the meat of the bulletins' language.

We have continued to demonstrate this cultural skewedness against one particular class in our examination of the visual elements of the bulletins. We have found in particular that there is a measure of isomorphism between a person's status and how that person will be presented in the bulletins. We have also more generally demonstrated that the lack of competitiveness between the services extends down to the most minute examination of technical inputs; that not only stories but the ways in which they are covered, the graphics they generate, the locations and interviewees they bring forth are extraordinarily similar from channel to channel.

In doing all of this we have not explicitly suggested that corrections to the above are beyond the reasonable, not to say conservative, expectations of professional practice since much of our evidence as to what could have been done is culled from the so-called quality press. Given the privileged nature of these forms of electronic news transmission, we have shown that in other areas other journalists, whatever their faults might be, do better at reporting the range of opinion and facts in industrial life.

To suggest that in some way we conditioned by our own prejudices the phenomena we have here documented is to say in effect that we failed to see the high-status supercaptioned interview with the rank-and-file worker, the considerate and extended interview with the monetarist economist, the language that claimed that a management was by its actions threatening us, the nation or the workforce.

It is significant that little attention has been paid thus far to the evidence on which we based these conclusions. The broadcasters especially have largely sought to counter the criticisms outlined above by attacking what they call our 'bias'. Of course having argued that the ideology of neutrality is impossible of performance in their case, we would not claim to exercise it ourselves. Our very interest in this area of broadcasting might be seen by some as clear evidence of a host of other attitudes and beliefs which can be attributed to us. But although we would deny little of this, the facts still remain. We did not anticipate the possible production of 'neutral' news, and still less would we in some way welcome such production; on the contrary we were arguing and demonstrating that the ideology of news which requires it to be neutral, unbiased, impartial and balanced merely leads to a 'naturalism' on the level of stylistics which hides its ideological components. How we stand as regards that ideological component is irrelevant, given the weight of our findings. Just as attention must be directed at the evidence we present rather than at assumptions as to our ideological stance, so, too, we would not argue that the broadcasters are engaged in simple-minded conspiracy to distort or bias their work. The prevailing professional ideology encompassed by the myths of impartiality, balance and objectivity allows the broadcasters to tacitly trade upon the unspoken and dominant ideology of our society – the liberal notion that there is a fundamental consensus. Our use of the term 'ideology' in this context and throughout refers to sets of ideas which represent or serve the interests of social groups or classes. It is not intended to convey the meaning of merely illusory or false thinking.[7]

News and the ideologies of the larger society are integrally related. As Gouldner states, 'news is defined against the tacit background of unspoken premises, and by the bench marks these provide'. Gouldner's theoretical point, which we are empirically substantiating, is that ideologies are the connecting link between the so-called 'facts' of the news and the background assumptions which enable us, the audience, to understand those 'facts'.[8]

Depending on the kind of ideology we hold about the nature of society, the ideologies speak to the 'events' by the news; and, on the other hand, they may refer to certain news-censored aspects of everyday life, 'recovering' certain underprivileged elements within it. Ideologies are thus a 'background' to the news – e.g. 'The News Behind the News', or 'The Big News' – that premises the reading of certain news-reported events.[9]

In attempting to refute the above position broadcasters rely centrally on the twin notions of actual 'events' occurring in the real world and the 'newsworthiness' of those events.

One can see that, at the centre of this controversy, as in others, the professional response is to hold up the shield of such values, in this case – news values. When this is challenged various responses are possible. The efficacy of the challenge can be denied; the terms of the debate can be changed; or the values themselves may be in part questioned, to give ground, as it were, in order to maintain the central position.

A clear example of this last position occurred when Jeremy Potter, the then Managing Director of Independent Television Publications, suggested in an IBA public lecture:[10]

> It used to be said, rather smugly by us British at the time of Goebbels, that you cannot get away with propaganda unless you have proper geese. But we have since learned that all communication is propaganda. There is no such thing as due impartiality on the screen despite the exhortation of successive Television Acts and the earnest endeavours of the I.B.A., and the B.B.C. and the companies. There is selection in every news bulletin.

Potter went on to suggest that 'unavoidable partiality and involvement are common to all media, not characteristics peculiar to television'.[11] Here we have a clear illustration of the professional rejection of a position because it is thought to be inherently untenable. But in responding to the difficulties of admitting television to be partial and involved, Potter adheres to another professional value, that of balance. This for Potter appears to mean making judgments on such things as how much violence to show on news bulletins and at what times. Although balance might normally be seen as having to do with the internal organisation of a programme or, perhaps, a channel, Potter seeks a check against any channel having a monopoly of control and hence in effect determining balance. A diversity of control provides a check against particular viewpoints predominating:[12]

All television is subliminal advertising and the responsibility of producers correspondingly immense. Whatever their standards, they cannot avoid a viewpoint. The viewer is continually registering in his mind situations which he may not realise that he has seen: women always in kitchens, coloured men always outsiders. We viewers are being got at all the time. This is the strongest of arguments in favour of diversity of control.

But if news is the presentation of balanced viewpoints (which our evidence would deny) what becomes of 'objectivity'? It becomes difficult to hold on to a notion of objective news in terms of the honest and accurate reporting of facts and events. Perhaps the attempt to hold on to it has something to do with the feeling that to depart from it in the name of a plurality of perspectives is to move towards a view of news as 'subjective'. This invites one to doubt the credibility of news and to question the authority of those who deliver it. Of course all the multiple subjectivities in the world would not add up to a new objectivity transcending these partial viewpoints. It is precisely this point to which Anthony Smith seeks to attend in *The Shadow in the Cave*:[13]

News is founded upon the idea of a homogeneous mass audience (in the sense that it has a common frame of reference for what constitutes a news 'event') listening to an account, as accurately ascertained as can be, of actual daily events. The whole idea of news is that it is beyond a 'plurality of viewpoints'. The fact that the world has to a great extent ceased to believe in the intellectual possibility of such objective facts does not mean that one can quickly devise a new set of organisations in which new, 'pluralist facts' can be gathered and disseminated.

Ten separate news bulletins would not provide a more *accurate* picture even if we listened to all of them. A society which demanded its news from ten separate perspectives would not be receiving *news*. Ten views of reality do not between them add up to a new 'objectivity' to exchange for an old one.

Smith's own practical solution to this dilemma is to merely suggest that the crisis of credibility can be resolved, first, by mopping up areas of criticism (say coverage of trade union affairs) into a revised national news; second by supplementing the news presentations of reality with documentary interviews and discussion programmes operating from varied perspectives. In place of news from a plurality of perspectives we are offered 'reality' from a plurality of 'genres'. It is a defence of a news genre (albeit sensitive to criticism) not a defence of objectivity that is proposed. This position is somewhat quiescent, since it does not address the homogeneity of the current news services with their shared and largely non-competitive reliance on a narrow range of views. Yet Smith does make it clear that a 'news' view of the world cannot in its nature be an 'objective-realistic' view:[14]

> News is a cultural discipline, choosing it an intellectual skill, collecting it a profession. Within the confines of the broadcasting institution the news organisation absorbs the institution's picture of the society and inherits the professional assumptions and methods of newsmen in other media. News is only one vessel in which broadcasting strives to catch reality. The answer to the problem of in-built 'distortion' in the disseminated picture of society must be to encourage other parallel 'genres' for the representation of reality.

The representation of reality in television news has come under more severe criticism in a series of articles in *The Times* by John Birt and Peter Jay.[15] News was held to be not simply incomplete or necessarily partial because selective. It was positively misleading and unhelpful because it created a 'bias against understanding'. Birt and Jay argued that television news carried a large number of stories in a thirty-minute bulletin, but in a narrow and limiting way which inhibits rather than aids appreciation of the issues presented:[16]

> Our economic problems, for instance, manifest themselves in a wide variety of symptoms – deteriorating balance of payments, a sinking pound, rising unemployment, accelerating inflation and so on. The news, devoting two minutes on successive nights to the latest unemployment figures or the state of the stock market, with no time to put the story in context, gives the viewer no sense of how any of these problems relate to each other. It is more likely to leave him confused and uneasy.

Birt and Jay argue that television journalism can be differentiated in terms of news, feature and issue journalism. These vary in terms of the generality of context in which information is communicated.

The news context is superficial, the feature context focuses upon particular instances (say, a famine in Ethiopia) and not on the general problem (in this case, world food resources). Issue journalism seeks to come to terms with the complexities of industrial and social problems. It is desirable but difficult to accomplish. It does not abandon the notion of a real world to be analysed and in that sense is not a matter of subjectivity: 'The realities one is seeking are abstract – macro-economic mechanisms, political philosophies, international strategies – and cannot be directly televised like a battle zone or a demonstration.'[17] In their view, news is not organised to give accounts of this reality. Instead of recognising the world as being one of interacting processes, news splits it into innumerable atomised facts and millions of tiny, discrete stories.

Yet, the *reductio ad absurdum* is not that we are offered a continuous stream of unrelated facts. Despite the maxim that news should separate fact from comment this is not possible. It is an empty myth. The news journalist does implicitly and explicitly blur the line between fact and interpretation. There is selection, compression, simplification of reported events. There are connecting links between statistical information, the events to which they purport to relate (say unemployment) and government policy and future prospects. Moreover there is the inherent problem of the relationship between language and reality:[18]

Even if selection [of stories] were random or could be based purely on market analysis of reader/viewer interest, the journalist would still face the difficulty that every sentence and every word carries connotations which go beyond what he can see, hear, touch, smell and feel. Interpretation is implicit in any use of language at all to describe the world.

Birt and Jay in writing of 'the bias against understanding' lay down the challenge to journalists to make the 'real world' more intelligible. The paradox they appear to embrace is that in the name of 'hard facts' about the real world television news is peculiarly uninformative and unreal. And yet there is another kind of bias which suggests itself to them as a consequence of actual news practices. It is a bias in favour of the powerful:[19]

Most current broadcast journalism is partial – it favours the views of one group at the expense of those of another. This is because, lacking a clear sense of its obligation to society as a whole, most journalism lives under the shadow of the state and the other main repositories of power in our society: the political parties; business; the trade unions; and so on. It might almost be called 'corporate journalism'.

If that is so, then while Birt and Jay might go on to write of news values as restrictive, simplistic and highly prejudicial, it is a picture of the world that is being conveyed. If this picture turns out to be one which continually favours some interest-groups at the expense of or to the relative exclusion of others, we may wonder whether the bias against understanding turns out to be a bias towards the powerful. The question might have to be put again: what kind of understanding is on offer? For it would not be true to suggest that no understanding is on offer. The ideological underpinnings of news production do in fact create a coherence which Birt and Jay are unwilling to acknowledge. It is not that the news programmes leave the audience bewildered. On the contrary, the agenda-setting function works to limit the range and density of information just so that it can be comprehended within a narrow consensus. As has been observed,[20]

Media neutrality and independence are therefore quite 'real' in the sense that their function is essentially to try to *hold the ring*, to sustain an arena of 'relative independence', in order that this *reproduction of the conditions* of political power can take place.

Content analysis

It has been a basic contention of our approach that the detailed examination of the output of television journalism can be used to demonstrate its ideology and practices. Some have suggested that this is not the case; that we have made assumptions as to the audiences' inability to view the output critically; that we have ignored and indeed have no way of knowing what goes on in the newsrooms; even that we are intending to create a statistical measure as a substitute for the editorial control of news decisions.

To tackle the last of these first, it has been claimed that in deciding what to cover there are a range of factors and values 'which an industrial editor must weigh in his mind, in general though not in statistical terms'.[21] This might seem to suggest that news values are unfathomable, locked as they are in the minds of news editors. If that is so then no amount of research would suffice to refute the claims by broadcasters that news is impartial and balanced. But by the same token the claims would simply be rhetorical, capable of neither confirmation nor denial. But this view misunderstands the whole nature of content analysis. We are not in undertaking such work implicitly suggesting that the broadcasters should abandon rule-of-thumb decision-making (whatever professional rhetorics are used to justify such internal criteria) for higher mathematics. The point of such counting is that while, for instance, checking whether there is parity in the number of interviews given to antagonists might only tap the surface of any distortion that may occur, yet where it does occur it is still worth drawing attention to. If there is imbalance at this crude level (as we showed to be the case in the Glasgow dustcart drivers' dispute) then the credibility of news coverage is challenged, so to speak, at the first line of defence. We are thereby demonstrating that although we would not expect the newsmen to measure their output in more refined sociological terms, yet the rule-of-thumb can sometimes lead them into major distortions. As the Annan committee reported:[22]

> the broadcasters were not guilty of deliberate and calculated bias. But that the coverage of industrial affairs is in some respects inadequate and unsatisfactory is not in doubt. Difficult as the reporting of industrial stories may be, the broadcasters have not fully thought it through. They too often forget that to represent management at their desks, apparently the calm and collected representatives of order, and to represent shop stewards and picket lines stopping production, apparently the agents of disruption, gives a false picture of what strikes are about. The broadcasters have fallen into the professional error of putting compelling camera work before the news. Furthermore, the causes why people come out on strike are often extraordinarily complex. No reporter does his job adequately if he interviews only the leading shop steward or union official. The fact that a strike is not backed by the union does not exonerate broadcasters from discovering why the work force is out.

In other words the time-honoured notions of journalistic practice do not seem to be working too well in this area.

While the main thrust of our work has been to look at the deep structure and agenda-setting function of the bulletins, we were also interested in devising ways of checking news coverage against other bases of information on what was happening in the world. Commenting on this approach Professor Elihu Katz has recently said that one of the functions of tracking social trends[23]

> is to create certain external criteria to use as a guide in the selection of stories and in assuring adequate coverage. Such indicators cannot be allowed to dictate to journalists, no more than audience measurements should do, but they are worth having around as a basis for professional judgments.

The point is that the tripartite division of the research tradition, between the sociology of broadcasting institutions, the sociology of audience response and content analysis, is basically unsatisfactory. Ideally participant observational studies of the production offices should be matched to content analysis and audience research relating to the same period. This has not yet been done. Our justification for concentrating on content analysis in the light of this tradition is simply that of the three branches it has been the most neglected. Without a body of content analysis research the other two divisions are in danger of addressing a vacuum – for what is it the studied producers produce? And what is it the audience reacts to?

The criticism that nothing can be learned of real social relations from the screen is so palpably absurd as to scarcely warrant responses. If that were true then in some sense the output would have no semantic component – would be in fact meaningless. For when it comes to the use of language and the visual treatment of news we do not argue that these are to be dismissed as surface phenomena. For us they are central to any attempt made to discover whether there is systematic distortion of news information. The spoken and visual vocabulary of news may be regarded as the outward and visible expression of newsroom codes and conventions and not as separate from them. Since the output clearly has meaning, then the production of that meaning can as clearly be studied on the screen as it can be by interviewing either producers or audiences.

The real failure of recent work such as that of Tracey and Schlesinger lies in their inability to relate their conclusions regarding the nature of broadcast institutions to what those institutions actually produce.[24]

We further take the view that an analysis of news output over an extended period should enable us to discover some of the rules governing the presentation, ordering and frames of reference which guide newsmen as they scan the world day by day. Just as news-producers argue that they cannot be expected to understand and work to these latent structures (and thereby hope to deny their very existence), so it is argued that the audience, too, is unaware of them. This last can then be made the basis of a critique of all broadcasting research which does not focus upon the decoding abilities of the audience. It is true, of course, that a variety of readings or viewings of any given piece of the output are possible, but before proper work on audience comprehension can be undertaken there has to be systematic documentation and mapping of the dominant modes of presentation and framing. Otherwise how can the study of the audience be made to precisely address the issues of routine absences and presences in the coverage?

Given the current state of knowledge of the audience it is possible both to argue that they do not truly comprehend the bulletins and that if they do the bulletins are not the sole influence upon them.[25] Such critics see our methods as implying a low assumption on our part of the audiences' ability to resist or renegotiate the preferred ideology offered up in the output. But the contrary is true. The argument outlined above is nothing more than a restatement of the classic reinforcement view. And, as in the case of those who argued reinforcement as the dominant effect of the media, it leaves aside the whole question of agenda-setting and itself hides behind notions of the overall unimportance of television to the viewers. For us this is nothing more than a failure of methodology. If researchers can show that little information is passed by the medium, then it could be the case not that little information is actually passed but that what is passed cannot be properly measured. We obviously take the latter view, at least for the present, and therefore stand by the need for as sophisticated and systematic a method of content analysis as can be devised. The fact remains that, despite recent developments, the history of sociological research of the audience concentrates on the audience's ability to decode without paying concomitant attention to the encoding of the messages. We believe that the work offered here is an essential step in tackling this problem.

Front page

While the longitudinal dimension of the study was on the whole regarded as unproblematic, a number of our critics hastened to point out the lack of a regional dimension. The bulletins, it was suggested, are like the front page of a newspaper and the regional magazines like the inside pages. It is argued that concentration on the national bulletins cannot give a true picture of the news because regional bulletins are complementary to network news. This view is espoused particularly by professional broadcasters who maintain that an apparent lack of depth at the national level will generally be made up for in regional bulletins, especially in those regions in which the stories occur. Such a view ignores the vital fact that national news by definition is the news that the large majority of people see and listen to for information on national issues.

While we do not agree that such complementarity can be maintained given the division between news and current affairs, nevertheless, during the period of our study, we did collect the local broadcasts of both STV and BBC Scotland and a short account of our findings on one week's coverage is given below in Appendix A. Basically we find that the similarity of professional practice between national and local newsrooms does not allow the argument that the latter deal with the news in markedly different ways – by using different inferential frames or reporting in greater depth – to be sustained.

It could further be argued that the considerable debate about the television news and the changes made in the bulletins since the period of our study have rendered our findings obsolete. We felt that another week's output would therefore provide us with a check on the scale of the alterations which had been made in bulletin formats, running orders, visual inputs and styles of presentation. The profiles which emerged tended in every major respect to strongly confirm the patterns which were described in Volume 1. In particular, ITN's main innovation, the *News at 5.45*, varied from the previous early bulletin in the predicted direction. The results of this monitoring are also given below in Appendix A.

Critique

There is another level of criticism of our approach which casts doubt on the value of content analysis that is not grounded in, or developing, some particular theory or another. Gouldner perhaps sums up the basic attitude of such critics when he writes: 'Given a commitment to protect understanding of the social world from the biasing interests of dominant societal groups, there is a tendency to surrender and sneer at primary research.'[26] These critics fall into two groups – those who hold that a general theory of the media is an essential prerequisite for doing any analytic work and those who argue for particular positions in cultural analysis (currently within semiotics or a variant of it).

The first of these positions suggests that analysing the dominant codes governing cultural production (in our case, news bulletins) is merely dealing with the surface phenomena of our society. The task of a general media theory is, in contradistinction, to begin to spell out the structural relationships which hold between given institutions and the rest of society. The aim in our area would therefore be to contextualise news production as merely one part of the larger structure of power and domination within our society. It is assumed that some general theory can be developed that allows the specification of such relationships within which detailed study of the output would fit.

The crudest version of this position appears to believe that the market forces, in economic terms, coupled with the institutions of the capitalist state operate so forcefully upon the media institutions that the reproduction of culture is almost a perfect mirror image of the mythic relationships of bourgeois society (e.g. sanctification of the family; the special position of the Church; notions of law and order; and a central cultural commitment to competition). While this simple 'base/superstructure' view of broadcasting might account for a small part of the output, it can in no way explain and analyse the inherent contradictions and varieties of permitted views and the surface openness which exists across the range of broadcasting output. For instance the view would be hard pressed to offer a reasonable account of the sophisticated processes at work whereby a play by Dennis Potter, say, will be elaborately produced at considerable expense by an organisation replete with managerial and editorial control levels, which then shelves it.

Of course it does at times appear that nothing more than a crude ruling class viewpoint is at work. From the minutes of the most senior policy-making committee of the BBC in the news and current affairs area in 1976 (as published in the *Leveller*[27]) we learn that the

Editor of News and Current Affairs (albeit 'for the first time in his career') suggests that[28]

> at the present juncture stories about this country's currency needed careful handling . . . He was inclined to suggest that they should always be checked first with the Treasury. It would be wrong in the present circumstances to put out a major news story of which the Government had no warning.

In the light of this sort of information it is difficult to break totally with the notion of some kind of reflexive ideological bias at least in the upper echelons of the media institutions. But it seems to be becoming fashionable to suggest that since the phenomenon of broadcasting ideology is so deeply embedded in the society, it is unforgivably crude to suggest any single person capable of biased decision-making within that ideology, even in meetings such as the one quoted. This view seems to us to have all the makings of the sort of liberal double-bind that characterised the debate about the reinforcement effects research of some decades ago which we mentioned above. It was argued that since the only observable effect of broadcasting was to reinforce the audiences' previous points of view and attitudes, there was thus no basis for mounting critiques of broadcasting power.

It seems a pity for instance that Stuart Hall and his group in their concern 'to demonstrate how the television discourse could not be "read back", either to its class origins or – worse – to class interests' should suggest that their work seeks 'to break with any simplistic notion of television "bias" (still to be found residually in *Bad News*) as though simply directed by "the ruling class".'[29] Yet as they themselves suggest their own analysis 'could have been faulted for underplaying the connections and relations between the ideology of the television discourse and the ideologies of particular class fractions'.[30] It is apparent that our work rejects any crude notions of 'bias' and reductions to class interests. Yet the relative autonomy of senior managers within the television institutions means at times that they must be able to act. To deny this is to consider them automata; and in this sense any general position must accommodate some notion of classes of actions on their part which systematically bolster one view of society rather than another. However, any work in this area which treats our detailed evidential documentation of television discourse as merely an exercise in spelling out 'bias' fails to grasp its major direction. We have empirically established that, at least with regards to industrial and economic stories, the overwhelming use of inferential frameworks, routines and presentational techniques which favour one side of industry rather than the other exist. In this sense, for whatever reasons, the ideology of one particular class, despite contradictions in the output, is dominant and preferred. Yet we would agree with Hall and others that those who wish to push a reductionist analysis to include all areas of output at all times somehow want a theory which in Sartre's words 'tells us everything and gives us nothing'. For such a general theory of the media turns out on examination to be a general theory of society.

Whilst agreeing that some general theories of society, especially those that stress the role of class structure and conflict, are more feasible than others, we cannot agree that such theories at present offer us the concepts to analyse the manifold variations of cultural reproduction in our society. Perhaps the most sophisticated exponents of such a general position are Murdock and Golding, who in their article 'Capital, Communication and Class Relations' move uneasily between asserting that 'control over material resources and their changing distribution are ultimately the most powerful of the many levers operating in cultural production', and the argument that[31]

> if news coverage of industrial relations is cumulatively
> unsympathetic to militancy, radicalism, or union activism in
> general, is it simply because of the hostility of the capitalist media
> entrepreneurs or even anti-socialist sentiment among industrial
> relations correspondents?

As they suggest:[32]

> A fuller explanation must look for the complex of inter-
> relationships between pervasive definitions of industry, the
> Nation, responsibility and the like, with trends in industrial news
> practice, the conventions of interview, film and narrative and so
> on.

It is just these later trends and conventions that we have addressed in our work. At this time it seems that moving from the macro-level successfully articulated by Murdock and Golding in their detailed examinations of the patterns of ownership and cultural monopoly to the micro-level of close content analysis such as we have undertaken is difficult. But however sophisticated such an analysis becomes, there is a fundamental difference of levels between institutional and societal forms and the routine content of particular genres. Any method which relies at base upon economic reductionism will be unable to explain the routine presences and absences in content. Yet the basic assumptions at work in both are the same. Neither approach needs to rely on any crudity in its understanding of the patterns of cultural power in this society.

Semiotic critiques

Aside from the general problem of economic determination, another critique of our work can be mounted from the position in cultural analysis of those who consider themselves structuralists or semioticians. Initially this work is grounded in the linguistic studies of de Saussure, who pointed out that language was coded in an arbitrary fashion; that in fact the sound 'd-o-g' or 'ch-i-e-n' had little to do with the animal meant (or signified) when those sounds are uttered. This is a general point; the relationship between the sounds and the concepts of any language are arbitrary – the sound is, as it were, an arbitrary sign. De Saussure saw this basic distinction between the thing signified and the signifier as being the crucial concept in a new analytic. 'I shall call it', he announced, 'semiology' (from the Greek for sign). He further suggested that 'linguistics is only part of the general science of semiology'; which was the view of the American logician Peirce, who called the science semiotics,[33] and who refined the basic notion of the arbitrariness of the sign and extended it beyond linguistics, by distinguishing a tripartite possibility in the relationship between thing signified and signifier. For Peirce the three divisions are symbolic, where the relationship is arbitrary, as in language on the Saussurian model; indexical, where the relationship is not arbitrary, but related, as for instance with a sundial signifying time, or a weather-vane wind; iconic, where the arbitrariness is further reduced and the signifier agrees most closely with the thing signified, as in a photograph. For Peirce any sign could contain elements of all these categories.

In recent years a large body of work has grown up from such beginnings. Roland Barthes is probably the best-known of semiologists, in popular terms, whose work, together with that of other European structuralists, has come to play an influential role in the attempt to decode and recover the hidden relationships which we take for granted in everyday communications, verbal and non-verbal. Barthes suggests, for instance, that in our society visual images rarely appear without accompanying text which tends to foreclose on a range of possible connotations that the image by itself might have.[34] Others have developed ever greater refinements of the tripartite division of Peirce, relying on a distinction between denotation and connotation in attempting to show that varieties of signifying practices do not merely reproduce varieties of meanings but systematically foreclose on such ranges of meanings. The object of this analysis is to open up the flexibility of structuralist accounts of cultural production and reproduction so that they are not reduced to some mirror image or homology of some other level of analysis. One such contemporary account is articulated by Rosalind Coward, who argues that present usages of the notion of ideology, no matter how sophisticated, fail to grasp that the processes of signification are themselves autonomous and have no necessary correspondence to other levels of structural analysis. In *Language and Materialism* by Coward and Ellis, it is suggested that the way forward for cultural analysis is to accept the insights of Lacan: 'The analysis of the proper relations of the signifier leads to the conclusion that no meaning is sustained by anything other than reference to other meaning.'[35] This seems for all practical purposes to be approaching a *reductio ad absurdum* wherein the promise of semiotic analysis to open closed areas is itself reduced to the mere documentation of a constantly fluid cultural process. But we may ask what point has such analysis? Ought it not to illuminate the larger structural relationships which allow of closings and thus allow those using the dominant ideologies of our society to trade upon the weaknesses of routine perceptions? Even if it is the case that all the relationships between signifier and thing signified are arbitrary in the sense of having no necessary or natural connection (which thereby destroys the validity of the basic Peircean divisions), nevertheless to suggest that all signifying practices are of themselves arbitrary and autonomous is to mistake the issue at hand. As Eco points out 'the core of the problem is obviously the notion of convention which is not coextensive with that of arbitrary link but which is coextensive with that of *cultural* link.'[36] Because the production of signs is arbitrary, it in no way means that the cultural practices of signification which take place *within a code* are also arbitrary and autonomous. For, to take this position, as Coward and Ellis seem to do, would be to assume that there is no meta-language at all and that cultural analysis is empty except for the absolute autonomy of signifying practices. The point of engaging in television analysis, or any other cultural analysis, is to reveal the subtleties and refinements of ideological closure and imbalance by revealing the various codes in operation. In doing so one shows how much broader than particular ideologies is the shifting of 'the semantic universe' – in Eco's phrase. However, the purpose remains clear – to open up significant closures: 'Semiotics in its double guise as a theory of codes and a theory of sign production is also a form of social criticism, and therefore one among the many forms of social practice.'[37]

Thus in the work of visual analysis undertaken above we continued to rely on the simple Peircean division of the relationship between signified and signifier. We did this not because we felt that the problems of so doing could be avoided, but because in the particular field of empirical analysis such a use reveals cumulative examples of the codes with which the dominant ideology works in the production of television news.

An adversary relationship

The history of this project has been one in which considerable hostility and attempted interference has characterised the reactions of the broadcasters. While it is flattering to be the object of such activity (sustained as it has been and undertaken at the high levels it has been), it is perhaps important at this point that the more general history of the relationship between broadcasters and broadcasting researchers should not be forgotten. It is in fact the case that even more than with most professional groups coming under the scrutiny of academics, broadcasters have not hitherto in any way welcomed such attention. But we are only the inheritors of this poor tradition, not its creators.

Tom Burns recently described the difficulties he encountered as a researcher studying the BBC. These included vetoing publication of his work on the Corporation, a ban that was lifted only after many years. He points out that this kind of experience is not uncommon for social scientists studying the media. He cites Paul Lazarsfeld's 1948 article in *Journalism Quarterly* on 'The Role of Criticism in the

Management of Mass Media'. In the light of our more recent experience, Lazarsfeld's comment still sadly stands:[38]

> If there is any one institutional disease to which the media of mass communications seem particularly subject, it is a nervous reaction to criticism. As a student of mass media I have been continually struck and occasionally puzzled by this reaction, for it is the media themselves which so vigorously defend principles guaranteeing the right to criticise.

In the light of Lazarsfeld's comments on the broadcasters' espousal of the right to criticise, we can only wonder what world-view, what institutional ideology led to the following sort of debate in one of the highest councils of one of the world's leading cultural organisations:[39]

> DG said there would be no sense in attacking *Bad News* in detail . . . he thought however that the ideology of sociologists was a subject which would repay a little study and hoped that it would be possible for a programme like 'Analysis' to tackle it . . . Desmond Wilcox felt it would be dangerous to launch a widespread attack on the discipline of sociology, which included some perfectly responsible practitioners. It should attack, where necessary, particular arguments and . . . the standpoint from which they were presented. Michael Bunce repeated his view that the BBC should counter-attack spurious communicators and academics . . . DG agreed that the BBC could examine the aims and politics of sociology.

That a basis for a sociological critique of broadcast news might exist at no time seems to have entered the apparently fevered discussion of the Editor of News and Current Affairs's fortnightly meetings in the BBC.

What has been offered up here is not a contribution to an unnecessarily small-minded debate, but a detailed and documented critique of the ideology and practice of current television journalism – a first step in the decoding of the all-pervasive messages of the electronic media.

Appendix A   Just One Week

Regional news: a Scottish sample

We viewed and analysed a week's output of *Scotland Today* and
Reporting Scotland which are STV's and BBC-Scotland's regional
news magazine programmes respectively. The period selected for
analysis was 15–22 May 1975. Although we collected regional
output at other times, this was done for specific purposes such as
comparing national and regional coverage of the Glasgow dustcart
drivers' dispute in the previous months. We gathered a complete set
of regional tapes during the week in May for the purpose of
systematically comparing the national with the regional output.

The tapes were viewed and logged according to the logging
procedure described in *Bad News*. The logging sheet conveys basic
information about the resources which are used in each news item
(technical resources and personnel), who actually appears and the
length and content of each story. This information is helpful in
assessing the priorities attributed to different stories. However,
most of the technical information about film, video-tape and other
inputs was not of central importance to this sample comparison,
which was more concerned with questions of structuring, story
content and presentation.

The news stories had to be categorised so that comparisons
between the two types of programme would be possible. The
categories used were broadly the same as those used in the main
national sample. They were developed from 'commonsense'
criteria which stemmed from what we knew of the professional
practices of the producers. We rejected the generation of categories
according to prior analytic criteria and followed as closely as
possible the division of labour practised within the newsrooms.[1]

In the newsrooms the basic discrete areas of reporting are

represented on the screen by different correspondents – diplomatic, industrial, economic, etc. This division of labour is not hard and fast. Some areas are discernible as story-types without having correspondents allocated to them – Human Interest and Disasters are areas of general reporting which routinely occur. Thus the system outlined was not totally delimited by the presence of an identifiable correspondent, but by a professionally identified strand of stories. In the regional news, identifiable correspondents are fewer than on the national news, and reporting tends to be done according to the availability of news personnel for a particular story, rather than by specialists in the field. We continued to work with the ten basic story categories, the only difference being the addition of a new sub-category (60) of Home Affairs for Religious Affairs.

This was because the period chosen for analysis coincided with the week in which the General Assembly of the Church of Scotland met. It should be noted that this does not necessarily reflect any sort of norm in the regional news and the reason why the Church of Scotland stories were not incorporated into any of the former categories was because of the large proportion of time devoted to the Assembly. This, as well as the fact that the Assembly was not covered as an ordinary news item (at least by BBC; see below), would, it was felt, distort the pattern one would have got in an 'average' week.

Both organisations producing the regional news (STV and BBC-Scotland) were visited in an effort to discover what were the assumptions which determined the output of the regional news magazines. Initially, interviews were conducted with Heads of News in both institutions. This was followed up by a day spent in the BBC-Scotland newsroom, and with a news reporter covering an industrial story.

The initial meeting with heads of department (called News Editors, although the day-to-day editing is done by someone else) were rather formal and they described what they saw as the role of regional news on television. Neither of the two news editors saw the regional news as being solely complementary to the main national news bulletins. But one got the impression that both of them implicitly assumed that all the 'really important' news had already been broadcast in the early news bulletins on both channels immediately preceding the regional programmes. If any story in the early evening bulletins was deemed to have a particular significance to Scotland and was not sufficiently covered, there was, they said, a 'fairly good chance' that it would be followed up in the regional news. The IBA *Handbook* has this to say about the local news:[2]

Local News programmes set out to cover rather more than a report of the day's news as seen on film and in the studio. Their value to viewers in each area derives from the information they give on a wide range of topics of recurring interest. These include detailed weather forecasts in areas with a significant number of farmers, fishermen and market gardeners, employment prospects, correspondence columns of the air, advice and discussion of legal rights and liaison with the local police forces in items which assist in crime detection.

The official BBC perspective on the subject is very similar. On both channels the news editors saw the regional news as having a more 'people-orientated' approach than the rather impersonal national news bulletins. They emphasised the content being something the audience could relate to on an immediate level. Perhaps this accounts for the fact that one can often hear regional accents (albeit of a rarified kind) on the regional news.

The actual output was, it seemed, the result of events and public tastes. In fact, the BBC news editor said that the news was to him 'whatever was of any interest to the public'. When questioned as to what he thought was of any interest to the 'public' he replied with words to the effect that it was something one had the 'feel' for, growing out of years of journalistic experience. All programme work was, he indicated, conducted against the backdrop of the anticipated reaction of an invisible audience. Thus a priority is given to events which will, it is assumed, tend to be of interest to a 'mass audience'. This, as our examination of the output shows, leads to a stereotyped formula of mass journalism, so-called human stories – folksy sentimentality in stories which reiterate or are thought to reiterate stereotypical images which abound in mass society. This, of course, has been part of the stock-in-trade of mass journalism for well over 100 years and occurs in the national news as well, but the emphasis is heightened in the regional news and plays an important part in the selection of events being classified as news. The news editor of STV said during the interview, '*Scotland Today* is a straight mix between news and human interest stories'. Even in the covering of events which do not lend themselves to the conventional categorisation of human interest, an effort is sometimes made to 'humanise' the stories. The relationship of producers to audience is characterised by an in-built need to reach a *modus vivendi* with the invisible audience, an audience deemed to be co-terminous with the entire society. The local geographical area, not necessarily being a microcosm of larger society, has different audience profiles from the national news and attention is paid to this. But this priority is often at odds with other objectives of the broadcasting organisation. The news editor of STV, after having stressed the importance of the public moods and opinion, also mentioned that in the day-to-day running of the organisation what was featured in the output was basically what six or seven people in the newsroom believed news to be.

Our visit to BBC-Scotland's newsroom showed that the selection of what was to be a part of the evening's broadcast was done by the editorial staff and the news team sifting through information provided in government handouts, Press Association wire services and the daily morning newspapers. Provision was made for someone to stand by in case an unforeseen story of importance arose. Once a general list of news events had been selected, individual reporters were then assigned. The newspapers consulted were both local and national, both the 'quality' and 'popular' press. But they did not include any newspaper which could be termed even broadly as the 'alternative' press (such as the *Morning Star*).

Almost every member of the news team had a background in press journalism, including experience in such papers as the *Daily Express* and the *Daily Record* and major local papers such as the *Belfast Telegraph*. Television journalists in Britain at the local level as well as nationally have inherited historically and through the processes of professional socialisation the assumptions and methods (where appropriate) of print journalists.

One week of local news: a content analysis

In our analysis of the structure of the national news in Volume 1, we drew several conclusions: (i) that the length and scheduled time of the news is a product of the historical place of the news in television output as a whole, the daily exigencies of scheduling and the need to cover extraordinary events; (ii) that profiles of national news represent a 'quality' mix of stories; i.e. the proportion of time devoted in the news to political, economic, industrial and foreign news is consistently much higher than that given to crime, human interest and disaster stories; (iii) that the structure on both channels is fairly stable from week to week. Although varying from category to category, it represents continuous and predictable levels of inputs.[3]

The local news has, for a variety of reasons, a different placing from the national news and the audience for each is much smaller although, region by region, it begins to match the audience for the networked bulletins. BBC's own research reveals that for 1973 approximately 800,000 watched the Scottish regional news magazine. Significant absences from national news can be covered in the regional news – for instance, during the dustcart drivers' dispute some strikers were interviewed in the regional news. But the national impression created by the networked bulletins nevertheless remained. For the rest of Britain, the strikers had no direct voice.

Essentially the regional news on both channels is part of the magazine programmes. Regional news on both channels occupies the slot (between 6.00 p.m. and 6.30 p.m.) which had traditionally been observed by the BBC as the 'toddlers truce' – that is, they leave the screen 'empty' to enable parents to get young children to bed without competition. The rationale given behind the magazine format was thus to give families something to watch which did not require a lot of attention and during which domestic tasks could be carried out simultaneously while glancing at the screen from time to time, watching an item here and an item there without necessarily watching the whole programme.

The length of the programmes reflects this. The average lengths of the regional news in the sample week were 23.76 minutes on STV and 26.2 minutes on BBC. The lengths varied from 21.73 to 28.43 minutes on STV and from 21.2 minutes to 34.5 minutes on BBC-Scotland. The variations in length are not usually as great as this. The news editor of BBC-Scotland explained that 22 minutes was nearer the norm but that that particular week was different because of the extensive coverage of the General Assembly of the Church of Scotland. It was explained that this was because BBC-Scotland had traditionally devoted a full programme to the Assembly (which, in its eyes, seemed to be a sort of substitute for a Scottish Parliament). STV, while covering the Assembly, did not give it quite as extensive treatment as BBC. In comparing variations in the length of regional news bulletins with national news bulletins of comparable average lengths, the former show a greater degree of variability.

The number of items appearing on the regional programmes varied considerably from day to day. This was especially true in the case of BBC-Scotland's *Reporting Scotland*, where during the particular week items ranged from 11 per bulletin to 21. On STV the variation was much less marked. The average number of items on BBC was 13.8 and on STV 15.2. This seems to contradict our earlier findings for the national news that, the longer the news, the greater the number of stories covered.[4] However, it would be a mistake to take the fewer items on BBC news magazine as an indication of greater 'in-depth' reporting. The variation in this case had again been caused by the extended coverage of the Church of Scotland Assembly. It is, however, significant to note that in comparison to national bulletins of similar length (i.e. the *Nine O'Clock News* on BBC and *News at Ten* on ITN) the number of items contained are similar, i.e. 12.2 for BBC and 14.1 for ITN.

The average duration of items was 1.5 minutes for *Scotland Today* and 1.9 minutes for *Reporting Scotland*. This is in fact quite similar to the mean item durations for national news bulletins of similar length. The distribution of item duration is also not very different from that in the national news bulletins. The majority of items are less than 1 minute in length. As in the national news bulletins, the BBC regional news bulletins have a slightly lower proportion of longer items than STV. However, the variations in item duration on regional bulletins are greater than on the national news, from 11 seconds to 8 minutes 15 seconds on STV and from 16 seconds to 7 minutes 25 seconds on BBC (this is excluding 10-minute extensions for the General Assembly of the Church of Scotland). It is difficult to say in the case of regional news whether the duration of an item is the best indication of the importance attributed to it. Sometimes items of over 5 minutes are put into the news for reasons other than their 'newsworthiness'. This is illustrated for instance on 22 May 1975 when there was a feature of over 8 minutes about farming on the Clyde valley which was not of any immediate news value (it was actually filmed a few months before it was shown). The STV news editor justified it being a part of the programme by saying that 'it provided a break from the monotony of urban life'. Generally, however, the longer items arise out of certain priorities in news gathering and news processing. Thus, the Conservative party's Scottish conference merited a five-minute item (BBC1, 16 May 1975) which was in keeping with the shorter

coverage in the national news. The variations also reflect organisational arrangements within respective newsrooms.

Content profiles of regional news

Figure A.1 is a content profile of the regional news magazines on
BBC-Scotland and STV respectively. Each column represents the
percentage of time devoted in the programmes to each category

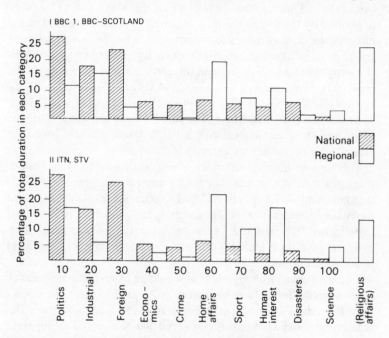

Figure A.1   Content profiles for national and regional samples

during the particular week. As is to be expected, local affairs
represents the single largest category (with the exception of
religious affairs, the reasons for which have been explained above)
in the output – 21.5 per cent on STV and 19.1 per cent on BBC. This
category includes all such matters as local government, consumer
news, environment and race. Most of the output in this category
during the sample week on both channels was concerned with the
local government reorganisation that was occurring in Scotland at
the time. The source of most of the information was press releases
from the Strathclyde Regional Council. However, an attempt

towards achieving balance was made in terms of interviews with people opposed to the reorganisation and by carrying out *vox pops*. 'Human interest' stories accounted for a large proportion of the output on both channels (10.1 per cent on BBC-Scotland and 17.5 per cent on STV). Compared to the national news (for which the figures for this category in all bulletins are 3.7 per cent on BBC1 and 3.1 per cent on ITN) the regional figures bear out what the respective news editors said about the regional news being more 'people-orientated'. The variation between BBC-Scotland and STV can be explained by the fact that BBC's *Reporting Scotland* is a part of the national news magazine programme, *Nationwide*, which tends to cover most of the outstanding 'human interest' stories, wherever they might happen. The 'human interest' stories were mainly of the type one might see in a popular newspaper – Nurse of the Year Award (BBC1, 19 May 1975), Bullock Runs Amok (STV, 22 May), Sporran Tax (STV, 20 May). The news editors see these stories as providing their audiences with a break from the humdrum and melancholy of modern industrial life.

Politics was another category which accounted for a significant proportion of the output, on both channels (12.1 per cent BBC-Scotland and 17.1 per cent STV). The sort of events covered were party conferences, parliamentary laws, etc., which were of special significance to Scotland or were occurring in Scotland. This category did not include political events arising out of local government affairs.

The amount of foreign news, as would be expected in regional or local news bulletins, was negligible on both channels. The reason why BBC had as much as 4 per cent had to do with the EEC referendum (which was only covered nationally and in separate programmes on the other channel) rather than with any actual reporting events occurring abroad. The rest of the story categories, i.e. economics, crime, disaster and science, formed a small part of the output on both channels.

A significant variation occurred in the coverage of industrial stories. The STV coverage was slightly above 5 per cent while on BBC it was around 15 per cent.

Generally, in comparing the content profiles of the two channels (with the exception of industrial and religious affairs) they seem to follow similar patterns. This tends to support the notion that the shape of a news bulletin has less to do with the patterns of events in the 'real world' than with patterns of professional practice. In comparison with profiles of the national news, these profiles are different on a few counts; while political and industrial and home affairs account for a large part of the output as in the national news, the proportion of foreign news is negligible and human interest stories are very much in the forefront. Industrial stories play an important part in the BBC output.

A detailed analysis of the 'industry' category was undertaken for the reasons given in the general design of our study. Here, it is necessary to examine this coverage to see to what extent the claim that it complements the network bulletins can be sustained.

In the week covered, industrial news accounted for 5 per cent of STV's output and about 15 per cent of BBC-Scotland's. The variation is most probably not the norm and reflects organisational differences in the respective newsrooms in relation to the availability of resources for that week. To arrive at any generalisation about the priorities of the organisations on the basis of a week's sample of output would be dubious. The average duration of each industrial item was 0.57 minutes on STV and 1.34 minutes on BBC. This contrasted with the figures for industrial items on the national news (1.18 minutes on BBC and 1.62 on ITN). Most of the items on both the regional news programmes were very short, not lasting more than 20 seconds.

Each industrial item was noted separately on an industrial logging sheet in an attempt to find out exactly what information was conveyed in the reporting of industrial news. As has been stated earlier, the scope of information was necessarily limited by the brevity of the items. The logging sheet itself was designed to convey information such as what the story was about, how many workers it involved, whether a dispute attributed causation, whether it was official or not, the unions involved and the kind of language used. An attempt was made to find out how much of this information was stated/not stated in the reporting of each individual story. This log provides an indicator of the range and amount of information provided by industrial reporting on television news.

There were 30 industrial stories in the week (14 on STV and 16 on BBC). These stories covered 10 disputes, redundancies, job creations and occupations. The unions involved were mentioned in only 2 of the stories (the NUM – BBC, 20 May, the Steel Workers' Union – BBC, 16 May). The number of workers involved were stated in 14 of the stories. The causes given for redundancy or dispute were in all cases except 2 attributed either to the government or to management. In the case of industrial disputes the official status of the dispute, or otherwise, was never given.

Thus, much the same lacunae as we have noted in the network bulletins recur at the local level. The reason given for this, by the news editors of the respective programmes, was either that the public did not want to know, or that exigencies of timing prevented any more details being reported. There is therefore little indication from this sample that regional news complements national news in the industrial area.

The main industrial stories in Scotland that week were about redundancies – the central ones being about the Chrysler Linwood plant and the British Steel Corporation (BSC). The Chrysler story, in which over 4,000 workers faced redundancy, was given similar treatment by both channels (15 May 1975 and 16 May 1975). BBC devoted 1 minute 12 seconds to the story over 2 days while STV spent 25 seconds on it in 1 day. Essentially these items contained reports of a Chrysler management statement that about 4,000 men were to be laid off, and that the main cause of the intended layoffs was the strike by the workers at Chrysler's Coventry plant. The second BBC item reiterated that this was the cause, quoting Chrysler's national management. The chief shop steward at Linwood was also quoted as expressing solidarity with the workers at Coventry. There was no mention of the unions involved.

The other main industrial story of the week was also about redundancies – British Steel Corporation workers had just held a demonstration in London, protesting about 4,000 prospective redundancies. This story was given a considerably more extensive coverage (at least in terms of time) than any other industrial stories that week. BBC-Scotland devoted 2.45 minutes on the day of the demonstration which was followed by a 5.5 minute item the next day. STV had one item over 5 minutes on the actual day of the march. The same story was reported nationally over three days in the early evening bulletins (on both channels) with BBC1 spending 4.5 minutes on it and ITN 3.9 minutes. Generally, the coverage on the regional news was more extensive as regards both time and information provided than the early national news. BBC-Scotland coverage included quotes from both union officials at a national level (Bill Sirs arguing that the situation was not a crisis and that he did not want any intervention from workers in any other industry) as well as a *vox pop.* with ordinary rank-and-file trade unionists. They, however, painted a rather different picture in terms of the outcome of the talks in London, which one of them described as 'anything but a victory'. However, most of the time on the second BBC item was spent interviewing an 'expert' (a sociologist) about whether it was possible to get around the redundancies by short-time working and work-sharing. No attempt was made to elaborate the reasons why the redundancies might occur except that they had been brought about by 'a general recession in the steel industry'. More significantly, there was no mention in either of the BBC items that the demonstration in London was backed up by a twenty-four hour strike by the steel workers in Scotland. STV's coverage provided some information concerning Sir Monty Finneston's views on the general economic recession causing the redundancies and reported the fact that there was a strike. The workers' point of view was 'represented' by Dr Bray, MP for Motherwell and Wishaw, who chaired the meeting following the demonstration.

The other industrial items were mainly concerned with local firms and received no mentions on the national news. There was a low correlation between the two channels with respect to stories reported. This reveals either rather arbitrary coverage or a significant lack of agreement on local 'news sense'. Of the 16 items of industrial news on BBC and the 14 items on STV, there were only 5 items which were reported on both channels. The 5 items in common were ones which were important enough to get 'widespread' public attention. This runs counter to the trend observed in the national news where the same stories appear on both channels. However, the same priorities were seen to be maintained in relation to the items that were common to both channels.

On the basis of this week's sample we can note certain trends in the manner in which regional news is presented and the similarity of these to those in the national news. There is an essential similarity in terms of overall informational mix between the two channels. This was seen in the analysis of the content profiles.

The major differences between the national and regional news are formal (i.e. regional news is not presented as a bulletin, but rather as a news magazine) and following from this structural difference is the difference in emphasis. National news presents itself to its audience as covering the 'serious news', whereas regional news on both channels is much less formal, presenting a larger proportion of 'human interest' stories. The output viewed and the content analysis confirmed the news editors' image (on both channels) of the regional news being more 'people orientated'. The extent to which the regional programmes could be said to have complemented the national bulletins was limited, although it did occur (the BSC and Chrysler stories, for instance). Generally, however, most of the items were selected according to regional news criteria and were not seen as an extension of the national news.

The coverage of industrial news, in the sample week, was, in terms of information conveyed, as sketchy as its counterpart nationally. There was little effort made to convey basic information – as was seen in the coverage of redundancies, especially in the failure to mention the unions involved or to obtain rank-and-file points of view. Much of the information given was in the form of reported management statements. While we would not claim that intentional distortion occurred in the regional news any more than in the national news, it is clear that closely similar professional routines and practices apply to the selection, processing and presentation of news and that there is no sense in which regional news can be said generally to give greater detail or provide more thorough treatment of the range of issues reported in the national bulletins.

Just another week

A number of changes in the news were heralded by the broadcasters and the press in the year following our six months of monitoring. A few of them, including the BBC's reversion to a single newsreader, simplified titles and a more 'matter of fact' style, were mentioned in *Bad News*. We then reported that there was no evidence that these changes had affected the basic pattern of the bulletins.[5] Subsequent changes on ITN looked as though they might be more far-reaching. Robert Kee's departure from *First Report* and Alastair Burnet's arrival as the presenter of an extended early evening bulletin were regarded as important by ITN. Indeed it seemed that the changes would allow significant innovations to occur.

With a view to assessing and comparing the news a year after the main study we recorded four days' output of national news on BBC and ITN from 31 August to 3 September 1976. We calculated profiles of item number and length, and content profiles using the same categories as earlier. We also drew up a list of interviewees to see whether there was any divergence in the hierarchical pattern which we had observed previously.

The figures for the average number of items for selected bulletins in the original sample (Sample 1) and the secondary sample (Sample 2) are given in Table A.1. In the case of the main evening

Table A.1   Number of items in each bulletin (weekdays)

	Sample 1	Sample 2
First Report/*News at One*	7.1	9.0
ITN early bulletin/*News at 5.45*	9.3	14.0
BBC1 *Nine O'Clock News*	12.2	13.3
ITN *News at Ten*	14.1	13.3

bulletins on each channel, there is no suggestion of a significant change. In the case of the ITN early evening bulletins there is the expected increase in the average number of items in Sample 2, based on the fifteen-minute instead of the ten-minute bulletin. The variation is expected because it conforms to the general principle that the number of items increases steadily with the length of the bulletins. Instead of further exploring the possibilities of a current affairs format, the extra time is devoted to more stories rather than to greater depth or analysis of the same number of stories. In fact, the fall in the average number of items in ITN's 1 o'clock bulletin suggests that there has been a move away from the tendency to treat fewer stories at greater length, which was one of the key characteristics of *First Report* in 1975.

This is also reflected in the figures for the average duration of items. Table A.2 again shows the strong similarity of pattern between the two samples, with the exception of the ITN bulletins at 1 o'clock. The average length of items in Sample 2 (2 minutes 12 seconds) is noticeably shorter than the average length of items in Sample 1 (2 minutes 40 seconds). However, the tendency to spend more time on fewer stories can still be seen in *News at One* when it is compared with the other bulletins.

Table A.2   Average duration of items (weekdays)

	Sample 1	Sample 2
First Report/*News at One*	2.40	2.12
ITN early bulletin/*News at 5.45*	1.00	1.00
BBC1 *Nine O'Clock News*	1.40	1.43
ITN *News at Ten*	1.35	1.36

We next compared the content profiles of the main evening bulletins on BBC and ITN, using the ten-fold categorisation based on professional practice in the newsrooms (see *Bad News*, Appendix I for details of this categorisation and how it was operated). The findings are given in Table A.3. The figures are based on the distribution of the number of items in each category rather than their relative duration.

Table A.3   Distribution of items by bulletins (weekdays), showing percentage of items in each category

	BBC *Nine O'Clock News*		ITN *News at Ten*	
	Sample 1	Sample 2	Sample 1	Sample 2
10 Political	21.6	1.9	21.1	3.8
20 Industrial	16.6	13.0	13.1	7.7
30 Foreign	21.1	29.6	25.9	25.0
40 Economic	9.8	3.7	7.6	1.9
50 Crime	4.5	11.1	5.1	13.5
60 Home affairs	6.9	14.8	7.2	17.3
70 Sport	7.5	13.0	7.4	13.5
80 Human interest	5.4	9.3	6.6	11.5
90 Disasters	5.1	3.7	4.4	3.8
00 Science	1.5	—	1.6	1.9
TOTAL %	100.0	100.1	100.0	99.9
n =	826	54	942	52

In this table there are some obvious differences between the two samples. On both channels there is a marked absence of political news in Sample 2 as compared with Sample 1, in which the political category was one of the largest. There is also a relative decline in the size of the industrial and economic categories. In contrast, there are more crime, home affairs, sport and human interest stories in the second sample. Some of the gross variations can be explained quite simply. Parliament was in recess at the time of the repeat study and this undoubtedly accounts for the lack of political news in Sample 2. This is because 'political' in the newsrooms is virtually synonymous with 'parliamentary'. The lead stories in the bulletins in Sample 2 were the Notting Hill carnival riots, the Hull prison riot, the Northern Ireland torture report and the riots in Cape Town. Therefore, much of the time which would have been filled by politics news in 'normal' circumstances (with a regular flow of parliamentary news) was taken up in these bulletins by home affairs, crime and foreign stories.

What is most significant about these findings is that they tend to confirm rather than contradict the conclusions of our study of longitudinal variations in content profiles.[6] We stated earlier that the three major categories of political, industrial and foreign news never occupy less than 50 per cent of total news time in any one week and usually account for much more. Conversely, it is rare (though not unknown) for any single other category to take up more than 10 per cent of the time in a week. If the home affairs stories are regarded as a substitute for political stories when there is a lack of parliamentary news, then this pattern is confirmed. It implies that the bulletin structures in September 1976 continued to reflect the professional norm that television news should have a category distribution which is more like that of the 'quality' than the popular press. It is interesting to note that the broadcasters interpret favourably, but without explanation, the close correlation between the leading stories of the main evening television bulletins and the front-page stories of *The Times* on the following day.[7] They imply that this consensus of 'news values' is evidence of quality journalism on television. We have already shown that this is misleading because, for example, *within* the same overall story distribution television displays tendencies noted in the popular rather than the quality press.[8]

The running order of the items in a bulletin has certain predictable features. We noted in *Bad News* that there was a strong tendency to lead with political, industrial and foreign news and to conclude with sport, human interest and science stories.[9] Again, this can be regarded as an expression of the professional norm that 'serious' stories should have greater priority, in keeping with television news commitment to a 'quality' profile. In our supplementary study we found that the placing of stories followed the predicted pattern. Moreover, there was the anticipated close correlation between channels such that on two days the lead stories were identical. On the days when they were not identical, the story chosen as a lead by one channel invariably appeared second or third in the running order in the competing bulletin. In the sample period all the payoff items on both channels fell into the home affairs, sport and human interest categories. From this brief sample we conclude that in the year following the main study there was no observable change in the relative priorities assigned to different story categories in terms of their placing in the bulletins.

In the main evening news bulletins during the four-day sample period there were interviews with 31 people on BBC and 24 people on ITN. The percentage of items with interviews is of the same order as the figures obtained in the 1975 study – between 30 and 40 per cent. The earlier finding that BBC has a larger proportion of items with interviews than does ITN is confirmed. There is also a notable similarity between the samples in terms of the way in which interviews are used, an observation which was also made in Volume 1 of our study.[10] First, spokesmen and opposition spokesmen are interviewed more frequently than either central figures or witnesses, for example, while experts and *vox pops* are used even more sparingly. Second, the seven interviewees who appeared on both channels in the four-day period were almost exclusively high-ranking politicians or public servants – J. Callaghan (Prime Minister), D. Howell (Drought Minister), B. Faulkner (former Northern Ireland Prime Minister), D. Costello (Irish Solicitor-General), Sir R. Mark (Chief Commissioner of Police). The other two interviewees were L. Murray (General Secretary of the TUC) and P. Shaw (an inventor). The news at this time continued to talk to the powerful. This is further illustrated by the fact that only two women were interviewed during this period and neither of them were named – a sign of low status in the cultural coding of television news. The other unnamed interviewees included a Black resident affected by the Notting Hill carnival riots, workers at Longbridge, prisoners and an unemployed worker. This is further evidence of a hierarchical ordering of those who appear on television to state their case.

Appendix B   Identifying Explanatory Themes

During the first months of 1975, the economic crisis was a persistent concern of all news bulletins. We took as our sample for the case study (see Part 1, above) all news items which directly related to the economy and to the political debates surrounding the management of the developing crisis. This sample was taken from the national television news of ITN, BBC1 and BBC2 from 1 January to 30 April 1975.

As with our earlier analysis of the first five months of 1975 (*Bad News*), there are some gaps due to technical failures which prevented the recording of some bulletins or parts of bulletins. However, the overall proportion of such gaps was very small and their occurrence within the sample was random. In addition, as this particular case study involved textual analysis, we were able to further reduce the small number of omissions in the case of BBC1 and BBC2 by using archive microfilm of programme scripts provided by the BBC. We dealt with an almost continuous flow of news from the three national television news networks, daily for four months. Our method of analysis in this area was to identify the different explanatory themes in the text of news bulletins. These themes are references to particular explanations of economic and political events and typically contain diagnoses and prescriptions. They point to specific causes and/or solutions of the economic crisis. The themes are limited in number and often references to the same explanation recurred throughout the four-month period from one bulletin to the next. Below, we give some examples of how they were identified and recorded:

Newscaster: The Chancellor, Mr Healey, has warned that wage increases are the main cause of inflation and that it is irresponsible lunacy to ignore this. He told a private meeting of the Parliamentary Labour Party at the Commons that there was a danger of inflation rising to double that of other Western nations; to ignore this, he said, would be to commit a very primitive error. (ITN, 17.50, 19 March)

This would be recorded as a *Reported statement* from Mr Healey which identifies *Wages* as *Cause*. Often a statement contained identification of both cause and solution. For example:

Industrial Correspondent: With wages now as the main boost to inflation, just getting down inflation to a reasonable level seems to imply tougher pay restraint. (BBC1, 21.00, 20 January 1975)

This would be recorded as a *Media statement* identifying *Wages* as *Cause*, and a *Media statement/Pay restraint/Solution*. By media statement we mean an opinion directly expressed by media personnel which is not attributed to other sources. The source of references to explanatory themes was often significant. In all of our analyses we identified the source of such references. Altogether there were four – *Reported statements, Media statements*, and, within interviews, *Interview questions* and *Interview responses*. For example an interview on ITN's *First Report*:

Interviewer: Now inasmuch as your reappraisal might lead to higher wage settlements, how much do you take into account the warning Mr Healey, your Chancellor, was giving only at the weekend that it was a wage inflation that was now the real danger to Britain's economy?
Interviewee: Well I have never accepted that wages are the root cause of Britain's economic difficulties. (ITN, 13.00, 27 February 1975)

Here we recorded *Interview question/Wages/Cause* and *Interview response/Wages/Cause/Negative*. Later on in the same interview we find the rejection of one framework there and the insertion of another:

Interviewee: But I do not accept, and I don't think the majority of trade unionists accept, that British economic ills are because there's wage inflation. It is because there is lack of investment and this is one of the things that we've been talking about at a recent seminar this morning.

Thus we recorded *Interview response/Wages/Cause/Negative* and *Interview response/Investment/Cause*.

It should be noted that excerpts of public speeches, addresses to conferences, etc., shown on film or video-tape are recorded here within the category *Interview response*. In the case of public speakers shown, not merely quoted, on the news, the same level of possible mediation of content operates as in the recorded interview in terms of the selection by the media of those parts of the speech or interview which are to be highlighted in the news report. If the interview is live (as is often the case in ITN's *First Report*) then the mediation of the interview as message occurs at least in terms of the structuring of the interview by the kind of questions asked and the direction in which the interviewer may push the line of argument – the agenda-setting function of the interviewer. Some further examples will serve to indicate the method of identifying the themes which occur in our sample period:

> News journalist: Sir Keith Joseph, the opposition's Head of Policy and Research, said that the government's reliance on the Social Contract and their delay in tackling public spending had meant that our recession and inflation would drag on while other countries had got over theirs faster. (ITN, 22.00, 21 April 1975)

Here we recorded, *Reported statement/Government expenditure/ Cause*.

> Newscaster: And it's been the final day of the debate on the Budget in the Commons. MPs were told by Sir Keith Joseph for the opposition that there had to be cuts in public spending. Here's Christine Eade of our Westminster staff.
> Reporter: Sir Keith's diagnosis of the national problem was that we were over-spending, over-taxing, over-borrowing, and overmanning. Yet because the government over-relied on the Social Contract our recession would drag on longer than other countries'. We would then need a more prolonged dose of medicine. Sir Keith believed that no Chancellor could prevent trade unions prising people out of a job but he ended his speech with seemingly greater sympathy for management, the ulcer people as he called them; the difference between their pay and those of the people they were supervising grew less. He concluded they

would either join the brain drain and go abroad or switch off mentally while staying here. (BBC1, 17.45, 30 April 1975)

For the newscaster's introduction we recorded *Reported statement/ Cut government expenditure/Solution*, and from the Westminster correspondent's report we recorded *Reported statement/Government expenditure/Cause, Reported statement/Taxation/Cause, Reported statement/Overmanning/Cause, Reported statement/ Borrowing by government/Cause* and *Reported statement/Wages/ Cause* (i.e. trade unions' wage demands cause unemployment and they 'price themselves out of the job').

Correspondent: Today is the day when the opposition set about the Chancellor and tell him what's wrong with his Budget and this the Shadow Chancellor did with gusto and with a mass of critical quotes. After the Budget, said Sir Geoffrey, the British people must be crying out come back Sir Stafford Cripps all is forgiven. The government had caught the English disease. A very high temperature of inflation at 20 per cent, chronic overweight in bloated public spending supported on crutches of overseas loans and that from a Chancellor who once complained about begging from the Arabs. Public spending was virtually out of control and if that went on we would be on the brink of hyperinflation. Mr Healey, said Sir Geoffrey, was facing the same problem as Errol Flynn. He was unwilling to reconcile his net income with his gross habits. What's more the higher taxes wouldn't mop up inflation. They will add fuel to the flame. So we all had to suffer this collective punishment which was, said Sir Geoffrey, a feature of the government's socialist society. (BBC1, 21.00, 16 April 1975)

From our last examples above, we recorded, *Reported statement/ Government expenditure/Cause* and *Reported statement/Taxation/ Cause*.

See also Tables B.1 and B.2.

Table B.1 Causes of economic crisis identified on TV news, showing references to problems identified by channel and form in which they appeared.

Problem identified	Media statement			Reported statement			Interview question			Interview response			Total all channels
	BBC1	ITN	BBC2	BBC1	ITN	BBC2	BBC1	ITN	BBC2	BBC1	ITN	BBC2	
Wages	7	4	3	28	17	11	2	8	2	1	10	3	96
(Negative)	—	—	—	(2)	(3)	(2)	—	—	—	—	(5)	1	(12)
Investment	—	3	—	3	8	3	—	2	—	8	5	—	33
Oil price	6	2	4	5	5	—	2	1	—	2	2	—	29
Government borrowing	2	1	—	7	3	3	1	—	—	2	1	2	23
Government expenditure	—	—	—	8	6	2	—	2	1	—	4	—	22
High taxation on industry	—	—	—	2	—	2	—	2	—	—	6	—	10
Price control	—	—	—	2	1	1	—	—	—	—	2	—	5
Overmanning	—	—	—	2	1	2	—	—	—	—	—	—	5
(Negative)	—	—	—	—	—	(1)	—	—	—	—	(1)	—	(2)
Speculation	—	—	—	—	1	1	—	—	—	—	2	—	2
Management	—	—	—	—	1	—	—	—	—	—	—	—	2
World recession	—	—	1	—	1	—	—	—	—	—	—	—	2
Tax evasion	—	—	—	—	—	—	—	—	—	—	2	—	2
High interest rates	—	—	—	—	—	—	—	—	—	—	1	—	1
Foreign imports	—	1	—	—	—	—	—	—	—	—	—	—	1

Table B.2 Policies or solutions to economic crisis identified on TV news, showing references to policies identified by channel and form in which they appeared

Proposed solution	Media statement BBC1	ITN	BBC2	Reported statement BBC1	ITN	BBC2	Interview question BBC1	ITN	BBC2	Interview response BBC1	ITN	BBC2	Total all channels
Voluntary wage restraint	2	3	1	75	62	45	7	28	11	9	27	17	287
(Negative)	—	—	—	(2)	(12)	(1)	—	—	—	(2)	—	—	(17)
Defend living standards	—	—	—	20	25	8	5	2	—	7	9	3	79
(Negative)	—	—	—	(4)	(2)	(1)	—	—	—	(3)	(3)	(2)	(15)
Expand public sector	—	2	—	10	12	3	—	—	—	6	10	4	47
(Negative)	(2)	—	—	(11)	(14)	(7)	—	(2)	—	(5)	(8)	(1)	(50)
Cut government expenditure	—	—	—	7	5	4	—	1	—	4	—	—	21
(Negative)	—	—	—	(1)	—	—	—	—	(1)	—	—	—	(1)
Reduce company tax	—	—	—	2	3	3	—	—	—	2	3	2	15
Better communication	—	—	—	1	3	3	1	—	—	6	—	—	14
(Negative)	—	(1)	—	—	—	—	—	—	—	(1)	(2)	(2)	(6)
Increase personal taxation	—	—	—	6	5	2	—	—	—	—	—	—	13
(Negative)	—	—	—	—	(1)	(1)	—	—	—	—	—	—	(2)
Tax the rich	—	—	—	2	3	—	—	2	—	5	—	—	12
(Negative)	—	—	—	(1)	—	(1)	—	(2)	—	—	—	—	(4)
Abolition of price control	—	—	—	4	1	3	—	—	—	3	—	—	11
(Negative)	—	—	—	—	(1)	—	—	(1)	—	(3)	—	(1)	(6)
Increased profits	—	—	—	2	1	2	—	—	—	2	2	1	10
Statutory wage control	—	—	—	2	1	—	—	5	—	—	—	—	8
(Negative)	—	—	—	(7)	(3)	(4)	—	—	—	(5)	—	(1)	(20)
Private sector investment	—	3	—	2	1	1	—	—	—	1	1	—	9
Import controls	—	—	—	3	3	—	—	—	—	—	—	1	7
Reduction of VAT rates	—	—	—	1	—	2	—	—	—	3	—	—	6
Stop export of capital	—	—	—	—	—	—	—	—	—	2	—	—	2
Lower interest rates	—	—	—	—	—	—	—	—	—	1	—	—	1

Appendix C The Events of Sunday 11 May–Saturday 17 May 1975

Saigon had been in the hands of the Provisional Revolutionary Government for about a fortnight when the week under consideration began, and the media's attention was still focused on South-East Asia. On Sunday 11 May every bulletin carried a small story from the area. Planes flown out of Saigon in the last hours before the arrival of the communists were reported as having arrived at Guam on board a United States carrier. America was expected to keep the aircraft, mainly helicopters, despite the demands of the Viet Cong that they be returned. Reports out of Washington emphasised that another of the Indo-Chinese states was about to become communist. It was Laos' 28th Constitution Day and the communist Pathet Lao were in evidence at the parade. In the German School six miles from Vientiane a group of cadets sat-in to protest the continued presence of the right-wing in the government. This followed the resignation of the Finance and Defence Ministers and took place against a background of refugees crossing the Mekong in advance of the takeover. Also on Sunday Phnom Penh Radio, now held by the Khmer Rouge, was reported as proclaiming its links with China, North Korea, Vietnam and Laos, which was seen as evidence of a setback to the pro-Soviet faction in the ruling Central Committee.

On Monday 12 May, the week's major story broke. The 10,000-ton American freighter *Mayaguez*, owned by the Sea Land Corporation, was seized by Cambodia in disputed waters in the Gulf of Thailand. The story of the seizure and the American attempt to rescue the crew of the ship dominated the week's news. On Tuesday and Wednesday it was the lead story in all bulletins but two and it again became the lead on Saturday in all but one of that day's bulletins.

BBC1 main bulletin at 9 o'clock on Monday broke the news. It announced that the vessel had been seized by a Cambodian warship 60 miles off the coast but only 8 miles from a small rock island called Ko Tang which both Cambodia and Thailand claimed. The bulletin said the *Mayaguez* had been taken to the Cambodian port of Kompong Som and recalled the 'USS *Pueblo* incident' and the so-called 'Tonkin incident'. President Ford called the seizure of the *Mayaguez* 'an act of piracy'. One hour later ITN reported reactions to the seizure from Congress, quoting the chairman of the Senate Foreign Relations Committee as saying that 'if a person shoots you, you've got to shoot back'. But the bulletin also mentioned other opinions in Washington which, in the quoted words of Senator Javits, suggested 'a little patience'.

Ford met with the National Security Committee in the early hours of Tuesday morning and that, too, was reported in the main bulletins. The number of American crewmen involved were variously reported as 39 and 40, a discrepancy which continued throughout the week and which was only made clear on Saturday when the crew was revealed as consisting of 39 men and a captain. The ship was believed to be under contract to the United States army.

The midday news on Tuesday (which, it should be remembered, was being broadcast at the end of the working day in Washington and in the middle of the following night in South-East Asia) revealed that the *Mayaguez* was at anchor off Ko Tang and that United States warships including the carrier *Coral Sea* were steaming into the area. Two Cambodian vessels had apparently escorted the *Mayaguez* to anchor off Ko Tang. During the day the response became clearer: 1,000 marines were to be transferred from Okinawa to American bases in Thailand. A United States reconnaissance aircraft had been hit (but only slightly damaged) by Cambodian small-arms fire. Later, either 100 or 150 marines reached Utapao, a United States base in Thailand, and the Sea Land Corporation, the *Mayaguez*'s owners, admitted that the ship's cargo included military supplies. This report was not repeated and was otherwise strenuously denied by the Americans, who only conceded that there were NAAFI-type supplies aboard. Through the day the Pentagon had remained unusually silent as to its plans but it was revealed that the President had been kept in close touch with the situation, having been woken at 2.30 a.m. and again at 5.30 a.m. All this took place against a background of hardening American attitudes in favour of a military intervention to rescue the ship and its crew, although there were reports of diplomatic activity with Peking to try and effect a peaceful hand-over. The last bulletin of the day reported that within the last few minutes the *Mayaguez* had started to move from Ko Tang.

This last report was not explained by the midday bulletins the following day, but by the early evening there was tape of a Pentagon spokesman explaining (sixteen hours after the event) what had happened. At 8.30 p.m. the day before (presumably local Washington time) United States planes had attacked with 20mm. fire a number of Cambodian vessels, sinking 3 and immobilising 4 others; 1, however, had got away to Kompong Som. The Pentagon said that this was in reply to hours of small-arms fire against the American planes but other reports suggested it was to prevent the Cambodians moving the crew of the *Mayaguez* to the mainland. One bulletin said that the Cambodians had prevented the Americans from rescuing drowning Cambodian seamen. The destroyer-escort *Holt* was now in the area and the Cambodian coast had been sealed off. At various times during the evening this basic action was filled out in the reports. It was revealed that three hours before it commenced President Ford, who had been entertaining the Dutch Prime Minister, had consulted with eighteen congressional leaders and told them he intended to use force. This either followed or preceded a warning to Phnom Penh, delivered via Peking, to desist.

Otherwise on the diplomatic front the United States appealed to the UN and there were continued reports of Thai annoyance at having their territory involved. The Thais called the sinking of the gunboats 'an act of piracy', but American public opinion was clearly behind the move. Senator Goldwater was seen saying that this incident was 'just a forerunner of every little, teeny, dinky country in this world beginning to take advantage of us because we didn't show strength in South Vietnam'.

Christopher Wain, ITN's defence correspondent, hypothesised as to how exactly the Americans might get the crew of the *Mayaguez* off Ko Tang. He revealed that it was a small, lightly wooded island 3¾ miles long by ½ a mile wide, with a hill 440 feet high in its middle.

The following day, Thursday, a marine operation of the sort envisaged by Wain took place, resulting in the recovery of both the *Mayaguez* and the crew. How Wain described the events of the day can be found on p. 282. While the marines were still pinned down on Ko Tang, President Ford, who was at a state dinner for the Shah of

Iran, changed from evening dress and went on television to say: 'The forces that have successfully accomplished this mission are still under hostile fire, but are preparing to disengage.'

The BBC reported that the attack on Ko Tang had begun after the Cambodian radio had said the ship would be released and ordered out of Cambodian waters. With the marines on the *Coral Sea* and the *Mayaguez* with its own crew both steaming towards Singapore, America was reported by the BBC's Washington correspondent John Humphrys to be 'in a mild state of euphoria' but some, like Senator McGovern, continued 'to be alarmed and puzzled as to why military action of this type was taken'. There were demonstrations against the action in Bangkok and protests from Lebanon and Denmark.

On Friday these diplomatic aspects were reported but not as the lead story. The Thais recalled their Washington Ambassador and the anti-American demonstrations continued in Bangkok. The first official film of the attack was available to the bulletins but doubts about the operation (especially the faulty Intelligence that seemingly was unaware that the crew were not on board the *Mayaguez*) drew further criticism. Henry Kissinger was quoted as saying, 'Come on, surely we must be able to do something right.'

Saturday's news programmes had the postscript, again as a lead story. The ship arrived at Singapore and Captain Miller and some crewmen were interviewed as the newsmen inspected the cargo. Derroll Castle, a sailor, said 'the people that took the ship were children as far as I'm concerned, 14, 15 years old'. The captain revealed that he had been nearly gassed by the United States planes seeking to prevent the transfer of the crew to the mainland, but that he had secured his own release by convincing the local Khmer Rouge that he was not carrying military supplies and that the *Mayaguez* was not a spy ship. He knew nothing of the battle on Ko Tang until the Thai fishing smack brought him and his men in sight of it.

The *Mayaguez* story did not halt the flow of other reports from South-East Asia, although these were often used to pay off the *Mayaguez* reports in the bulletins. Before the ship was seized, the early Monday bulletins carried news of six ships, loaded with some of the 200,000 South Vietnamese refugees said to have fled the Provisional Revolutionary Government, which slipped their moorings in Singapore and were heading back to Saigon. They were the first to do so.

Sandy Gall, trapped in Ho Chi Minh City, as Saigon was now officially called, phoned a report to say the 'city is wallowing in the euphoria of peace'. On Tuesday the British Foreign Secretary, James Callaghan, announced that the United Kingdom was recognising the new government in South Vietnam as soon as the evacuated British Embassy staff could be returned from Singapore. The Provisional Revolutionary Government said all embassies would be handed back to any government that recognised them. On Thursday Gall reported that the British Embassy was occupied by troops and the PRG's committee for finance and economy.

On the day that Britain recognised them, the PRG asked Algeria to look after their assets in America. But more importantly, a three-day victory celebration began with the President of North Vietnam, and Lee Duk Toh, the Paris Viet Cong negotiator, attending a parade which was also watched by an estimated crowd of 1 million. United States deserters were reported as driving some of the trucks. On the Friday there were fireworks and the bulletins had the first film of the city since the PRG had taken over. It contained footage of General Minh handing over power as well as street scenes. It was also reported that the port of Saigon would reopen on the Sunday. On the Saturday there was one report that the curfew in the city which had so far been a dead letter was being imposed strictly for the first time.

The story of the *Mayaguez* obviously constituted the major part of the news from Cambodia but there were other eyewitness reports and analyses to be made of what was reportedly happening in Phnom Penh. On the Monday, before the *Máyaguez* had been seized, Robert Kee (on a peg that Phnom Penh radio had announced that it was ready to accept aid) interviewed a pro-Khmer Rouge Cambodian about the depopulation of the capital. That evening in *News at Ten* there was an interview with a Swedish journalist who had been in the city during the evacuation. He said: 'I am sure that thousands of sick and wounded people just died in the street. I saw bodies along the street'. The following day, Kissinger was accusing the Khmer Rouge of atrocities without referring to the *Mayaguez*.

Following the reports of Laos' constitution day on the Sunday, there were further situation reports on the Monday showing the presence of the Pathet Lao in the capital; on Tuesday more units including police were in revolt against right-wing members of the government but the big Laotian story (although it was used as a

Mayaguez peg) broke on Wednesday and remained unresolved at the week's end. Three American aid officials were being held hostage in Savannakhet by students, who were demanding, with the military units, the resignation of the non-communist members of the government and the expulsion of all Americans. At Luang Prabang, the ceremonial capital, a United States aid office was smashed by 3,00 rioters who seized rice. The United States said it would begin running down its embassy by the end of the week. Despite early reports on Wednesday that the men had been released, it transpired they were now being held in their homes, and, there being no reports on the Friday, the BBC carried a situation report from Michael Sullivan on Saturday which said that the United States was still arguing for their release and that 1,000 members of the Royal Lao Air Force had joined the anti-right demonstrations.

News from Thailand was of course overwhelmed by the *Mayaguez* as well, but Kukrit Pramoj, the Prime Minister (apart from ordering the American marines to leave Utapao the moment they arrived and complaining furiously afterwards) also made some gestures of friendship to his neighbours, now all communist. On Friday he welcomed a three-man delegation from the PRG of South Vietnam.

The only other foreign diplomatic stories were that Teng Hsiao Ping, Number 3 in the Chinese communist hierarchy and according to Jim Biddulph, the BBC's diplomatic correspondent, Chou's likeliest successor, became the first senior Chinese leader to visit Europe since the revolution when he arrived in Paris on the Monday. And on the same day the BBC lunchtime bulletin exclusively reported that two United States vessels were on a courtesy visit to Leningrad, the first since the end of the Second World War.

Three interrelated domestic stories also ran through the week: one concerned the motor industry and two strikes in the Midlands; the second plotted the exchange rate of the pound and the cost of living figures released on the Thursday; and the third covered, via reports of speeches and explanatory features of various sorts, the debate about Britain's continued membership of the Common Market, which was to be finally decided some three weeks after this period in the 6 June referendum.

The industrial stories were prefaced by the then Prime Minister, Harold Wilson, who in a current affairs interview on the Sunday morning said *inter alia* that he was 'horrified' that a proposal for worker participation from the Chrysler management had been 'turned down out of hand' by the workers at the company's Ryton plant in Coventry, who were to strike over wage rates on the Monday. The Prime Minister's interview with Peter Jay for London Weekend Television's *Weekend World* (and another interview on BBC's Radio 1, which was quoted once) led all the Sunday bulletins on both ITN and BBC. On the Chrysler situation he said, 'I utterly deplore what is going on', and revealed that he had privately talked to Chrysler's top American management about the company's future in Britain.

On Monday there was no cash offer such as the men were demanding so the strike went ahead, and the shop stewards made no move to bring forward a Thursday meeting to reconsider the situation. As a result of the Monday meeting of 140 stewards, 4,000 men at the engine plant were out and the bulletins reported that layoffs were likely at assembly plants both in Coventry and in Scotland at Linwood. Bob Morris, the Convenor of Stewards, was interviewed and said 'this strike will go on'. As to the company offer on worker participation Frank Chater, the local AUEW official, in interview said there was 'no opposition in principle to the company's suggestion' but that there would be no talks on the matter until the main issue of pay was on the negotiating table. As Morris put it to ITN, 'We are on strike for a living wage. Full stop.' He was also quoted by *First Report* as saying he was absolutely stunned by Mr Wilson's 'outrageous' interview of the previous day. *First Report* said that 6,000 men were already laid off at Chrysler and *News at Ten* suggested that 10,000 could be idle by the weekend.

On Tuesday 700 door hangers were reported as being laid off at Linwood, and Mr Foot, the Employment Minister, called in the Commons for a return to work. It was also reported that Jack Jones and other trade union leaders would be meeting the Chrysler management on the following day. The main BBC1 evening news said this was 'to try and reach a peace formula'. The BBC also had an exclusive interview with one of the strikers' wives, Mrs Sheila Williams, whose husband was a £50 a week machinist. She told of her plan to picket the meeting of the stewards due for the following day. But the midday BBC bulletin on the Wednesday described the demonstration as modest and the film on both news services revealed only about eight wives, evenly split between pro- and anti-, having a slanging match in front of the factory gates. Eddie McCluskey, one of the stewards at the meeting, was interviewed and said that if the wives were to 'approach the company and suggest that their husbands get the rates of pay applicable in the Coventry district they'll end the strike very easily'. All 144 of his colleagues voted to recommend that the strike should continue to the mass meeting scheduled for Thursday. 'We are going to suggest that our fight is going to continue. Full stop', said Mr Morris.

Without prejudice to the Tuesday reports of door hangers being laid off, the Wednesday bulletins reported 1,800 night-shift and 2,000 day-shift workers laid off as the first affected by the strike. Mr Jones denied that the high-level meeting with management was being called to solve the strike, which he said could only be done in Coventry. The meeting was to discuss the worker participation plan and at its end both he and the Managing Director of Chrysler UK, Mr Gilbert Hunt, agreed that they had not discussed the stoppage. This news, exclusively carried on BBC2's *News Extra*, had both men saying they hoped for an early resumption of work. Earlier in the day Mr Hunt had told the Commons' Committee on Trade and Industry that the company intended to build a new model in the UK and that they wanted £35 million from Finance for Industry for that purpose. He also confirmed that Mr Wilson had been in contact with his American boss.

In repeating the notion that the London meeting was going to have the strike 'high on the agenda' although it was 'ostensibly' to discuss the other plans, Robert Kee on *First Report* explained that the men wanted £8 a week at once although their current contract did not expire until 1 July, at which time, Kee announced, they would want a further £15. The company was not even prepared to make an offer until 23 May, aside from the worker participation scheme. Maurice Edelman, the MP for Coventry North-West, suggested in an interview on this programme that inadequate communication was a keynote of the situation at the factory.

Kee's error as to the men's demand was corrected the following day, Thursday. The claim was for £8 a week as part of a £15 a week rise. At the mass meeting the strikers voted overwhelmingly to continue, with 50 against. Morris, addressing the crowd, said:

the manipulation of the press, the mass media in vision, and the unprecedented intervention of the First Minister of the Land – who spoke about something when we weren't even on strike. Mr

Wilson, your platitudes and your attitudes and your political inspiration, you horrify me.

At this meeting the workers agreed in principle to the company's participation scheme and were also advised, as Kee pointed out at the end of the report, on how to draw their social security.

On Friday, in addition to the 4,000 strikers, 8,000 were reported as being laid off and the stoppage was said to be costing £1 million a day. In New York a Chrysler spokesman said the company intended to continue United Kingdom operations despite union troubles.

Virtually every report on Chrysler in the early part of the week was coupled with the reports on the strike, also in Coventry, of 700 clerical employees of Dunlop Engineering. This stoppage had halted production of suspension units for all manufacturers except Fords but had mostly affected Leyland cars, with the result that an increasing number of BLMC workers were laid off during the week. On Monday the strikers turned down a new offer of £7 per week for women and between £7.35 and £8.51 for men because it was still short of their demand for £10 a week for both sexes. There were at this point some 12,500 BLMC workers laid off, a figure which fluctuated to 13,000 in a later bulletin, and finished with an increase that day of 1,700, at above 14,000. Dunlop itself was also affected, with 2,000 being made idle. On Tuesday the 1,700 was confirmed as being 1,500 and the figure of £25 million in lost production was mentioned.

On Wednesday the BLMC layoffs had climbed to 15,000 and new talks for the Thursday were announced. This meeting, which lasted twenty-six hours, yielded a proposal which the stewards agreed to recommend to the members, but the layoffs continued, with 2,000 more that day bringing the total to 16,500 (or 18,000 in another bulletin). The Maxi, Marina, Allegro, 1822 (now Princess), Toledo, Spitfire and TR6 lines were halted. But on Friday the strikers met and accepted the recommendation which did agree to equality of the sexes by November and a £40 a week minimum by that date. Dunlop would be back by Monday and British Leyland in full production again by Wednesday. In lost production the strike had cost an estimated £30 million at showroom prices.

There were two stories arising out of the government's acceptance of Lord Ryder's recommendations on British Leyland the previous month. Heseltine, the Conservative spokesman on industry, asked his opposite number Tony Benn how many jobs would be lost through the implementation of the Ryder proposals. Heseltine put the figure at 33,000. On Monday Mr Geoffrey Robinson resigned as Manager of the Jaguar car division because of the Ryder recommendation that one single luxury car division should be created out of Jaguar, Rover and Triumph. On Wednesday the BBC carried the story that BLMC had lost £43 million in the six months to March, mainly incurred through the closure of the Spanish factory. But BBC2's *News Extra* also had an upbeat feature to celebrate the fiftieth birthday of the MG. The first model in 1925 had cost £350, the current MGBGT £2,670.

There were two stories about lockouts. On Tuesday the printers who work directly for the Bank of England making notes were 'suspended' after refusing a new work deal and the Independent Television Companies said that if the Association of Television Technicians' strike over the spring Bank Holiday (because of unfulfilled clauses in the previous year's agreement) went ahead, the workers 'won't be able to resume work', until the claim was withdrawn. This was on the Friday.

Action was also agreed by the firemen. In pursuance of a wage claim they refused to undertake prevention duties (that is, advice and inspection work) for three months. On the same day, Tuesday, 100,000 bank employees were reported as rejecting a 20 per cent offer because they wanted 25 per cent. On Monday the three rail unions rejected what one bulletin called 'a Social Contract' pay offer of 21 per cent because they were claiming 30 per cent. One of their leaders the same day spoke out against 'irresponsible' trade union demands, a story kept largely separate from the rejection. Among the wage agreements reported during the week were 130,000 engineering workers agreeing to an 18 per cent increase and 60,000 Scottish schoolteachers agreeing a rise of just over 20 per cent, i.e. £6 a week. The post office engineers agreed 18 per cent with threshold consolidation payments taking the level to 25 per cent at a cost of £83 million in a full year to begin in July. It was within the Social Contract, according to the post office management. All these took place on Monday. Post office workers in general on Friday gave their approval to mechanical letter-sorting, which for years they had rejected. Their General Secretary, Tom Jackson, was reported as saying that without the introduction of mechanical letter-handling the second delivery would be abandoned and with it 7,000 jobs, and the whole parcel service would be placed in jeopardy, with a further threat to 17,000. They also agreed on Saturday to shelve a demand for a productivity deal.

The armed forces were given a pay rise to keep rates in line with civilian wages. Backdated to 1 April and announced on the Friday, it was the first rise for three years. Then the forces had been awarded 45 per cent; now they had a further 29 per cent on average but some ranks got up to 34 per cent excluding an increase for the 'X' factor (which was described as dangerous or specialised work). Women got only 5 per cent for this. A private was to get £450 more a year and a full colonel over £1,900.

At Newbury, stable lads managed to persuade members of the BBC's own union, the Association of Broadcasting and Allied Staffs, not to cross the picket lines for the Saturday meeting, it was reported on Friday. As a result there was no television coverage from the track.

The British Steel Corporation plan to reduce jobs in the industry by 20,000 surfaced in a number of stories during the week. The nationalised industry chairmen met under Richard Marsh on the Monday and on the agenda was the row that the steel plan had provoked between Sir Monty Finneston, the BSC chairman, and Tony Benn, the Industry Minister. Marsh when interviewed denied that this was prominent and emphasised the regularity of the meeting. Two days later Marsh told the parliamentary press lobby that interference by government was a major problem for the nationalised industries. On Tuesday Labour MP Roy Hughes was reported as seeking the sacking of Sir Monty, and Employment Minister Michael Foot (in his capacity as an MP from a steel constituency) led a delegation to discuss the proposals with Sir Monty; 5,000 jobs were threatened by the plan in the Ebbw Vale, Foot's constituency. *News Extra* carried a report on the closure of a Lancashire steel mill at Irlam. After one year, 80 per cent of the workers made redundant had no work in the town and 22 per cent were on the dole without any work at all. One of the unemployed and one of the few to find work in Irlam were interviewed. On Friday thirty-one delegates of the Steel Workers Action Committee met to discuss campaign tactics to save other jobs. One, Eric Wilson, said that they were going to ask railmen and dockers not to unload foreign steel. Some 3.5 million tons of steel had been imported over the previous year. The BSC was losing £2.5 million a month. The TUC steel committee were to meet the BSC the following week.

There was little news of overseas industrial affairs during the week except that on Wednesday ITN carried reports from the strike-hit Olympic site in Montreal. Attempts by the Quebec government to combat corruption in the Labour unions in the province had provoked stoppages on the Olympic site. There were reports of the possible cancellation or transference of the games. But despite the six-day strike by 5,000 builders this was not considered likely. The previous day ITN had carried reports of a riot in connection with another Montreal strike in which 500 workers overturned cars and took hostages as the police used tear gas against them. The strike, against an aircraft factory, was in its sixteenth month and the pickets were demanding an end to it.

There was one upbeat industrial story in the week (discounting the celebration of MG's fiftieth year mentioned above). In addition to the Chrysler and Dunlop strikes ITN mentioned stoppages at GEC and Massey-Ferguson by way of introducing a report on the workers' co-operative at the Triumph Motor Cycle factory at Meriden. Trevor MacDonald, the reporter, after interviewing the worker who was now chairman, Dennis Johnston, said the experiment was 'a significant marker in a new industrial phase'.

Other non-dispute industrial items included coverage of the troubles of the footwear industry. There were questions in the Commons on Thursday about the industry and the BBC carried a feature. At one major manufacturer 50 workers were being paid off and at another Bristol factory 200 out of 800 were scheduled to lose their jobs. Four were interviewed. It was pointed out that unlike other countries, the United Kindgom had no protection against shoe imports with the result that, for instance, Britain sold 70,000 pairs to Japan while they sold 200,000 here. But the main problem, explained Mrs Christine Lory of the Footwear Federation, was Eastern European dumping.

Another firm in trouble was bailed out by the government. On Wednesday the government acquired 50 per cent of the voting and 60 per cent (also reported as 62.5 per cent) of the non-voting shares in Ferranti, the electronics company, for £9 million and advanced a further £6 million as a loan. This followed action in September 1974 when the government had guaranteed the company's £12 million overdraft. Sebastian De Ferranti ceased to be managing director although he remained chairman. Michael Heseltine, MP, described the deal as unnecessary and expensive. The company employed 16,000. During the course of announcing this in the Commons Tony Benn, the Industrial Minister, attacked Winston Churchill Jr, MP, for his remarks about redundancies at Ferranti. He spoke of 'a hatred of working people' and argued that well-paid and secure people were not strongly placed to demand redundancies in British Industries. This was but one of the Benn stories of the week. The Prime Minister in his interview on Sunday had said, 'Mr Benn, I think, has many of the qualities of a great Old Testament prophet without a beard who talks about the New Jerusalem he looks forward to in a future time'. (Mr Heseltine's demands for a redundancy price on the implications of Ryder for British Leyland on the same day has been mentioned above.) Benn's response to this was to quote sections of the Prime Minister's own speech to the 1973 Labour party conference as part of his argument for the guillotine motion on the controversial Industry Bill in the House on the Monday night. The government got a majority of 24 for the motion and in BBC2's *News Extra* correspondent Christopher Jones described Benn's handling of the debate as 'a very considerable parliamentary performance'.

Before the debate took place Clive Jenkins, addressing the annual conference of his own union, ASTMS, sharply criticised the press for what he was quoted as calling the character assassination of Mr Benn. Benn was involved in another row in the course of the EEC referendum campaign which will be dealt with below.

The only internal news from individual unions came on Saturday. After a much-publicised debate the AUEW, by the casting vote of its president Hugh Scanlon, decided to keep the voting (for officials) by branches, which the bulletins said was the wish of the militants. The moderates (in the bulletins' usual language) had wanted postal elections.

There were stories about two critics of the power of the trade unions in general, both of whom were prominent socialists. Tom Bradley, MP and recently elected president of the white collar rail union TSSA, was quoted as saying that 'to demand a larger slice of a smaller cake was to deny many a portion at all'. In an interview on *News Extra* on Monday he said he was 'reminding some unions that they do have responsibilities'. *First Report* on Friday interviewed Paul Johnston because of his attack on trade union leaders which had appeared in the week's *New Statesman*. He had written: 'powerful men who conspire to squeeze the community are gangsters. Let's identify them as such.'

This theme was part of the coverage of the meeting of the TUC's economic committee on the Wednesday. Attacks on the government for failing to keep their side of the Social Contract were reported as having taken place inside the committee but no real proposals emerged except that, as Ian Ross, the BBC's correspondent, put it, 'yet another circular to member unions' would be sent out.

The alternative to the Social Contract was presented as a statutory wage policy and the failings of the Contract were often coupled with a call for this by interviewees. In his interview on the Sunday the Prime Minister had denied any plans for such a policy. On Monday Sir Cyril Kleinwort, interviewed by *First Report* on the falling pound, spoke of the 'almost irresponsible demands and strikes we are seeing at this particular time'. On Tuesday, sandwiched between reports on the CBI survey of 1,200 businesses (70 per cent of whom reported that they were working at less than full capacity) and a fall of 0.5 per cent in favour of the pound on the dollar exchange (because of the *Mayaguez* affair), the Leader of the House was reported as saying that the economy was improving, on the BBC1 *Nine O'Clock News*. The same day Sir Frederick Catherwood, speaking at a conference in London on exporting, was quoted as saying that there would be pressure 'for some kind of new pay policy within the month'. ITN found a 'Swiss bank economist' to comment on the falling pound. In interview he described the Social Contract thus: 'the Social Contract which doesn't seem to function at all'. Commenting on the CBI report mentioned above, which also found 38 per cent of the responding companies foreseeing redundancies, 50 per cent preparing to invest less in building and 25 per cent less in plant and machinery, Sir Donald MacDougall, the CBI's chief economic adviser, explained: 'of course one other reason why labour employment is going down is that firms are shedding labour because they're short of cash and they're faced with very large wage increases'. Other factors mentioned in the reporting of the CBI survey were that 90 per cent of firms said there had been increases in costs, 80 per cent mentioned a shortage of orders, and the report, according to ITN, put 'the blame for the recession on pay increases'. However, the economic and industrial correspondents did point out that in a couple of respects, such as cash-flow problems, the report was less 'gloomy' than a similar survey in January.

On the Wednesday, the day when the TUC economic committee met, Ian Ross used government figures which were due to be published the following Monday showing prices rising at 20 per cent while wages were going up at 33 per cent. The CBI Director-General, speaking at Cambridge, was reported as warning the government that it could not go on disregarding the views of industry. He was reinforcing a previous statement by the CBI's Chairman, Lord Watkinson.

On Thursday Shell reported a 31 per cent drop in profits in the first quarter of 1974. Instead of £319 million they had made £220 million. On the Friday, following the cost of living index report, Peter Walker called for a statutory incomes policy while Joe Gormley said that he would not accept that wage rises automatically caused inflation. On Saturday Denis Healey was interviewed for American television and ITN used the tape. He took the opportunity to hit at heavy wage settlements. Margaret Thatcher used the opportunity of the Scottish Tory conference, to hit at 'unbridled socialist inflation' and issued a call 'to tackle militancy at its source'. Her speech was filmed. Jack Jones also spoke on the Saturday, calling, it was reported, for a positive union response to the economic crisis and suggesting a flat rate across-the-board ceiling for wage increases.

These reports took place against a tapestry of statistics.[1] First, all week the fluctuations of the pound were reported. Before the exchanges opened the BBC carried a feature on the effect of the falling rate on foreign holidays. On the Sunday Roger Davies, the marketing director of a tour company, was interviewed and revealed that holidays in Spain were attracting a 2 per cent surcharge and holidays in France a 10 per cent surcharge. This followed the report that Gordon Richardson, the Governor of the Bank of England, had flown out to Basle for the regular meeting of the Central Bankers. The Prime Minister's interview was also seen as relating to the question of the slipping pound, for on the Monday the drop of the currency to new lows against the franc and the Deutschmark was seen as making the interview a failure as far as the restoration of confidence went. At the start of the day the pound fell to 75 per cent of its December 1971 value against the currencies of our principal trading partners. There was a rush to buy shares in firms with large overseas holdings as a hedge against this depreciation which forced the *Financial Times* Index up 9 points at lunchtime. The Bank stepped in to hold the rate but not massively. And the Central Bankers were reported as calling for more stringent anti-inflation measures. The Speaker of the House, Selwyn Lloyd, refused a Conservative request for an emergency debate on the situation in order not to exacerbate the jitteryness of the market. The Tories claimed that over £3 billion had been added to the government's deficit by recent measures. These included help to British Leyland and the nationalisation of the North Sea oil industry. Another factor mentioned was the uncertainty created by the referendum campaign.

An exchange dealer for one of the British clearing banks said in interview that 'the speculator is nowhere near as in evidence as he has been in the past'. It seemed as if Arab institutional funds held in sterling were being switched to other currencies, and this was suggested as a prime cause of the run. The Arab nations held over £3,000 million in sterling in December 1974. On this basis Angela Rippon interviewed Aubrey Jones as an expert on Arab business. He said that he felt that the Arabs had confidence in Britain and a great respect for British technology. That evening, as reported on *Newsday*, Sir Geoffrey Howe called for a coalition government, which *News Extra* also mentioned.

On the Tuesday the pound fell a further point, by 25.1 per cent against its December 1971 value. This worsened to 25.2 per cent by the end of the day. But the dollar also fell. Gordon Richardson returned from Basle but refused to comment. It was also reported that the prices charged by industry were up by over 5 per cent during the last three-month period but as only 0.5 per cent in the last month was due to increased import costs, it was suggested that wages accounted for the major part of the rise. The Prime Minister announced that there would be a debate on the economy the following week.

On *News Extra* that night Dominic Harrod speculated about the trade figures due on the Wednesday. He said that anything under £200 million in the red could be considered comparatively good. And on the Wednesday his guess was confirmed. The visible trade gap for April 1975 was £289 million but invisible earnings were £120 million – leaving £169 million, twice the March figure but still much better than the figures for the months at the end of 1974. In response the pound rose to finish at 25.1 per cent below the December 1971 rate. On the Wednesday this upward trend continued and the pound finished at 24.8 per cent below the December 1971 rate. The dollar, too, recovered with the rescue of the *Mayaguez* crew. On Thursday Otto Emminger, the German banker who was president of an OECD working party, was quoted as saying that there was no crisis atmosphere surrounding sterling, and that the balance of payments prospect looked better.

On Friday the cost-of-living index figures were issued. They contained a record single-month rise of 3.9 per cent between March and April. Rates increases accounted for 1 per cent of this rise, council rents for 0.2 per cent, electricity price increases for 0.14 per cent and insurance premium increases for 0.13 per cent. Coal, coke, beef, school meals, public transport fares, TV licences also contributed. Fresh vegetables had gone up 8.6 per cent. These figures gave an annual inflation rate of 21.7 per cent but over the preceding six months the rate had been 27.5 per cent and over the last three months 34.5 per cent. The pound fell to 24.9 per cent of its December 1971 value. This cost-of-living increase was the largest ever recorded since records began in 1947. It put Britain at the top of the international inflation table in front of Italy and well before countries like West Germany with a rate of 6 per cent. Denis Healey had estimated that the Budget would add a further 2.75 per cent to the cost-of-living index and that, it was reported, was yet to come. ITN on the Friday followed its feature of Thursday on how advantageous it was for Calais women to shop in Ramsgate because British prices were still half those of France with a report on the tour surcharge problem similar to the one carried by the BBC the previous Sunday. These two stories involved interviews with Frenchwomen, British butchers and another tour operator. That evening, Friday, *News Extra* interviewed financial journalist Bill Horewood on what strategies families could adopt for savings in such a period of inflation.

The third major domestic theme of the week concerned the Common Market and the referendum which was scheduled for 6 June. The stories on this topic fell into two groups. First, there were speeches by pro- and anti-Marketeers dealing either with the economics of Britain's membership or the political consequences of the campaign. Second, both services ran information features on these aspects of the event.

There were Common Market and referendum stories each day of the week. Mr Wilson in his interview on the Sunday concentrated on the problems posed for the government by the division caused in the Cabinet on the issue. He said that after the referendum all Cabinet ministers would have to get back into line. The issue of Britain's EEC membership was presented as causing the Labour party more problems than the Conservatives, although the pro- and anti- factions contained prominent members of both parties. On the Sunday, anti-EEC Cabinet minister Peter Shore was quoted as saying that within a few years of continued membership Britain would be paying 25 per cent of the Common Market's revenue while receiving only 15 per cent of the benefits.

On the Monday Fred Peart, a pro-EEC minister, was seen arguing in a speech that Britain's food supplies would be best protected by remaining in the Community. The Farmers' Union President, Sir Henry Plumb, was reported as saying that the pound would fall to frighteningly low levels if Britain voted No to membership. Frank Allaun, the MP for East Salford, was quoted as saying that the rest of the countries in the Community 'have their beady eyes on our oil'. Eric Heffer raised the issue of secret plans for steel. He claimed that the Commissioners in Brussels were not revealing plans for a cutback on British steel production, because such schemes would be unpopular. Douglas Jay was reported as saying that every staple foodstuff would be cheaper if Britain had remained outside. The National Referendum Campaign, the umbrella organisation for the antis, claimed that since Britain had been part of Europe £519 million had been invested there by British business, while only £109 million had been invested here by other Europeans. The Foreign Secretary at a press conference that day was reported as saying that he expected 'the British electorate to give a resounding yes' on referendum day.

On the Tuesday the Britain in Europe Group, the umbrella organisation for the pros, had its first press conference. Before the cameras were leading members of all three parties – Roy Jenkins, Edward Heath and Jeremy Thorpe. Since the day was also one in which the pound was slipping badly, their comments addressed themselves to how much more fragile the situation would be if Britain voted to leave the EEC. Against this the Get Britain Out Campaign, part of the National Referendum Campaign, introduced the press to representatives of an anti-EEC New Zealand Group, who argued that New Zealand farmers would welcome a restoration of the special relationship with Britain.

In response to Mr Heffer's suggestion of withheld schemes and secret agreements with Cabinet members, the officials in Brussels denied that they had any plans for British steel that were not already known. The Foreign Office also issued a statement of denial. On the Wednesday Edward Heath was quoted as saying that 'one stark political consequence [of a No vote] must be Mr Wedgwood Benn and his world swamped with ration books and state directives'. Mr Eric Deakins in a filmed speech said that the protective shield of the EEC, and the Commonwealth before it, had been bad for British business. In other speeches quoted from the Wednesday, Mrs Shirley Williams said that after the vote ministers must be prepared to agree with the decision or resign. She announced that she was prepared to do so. Mr Alf Morris, another Labour MP, said that in three years food prices had gone up 45 per cent in Britain but in Norway and Sweden they had risen half that amount in the same period. The two Scandinavian countries were not members of the Community.

On the Thursday the non-nationalised British steel industry, which employed about 70,000 workers, said it was in favour of remaining in the EEC. Mr Callaghan was recorded at a miners' conference. He addressed himself to the prospect of New Zealand food supplies: 'They'll send us the food, yes, we've got the entry for the food, but they want, and why the hell not, they want a fair price for it'. Another Labour MP, Mr Sedgemore, was quoted as saying that continued membership would mean the Chancellor would have to pursue a ruthless policy of unemployment. Figures were issued which revealed that in the previous three months Britain's trade deficit had been £470 million with the EEC but there was a surplus on trade with the rest of the world of £230 million.

On Friday Michael Foot said that to remain in the Common Market would mean being sucked into a coalition method of governing our economic affairs. Michael Heseltine said that we would be able to control the economy ourselves but that our inflation rate was entirely our own fault. Douglas Jay said that the balance of trade would continue to be bad as long as we remained in. Mr Maudling at the Scottish Conservative party conference repeated that a No vote would mean extreme socialism. Mr Benn, on his part, attacked Mr Heath. He said none of Heath's seventy-one predictions on the advantageous consequences of joining the Market for trade, investment, jobs or regional development had come true.

Sir Geoffrey Rippon, quoting a survey of British business chief executives (95 per cent of whom believed Britain should remain in Europe), said unemployment would increase if we left. He was filmed, while all the rest of Friday's speakers were quoted verbally in the bulletins.

As part of a series of stories on Eire, ITN interviewed Garrett

Fitzgerald, the Irish Foreign Minister, on the consequences for
Ireland if Britain voted No. 'It's important to Ireland', he said, 'that
Britain should remain in.' *News Extra* also carried a story on the
Irish dimension from the Ulster Border, which is crossed by over
£200 million of goods a year. Interviews were given by a border
farmer on the effectiveness of trying to close the border to trade and
by a woman shopper from the Republic on the advantages of the
cheaper food in Ulster. The day before, ITN had featured the Irish
currency. Since the previous December, when Britain had stopped
maintaining the value of Irish-held sterling, Eire had reduced its
sterling holdings by £150 million. George Colley, Opposition
finance spokesman in the Dáil, was interviewed.

On the Saturday there were a number of campaign speeches. Mr
Heffer was reported as adding his voice to the warnings of increased
unemployment if the vote was Yes. Mr Crosland said that voting No
would be a grotesque blunder and Mr Thorpe commented that the
debate in general reminded him of the politicians of the Weimar
Republic: it avoided all real discussion of the real economic issues
facing the country. Mr Powell was filmed addressing a meeting.
'Don't be simple, rub your eyes and look around you,' he said, 'use
your loaf.' He was arguing the need for a No vote.

The features that backed up this parade of speeches begun on the
Monday of the week being studied. Mr Jay's remarks were used as a
peg by *News at Ten* to explain, with the help of interviews with Mrs
Shirley Williams and a former Ministry of Agriculture official, Sir
John Winifrith, the ins and outs of the argument about food prices.
Summing up, Jon Lander, the ITN correspondent, said, 'In the end
in this argument you pays your money and you takes your choice.'

On the Tuesday BBC1's main bulletin ran a feature on the two
umbrella organisations, the National Referendum Campaign and
the Britain In Europe campaign. That day Robert Kee in *First
Report* opened his 'EEC Postbag' and answered readers' letters.
These were concerned with the food price argument and in the
studio he had Sir Geoffrey Rippon and Mr Norman Buchan for an
extended debate on the issue. ITN in *News at Ten* endeavoured to
unravel the EEC balance of trade statistics which were being used
during the week. Although the feature admitted that the balance
was adverse there were advantages, it was suggested, as in our iron
and steel exports to the Community, and the figures were anyway
distorted by such things as the three-day week at the beginning of
1974, a general price rise worldwide in foodstuffs and the

Flixborough disaster which, because of the unique nature of the plant, necessitated importation to make up the losses caused.

On Wednesday there was news of how the referendum itself was to be conducted. The count was to start at 9 a.m. on the morning of 6 June and the mass of the results would be known by that evening. MPs would be allowed to observe the count, which would take place at one of sixty-eight counting units throughout the country. Finding buildings large enough to accommodate the count was causing some difficulties. Kent had opted for an aircraft hangar. South Yorkshire for the Doncaster racetrack building. Sir Philip Alan, the Chief Counting Officer, was interviewed on the difficulties of how close a vote would necessitate a recount. The whole problem of the referendum count was used by BBC *Nine O'Clock News* as a peg for a story on the regional reorganisation of Scotland. This was due on the following day and the film examined how the new area of Highland, containing one-third of the land but only 130,000 of the people of Scotland, would cope.

On the Thursday Kee opened his postbag again and dealt himself a range of queries from the possibility of a return to shillings and pence to freedom of religion in the Community. That night *News at Ten* carried a feature on how the Euro-Parliament worked and in interviews with Dr Fitzgerald, in his capacity as a member of the EEC Council of Ministers, and Peter Kirk, the Conservative MP who was leading the British group, pointed to some emergent tensions between Strasbourg and Brussels. There were no features on Saturday.

Thus the main foreign story of the week came from South-East Asia and three domestic stories, industrial troubles, the economy and the referendum also received extensive coverage. Nothing else received coverage as heavy and only two of the news items listed below were used as lead stories, each on only one early bulletin.

There were the following reports from Northern Ireland during the week. On Sunday the Provisional IRA claimed responsibility for the killing on the previous day of a twenty-year-old policeman, Paul Grey, in Londonderry. Grey's death (he was the first officer to be shot during the four months of the ceasefire) renewed speculation that the truce might be ending. On the Monday the Secretary of State for Northern Ireland, Merlyn Rees, responded by threatening a slowing up of the release of detainees, 247 of whom had been released since the truce began but 300 of whom were still being held in Long Kesh. A judge also granted a defence application to move the Birmingham bomb trial to Lancaster. On the Wednesday PC Grey was buried and the IRA issued a statement saying that the killing was in line with its policy if the ceasefire was not honoured by the Army. That night a Catholic pub on the outskirts of Belfast was bombed by the Protestant Action Force. A nineteen-year-old girl lost a foot but there were no deaths. On the Thursday Rees met with Garrett Fitzgerald, the Irish Foreign Minister, but no definite action was taken.

The reorganisation of Scotland's local government merited one story in addition to the report from the new Highland region referred to above. ITN carried it on the Strathclyde regional news on the day it came into effect, Friday, and interviewed Dr Laurence Boyle, the new region's chief executive officer. On the Thursday the Scottish Conservative party began its annual conference in Dundee, from which speeches by Mr Maudling and Mrs Thatcher were reported. Only the BBC carried reports from the opening of the conference and interviewed the chairman of the party, which was now commanding less of the popular Scottish vote than either Labour or the SNP and had only 16 of the 71 Scottish seats in Westminster.

At the beginning of the week the NALGO leader, Geoffrey Drain, attacked the Environment Minister, Mr Crosland, for his remarks about 'the party being over' for local government. Mr Drain said that for most of his members the party had never begun. Apart from reporting this speech in quotation it was made the peg for a story on *First Report* about rate increases in Cardiff which had provoked the formation of citizen groups questioning the efficiency of local government. Various members of the city council and the groups in question were interviewed. Drain's remarks were also used by *News Extra* for a situation report of the bankruptcy of New York City and the attendant cutbacks in services there (despite the fact that an 8 per cent sales tax went directly to City Hall).

On the Tuesday it was reported that London Transport fares would rise by 25 per cent in November.

The chairman of the Building Societies Association was quoted on the Wednesday as warning that mortgage rates might be substantially increased to combat the attractiveness of the government's inflation-linked savings scheme which was being introduced over the coming months. On the Friday his general secretary was interviewed following the announcement of record deposits in April and said, 'I think the 11 per cent mortgage rate is going to remain stable for the rest of the year.' Deposits were up from £274 million to £406 million, and the highest number of loans had been recorded, too.

The main consumer story was that over the coming six months the price of sugar would fall by 20 per cent; that is to say, by as much as 6½p. on a two-pound bag. The Commonwealth price was £260 a ton, it was announced on Tuesday, while the world price was £180 a ton; government subsidies would make up the difference to the refiners.

There were two drinking stories. On Tuesday the High Court ordered Bulmers and Showerings to no longer call their cider 'champagne'. A champagne spokesman was interviewed. And on Friday *First Report* told how the Campaign for Real Ale (CAMRA) had persuaded Courage to reinstate hand pumps in pubs in London and Reading. A brewer and publican were interviewed.

As to health stories, the announcement on the Tuesday that the Department of Health and Social Security was to phase out the last 430 private beds in the National Health Service was used by *News Extra* as a peg to examine the growth of private hospitals. An official of the Private Patient Plan, the administrator of the London Clinic and the chairman of a small clinic in Colchester were all interviewed.

The same day the President of the General Dentist Council was quoted as warning that dentists could be liable for errors in anaesthetising their patients and should therefore work with qualified anaesthetists. On the Wednesday, as only *First Report* noticed, the Birth Control Trust published a pamphlet recommending that the birth control pill be taken off prescription. Professor Peter Huntingford in interview said, 'I don't really believe that the availability of the pill will affect moral standards.' On Thursday, pegged to Nestlés' annual meeting in Switzerland, *News Extra* carried a feature on the dangers of feeding babies artificial milk, attacking particularly the company's aggressive sales techniques in societies lacking basic hygiene facilities.

More than 1,000, or alternatively 'several thousand', blind people marched two miles to lobby Westminster on the Thursday about their supplementary benefit. They were demanding £5 a week instead of the £1.25 which they currently got and which had gone up only 50p. in twenty-eight years. It was the first time since 1920 that they had met with MPs. Some of the marchers were interviewed.

The big education story of the week (carried in most bulletins on the Thursday) came when over 500 police in thirteen coaches arrived at the Warwick University campus to end a twenty-five-day sit-in by 200 students in the administration building. They were protesting against a £2 a week rent rise and had caused the postponement of finals, but on the arrival of the police, some in full riot equipment, the students left and occupied the adjacent arts centre building instead. On the Saturday the BBC had an exclusive interview with the Education Secretary on the growing problem of teacher unemployment. Fred Jarvis, the NUT leader, had called the training of surplus teachers and their subsequent unemployment 'the height of folly'.

The major defence story of the week, apart from the armed forces' pay rise, was the decision announced by the Minister, Roy Mason, on the Thursday to go ahead with the naval version of the Harrier jump-jet. The United States marines had over 100 land Harriers and the expansion of the programme meant 3,000 extra jobs at Hawker Siddeley, Rolls-Royce and Ferranti. There was also the possibility of another 1,000 jobs if Iran decided to buy the plane. In interview Mason explained the need for the naval version to attack the Russian spy plane, the Bear, which could otherwise co-ordinate Russian submarine attacks on NATO vessels from beneath the horizon. 'There's no additional defence expenditure', he said.

Flooding following heavy rain was reported from a number of Home Counties on the Saturday. But the week's biggest disaster story was the government's report on the Flixborough chemical explosion on the Monday. This was dominating the day's news until the first reports of the *Mayaguez* came in in time for the main evening bulletins. The report firmly blamed the Nypro company for the disaster and Nypro, part-owned by the British and Dutch state mines, accepted the blame. A makeshift pipe, installed in the absence of any qualified works engineer, had been responsible for the explosion, which killed twenty-eight people. The Under-Secretary for Employment said in the House that had the legislation now passed been in existence at the time of the disaster, Nypro would have been prosecuted. The report recommended that black boxes, of the sort used on aircraft, be installed in chemical works. Leslie Granger, Nypro's managing director, was interviewed and the BBC science correspondent explained what steps to increase safety the industry had itself taken since the explosion. The implications of the disaster for the balance of trade has been otherwise referred to. On the Tuesday the company announced that they would rebuild the plant at a cost of £30 million.

On the Friday the BBC had 'spectacular' film of a fire at a Canadian cosmetics factory which caused over £1 million of damage. The same day the bulletins reported a train crash in Yugoslavia in which 13 people died and 169 were injured when a bridge crossing a flood-swollen river collapsed. In Sweden the previous day 8 people, 7 of them children, had died in another train crash 100 miles south-west of Stockholm. That day also saw the try-out of an exact replica of *Locomotion 1*, the first steam engine, on a specially built track at the open-air museum at Beamish in County Durham. It was built by 250 volunteers at a cost of £25,000 to celebrate the first run of Stephenson's original locomotive on 27 September 1825. Also on the Friday, the BBC reported that the niece of Graf Zeppelin had had difficulty launching a hot-air balloon in Switzerland.

In the courts the Prime Minister settled a libel action against the *Daily Express* for two articles which contained innuendo about a land deal speculation. The paper apologised and said no such innuendo had been intended. At Chester a murder trial was halted when a juror revealed that the family of the prosecution's main witness was known to him. In the Court of Appeals on Tuesday Lord Denning argued that the distinction drawn by an inferior court between industrial picketing and picketing for other causes should not stand. On Wednesday, as they alone reported, the BBC apologised to Frank Sinatra in the High Court for linking him without foundation with the Mafia in a *24 Hours* story. ITN reported that day on how the search for the rapist who had been terrorising Cambridge was going. The superintendent in charge of the case was interviewed. On the Thursday Mr Justice Morris caused a storm when he said, in sentencing five black youths for 'robberies on unaccompanied women', that whole areas of South London had been transformed from peaceful communities by immigrants settling in them. He later apologised and exonerated the majority of the immigrant community, but the chairman of the Race Relations Board, Mark Bonham Carter, was quoted as saying that 'the remarks of a highly placed judge would do more to foster racial tension than the offences of five underprivileged youngsters'.

On the Sunday the police were hunting an escaped patient from Rampton in Nottinghamshire. On Wednesday sixty-five leading Anglican theologians wrote an open letter to the Archbishops warning against upgrading the official Church of England attitude towards the rite of exorcism. As Professor Geoffrey Lampe, one of those involved, explained in interview, 'to try and treat people who are psychologically disturbed and disorientated by means of exorcism is in fact playing the occultists' game.' It was dangerous to encourage belief in powers which might deprive men of their normal responsibilities, the theologians claimed.

Michael Abdul Malik, known as Michael X in Britain, was hanged on the Friday in Trinidad for the murder of his cousin after three years of trials and appeals. He had been jailed in Britain in 1968 for inciting racial hatred and had fled to the island in 1970 when facing robbery and blackmail charges. The body of a sometime Conservative MP's daughter, Gayle Benson, had also been found in the grounds of Malik's home.

On the Thursday thirty-six modern masterpieces, including works by Cézanne, Renoir and Van Gogh, valued variously at £3–£3.5 million, were stolen from an art gallery in Milan to which they had only just been returned after being recovered by the police following an identical theft three months earlier. On the Tuesday the National Gallery for the first time displayed its paintings outside London by opening an exhibition in the Long Gallery of Montacute House in Somerset.

The remainder of the week's reports from abroad included news on Wednesday of a shooting near Guernica in the Basque provinces of Spain in which one policeman and three others died. The policeman was the fifth to be killed in the area in just over a month. On the Friday ITN reported that the ruling council in the ex-Portuguese colony of Angola was to bring in emergency regulations to prevent a repetition of the inter-communal violence that had killed an estimated 500 at the end of the previous month.

Reports from the Middle East said that on the Tuesday, for the second time in twenty-four hours, the Israelis had crossed into Southern Lebanon and seized guerrilla suspects from a village near Tyre. They kidnapped three people in that raid, five people in the day before's. On the Friday twenty people were injured in an explosion in an arms factory in Tel Aviv. Although the PLO claimed responsibility, the Israeli police said it was an accident. On the Saturday seven children were killed playing with an unexploded bomb near the Lebanese village of Aitroun, close to the border. A bomb on a Dead Sea beach injured ten.

On the Sunday a big security operation was mounted at

Heathrow Airport, London, as King Hussein of Jordan flew in from Miami and Washington on a private visit. Troops and police were involved. On Friday the BBC had an exclusive with their reporter David Sells, the first Western television man allowed into Kurdistan. After years of war between the Kurds and the Iraqis two months prior to Sells's visit the Iraqi leader Sadam Hussein had unexpectedly reached agreement with the Shah. Since the Shah had been the main supporter of the Kurdish rebellion, his withdrawal meant the collapse of the revolt. Sells toured the now pacified area.

Also on Sunday, Greek Cypriots in London demonstrated in Hyde Park for the early implementation of United Nations resolutions on the island. Lord Soper addressed the rally.

A group of six Labour and Conservative MPs met with Trade Secretary Peter Shore on Wednesday. Led by Tom Williams, they had been to Sri Lanka to investigate conditions on the tea plantations, many of them British-owned. They recommended immediate improvement of medical conditions for the workers, who earned 36p. a day for men and 27p. a day for women. They also complained that Granada's *World in Action*, which first drew attention to the miserable plight of the plantation workers, had been too selective. Sir Dennis Forman of Granada Television, interviewed by *News Extra*, said the MPs had not bothered to speak to them and that they had been misinformed in Sri Lanka. However, he was pleased that they confirmed the essential television case against the plantation owners.

Tea of a different kind figured in ITN's coverage of the Queen's visit to Japan. This tour was drawing to an end at the week's start and all bulletins reported the Queen and Prince Philip's departure from Tokyo on the Monday and her return via Anchorage in the early hours of Tuesday morning. But ITN further carried film reports of her last activities in Japan. The tea ceremony happened 'earlier in the weekend' and was shown on the Sunday, and her visit to a major Shinto shrine, a strange medieval football match and the pearl divers of Kobe was used on the day of her return.

The week's sports news was as follows: on Sunday England beat Cyprus at soccer in Limassol and Niki Lauda won the Monaco Grand Prix in a Ferrari, but Fittipaldi was still in the lead for the world championship. In the Sunday League cricket, Glamorgan, Kent, Northamptonshire, Somerset, Worcestershire and Yorkshire beat Surrey, Middlesex, Sussex, Gloucestershire, Lancashire and Derbyshire.

There was a climbing accident in the Himalayas. Two of the army's team assaulting Nuptse were killed in a rock fall. This tragedy was repeated on Saturday when a third officer and a Gurkha were killed and the climb was abandoned. On the same day, Saturday, a thirty-five-year-old Japanese housewife, Mrs Yanko Tabey, reached the summit of Everest.

On Monday Britain was beaten by Spain in the Davis Cup. On Tuesday Scotland beat Portugal 1–0 in a friendly. On Wednesday ITN exclusively interviewed Linda Mottram, the daughter of a famous tennis star, who was doing well at the national hard court championship at Bournemouth. On Thursday Middlesex's wicket keeper Murray broke the record for catches by taking his 1,235th against Somerset. The record was thirty-eight years old. On Friday there was a tennis story that reached every bulletin. At the hard courts championship Ilie Nastase and Roger Taylor both had arguments about line calls, but Nastase was so furious he was disqualified. He and Captain Mike Gibson, the chief umpire, were both interviewed.

On the Saturday, apart from the climbing stories cited above, there were domestic soccer internationals including the first game played in Belfast for four years. In this, Northern Ireland held England to a 0–0 draw. At Cardiff Wales held Scotland to a 2–2 draw. The London Transport and British Rail crews in the London area announced that they would not be running trains out to Wembley for the Scotland England match since a guard had been badly injured on the last occasion. In Rugby League the first premiere championship was won by Leeds (26) against St Helens (11). Mohammad Ali beat Lyle in a championship fight at Las Vegas. In Australia England beat New South Wales at the start of the Rugby Union tour. Because of the floods and heavy rain much cricket and tennis was disrupted and only one Benson & Hedges Cup match was finished. There was a fire at the Newmarket stables of Bruce Hobbs but no horses or people were injured. And Princess Anne competed in the army horse trials at Tidworth Park.

There remains but one story. On the Tuesday night *News at Ten* finished thus:

> Finally, there's been another sign in the City of the way things are going in our changing financial circumstances. A Saudi Arabian prince has become a director of a British merchant bank. He's the son of the Saudi Finance Minister. After he and Arab

associates bought a 25 per cent interest he joined the Board of the bank of Edward Bates & Sons. His fellow directors will know him as Prince Abdullah Bin Musaid, Bin Abdul Rachman.

Notes

Introduction

1 T. Burns, *The BBC: Public Institution and Private World*, Macmillan, London, 1977, p. 206.

1 Introduction: The Economic Background

1 T. Burns, *The BBC: Public Institution and Private World*, Macmillan, London, 1977, p. 202.
2 For a more detailed account of each of these approaches see A. Gamble and P. Walton, *Capitalism in Crisis*, Macmillan, London, 1976.
3 See, for example, A. W. Phillips, 'The Relationship Between Unemployment and the Rate of Change of Money Wage Rates in the U.K., 1861–1975', *Economics*, vol. 25, no. 100, 1958, pp. 283–99; and F. W. Paish, *Studies in an Inflationary Economy*, Macmillan, London, 1962.
4 *Financial Times*, 1 August 1973.
5 F. Cairncross, in the *Guardian*, 8 October 1976.
6 *The Economist*, 4 November 1972.
7 See, for example, D. Yaffe, 'The Crisis of Profitability', in *New Left Review*, 80, July–August 1973; and P. Mattick, *Marx and Keynes*, Merlin Press, London, 1971.
8 *Daily Express*, 14 February 1975.
9 Yaffe, *op. cit.*, p. 54.
10 *Politics and Money*, vol. 2, no. 2, 1971, p. 11.
11 *Observer*, 25 May 1975.
12 *Investors' Chronicle*, Editorial, 11 September 1974.
13 Figures from London and Cambridge Economic Bulletin, *The Times*, 27 June 1972.
14 *Guardian*, 13 February 1974.
15 For a theoretical account see M. Friedmann and A. Schwartz, *A Monetary History of the United States*, Princeton University Press, 1963; also A. Walters, *Money in Boom and Slump*, Institute of Economic Affairs, London, 1969.
16 *Observer*, 25 May 1975.
17 *Guardian*, 6 October 1976, p. 8.

18 *Sunday Times*, 'Business News', 20 January 1974.
19 D. Jackson, H. A. Turner and F. Wilkison, *Do Trade Unions Cause Inflation?*, Cambridge University Press, 1972.
20 *Financial Times*, 30 April 1975.
21 Price Commission Report for the period 1 December 1974–28 February 1974, p. 4.
22 *Ibid.*, our italics.
23 The effect of direct wages for the previous quarter had been calculated by the Price Commission as 33 per cent.
24 *Morning Star*, 30 April 1975.
25 *Daily Telegraph*,30 April 1975.
26 The critical political arguments at this time did not in fact involve the discussion of commodity prices such as oil, since everyone was agreed that oil prices were a problem. This may account for the high number of direct media statements in this area. The high number of statements in relation to wages as a problem and the low number to industrial investment says more about the ideological standpoint of the news.

2 Wages and Prices Figures

1 BBC1, 21.00, 20 January 1975.
2 For all the coverage in January the figure given by the BBC for the increase in retail prices was 18.3 per cent. The figure quoted in the *Financal Times* and on ITN was 19.1 per cent.
3 F. Cairncross, *Guardian*, 8 October 1976.
4 *Guardian*, 20 March 1975.
5 The industrial editor of ITN had similarly commented in January that the comparison between *average earnings* and prices was the one 'which really counts' (ITN, 22.00, 21 March 1975).

3 From Diagnosis to Prescription

1 The remaining references were reported statements from Robert Carr (ITN, 22.00, 21 January 1975) and a firm of stockbrokers (ITN, 13.00, 24 April 1975) and an interview response from Robert Carr (ITN, 13.00, 21 January 1975).

4 Pointing the Finger: Evaluations and Judgments

1 Cmnd 6753, HMSO, London, 1977, p. 273.

5 'Who Gets On?': Conclusion

1 For these reasons we have recorded interviewees and those filmed speaking to conferences in the same category, 'Interview', as we did in the analysis of explanatory themes in Chapter 3.
2 None of the four interview situations on Budget Day was actually concerned with the Social Contract. They were included in the sample

because they occurred in the news bulletins as part of a 'Budget package', a key part of which was the discussion of the working of the Social Contract as reflected in the Chancellor's Budget measures. In terms of collecting a strictly correct sample, these interviews then had to be included. Considering those interviews within the sample as a whole which *do* relate directly to the Social Contract, the point about the narrow range of access is heightened.

3 The tendency to give different treatment to the medical profession from that which normally characterises coverage of trade unions has been noted elsewhere in this study. See, in particular, Part II, 'Hear It This Way', pp. 179–80.

4 Only in the ITN's reference (one in each case) to 'shopkeepers', 'moderate miners' and 'left-wing' miners' are the views of the workers and other occupational groups noted. These are cases where opinions of 'feelings' are attributed to a group defined by the newsroom rather than direct quoting of a particular statement. Of a similar nature is BBC1's speculative reference to the views of 'hard-headed financial and political observers'.

5 In terms of the proportional representation of the parliamentary parties, it should be noted that three of the Labour MPs are quoted only once and in the context of the parliamentary debate on the Queen's pay (parliamentary criticism of the royal family as a recipient of state aid being restricted to the Labour back-benches), as are two Conservative MPs and the Liberal Jeremy Thorpe (these three quoted as defending the increase in the Civil List).

6 See the British Leyland case study in Glasgow University Media Group, *Bad News*, Routledge & Kegan Paul, London, 1976, Chapter 7, pp. 243–56.

7 *The Task of Broadcasting News*, a study for the BBC General Advisory Council published by the BBC, May 1976, p. 12.

8 This is not to say that ideology and the production of world views operates only at the level of the explicit explanation of the social and economic world, and that what is taken as sensational and dramatic is somehow natural and pre-given. Sex and violence, for example, are dramatic angles in many news stories, but we must ask what kind of a society and what is its history which generates an obsession with these and with property and control as key elements of both. The particular form and content of what is taken as sensational is obviously socially and historically determined and presumably the need to seek out and present the sensational and dramatic is as well.

9 See p. xiv above.

6 News Ideology: Neutrality and Naturalism

1 For our use of the term 'ideology' in this context and throughout this study, see p. 402.

2 N. Chomsky, *Reflections on Language*, Pantheon, London, 1976, p. 4.

3 This is well illustrated in R. H. Robins's paper, 'Malinowski, Firth and

the "Context of Situation" ', in E. Ardener, *Social Anthropology and Language*, Tavistock, London, 1971, pp. 33–46.

4 In Malinowski's own work this is probably best exemplified in *Coral Gardens and their Magic*, Allen & Unwin, London, 1935.
5 D. Hymes, 'Sociolinguistics and the Ethnography of Speaking', in Ardener, *op. cit.*, p. 51.
6 D. Hymes, 'On Communicative Competence', Pride and Holmes (eds), *Sociolinguistics*, Penguin, Harmondsworth, 1972, p. 272.
7 L. Wittgenstein, *Philosophical Investigations*, Blackwell, Oxford, 1963, p. 11e.
8 R. Brown and A. Gilman, 'The Pronouns of Power and Solidarity', in P. P. Giglioli (ed.), *Language and Social Context*, Penguin, Harmondsworth, 1972.
9 E. Goffman, *Frame Analysis,* Harper & Row, New York, 1974, p. 21.
10 Goffman, *op. cit.*, p. 21.
11 Goffman is now working in this area and has produced an extended paper on 'Gender Advertisements' in *Studies in the Anthropology of Visual Communication*, vol. 3, no. 2, autumn 1976; cf. also E. Goffman, *Gender Advertisements*, Macmillan, London, 1978.
12 A. Smith, *The Shadow in the Cave*, Quartet, London, 1976, p. 176.
13 We showed in Chapter 7 of Volume 1, *Bad News*, Routledge & Kegan Paul, London, 1976, how the characteristic inferential framework of industrial reporting utilises limited aspects of a dispute to create a 'dominant view'.
14 S. Hall, I. Connell and L. Curti, *The 'Unity' of Current Affairs Television*, in Working Papers in Cultural Studies No. 9, University of Birmingham, spring 1976, p. 53.
15 M. A. K. Halliday and R. Hasan, *Cohesion in English*, Longmans, London, 1976.
16 J. McH. Sinclair and R. M. Coulthard, *Towards an Analysis of Discourse*, Oxford University Press, 1975.
17 For a detailed model of the variables governing turn-taking, cf. H. Sacks and E. Schegloff, *On Turn-Taking in Language*, Mimeograph, December 1974.
18 *Class, Codes and Control*, Routledge & Kegan Paul, London, 1971, is a collection of some of B. Bernstein's most important essays.
19 N. Dittmar *Sociolinguistics*, Arnold, London, 1976, p. 24.
20 *Ibid.*, pp. 104–5.
21 *Ibid.*, p. 28.
22 *Ibid.*, p. 185.
23 For a further incisive critique of Bernstein's work see A. D. Edwards, *Language in Culture and Class*, Heinemann, London, 1976, pp. 86–122.
24 This is reiterated in a recent pamphlet, *The Task of Broadcasting News*, BBC, London, May 1976.
25 Dittmar, *op. cit.*, p. 24.
26 For a general discussion of the relevance of this theory to the media see B. Winston, *Dangling Conversations – Hardware/Software*, Davis-Poynter, London, 1974.

27 C. E. Shannon and W. Weaver, *The Mathematical Theory of Communication*, Urbana, University of Illinois Press, 1949.

28 E.g. ITN, *News at Ten*, 21 March 1975.

29 There is an exceptional reference, outside the sample period, to a dispute which led to a lockout. An item on *News at Ten* on 13 May 1975 began: 'And at home there's a new problem for the pound in your pocket. The 100 craftsmen at the Bank of England's only printing plant for £20, £10, £5 and £1 notes have stopped work because of a pay dispute.' Only later do we learn that the union see it differently, but even this information is strongly qualified when the reporter says, 'The trouble, according to the unions, has led to the Bank locking them out' (ITN, 22.00, 13 May 1975). Another clear case of an employer's action occurred in the dispute between the commercial television companies and technicians but the term 'lockout' was avoided. For example, a report on *News at Ten* in May 1975 announced that 'Independent Television Companies have said that if technicians go ahead with the planned strike over the spring bank holiday, they won't be able to resume work until their claim is withdrawn' (ITN, 22.00, 16 May 1975).

30 H. Sacks, Mimeographed Lectures (unpublished), University of California.

31 R. Tyrell, *The Work of the Television Journalist*, Focal Press, London, 1972, p. 31.

32 IBA internal documents dated 8 October 1976 and 4 February 1977.

33 R. Collins, *Television News*, BFI, London, 1976, p. 47.

34 See *Bad News*, pp. 4 ff.

35 *Ibid.*, p. 6.

36 See, for example, S. Cohen, *New Society*, 9 September 1976.

37 Their viewing is the subject of a study by J. Blumler and A. Ewbank, reported in *British Journal of Industrial Relations*, vol. 8, no. 1, 1970.

38 BBC2, 23.05, 14 May 1975.

39 BBC1, 21.00, 13 May 1975, Items 14, 15.

40 See Chapter 4 in this volume and *Bad News*, Chapter 7.

41 This view has been endorsed recently by the BBC in *The Task of Broadcasting News*, pp. 9–10:

> News seeks above all to answer the questions WHO, WHAT, WHERE, WHEN, and HOW. It is primarily concerned with new facts and the factual background to them. Its interest in the question WHY is confined to the audience's urgent interest in understanding what has just happened within the bounds of immediately available information. The subsequent debate may itself make news, but the continuing broadcast reflection of the controversy about the issues, the deliberately balanced presentation of opposing points of view after the event, is left to a different group of journalists in the BBC's Current Affairs Groups in radio and television.

7 Assembling the News Text

1 BBC Radio News, *News Guide*, mimeo, BBC, London, May 1972.

2 Quoted in R. Tyrell, *The Work of the Television Journalist*, Focal Press, London, 1972, pp. 40–1.
3 See M. A. K. Halliday, 'Language Structure and Language Function' in J. Lyons *New Horizons in Linguistics*, Penguin, Harmondsworth, 1970, and *Explorations in the Function of Language*, Arnold, London, 1973.
4 Cf. D. Crystal and D. Davy, *Investigating English Style*, Longmans, London, 1969, especially Chapter 7, 'The Language of Newspaper Reporting'.
5 With CEEFAX, ORACLE and VIEWDATA this circumstance will change. However, during the period of our study this involved a minute fraction (less than 1 per cent of the 17.7 m licensed sets in 1975–6). Market research indicated that by the end of 1977 the total of teletext receivers and adaptors may have reached 50,000 (see *Sunday Times*, 27 February 1977).
6 Cf. Television Act, 1974, Rules Concerning Advertisements, paragraph 4: 'Advertisements shall not be inserted otherwise than at the beginning or the end of programmes or in natural breaks therein.' Leaving aside the nicety of the fit between the professional ideology of television journalism and the notion of naturalness, there remains the unanswered question of whether the news has a 'natural break' at all. Our findings in *Bad News*, Routledge & Kegan Paul, London, 1976, Chapter 4, would indicate that it does not.
7 There was an exception. The interpretation of the armed forces' pay rise was as follows:

> The Government Review Body said that pay rates for the armed forces had fallen behind civilian levels and, while they took the social contract into account, servicemen should not be treated less favourably than the rest of the community. (ITN, 22.00, 16 May 1975)

8 See Chapter 10, Part III for a detailed discussion of visual inputs to titles and openings.
9 E.g. ITN, 20.20, 1 January 1975; BBC1, 21.00, 16 January 1975; BBC1, 21.00, 21 March 1975; ITN, 22.00, 17 April 1976.
10 E.g. BBC1, 21.00, 24 January 1975; BBC1, 21.00, 28 February 1975; ITN, 22.30, 1 February 1975.
11 E.g. BBC1, 21.00, 28 February 1975.
12 See BBC1, 21.00, 24 February 1975; BBC1, 21.00, 14 January 1975; BBC1, 21.00, 2 February 1975; ITN, 22.00, 24 February 1975.
13 P. Schlesinger, 'Newsmen and their time machine', in *British Journal of Sociology*, vol. 28, no. 3, September 1977.
14 See BBC1, 21.55, 30 March 1975; ITN, 22.00, 27 February 1975; ITN, 22.00, 21 March 1975.
15 See BBC1, 21.00, 18 April 1975; BBC1, 21.10, 29 April 1975.
16 For systematic discussion of labelling theory and its use and limitations, cf. I. Taylor, P. Walton, J. Young, *The New Criminology*, Routledge & Kegan Paul, London, 1973, Chapter 5. For a discussion of the limitations of social psychology and the labelling approach with special

reference to the mass media, cf. N. Armistead (ed.), *Reconstructing Social Psychology*, Penguin, Harmondsworth, 1974, especially the articles by G. Murdock, H. Resler and P. Walton.

17 Ralph Dengler, SJ, 'The Language of Film Titles', *Journal of Communications*, summer 1975, pp. 51–60.

18 E.g. ITN, 22.00, 3 April 1975. Between Items 3 and 4.

19 Tyrell, *op. cit.*, p. 37.

20 Gaye Tuchman describes the 'presentation of conflicting possibilities' as one of the strategic procedures used by newsmen to claim objectivity; see 'Objectivity as Strategic Ritual', *American Journal of Sociology*, vol. 77, no. 4, pp. 665 ff.

21 There is a further illustration of this usage in Table 7.4 in the opening sentence of the *News at Ten* report.

22 E. A. Schegloff, 'Sequencing in Conversational Openings', *American Anthropologist*, vol. 70, no. 6, 1968.

23 See for example V. Propp, *Morphology of the Folktale*, Indiana Research Center in Anthropology, Bloomington, 1958.

24 *The Task of Broadcasting News*, BBC, London, 1976, pp. 9–10.

25 R. Williams, *Keywords*, Fontana, London, 1976, p. 275.

26 Including D. Morley in his discussion of the 'event orientation' of the media in 'Industrial Conflict and the Mass Media', *Sociological Review*, May 1976.

27 J. L. Austin, 'Performative-Constative' in C. Caton (ed.), *Philosophy and Ordinary Language*, University of Illinois, Urbana, 1963.

28 M. A. K. Halliday, *Explorations in the Function of Language*, Arnold, London, 1973, p. 20.

29 BBC1, 21.00, 25 February 1975.

8 News Talk: Vocabulary and Industrial Action

1 L. Wittgenstein, *Philosophical Investigations*, Blackwell, Oxford, 1973, p. 223e.

2 I. L. Horowitz (ed.), *Power, Politics and People*, The Collected Essays of C. Wright Mills, Oxford University Press, New York, 1967, pp. 433–4.

3 'The Task of Broadcasting News', pp. 9, 12.

4 *Ibid.*, p. 452.

5 Volume 1, *Bad News*, Routledge & Kegan Paul, London, 1976, p. 169.

6 H. Sacks, 'On the Analysability of Stories by Children', in R. Turner (ed.), *Ethnomethodology*, Penguin, Harmondsworth, 1975, pp. 216–32.

7 See *Bad News*, pp. 193–200.

8 A. Blum, *Theorising*, Heinemann, London, 1974.

9 ITN, 22.30, 7 January 1975.

10 E.g. frequently quoted differences in colour terms. See J. Lyons, *Introduction to Theoretical Linguistics*, Cambridge University Press, 1971, pp. 56–8 for a discussion of this point.

11 Figures for the words counts are rounded to the nearest ten words.

12 E. Goffman, *Frame Analysis*, Penguin, London, 1975, p. 44.

13 G. A. Miller, 'Statistical Indicators of Style', Chapter 10 in N. N. Markel (ed.), *Psycholinguistics*, Dorsey Press, Homewood, Ill., 1969.

14 See *Sunday Times* Business News, 20 March 1977.

15 O. Findahl and B. Hoijer, *Fragments of Reality: An Experiment with TV News and Visuals*, Audience and Programme Research Dept, Swedish Broadcasting Corporation, 1976, pp. 14–15.

16 P. R. Hawkins, *Social Class, the Nominal Group and Verbal Strategies*, Routledge & Kegan Paul, London, 1977, p. 45. See also D. Henderson, 'Contextual Specificity, Discretion and Cognitive Socialization', *Sociology* 4, 3, 1970.

17 O. Findahl and B. Hoijer, 'Effect of Additional Verbal Information on Retention of a Radio News Program', *Journalism Quarterly*, vol. 52, no. 3, Autumn 1975.

18 *Report of the Committee on the Future of Broadcasting* (Annan Committee), Cmnd 6753, HMSO, London, 1977, p. 272.

19 See for example BBC1, 21.00, 22 January 1975 and ITN, 22.00, 3 February 1975.

20 This is in keeping with the 'events' orientation of industrial news which we noted in *Bad News*, p. 19.

21 A. J. Liebling, *The Press*, Ballantine, New York, 1975, pp. 92, 240.

22 Cf. A. Gouldner, 'Reciprocity and Autonomy in Functional Theory', in L. Gross (ed.), *Symposium on Sociological Theory*, Harper & Row, New York, 1959, p. 270.

23 H. F. Moorhouse, 'Attitudes to Class and Class Relationships in Britain', *Sociology*, vol. 10, no. 3, September 1976. (See also a forthcoming book on industrial relations and the media by P. Hartmann.)

24 Moorhouse, *op. cit.*, pp. 477–8.

25 H. Gerth and C. W. Mills, *Character and Social Structure*, Routledge & Kegan Paul, London, 1954, pp. 116–18; referred to in R. Hyman and I. Brough, *Social Values and Industrial Relations*, Oxford University Press, 1975, pp. 206–7.

26 This usage has occurred more recently, in quotation at least, in the quality press. See for example *The Times*, 4 August 1976. At the time of writing it does not appear to have been used in television news reporting.

9 Measuring the Visuals

1 See Volume 1, *Bad News*, Routledge & Kegan Paul, London, 1976, pp. 26 ff.

2 *Report of the Committee on the Future of Broadcasting*, HMSO, Cmnd 6753, London, 1977, p. 277 (italics in original).

3 *Bad News*, pp. 384 ff.

4 E.g. Table 1, pp. 52–64 in S. Heath, 'Film and System Terms of Analysis', *Screen*, spring 1975.

5 See below, Chapter 14 'Conclusion', p. 415, for a fuller discussion of the Group's rejection of post-Peircean semiotic methodology.

10 Halting the Flow

1 *Television News*, BFI Television Monograph 5, London, 1976, p. 36.
2 *Ibid.*, p. 36.
3 Although the use of Alastair Burnet and the arrival of Anna Ford might indicate that, at least, on ITN this might be changing.
4 *Report of the Committee on the Future of Broadcasting* (Annan Committee), Cmnd 6753, HMSO, London, 1977, p. 282.
5 Except possibly on Tuesday. The archive tape is damaged.
6 Now that distinction would probably have to go to the revamped *News at 5.45* on ITN.
7 See below, p. 274, chapter 11 'Good Evening'.
8 ITN have currently reversed this and name the senior members of the production team, but at the time of going to press it was still true of the BBC.

11 'Good Evening'

1 *New Yorker*, 21 February 1977, p. 70.
2 Christine Eade, a member of the BBC's political staff, was the only woman in this group, but she does not appear in the sample.
3 The figures do not include further correspondent and reporter inputs. These can include voice-over film or tape, to camera appearances on film or tape or live from an OB, all of which are discussed in Chapter 12 below. The one exception to this is the shot of Brunson on film listed in Table 11.1
4 Footage of marines in Okinawa and Utapao had been used on earlier bulletins. The remark is intended without prejudice to any other footage that might have been available but relates only to what was shown on British television.

12 Still Life

1 Since no 'other photographs' were used on Sunday 11 and Saturday 17 May, these figures relate to weekday usages and compare with duration figures, which are based on weekday usages only (see Table 12.2).
2 G. Slessenger: 'A BBC Analysis of the Glasgow University Media Project Report', December 1975.

13 'Truth 24 Times a Second' – 25 Times for Television

1 *Report of the Committee on the Future of Broadcasting* (Annan Committee), Cmnd 6753, HMSO, London, 1977.
2 Michael Tracey, *The Production of Political Television*, Routledge & Kegan Paul, London, 1978, p. 16.
3 Glasgow University Media Group, *Bad News*, Routledge & Kegan Paul, London, 1976, Appendix 2.
4 ITN are now supercaptioning the majority of speakers.

Conclusion: Ritual Tasks

1 *Bad News*, Routledge & Kegan Paul, London, 1976, p. 9.
2 Anthony Smith, *The Shadow in the Cave*, Quartet, London, 1976, p. 143.
3 Richard Collins, *Screen Education*, winter 1976/77, no. 21, p. 80.
4 The Annan Committee, *Report of the Committee on the Future of Broadcasting*, Cmnd 6753, HMSO, London, 1977, p. 276.
5 *Ibid.*, p. 277.
6 S. Hall, *The Report of the Committee on the Future of Broadcasting*, NUQ, summer 1977, p. 272.
7 There is a useful summary of the history and meaning of the word in R. Williams, *Keywords*, Fontana, London, 1976, pp. 126 ff.
8 A. Gouldner, *The Dialectic of Ideology and Technology*, Macmillan, London, 1976, p. 111.
9 *Ibid.*, p. 112.
10 ITV, 'Critics and Viewers', *Independent Broadcasting*, May 1975, p. 17.
11 *Ibid.*, p. 17.
12 *Ibid.*, p. 17.
13 Smith, *op. cit.*, p. 176.
14 *Ibid.*, p. 174.
15 Peter Jay and John Birt, *The Times*, 28 September 1975, 30 September 1975, 1 October 1975, 2 September 1976, 3 September 1976.
16 'Can television news break the understanding barrier?', *The Times*, 28 February 1975.
17 *Idem.*
18 'Why television news is in danger of becoming an anti-social force', *The Times*, 3 September 1975.
19 *Idem.*
20 Curti, Hall, Connell, 'The Unity of Current Affairs Television', in *Cultural Studies 9*, University of Birmingham, spring 1976, p. 92; italics in original.
21 Cox, 'Bad News – or poor Scholarship?', *Independent Broadcasting*, December 1976.
22 Annan, *op. cit.*, p. 272.
23 *Social Research on Broadcasting: Proposals for Further Development*, BBC, London, 1977, p. 67.
24 Michael Tracey, *The Production of Political Television*, Routledge & Kegan Paul, London, 1978; Philip Schlesinger, *Putting 'Reality' Together*, Constable, London, 1978. Both these works do little but regurgitate professional notions of production. Given the general lack of production understanding, it is little wonder that no insights into its processes are forthcoming. The continued failure of this research tradition to take cognisance of what is actually produced reduces its usefulness to the level of academic journalism which pessimistically accepts the professional view that no real change is possible under present society.
25 Findahl and Hoijer, 'Fragments of Reality', Swedish Broadcasting Corporation, 1976, p. 48. Even this work reveals that careful

presentation can heighten viewers' perception and memory of causes, for instance.

26 Gouldner, *op cit.*, p. 116.
27 *The Leveller*, London, January 1978, pp. 14 ff.
28 *Ibid.*, p. 15.
29 Stuart Hall *et al.*, 'Debate', *Screen*, London, winter 1977/78, p. 113.
30 *Idem.*
31 Murdock and Golding, 'Capitalism, Communication and Class Relations', in Curran, Gurevitch and Woollacott (eds), *Mass Communication and Society*, Arnold, London, 1977, p. 20.
32 Annan, *op. cit.*, p. 35.
33 B. Winston, *Dangling Conversations*, vol. 2, Davis-Poynter, London, 1973, p. 42.
34 R. Barthes 'Rhetoric of the Image', in *Image, Music, Text*, Fontana, London, 1977; and T. Pateman, 'How To Do Things with Images' in *Theory and Society*, forthcoming 1979.
35 R. Coward and T. Ellis, *Language and Materialism*, Routledge & Kegan Paul, London, 1977, p. 3.
36 U. Eco, *A Theory of Semiotics*, Macmillan, London, 1977, p. 191.
37 *Op. cit.*, p. 298.
38 Cited by T. Burns, *The BBC*, Macmillan, 1977, p. xv.
39 *The Leveller*, *op. cit.*, p. 17.

Appendix A Just One Week

1 For a recent study of the BBC newsroom, see P. Schlesinger, *Putting 'Reality' Together: BBC News*, London, Constable, 1977.
2 IBA, *Handbook*, 1975.
3 olume I, *Bad News*, Routledge & Kegan Paul, London, 1976, pp. 85–6.
4 *Ibid.*, p. 88.
5 *Ibid.*, p. 139.
6 *Ibid.*, pp. 107–12.
7 *The Task of Broadcasting News, a study for the BBC General Advisory Council*, BBC, May 1976, Appendix I.
8 *Bad News*, p. 190.
9 *Ibid.*, pp. 112 ff.
10 *Ibid.*, p. 136.

Appendix C The Events of Sunday 11 May – Saturday 17 May 1975

1 See Chapter 2 for a further discussion of the significance of such uses of the three-day week statistics.

Index